The History of Limerick City

by

Séan Spellissy

The Celtic Bookshop

'specialising in books of Irish interest'

Limerick City

First published by
The Celtic Bookshop,
2 Rutland Street, Limerick City, Republic of Ireland.
Tel: 061-401155 Fax: 061-340600.
e-mail: celticbk@iol.ie

ISBN 0 9534683 1 3

Printed in Ireland by SciPrint Ltd., Shannon, Co. Clare

Dedicated

To My Friends

Lynda, Majella and Marese,

To My Cousins

Tara and Katie Spellissy,
in Lowell, Massachusetts

and

My Sister

Sinead Spellissy

The author's previous publications include:

Clare, County of Contrast	*(1987)*
Limerick, The Rich Land	*(1989)*
A Portrait of Ennis	*(1990)*
Suicide: The Irish Experience	*(1996)*
The Merchants of Ennis	*(1996)*
The Ennis Compendium	*(1998)*

Contents

Publisher's Note

Limerick City is one of the most historic cities in Ireland, with a dramatic and interesting history and a variety of important historical sites. However many people, throughout the country remain unaware of Limerick's rich heritage. There is no book which outlines in a concise, accurate, informative and entertaining fashion, the history and attractions of the city. To redress this problem, we have commissioned the eminent local historian, Séan Spellissy to compile this historical book. The *History of Limerick City* chronicles the story of the city from its foundation by the Vikings, right up to modern times, and also details the lives of many individuals who contributed to the colourful history of Limerick City.

Caroline & Pat O'Brien
The Celtic Bookshop

JIM KEMMY
Shannon Development Photo Library

Introduction

This new book by Séan Spellissy charts the story of a city which has inspired many writers, whose history has been researched and recounted with great enthusiasm, particularly in recent years.

There is a great appetite for local history in Limerick and rightly so. It is a natural thing to want to know how our place came to be what it is today and how the millions of people who lived here before us contributed to its development. The character of a city, rather like that of a person, is formed by various influences it encounters through the various stages of its life. Like a person, it continues to grow and change as it develops.

Limerick's history is the stuff of drama. From the encounters of the invading Vikings with the equally blood-thirsty natives in the ninth century through the growth and defence of the walled town right up to the development of the modern technological-age city the story has variety and colour.

This book, *The History of Limerick City*, captures that colour and the many dimensions of the lives people led here before us. It is a textured history, telling of battles long ago, but also of the everyday lives and concerns of people of different classes and different levels of wealth and poverty. It tells us about the many crafts practised, the development of hospitals and schools, how modes of transportation changed through the years, and much much more.

Séan Spellissy pays tribute to others who, like himself, have developed and fed our appetite for knowledge of our history. He acknowledges especially those recently gone from our midst: Kevin Hannan, Seamus O'Cinneide and Willie Gleeson. He rightly gives pride of place to the late, great Jim Kemmy, who made such a huge contribution to enlightening us about our past.

Jim Kemmy loved Limerick, its people and its history. This shines through in his dedicated work on the *Old Limerick Journal*, *The Limerick Anthology*, *The Limerick Compendium* and much more. It was an integral part of the flow of his life and of his conversation. It was no bother to Jim to edit on trains, before meetings, at midnight after canvassing the city streets for an election.

It is a great honour for me to have been asked to write this preface. My work is to help to carry on Jim's political legacy. His legacy as a historian is very much alive as well with the continuing publication of the *Old Limerick Journal.*

History is always in the making and Limerick, at the present time, is involved in a period of quite significant change. Urban renewal has rejuvenated the physical heart of the city in recent years and this process is ongoing. Appropriately, the River Shannon is given central focus again as it was central, in the past, to so much of the city's changing fortunes.

Read this book to savour the identity of Limerick and its people. It is a picture of variety and change, as much about now as then, us as them and how we are all connected. As we look forward to a new millennium, a look back will help us on our way.

JAN O'SULLIVAN.

*SARSFIELD BRIDGE AND RIVER SHANNON - **Limerick City Museum***

Preface

The History of Limerick City, owes its origins to a suggestion by Pat and Caroline O'Brien of Celtic Books, 2 Rutland Street, Limerick. In 1997 they republished P.W. Joyce's *Social History of Ireland* and John Dalton's *Illustrations Historical and Genealogical of King James's Irish Army*. They were familiar with my *Limerick the Rich Land* (1989) and suggested that I should write a history of Limerick City. The O'Briens may be relative newcomers to the world of publishing but their premises at 2 Rutland Street housed the printing presses of Henry Watson and D. S. Mahony in 1813. The *Limerick Chronicle* was printed here, by Henry Watson and, later, by a printer named Hall.

Booksellers, newspapermen and printers have left us their own memorials, the printed word. The earliest newspaper in the city may have been a news-sheet in which bulletins and proclamations were published during the siege of 1691. This publication is believed to have been printed on a mobile press. The credit for producing the city's first newspaper is usually ascribed to a Dubliner named Brangan. In 1716 he published the *Limerick Newsletter*, a newspaper that seems to have been rather short-lived as only a single copy of the first issue survived into modern times. Richard Wilkins was the first bookseller noted in the city, during the 1660s and 1670s. He emigrated to Boston, Massachusetts, about 1680. George Roche was listed as a Limerick bookseller in 1710 and 1730; Rebecca Nicholls was recorded as a bookseller in 1719; Thomas Ross was a bookseller in 1729; and William Farrier[†] was described as a bookseller and bookbinder between 1729 and 1754. From 1748 onwards, William Farrier was listed as William Ferrar in the subscribers' lists. Josiah Sheppard was a bookseller and publisher, opposite the Exchange, and published Rowe's *Devout Exercises of the Heart* in 1740. Joseph Sexton, a papermaker in the city, between 1747 and 1782, had two paper mills within the Liberties, one built in 1747, the other in 1749, and was married to the daughter of Henry Long, a printer. In 1763 C. Harrison was a bookseller in Limerick; J. Hurley was a bookbinder in 1769; Catherine Long was listed as a bookseller, between 1769 and 1774; M. Lisse or M. Lisle, an engraver and drawing master, from Paris, died in Limerick in 1774; and George Rowland, a printer, died in 1792, at the age of eighty-five.

Andrew Welsh printed *the encouragement of the ladies of Ireland to the woollen manufactury*, at the *Sign of the Globe* in Quay Lane, in 1721. This was the first book printed in Limerick and Andrew Welsh was not alone one of the city's first printers but the father and grandfather of other printers. In 1722 Samuel Terry entered into a partnership of sorts with L. Bixou (alias L. Tabb) and published *The Libertine School'd*. Both gave their address as Baal's Bridge and were also partners in the publication of *A Sacremental Cathechism* in 1723. John Cherry was a printer in Pery Street between 1761 and 1769 and was listed in *Ferrar's Limerick Directory 1769*. Matthew Eyres was a journeyman printer from Cork. He lived in Limerick during the 1760s and worked for John Ferrar until he returned to Cork in 1771.

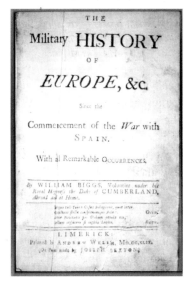

MILITARY HISTORY OF EUROPE, BY WILLIAM BIGGS. PRINTED BY ANDREW WELSH IN 1749, ON PAPER MANUFACTURED BY JOSEPH SEXTON - *Limerick City Museum*

Andrew Welsh, Junior, the son of Andrew Welsh, was a bookseller, newspaper proprietor, printer and publisher, with business premises in both Cork and Limerick. His Limerick establishment was in the Irishtown, above the Market House. He was the owner of the *Limerick Journal* which he printed from 1739 to 1749; changed its name to the *Munster Journal* in 1749; took his son, Thomas

[†]Obviously a misprint for *Ferrar*

RARE EIGHTEENTH-CENTURY LIMERICK
PRINTING. 1724
Limerick City Museum

Welsh, into partnership in 1757; published the *Munster Journal* with his son until 1769; and died in 1772. Andrew Welsh, Junior, published an edition of John Ferrar's *History of the City of Limerick* and was succeeded by his son, Thomas Welsh, who continued to publish the *Munster Journal* until 1784. John Ferrar was a writer, bookseller, newspaper proprietor, printer and publisher whose first premises was located near the Exchange. He moved to the New Printing House in Quay Lane, from 1769 to 1785, and later lived in Sir Harry's Mall. On 25 December, 1786, he was living in Sir Harry's Mall when he wrote the preface to *The History of Limerick, Ecclesiastical, Civil and Military*. Kevin Hannan described John Ferrar's preface as being ecumenical in tone but on reading it myself I came to the conclusion that John Ferrar was, in all probability, a Freemason.

His reference to the Supreme Being and the need for toleration was in line with masonic thinking. He is best known as a Limerick historian, publisher of both a history and a directory of Limerick, and the founder of a newspaper that is still published two centuries later. He founded the *Limerick Chronicle* in 1768. This continued to appear twice a week, for almost a century afterwards, and was eventually taken over by the *Limerick Leader* and is now its Tuesday edition. John Ferrar was a son of William Farrier and he retired from, and sold, his printing business in 1785. Edward Flin started a new newspaper, using an old name, the *Limerick Journal*, in 1779. It remained on the market until 1819. The *Limerick Herald* and *Munster Advertiser* was printed by Robert Law of Mill Lane in 1788. He had no connection with it in 1789 but it continued to appear until about 1795.

Maurice Lenihan (1811-1895), the historian, was editor and owner of the *Limerick Reporter and Tipperary Vindicator*, from 1841 up to the time of his death fifty-four years later. He published the *Tipperary Vindicator* in Nenagh from 1844 to 1850 when he incorporated both newspapers. Jeremiah Buckley founded the *Limerick Leader* in 1889 but its first issue, dated Friday, August 9, 1889, had to be published by a rival printing firm, MacNamara and Brunard's, on the opposite side of the same street, Patrick Street. In 1940 Ivan Morris became the editor of the *Limerick Weekly Echo* which had long been the *Limerick Chronicle's* main competitor. The *Limerick Leader* now has its offices at 54 O'Connell Street and

SYLVESTER O'HALLORAN -
Limerick City Museum

the *Limerick Post* newspaper is located within the former town hall in Rutland Street.

Limerick born writers have had national, even international, reputations. Richard Creagh (1525-1585) was ordained in Louvain; served as a priest in his native city from 1557 to 1562; was created archbishop of Armagh, in Rome, in 1564; escaped from the Tower of London on one occasion; and later died in that self-same prison, possibly by poisoning. He wrote *De Lingua Hibernica* and *Topographia Hiberniae*, the manuscripts of which are now in Trinity College Dublin, unpublished. He was the author of *An Ecclesiastical History*, which was published. Sylvester O'Halloran (1728-1807) is mentioned elsewhere in the text as a historian but he also published a medical book in 1750, *A New Treatise on the Glaucoma, or Cataract in Ireland*. Joseph Timothy Haydn (1786-1856) was educated abroad, became a journalist and co-operated with F.W. Conway in the production of a theatrical journal, *The Stage*. In 1828 he edited the *Dublin Evening Mail* but by 1834 he had returned to Limerick where he published the *Limerick Star and Evening Post* newspaper, in partnership with W.D. Geary. This was the newspaper Gerald Griffin worked for at the time of the *Colleen Bawn* trial. Joseph Timothy Haydn was the sole proprietor of the *Limerick Times* before he emigrated to London in 1839. He published his *Dictionary of Dates* in 1841 and this had run to twenty-five editions prior to 1900. His most famous editorial work, however, was his 1849 edition of *Lewis's Topographical Dictionary* which was published in eight volumes. This detailed the cities, towns, villages, parishes and baronies of Great Britain and Ireland and is still a valuable reference work today. Edward Fitzgibbon (1803-1857) was a keen fisherman, a nineteenth-century Kevin Hannan. He wrote on angling, often using the pseudonym 'Ephemera', for the *Observer* and *Bell's Life in London*; published his *Handbook of Angling* in 1847 and the *Book of Salmon* in 1850; and edited Walton's *Compleat Angler* in 1853. John Francis Waller (1809-1894) was an editor of *Dublin University Magazine* and the poet who published *Ravenscroft Hall* (1852), The *Slingsby Papers* (1852), The *Dead Bridal* (1856) and *Peter Brown* (1872). He is responsible for many of the entries in the *Imperial Dictionary of Universal Biography* and was an editor of *Goldsmiths Works*. Marie Dolores Eliza Rosanna Gilbert (1818-1861) is better known to history as Lola Montez. She published *The Art of Beauty* (1858) in New York and is believed to have had her autobiography, the

Autobiography and Lectures of Lola Montez (1858), ghost-written by Rev. C. Chauncey Burr. Fitzjames O'Brien (1828-1862) was a poet who ran through his inheritance before becoming a journalist in London. He emigrated to America; wrote a play, *A Gentleman from Ireland*, which was well received; and died, fighting on the northern side, with the Seventh New York Regiment, during the civil war in America. Michael MacDonagh (1860-1946) was a biographer and nationalist whose books mirrored his interests, *The Speaker of the House* (1914), *The Irish at the Front* (1916), *The Irish on the Somme* (1917), *The Life Of William O'Brien* (1928) and *Daniel O'Connell and Catholic Emancipation* (1929). Minnie Dorothea Spaight Conyers (1871-1949) wrote a series of novels dealing with horses, hunting and Anglo-Irish Ireland. *Peter's Pedigree* (1904), *The Boy, Some Horses and a Girl* (1908) and *Old Andy* (1914) are but a few of many written in similar vein.

Limerick has lost several of its historians since I wrote *Limerick, The Rich Land* in 1989. Willie W. Gleeson (1905-1991) remembered the days of the Black and Tans and committed many of his memories to paper. Yann Philippe Mac Bradaí, half-Breton, half-Irish, had a brief moment of glory on 15 January, 1983, when his discovery of the Sarsfield-Spencer connection was published simultaneously in the *Limerick Leader, Irish Press, Evening Press* and *Cork Examiner.* Yann Philippe had worked as a night porter in England, France and Ireland, an occupation that allowed him the time and opportunity to carry out research in the various archives. He was a genealogist specialising in the ecclesiastical families of Ireland and had spent the best part of thirty years working on this project. In 1986, 1987 and 1988 he had published other material on the lineage on the Princess of Wales, the Duchess of Kent and their consorts in the *Limerick Leader, Sunday Tribune* and *Sunday World*. He

ROBERT HERBERT, CITY LIBRARIAN FROM 1939 TO 1956. - Limerick City Museum

died at his desk in Hanratty's Hotel, Glentworth Street, his work unfinished. Wherever he went, he brought his large briefcase with him. This contained several hundred A3 sheets which comprised his manuscript. On one side of each sheet was a genealogical chart and on the other side was a *precis* on each individual mentioned. Yann Philippe Mac Bradaí constantly revised this work as he uncovered more details on "his" families. After his death, the briefcase turned up in his house, empty, his life's work dumped.

Seamus Ó Cinnéide (1925-1992), journalist and poet, was born in Mungret

ARCHAEOLOGICAL EXCAVATIONS IN KING JOHN'S CASTLE - Shannon Development Photo Library

Street. He wrote in both Irish and English in the *Limerick Leader*, was the newspapers theatre critic, social commentator, local historian and satirist; was a lifelong admirer of Eamon de Valera (1882-1975) and detested hypocrisy of any kind, often lampooning the pretentious. A noted eccentric and a lover of Irish music, song and dance, Seamus was "known to the stones in the road". To travel with him was an experience rarely forgotten; people would appear from nowhere in remote areas, just to speak to him; and the pints would pile up in front of him as he was too busy talking to sip from a glass. He co-authored *Stair agus Béaloideas - Páirtin agus Miliuc, The History and Folklore of Parteen and Meelick*, with Dónal Ó Riain, and was the author of several hundred articles, on folklore and local history, in the *Limerick Leader*, and local, meaning County Limerick or County Clare, publications.

The Old Limerick Society was founded in 1943 to create and foster an interest in everything pertaining to Old Limerick; to promote the study of its history and antiquities; and to acquire and conserve local books, documents and plans. It produced a magazine in December 1946, petered out in 1953, and was revived in 1979, producing its own publication, *The Old Limerick Journal*, in December 1979. Jim Kemmy was the editor, Kevin Hannan, consultant editor, Joe McMahon, associate editor and John Keane was the circulation manager. The first editorial committee was formed by Michael McInerney, Patsy Harrold, Pat Feeley, W.W. Gleeson, Kevin

KING JOHN'S CASTLE, FROM A LITHOGRAPH BY SAMUEL BROCAS, 1826 - Limerick City Museum

O'Connor, Dolly Stewart, Ernest Kelly and Joe Hartnett. Kevin Hannan (1920-1996), a keen fisherman, was the *Limerick Leader's* angling correspondent in the 1950s, and was a prolific writer who documented the history of his native city in numerous articles in the *Limerick Chronicle, Limerick Leader, North Munster Antiquarian Journal, Old Limerick Journal* and other publications. I was at the launching of his last book, *Limerick Historical Reflections,* which was published on 23 February, 1996. Kevin died in St. John's Hospital, on Wednesday 6 September, 1996. He had been admitted to the hospital a week earlier, missing the launch of Mary Fennelly's *Limerick Lives* (1996), the last book on which he had worked. People have described himself and Jim Kemmy as being like chalk and cheese, yet few missed him more than Jim Kemmy who spoke of him in the following terms;

> He was the best local historian we had. By any standard Kevin Hannan was a remarkably gifted and versatile man - historian, tailor, writer, nature-lover, traveller, poet, fisherman, story-teller, artist, he has filled all these and many more roles with distinction and without turning a hair or changing gear. He was a true renaissance man. Because of his single-mindedness and enthusiasm he often found himself at odds with his colleagues, be they fishermen or historians. He set his face firmly against modern poetry, and was a severe and vocal critic of the sculpture that has appeared on our streets in recent years. He saw little merit in modern poetry and prose, and dismissed almost all of today's art as dross.
>
> In recent years he became a controversial figure in Limerick life because of his public stances. When embroiled in battle he enthusiastically tackled all comers and brought the full range of his formidable Victorian vocabulary into play in these encounters.
>
> I often found myself poles apart from him on many issues. But our differences never blinded me from recognising his unique and tireless contribution to his native city, and I was not alone in admiring his zest for life, his boundless energy, his writing verve and his mental serenity.
>
> He was a great friend, a delightful companion, and I will miss him.

Jim Kemmy died, suddenly, on Thursday, 25 September, 1997, after a long illness from which he seemed to be recovering. He loved his native city with a passion; was a committed socialist, with a strong anti-nationalist tendency; was a fervent believer in the total separation of church and state; was mayor of Limerick on two occasions, comparing himself to Matt Talbot in deciding to wear the chains, but not the robes, of office, was a major advocate of conservation, serving on every committee of benefit to the city, and was a passionate worker for the disadvantaged, regardless of political affiliation. Jim was a stonemason, historian, writer, publisher and editor of the *Old Limerick Journal*. In 1996, as mayor, he awarded my book, *Suicide, the Irish Experience*, a civic reception. On remembering the review Noel Browne had given the book he joked that if I'd produced this book thirty years earlier the confraternity would probably have burned it in the Potato Market and that I'd have been excommunicated, that is if I were a church-goer at that stage. Jim died as he had lived, without benefit of clergy, stalwart to the last. His body remained on view in Griffin's funeral parlour until his cortege moved to Mount St. Lawerence, making a brief stop outside the *Pike Inn*, his campaign headquarters and clinic, *en route*. Jim was buried after a secular graveside ceremony witnessed by about six thousand people who had crowded into Mount St. Lawrence. He would have appreciated his obituary in the *Irish Post*, of October 4, 1997;

> Limerickman Jim Kemmy would have been amused to hear the various tributes paid to him this week by Ireland's great and good because, for much of his political life, he was an outsider - a socialist in a politically conservative climate, a social liberal in a socially conservative city and a radical within the Labour Party.
>
> He was just 61 when he died last week in a Dublin hospital after a long illness and it is fair to say that London started him out on his long road as an outspoken activist .... That city also helped him develop a passion for reading and friends recalled how he would often arrive home on holidays in Limerick with a suitcase crammed with works by the likes of Marx, Connolly, Engels and Larkin.
>
> He returned for good in 1960 and three years later joined the Labour Party he would eventually chair. His range of campaigns was broad, his commitment total.

Despite the deaths of both Kevin Hannan and Jim Kemmy their journal still survives. *The Old Limerick Journal* and the Old Limerick Society is in the capable hands of a new chairman, Tom Donovan, and editor, Larry Walsh, and a committee composed of Richard Ahern, Tony Browne, John Curtin, Liam Irwin and Des Ryan. The Limerick Field Club was founded in 1892, changed its name to the North Munster Archaeological Society, and is now known as the Thomond Archaeological Society. The journal of the Limerick Field Club later became the *North Munster Antiquarian Journal*. In 1919, following World War I, the society disbanded. It was revived in 1929 and from 1938 was known as the Thomond Archaeological Society. This group has its own publication, the *North Munster Antiquarian Journal*, which was produced by an editorial committee into the 1940s. Robert Herbert was born in Dublin; became the city librarian for Limerick in 1938, and was the first editor of the *North Munster Antiquarian Jou-*

rnal in 1945. He was succeeded by Dermot Gleeson and the present editor, Etienne Rynne, who has consistently produced a quality publication for over thirty years. Denis Leonard and the Limerick Civic Trust have published a lot of new material, including several books, such as *Georgian Limerick* (1996) and *Remembering Limerick*

THE SHANNON, FROM ST. MARY'S CATHEDRAL.
Limerick City Museum

(1997). Other books and publications not mentioned in this introduction are listed in the bibliography.

I would like to take this opportunity to thank Tony Browne, Brian Ó Dálaigh, Gerry O'Leary and Larry Walsh for unearthing material used in this book which I might not have found otherwise. Tony walked the Plassey Bank and explored the graveyards of Kilquane, Killeely and Rossbrien with me. He also accompanied me on several walks through the city and is, in the best sense of the words, a nineteenth century gossip. He knows more about the old families and big houses of Limerick, and the adjoining counties than anyone else I have ever met and has just started to write his long-promised book on that subject. Brian

PLASSEY CAMPUS, IN THE EARLY 1990s. Shannon Development.

11

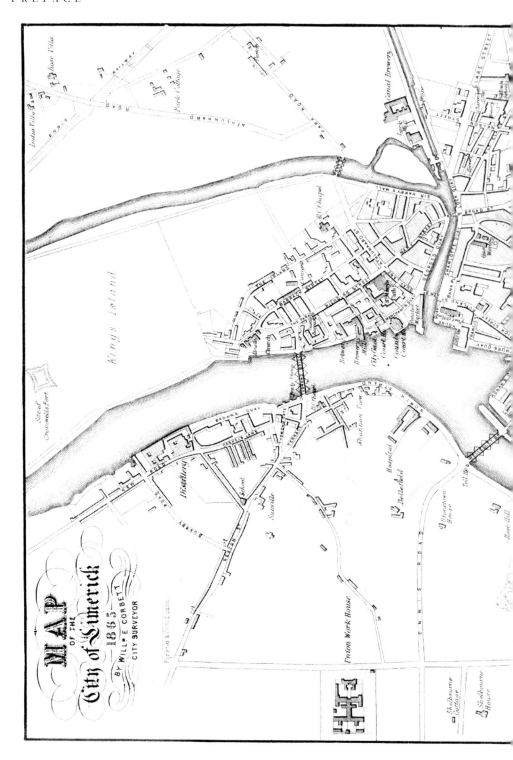

Ó Dálaigh has written extensively on Ennis; is the author of *Ennis in the 18th Century, Portrait of an Urban Community* (1995) and editor of the *Corporation Book of Ennis* (1990), is currently preparing a book on early travellers to Clare, and sent me details he had discovered of travellers who had visited Limerick in 1716, 1732 and 1844. Gerry O'Leary of Tralee supplied me with material on the origins of the place-name, Smerwick, that provided an interesting insight on Viking traders operating from Limerick. Larry Walsh curator of Limerick Museum, Michael Holland of the Hunt Museum, and Frankie O'Gorman and Gwen Walsh of the Shannon Development Company provided many of the photographs and I would like to thank them and their company for being so helpful. Each of the photographs supplied by them is acknowledged with a credit in the text. Noreen O'Neill of the City Library helped me to select several of the illustrations scattered throughout *The History of Limerick City* and Caroline Collins, her colleague, suggested various sources to augment my Limerick material. I'm sure Chris O'Mahony wished his Limerick Regional Archives were not so near the City Library as I popped in so often. Desmond M. Long provided me with details of John Raleigh's role during the War of Independence and proof-read some of my text. Tony Browne, Des Ryan, David Lee, Sean Downes, Denis Leonard, Rev. John Leonard, Larry Walsh, Rev. Donough O'Malley, Pat O'Brien, Caroline O'Brien, Geoffrey G. Ashton and Liam Irwin proof-read the original manuscript. They made various suggestions on the suitability of my text that resulted in the deletion of material that was not really relevant to the city's history, corrected my errors and drew my attention to several omissions. I am extremely grateful to them and am taking this opportunity to thank them for their time and effort. Any mistakes that remain in the text are my own and I will take full responsibility for them.

Last, but by no means least, I must thank my friends for their perseverance. Lynda O'Leary walked me into a surprise birthday party which I had been reluctant to celebrate, pleading the book as an excuse. My sister, Sinead Spellissy, and Gerry Malone helped her to set up the ambuscade with the connivance of Josie Lucas and Margaret Hurley. Sinead and Gerry were both very generous with their time and often let me off for a day to conduct my research. I am also indebted to two of my friends, each of whom has a remarkable knowledge of herbs and herbal medicine. I spent several years collecting information on the history and wild plants of the Aran Islands and both of these ladies are looking forward to my publication of a herbal book, sooner or later. Both have practices in Limerick. Majella Stackpoole and Marese McElduff are my mentors on the Aran plants and told me about the growth of alternative medicine in Limerick. Majella Stackpoole is an aromatherapist at 5 Greenpark View, Ballinacurra, and Marese McElduff is an acupuncturist at 1 Raheen Gardens, Raheen and also has a practice at 3 St. Anthony's Terrace, Ennis. She has written about traditional

Chinese medicine which can be traced back to over to 4000 years BC and was highly developed by 450 BC when the major classic, the *Nei Ching Su Wen*, was compiled.

In the normal course of events Jim Kemmy would have written the introduction to this book. I was delighted when his designated political heir, Jan O'Sullivan, said she was willing to do so and would like to take this opportunity to thank her. I would also like to thank the following people for helping me in the preparation of *The History of Limerick City*:

Phil Aylward,
St. John's Hospital.

Betty Brislane, St. Mary's Cathedral.

Tony Browne, Lifford Park.

Kathy Canavan, King John's Castle.

Margaret Casey, O'Connell Avenue.

Síobhán Carroll, Limerick Corporation.

Sean Clancy, Kilrush.

Collette Cotter, O'Mahonys' Bookshop, Limerick.

Dr. Frank Counihan, Ennis.

Pat Dempsey, Limerick and Quilty

Des Derwin, Dublin.

Owen Devereux, University of Limerick.

Catherine Doherty, Corravorrin, Ennis.

The Dore Family, Willsbrook, Limerick.

Noreen Elleker, St. Mary's Cathedral.

Alexandra Escher, Kilshanny.

Dolores Fox, St. John's Hospital.

Mary Hannan, Pennywell Road.

Kay & Ted Hanrahan, Ashbourne Park.

Larry Hayes, Castletroy Golf Club.

Gerald Healy, Monaleen National School.

John Kerin, Beechpark, Ennis.

John Leamy, Garda Station, Henry Street.

Evelyn Lee, University of Limerick

Philip Lucas, Ennis.

Mary Lynch, Texas Steakout.

Paddy Lysaght, Osmington Terrace.

Brendan Martin, City Library, Limerick.

Niall MacCullough, Ennis.

Leslie McCrum, Ennis.

Catherine McDermott, Haddington Road, Dublin.

Michael Meaney, Lissycasey.

Jean Mulholland, Limerick & Shannon.

Dympna Moroney, Clare F.M. Radio.

Mick O'Brien, Creagh Avenue, Killeely.

William O'Callaghan, Pike Treaty Anglers.

Cormac O'Connell, Clare F.M. Radio.

Ciaran Mac Gonigal,
Hunt Museum.

Síobhán O'Dwyer,
Castletroy Golf Club.

Sylvie O'Dwyer,
Kilrush, Co. Clare.

Dr. Rory O'Keeffe,
Ennis.

Marie O'Kelly,
City Library, Limerick.

David O'Mahony,
O'Connell Street,
Limerick.

Seamus O'Reilly,
Clare County Express,
Ennis

Jan O'Sullivan,
Limerick.

Mary Qualter,
Galway County Library

Arthur Quinlan,
North Circular Road.

Dr. Etienne Rynne,
Ennis & Athenry.

Noel Scanlon,
Murphy O'Laoire

Architects, Limerick.

Derek Sexton,
Limerick and Dalkey.

Dean Maurice Sirr,
St. Mary's Cathedral.

Gordon Spillane,
St. John's Hospital.

Miriam Stack,
University of Limerick

Isobel Stokes, Ennis.

Dick Tobin,
Limerick Corporation.

Reg Turner,
Croom and Limerick.

Susan Ward, Ennis.

Evelyn Lee,
Press Officer,
University of Limerick

Paul Adams,
General Manager
Shannon Heritage.

Denis Leonard,
Civic Trust Limerick.

Frankie O'Gorman,
Shannon Development.

Gwyn Walsh,
Shannon Development

Larry Walsh,
Limerick Museum

John Pierse,
Listowel

Vincent O'Shaughnessy
SciPrint Ltd.

Liam Nolan,
SciPrint Ltd.

Gary Kirby,
SciPrint Ltd.

All the staff at
SciPrint Ltd.

Paul Hyde,
ArtWorks Design Co.

Fr. John Leonard,
Dooradoyle.

Fr. Donagh O'Malley,
Our Lady of Lourdes,
Rosbrien.

Peter McNamara
The Hunt Museum

Limerick Corporation

I could not have written this book without the help of these people and others who go
unmentioned.

Séan Spellissy.

The Abbey River. Limerick City Museum

Island Settlement to Modern City - a Chronology

Vikings are the acknowledged founders of the original port and fledgling town from which the modern commercial city of Limerick evolved. In 812 they plundered a small settlement on the southern end of an island off the eastern bank of the Shannon River, the selfsame island to which they later returned as settlers and traders. This island was later named King's Island in honour of an English monarch; may have been called *Odensay*, Odin's Island, to commemorate the Viking god; was once noted as *Inis an Ghaill Duibh*, the island of the dark foreigner: is mentioned in the ancient records of the city as *Inis Sibtond*, *Inis Sibhtonn*, *Inis Sipont* and *Inis Uibhtonn*; and is familiarly known as *The Island* to all the people of Limerick. By the middle of the ninth century the Vikings had turned their crude settlement into a major maritime station and surrounded it with walls and towers. It proved to be an ideal base from which to handle the Viking trade from Atlantic Europe and gave the Vikings access and control of the Shannon Basin.

   Archaeology, folklore, history and mythology, confirm the presence of earlier settlements in the immediate vicinity. The earliest map of Ireland was prepared by an Alexandrian astronomer, Ptolemy, about 150 AD and shows a place called Regia on the approximate site of the later city of Limerick. The legendary Immar, Yvorus or Yuours, is said to have founded a city here in 155; Cormac Mac Airt fought a battle nearby in 221 and St. Patrick baptised an Eoghanacht chief, Carthann the Fair, and his infant son, Eochaidh Bailldearg, in Singland, Saingeal's Fort, in 434. The place-name of *Ros da Nochoilledh* or *Ros Dá Saileach*, the promontory of the two sally trees, seems to have predated that of Limerick and was used into the ninth or tenth century. *Luimneach*, however, is an older place-name. It can be dated back to at least 561, when an ancient poem mentioned how the body of St. Cuimin Fada was carried up the Luimneach on a boat. The name originally applied either to the Shannon Estuary or to a specific section of the Shannon River and is, more than likely, a derivative of the rather prosaic *Loimeanach*, the bare marsh. There are other explanations of the place-name *Luimneach*. The most fanciful details how the warriors of Connacht and Munster met on the banks of the Shannon to compete in war games; threw off their *luimneach liathghlas*, their grey-green cloaks, to play, became so engrossed in their sport that they forgot about the rising tide and only noticed what was happening as their grey-green cloaks were swept out of their reach in what appeared to be a grey-green rush of water. *Luimneach* has also been translated as the steed's leap because of a folk tale that relates how a horseman coaxed his mount to jump the Abbey River. The place cropped bare by horses is another explanation for *Luimneach* derived from the somewhat similar *Lom an Eich*. A tribe called the *Tuath Luimnigh* once had their territory on the southern shore of the River Shannon, were ruled by two chiefs, Ó Cadhla and Ó Máille, and may have been perpetuated in the place-name *Luimneach*.

Limerick is either a variant of the Norse term *Laemrich*, *Hlimrek* or *Allymrick*, meaning the rich land, rich soil or rich loam or a Norse corruption of the original *Luimneach*. In the latter instance the Norsification of *Luimneach* has been paralleled in Dublin, where the Viking name of that city was *Dyflin*, a debased version of *Dubhlinn*, the black pool. Thormodr Helgason, a Viking sea-king, established the first permanent stronghold on Inis Sibhtonn in 922. He was known to the native Irish as Tamar Mac Ailche and, with Limerick as his headquarters, he raided the length of the

STONE AXE FOUND AT CURRAGHGOWER. THIS STONE IMPLEMENT PREDATES THE LEGENDARY FOUNDATION OF 155 AND PROVES MAN HAS LIVED HERE SINCE PREHISTORIC TIMES, POSSIBLY SIX THOUSAND YEARS AGO.
Limerick City Museum

Shannon from Lough Derg to Lough Ree. His Vikings pillaged the ecclesiastical settlements along the banks of the Shannon and its tributaries. They carried their longships across the falls on Ireland's mightiest river, and made forays inland to plunder Meath and Connacht for treasure or captives whom they could hold, sell or trade as slaves. In 924 Tamar mac Ailche defeated a rival fleet sent against him by the Vikings of Dublin. By then the province of *Mumhan* was teeming with Vikings and there was not a harbour, landing-place, dún or fastness without its attendant fleet of Danes or pirates. It was from this period onwards that the Scandinavian term *stadr*, meaning a place, was added, as the termination *-ster*, to the place-names of three provinces creating *Mumhan-ster*, *Laighen-ster* and *Uladh-ster*, or Munster, Leinster and Ulster. In 930 another fleet of Vikings arrived into Inis Sibhtonn under the leadership of Ivar and his three sons Dubhchenn (Blackhead), Cú Allaidh (Wild Hound) and Aralt (Harold). They augmented Tamar's forces and both groups acted in concert to resist any attempts to curb their growing power or independence. In 933 Olafr Cenncaireach, Olafr Scabbyhead, dominated the midland region from his base on Inis Sibhtonn. In 934 he led his men on a rampage through Roscommon and transported his fleet from the Shannon to Lough Erne. During the depths of winter in 936 he had his longships carried from Lough Erne to Lough Ree, via Breifne. Olafr Gothfrithsson, the Viking king of Dublin raided Clonmacnoise in 936, an intrusion that was resented by Olafr Cenncaireach and the Vikings of Limerick. In August of 937 the Viking fleets of Dublin and Limerick met in battle on Lough Ree. The Vikings of Limerick were defeated, Olafr Cenncaireach was captured and the Limerick longships were broken up by the victors. By then the Vikings of Limerick had established a series of settlements scattered over what are now the counties of Limerick, Kerry, and Tipperary,

VIKING AXE HEAD, WITH WOODEN HANDLE.
Limerick City Museum

had organised themselves in the same way as the Irish tribes and had started to integrate with the natives by giving their names an Irish form. Their city, Limerick of the Swift Ships or Limerick of the Riveted Stones, rivalled Viking Dublin in many respects. As the Vikings consolidated their position the Irish fought or allied with them as circumstances dictated. An uneasy trading alliance between the two different peoples became an uncertain friendship and Limerick and Munster prospered apace.

*IRISH BRONZE AXEHEAD AND A STONE MOULD OF THE TYPE USED TO MAKE FLAT AXEHEADS ABOUT **4,000** YEARS AGO*
The Hunt Museum

The province of Munster was once dominated by a loose federation of dynastic groups known as the Eoghanacht or Eoghanachta. They derived their name and descent from Eoghan Mór, occasionally named Mogh-Nuadhat, who is said to have been responsible for the division of Ireland into two halves during the late second century. Eoghan divided his half, the southern portion, between several groups who maintained control over the occupied areas, taken from earlier peoples, by planting kingdoms in their midst. The eastern Eoghanacht held the richest of the Munster lands, those of east Limerick, Tipperary and north Cork, had become the most dominant of the Eoghanacht dynasties by the seventh century, was at its most powerful and influential peak from about 700 into the early 900s but had gone into decline after Cormac Mac Cuileannáin, king-bishop of Cashel, was killed at the battle of Belach Mughna in 908. Cormac Mac Cuileannáin, had attempted to make himself high-king of Ireland and when he had fallen in Leinster several other Eoghanacht chieftains had perished with him. Their deaths could not have come at a worse time for the Eoghanacht because as their dynasty was crumbling another was emerging from obscurity, the Dal gCais. The Dal gCais, seed of Cas, or the Dalcassians, were descended from the Déisi whose territory had extended from Waterford, through Tipperary, to Limerick. The Déisi divided into two groups, the eastern Déisi who founded the kingdom of Desmond and the western Déisi who were based in east Limerick. By 713, the year the Déisi killed Cormac Mac Ailell, the king of Munster, at Carn Feradaig (Carnarry), the western Déisi had split into two other divisions. The Déis Deiscirt identified with the Uî Fidgente and other peoples of Limerick and the Déis Tuaiscirt eventually became the Dal gCais, named after a fifth century king of north Munster. From 744 onwards the Déis Tuaiscirt established themselves in east Clare and in 934 they were first recorded in the annals of history as the Dal gCais. In 943 Cinnéididh Mac Lorcan, chief of the Dalcassians, entered into an alliance with Ceallachán, king of Munster, against the Vikings. In that year the men of Munster defeated the Vikings in the battle of Singland, drove them back behind the walls of their city and forced them to pay a heavy contribution to avoid retribution. Coinage was an alien tradition to the Irish but the Vikings had introduced coins into the country during the ninth century and imported even more during the tenth century. The earliest Viking hoards date from about this period and coins passed freely amongst the Viking colonists during the eleventh century. The native Irish, however, were reluctant to use coinage until almost into the sixteenth century.

The Vikings of Limerick may have named Smerwick in West Kerry, according to a Miss Hickson who was the local secretary of the Kerry branch of the Royal Society of Antiquaries in 1892. She wrote in the society's journal, of that year;-

> ... Smerwick, there can be no question that its second syllable is the common corruption of the old Scandinavian word *vik* for a creek or bay, which appears as *wick* in so many places on the coast of the two islands. The only question therefore is from whence came the first syllable of the word that is *"smer"*. Taylor, in his valuable (though of course not infallible) "Words and Places" says that it is a corruption of smar, the Scandinavian word for butter, and he supposes that the place was called Smarvik by the Danes, who probably traded there with the native Irish for that article. This derivation has been laughed at by Irish writers as an "impossible one", although one can hardly understand for what reason it should be considered so. The Danish kingdom of Limerick in the ninth and tenth centuries lay within less than twenty miles by sea of Smerwick, a short distance for its subjects, adventurous sea rovers, and merchants, to traverse, and it is only reasonable to suppose that they traded with the native Irish of the western coast for all kinds of agricultural produce. At the same time, certainly, they had better grazing grounds near their city than they could find in Kerry, but perhaps the native Irish of Awney and Kilmallock contested the Danish right to these too hotly to make them profitable, and so the *Dubh Gall* may have had to turn to the Kerry pasturages. The Lochlanners, whose dwellings "Viator" found traces of on the headland of the wick, were likely to have been merchants, or the agents of merchants from the Lochlanners' kingdom of Limerick, in AD 853-968.

Twenty years later P.W. Joyce stated that the Irish name of the village was *Ard-na-caithne*, the height of the arbutus, but it was generally known as Smerwick.

Ceallachán, king of Munster, was a folk hero who was notorious for forming alliances with the Vikings whenever he found it convenient to do so. He destroyed as many churches, killed as many people and took as many slaves as the most notorious of the Viking raiders. In 944 he turned on his former ally and killed two of Cinnéididh Mac Lorcan's sons. Two more of Cinnéididh's sons were killed by Congalach, the king of Tara, in 950. Cinnéididh died in 951 and in 954 Ceallachán died and was succeeded, some years later, as king of Munster, or king of Cashel, by one of Cinnéididh's sons, Mahon. By then the origins of the Dalcassians had been all but forgotten; an elaborate mythology had been constructed to further their claims to be of Eoghanacht descent; and their

The Abbey River, flowing from Sir Harry's Mall, past Baal's Bridge, with George's Quay (or Barrington's Mall) to the left, Charlotte's Quay to the right and Matthew Bridge and Rutland Street in the foreground. The Granary and St. Michael's Graveyard can be seen behind Rutland Street. **Shannon Development Photo Library.**

military and political successes ensured that Mahon was able to contest with several others for the kingship of Munster. Cinnéididh Mac Lorcan was referred to as king of Thomond and "royal heir" of Munster at the time of his death. He was succeeded by another son, Lachtna, who was killed, by rival claimants within the Dalcassian ranks, in 953. Mahon succeeded to the Dalcassian kingship while Ceallachán was succeeded by Máel Fothartaig (who was killed by the Osraige in 957), Dub Dá Boirenn mac Domnaill (slain in 959), Fer Gráid (killed in 961) and Donnchad, the son of Ceallachán, who died in 963. Mahon and his chief rival, Maél Muad mac Brian, were both members of west Munster dynasties. Mahon had seized the lands of Eoghanacht Caisil and occupied the old stronghold of Cashel in 964. Maél Muad had allied himself with Donnubán of the Uí Fidgente and the Vikings of Limerick. In 967 Mahon moved against Máel Muad and his allies, defeating them at the battle of Sulchóid. He drove the Vikings back into their city which he then proceeded to attack, sack and burn. In 969 he forced Donnubán of the Uí Fidgente to hand over hostages and, for a brief period, expelled Ivar, the king of the Limerick Vikings, from the rebuilt city; allied himself to the Éli, the Déisi and the Vikings of Waterford; and was the undoubted ruler of north and east Munster. In 972 he was one of the three men who controlled the province, the other two being Máel Muad and the king of the Déisi. The Eoghanacht and Uí Fidgente allied themselves with the Vikings of Limerick in 974 and two years later Donnubán captured Mahon by treachery. Mahon was executed by Máel Muad and Mahon's brother, Brian, succeeded him

BEAL BORU, THE FORT IN WHICH BRIAN BORU IS BELIEVED TO HAVE BEEN BORN AND REARED.
Limerick City Museum

as king of the Dalcassians, Thomond and Munster.

Brian Mac Cinnéididh (941-1014) had attacked Limerick in 967 and driven out the inhabitants. He sacked it again, in 968, but this time forced its occupants to part with some of their accumulated treasures. Brian is better known in history as Brian Bóru, Brian of the cattle tributes, and he allowed the Vikings to remain in Limerick on payment of an annual tribute, 365 tuns of wine each year. As each tun comprised thirty-two gallons, this amounted to 11,680 gallons of wine a year. Brian Bóru was more anxious to curb the power of the Vikings rather than to drive them out of the country. His capital was based in his father's old seat, Kincora, now the town of Killaloe in County Clare, and his people, the Dal gCais, once a tributary people of the Eoghanacht, now eclipsed their former overlords, due to Brian Boru's efforts and the earlier ones of his brother Mahon, father Cinnéididh and grandfather Lorcan. Scattery Island, in the mouth of the River Shannon, was over sixty miles west of Limerick. It held a mixed population, ecclesiastics and Vikings, and should have developed into another city such as Limerick. The Vikings of Limerick used it as a secondary base and refuge in time of war. In 977 Brian Bóru attacked the island and killed all of its inhabitants, a total of 600 or 800 people, a catastrophe from which Scattery never recovered. On this island he also killed the Viking king, Ivar, and his two sons, all Christians, and desecrated the ecclesiastical site on which they had sought sanctuary. In 978 he defeated the Uí Fidgente and killed Máel Muad, Mahon's executioner. From 982 onwards Brian concentrated on consolidating his grip on Munster. He came into conflict with Maelsechnaill, the king of Tara, when he campaigned against Osraige provoking Maelsechnaill into an attack on the Dalcassian inauguration place at Magh Adhair, near Quin. In 983 Brian attacked Connacht and Bréifne and in 984 he formed an alliance with the Vikings of Waterford. He and his Norse allies penetrated Uí Chinnesláig, Osraige and

THE CATHEDRAL AND ROUND TOWER ON SCATTERY ISLAND. Limerick City Museum

Leinster, ravaged Maelsechnaill's territory of Meath; captured the king of Osraige, Gilla Pátraic, and took hostages from both Leinster and Osraige. In 988 Brian Bóru suppressed several rebellions in Munster; deployed a large fleet on the Shannon to attack Connacht and Meath; and prepared to wage a series of expeditions against Maelsechnaill and his other enemies. In 985 he was attacked by the Déisi, the very group from which the Dal gCais evolved. He quickly dispersed his attackers, drove their king into Waterford and ravaged their territory. By 987 he had taken hostages from Cork, Emly and Lismore and from 988 onwards he was at war with Maelsechnaill. Brian Bóru had become the most dominant figure in Munster and the southern half of Ireland by 996 and Maelsechnaill was eventually forced to acknowledge him as such. The pair met at Clonfert in 997 and agreed to divide Ireland, leaving Maelsechnaill to rule the northern half and Brian in control of the southern half. In 999 Brian crushed a revolt by the Leinstermen and their allies, the Vikings of Dublin. Brian plundered the city of Dublin in February 1000, burned the fortress and expelled Sitric, the king of the Dublin Vikings. Sitric returned to Dublin shortly afterwards, entered into an alliance with Brian and was amongst the vast army, many of them former enemies, Brian used in order to isolate Maelsechnaill. In 1002 Maelsechnaill was forced to submit and Brian Bóru became the high-king of Ireland. The northern Uí Neill, the Ulaid and the Oirghialla retained their independence but a series of expeditions, between 1005 and 1011, eventually forced them to acknowledge Brian Bóru as their ruler. By then Brian had made himself the overlord of all Ireland. An unknown scribe had made a note to this effect in the *Book of Armagh* in 1006 when he described him as *Brian imperator Scottorum*, Brian emperor of the Irish.

The men of Leinster and the Vikings of Dublin revolted against him in 1014. The Vikings of Limerick had renewed their alliance with Brian in 1005; helped him in his campaign against the people of Ulster; and were numbered amongst his allies at the epic battle of Clontarf, on Good Friday, 23 April, 1014. Brian Bóru and his son, Murchadh, were killed in a pyrrhic victory which saw the Leinstermen and their Viking allies routed. Máel Mórda, the king of Leinster, and his Norse allies, Sigurd and Brodar, were killed but Sitric, the Viking of Dublin, had kept himself and his forces safe by taking refuge behind the walls of his city. Sitric and his Vikings had sought reinforcements from their kinsmen of the Isles. Brodar and Ospak had come to his support from the Isle of Man and Sigurd, the earl of the Orkneys, had brought his fleet to Dublin on Palm Sunday.

St. Mary's Cathedral, towering over the County Court-House. Shannon Development Photo Library.

Maelsechnaill had quarrelled with Brian Bóru prior to the battle and had led his forces homeward before hostilities commenced. The rulers of Ulster, the Munster kingdom of Osraige and most of Connacht had also refused to participate in the battle which was primarily a revolt against Brian Bóru and Dalcassian supremacy. Clontarf was mainly concerned with the internal struggle for sovereignty while the Viking role was of secondary importance as most of them had merely supported the rebellion of the Leinstermen. Long before then Viking colonists had been assimilated into an Irish way of life, acknowledged native kings and sub-kings as their overlords and had become a political force in many of the areas in which they had settled. The Irish admired the Vikings as merchants and mercenaries, fought or allied with them as circumstances dictated, imitated their vessels and traded with them in their own ports for overseas goods. An uneasy trading alliance blossomed into uncertain friendship between the Vikings and the native Uí Fidgente after the battle of Sulchóid in 967. The ruling houses of

STONE TRIAL PIECE, WITH ATTRACTIVE ILLUSTRATIONS. Limerick City Museum.

both peoples intermarried and the resulting friendly relationships softened the Viking prejudices against Christianity. When the Vikings converted to Christianity they adopted St. Munchin of the Uí Fidgente as their patron saint. One of their number, Gilbert or Gilla Easpuig, was consecrated bishop of Limerick in 1106 or 1107. Scattery Island, the secondary Viking settlement founded by the Vikings, was united with the bishopric of Limerick in 1195. It formed part of the parish of St. Mary and remained within the jurisdiction of the Limerick Corporation until 1854. It was then annexed, by order of Privy Council, to the Barony of Moyarta, County Clare, in November of that year. Some Viking descendants are said to live on, or close to, Inis Sibhtonn to the present day and are widely known as the Danes of Limerick. They were driven outside the walls of the city during the seventeenth-century Cromwellian occupation but settled on a long narrow tract of land, nearby, the riverside district of Park. This region straddles the three townlands of Lower Park, Rhebogue and Singland, lies to the north-east of the old city, is bounded by the River Shannon to the west and lay outside the city boundaries until 1840. Limerick's Scandinavian past is reflected in surnames such as Costelloe, Cotter, Doyle, Godfrey, Hally, Harold, Hastings, Howard, Kenrick, MacAuliffe, Nihill, O'Brouder, O'Loughlin, and Setright. The surnames of some of the oldest families in Park are a blend of native, Viking and Anglo-Norman origin. The Cunneens are said to have been associated with the area since the time of St. Patrick, the Shannys were members of a select group, the Abbey Fishermen, who fished the Shannon for salmon, the Clancys reserved their own Catholic burial-plot within the confines of the Protestant Cathedral of St. Mary, the Hannan name will always be associated with that of the late Kevin Hannan, the city's foremost modern historian and the Cross, Cusack, Cussen, Danagher, Gallagher, Hynes, Kane, Keehan, Kenny, Lawlor, MacMahon, MacNamara, Mullally, O'Halloran, Quilligan, Ryan, Troy and Woods surnames have been woven into the fabric of Park life for centuries.

The rise of the Dal gCais had turned the Vikings of Limerick into a tributary people under Dalcassian rule. The battle of Clontarf, however, marked the decline of Viking and Dalcassian power. Brian Bóru had great military ability, was able to command loyalty and support from former enemies (such as the Vikings of Limerick), was an able manipulator of churchmen and had broken the Uí Neill domination of the country and high-kingship which had persisted for centuries. But for his untimely death at Clontarf he might have established a strong centralised monarchy. The dynasty he founded never achieved the same level of power and even though his heirs described themselves as kings of Ireland they were merely *rithe co fresebra*, kings with opposition. None of them ever became undisputed monarch of all Ireland and Brian Bóru's achievements and subsequent death simply opened a pathway to the high-kingship for dynasties other than his own. He was succeeded by his son Teige who died in 1023, probably at the instigation of Donnchadh, the half-brother of Sitric, the Viking

LIMERICK HALF-PENNY, DATING FROM THE REIGN OF KING JOHN. Limerick City Museum.

king of Dublin and nephew of Máel Mordha, king of Leinster. Brian had married Gormlaith (c. 955-1042), a princess of Leinster who had previously been married to Olaf Cuarán, the Viking king of Dublin and Brien's chief rival, Maelsechnaill. Donnchadh was the son of Brian and Gormlaith and had succeeded to the throne of Munster after Teige's death. Teige's son, Turlough, eventually deposed Donnchadh, with the aid of Dermot, the King of Leinster and the former king died while on a pilgrimage to Rome in 1064. Turlough seems to have been the first of Brien's family to use the surname *O'Briain*, descendant of Brian, a name famous in the annals of Munster and Ireland as O'Brien. Eleanor Hull's *History of Ireland* credits Donnchadh Cairbreach O'Brien (1194-1242) as being the first to adopt the O'Brien surname. Turlough O'Brien laid claim to the high-kingship in 1072, forced Ulster to pay him tribute and dominated most of the provincial kings and chieftains. He remained a high-king with opposition and died, at Kincora, in 1086. He was succeeded as king of Munster by his son, Murtagh

Mór. Murtagh Mór O'Brien spent most of his reign contesting with Domhnall mac Lochlainn for the high-kingship of Ireland, a contest that was almost resolved at Lough Neagh in 1090 when Domhnall recognised Murtagh Mór as the monarch of Munster, Leinster and Connacht. The peace was short-lived as both Domhnall and his rival were determined on the high-kingship. Murtagh Mór O'Brien died in 1119 but his reign and that of his father, Turlough, had unfortunate repercussions on Kincora which was the seat of the kingdom of Thomond. Kincora had been located on the summit of the hill on which part of Killaloe now stands. It was rebuilt and strengthened by Brian Bóru in 1002 but was destroyed by the men of Connacht in 1016. As Turlough and Donnchadh O'Brien fought for the throne of Munster in 1062 the restored Kincora was burned by Aodh O'Connor. It was sacked by Rory O'Connor in 1081 and burned, yet again, by the men of Breifne in 1084. Domhnall mac Lochlainn destroyed Kincora in 1088 but long before then it had become a secondary capital for the O'Briens. Brian Bóru had been crowned in Cashel in 977 and his descendants had retained it as the seat of their kingdom of Munster. Murtagh Mór O'Brien had established a new capital in Limerick by 1100 and in 1101 he gave his former capital of Cashel to the Church. In 1107 Kincora was struck by lightning and set on fire but it had been repaired by 1114 as Murtagh Mór was then in residence. He was in poor health at the time as illness had reduced him the condition of a skeleton. Dermot O'Brien, his brother, assumed control of the kingdom for a brief period but the more warlike Murtagh Mór wrested the power back into his own hands. In 1116 Turlough O'Connor burned both Kincora and Beal Bóru. Murtagh Mór O'Brien died in 1119 and in 1124 Connacht's Turlough O'Connor returned to attack the ancient Dalcassian stronghold of Kincora. This time he took the fort, levelled it completely and threw the stones and timbers of Brian's great palace into the waters of the River Shannon. Murtagh Mór O'Brien was the last of Brian's line who could truthfully claim to be king of Ireland. His successors were kings of Munster, kings of Thomond or kings of Limerick but the size of the kingdom they administered

SILVER PENNY FROM THE LIMERICK MINT, STRUCK DURING THE REIGN OF KING JOHN. Limerick City Museum

fluctuated in accordance with their fortunes. Under Murtagh Mór O'Brien the territory of Thomond included most of the later county of Clare, with the exception of its northern and north-western regions, and all of the later counties of Limerick and Tipperary, extending into Offaly, a district co-extensive with the diocesan territories of Emly, Killaloe and Limerick. By 1201 Thomond had shrunk to a region comprising most of Clare (with the exception of the Burren, Corcomroe and Tradraighe) and some parts of south Galway.

Dermot O'Brien succeeded Murtagh Mór as king of Munster and reigned as such up to the time of his death in 1148. He had six sons, two of whom succeeded him as kings of Munster. Conor na Cathrach O'Brien was king of Munster and Leinster and died in Killaloe in 1142. Conor na Cathrach's son, Murtagh, was king of Thomond and was killed at Moinmore in 1151. Conor na Cathrach's brother, Turlough O'Brien, succeeded him as king of Munster and another brother, Teige Glae O'Brien, the progenitor of the O'Briens of Aran, succeeded Murtagh as king of Thomond in 1167. In 1153 Turlough O'Connor, the king of Connacht, laid siege to the city of Limerick and forced its Viking inhabitants to renounce the O'Brien authority and drive Turlough O'Brien west of the Shannon River. Turlough O'Brien abdicated in favour of his son, Murtagh Dun na Sgiath, in 1165 but regained the kingdom for himself in 1166. He died in 1167 and was succeeded by Murtagh who was killed by his cousin, Conor O'Brien, in 1168. Domhnall Mór O'Brien succeeded his brother, Murtagh. He blinded another brother, Brian na Sléibhe, who had just been inaugurated as king of Ormond, rendering him unfit to rule under Brehon Law. Domhnall Mór O'Brien was the last of the O'Briens to reign as king of Munster. From 1169 to 1173 he was at war with Connacht. He swore homage and allegiance to Henry

OLD THOMOND BRIDGE. Limerick City Museum

II (1154-1189) at Cashel in 1172. This was done mainly to achieve new allies but, in the process, gave Anglo-Normans their first foothold in Munster. In 1171 Robert Fitzstephen and his band of Anglo-Norman adventurers and mercenaries came to Limerick to help Domhnall Mór. Pope Adrian IV had encouraged the Anglo-Norman invasion of 1169 after Henry II had proposed that he enter the country, subject its people to law and extend the boundaries of the Church to a rude and ignorant people. In 1152 Ireland was divided into thirty-six ecclesiastical sees with four archbishoprics Armagh, Cashel, Dublin and Tuam. Cardinal Paparo, the Papal Legate, was aware of how the Irish Church had the organisational ability to attend to its own pastoral needs. His report on the true state of affairs in this country was either falsified or misunderstood by the pope who granted Henry II's envoy, John of Salisbury, the bull *Laudabiliter* of 1156, a document that gave approval to the proposed conquest of Ireland. In May of 1169 Robert Fitzstephen, Hervey de Montmorency and Maurice de Prendergast landed their forces at Bannow Bay, County Wexford. Richard de Clare (Strongbow) landed near Waterford in August, 1170 and Henry II came ashore at Crook, close to Waterford, on 17 October 1171.

Domhnall Mór O'Brien turned on his Anglo-Norman allies in 1174 and drove them out of the city. He then burned Limerick declaring that it would no longer be a nest for foreigners and killed 1700 men, under Strongbow's command at a battle near Thurles. The Anglo-Normans returned to Limerick in 1175. Raymond le Gros and the king of Ossory forded the Shannon, and obtained booty from the inhabitants, the resident Vikings or Ostmen, who welcomed their arrival. The hostile Irish admired their bravery but this time the Anglo-Normans decided to secure the city by establishing a garrison within it. Raymond le Gros abandoned the city after the death of Strongbow. Domhnall Mór O'Brien, to whom it had been entrusted, destroyed the bridge and burned the city in 1176, after the Anglo-Normans left. It took the latter twenty years to recover it. Long before then Domhnall Mór realised that his erstwhile allies were his most dangerous enemies. This realisation was confirmed when Henry II gave a grant of the kingdom of Limerick to Herbert Fitzherebert, who seems to have resigned his uncertain inheritance in favour of Philip de Braose, who was granted the kingdoms of Limerick and Thomond by the council of Oxford in 1177, the same year in which Henry II confirmed his youngest son, Prince John, in the lordship of Ireland. John retained this title throughout the remaining years of his father's reign, most of Richard the Lionheart's reign (1189 - 1199) and his own (1199 - 1216). He was also Count of Mortain, in Normandy, from 1189 - 1199 but was deprived of his Norman and English lands in 1194 and 1195 for trying to usurp his crusading brother's throne. In 1185 John brought another Anglo-Norman army into Ireland, accompanied by many prospective settlers and Giraldus Cambrensis (c. 1147 - c. 1223). Giraldus Cambrensis was the author of *Topographia Hibernica* (Topography of Ireland) and *Expugnatio Hibernica* (Conquest of Ireland) and had first come to Ireland in 1183. He had visited his uncle, Robert Fitzstephen, in Munster, possibly during the earlier visit. Giraldus Cambrensis, Gerald of Wales or Giraldus de Barri is best described as an early propagandist who misrepresented Ireland and its history on behalf of his patron, Henry II. John F. O'Meara translated his works in *Gerald of Wales - The History and Topography of Ireland*. In the preface Giraldus de Barri thanked Henry II for sending him to Ireland with John in an obsequious address using all of his overlord's titles. He described the Shannon as the chief river of the country and said that it originated in a large lake that divided Connacht from Munster. It flowed in two different directions, according to Giraldus, and one arm flowed southwards, past Killaloe and Limerick, separating the two Munsters from one another for a distance of over one hundred miles. He referred to the dominance of the Norwegian colonists from whom the Ostmen of Limerick were descended and stated they had arrived into Ireland disguised as traders. They occupied the seaports, led by three brothers, Amelavus, Sitaracus and Yvorus, who were the founders, respectively of the cities of Dublin, Waterford and Limerick. Norwegian settlers spread outwards from these secure bases and went on to build other settlements throughout the country. They then went to war with the native Irish and the latter defended themselves by developing the use of battle-axes.

Giraldus suggested that the kings of Britain had a twofold claim on Ireland since ancient times, that the Irish went into battle naked and unarmed until they had been taught to use short spears, darts and big axes by the Norwegians and Ostmen; that the inhabitants of this country were a wild and inhospitable people who were ignorant of the law and the rudiments of the Christian faith and that there had been no arch-bishoprics in the island until John Papiro had established four *pallia* here in 1152. He referred to the incomparable skill of the people in making

GROAT, A SILVER FOUR-PENNY PIECE, FOUND NEAR SIXMILEBRIDGE, COUNTY CLARE.
Limerick City Museum.

musical instruments, but most of his material was concerned with regurgitating old myths and downgrading the Irish and their abilities. He also wrote of the great number of people who were maimed and left a description of a freak attached to Domhnall Mór O'Brien's court, a woman who had a beard down to her waist and a crest of hair running along the length of her spine. Despite her infirmities she was very feminine and was not a hermphrodite.

John ignored Domhnall Mór O'Brien's position as king of Munster and granted five cantreds and a half of the Irish rulers lands to Theobald Walter, the progenitor of the Butlers of Ormond. Domhnall Mór defeated the English prince's forces in the same year, 1185, and then resumed his attacks on Connacht by invading Galway. Thomond was attacked by the Connachtmen under the leadership of Cathal O'Connor who ordered the burning of the O'Brien palace and town at Killaloe. Domhnall Mór O'Brien seems to have had a tempestuous and contentious life up to the time of his death in 1194. He may have been the first of the O'Brien kings to realise that he would be unable to hold Limerick as he had ceded his former palace to the church long before he died. He had nine sons, four of whom succeeded him as king of Thomond. Murtagh Dall, his immediate successor, was captured by the Anglo-Normans and blinded at the instigation of Conor O'Brien, thus becoming ineligible to rule. Conor Roe succeeded Murtagh Dall in 1194 but was dethroned in 1198 and killed by his nephew in 1201. It was during the brief reign of Conor Roe O'Brien that the Anglo-Normans took possession of the city which Henry II had reserved for himself even as he signed the treaty of Windsor in 1175. Limerick did not become an Anglo-Norman stronghold during Domhnall Mór's lifetime as he was too powerful. Until then, the Anglo-Norman presence remained insecure although the new invaders cultivated the city's Ostmannic population, the descendants of the Vikings. As the O'Briens fought amongst themselves for the kingdom of Thomond the Anglo-Normans re-entered the city in 1195. John had been designated Lord of Ireland, a title which suggested that the English kings

A GROAT, A SILVER FOUR-PENNY PIECE, FROM THE REIGN OF EDWARD IV. Limerick City Museum

thought of the country as a feudal lordship rather than as a kingdom. John, initially, showed little interest in his Irish fief as the pope was technically it owner. He alienated many of the chieftains who had met him in Waterford when he landed there on 25 April, 1185. He had treated them quite rudely, deprived them of their lands; and drove them into the armed camps of his enemies, the O'Briens, MacCarthys and O'Connors. By 1195 his attitude had changed considerably as he had been stripped of his English and Norman possessions. In that year the MacCarthy of Desmond drove the Anglo-Normans out of the city. They returned shortly afterwards but by then Richard I was having problems with the Anglo-Norman barons of Ireland and his own brother. John had rebelled against Richard the Lionheart in 1193 and 1194 and in 1195 Richard's representatives, John de Courcy and the son of Hugh de Lacy, successfully led an army against the Anglo-Normans of Leinster and Munster and destroyed John's land in Ireland. John later revenged himself on them when he succeeded to the English throne. By 1196 the Anglo-Normans were in secure possession of the city of Limerick, apparently with the consent of Conor Roe O'Brien and his kinsmen.

In 1197 Limerick is said to have received its first charter and installed a mayor, Adam Sarvant, and corporation under John's stewardship, ten years before London installed its own mayor and corporation. There is no evidence, however, to support this mayoral myth. John succeeded to the English throne in 1199. During his reign the constitution of the first shires or counties began with the intention of making English law effective in Ireland. William de Burgo married a daughter of Domhnall Mór O'Brien. He received a grant of lands in County Limerick from King John, built a castle in Castleconnell in 1201, and

KING JOHN'S CASTLE DURING THE 1980s. NOTE THE CORPORATION HOUSES WITHIN ITS WALLS AND ST. MARY'S COURT TO THE RIGHT OF THE CASTLE. **Shannon Development Photo Library.**

33

was confirmed in the ownership of his lands in 1209 and 1211. He was also the founder of an Anglo-Norman enclave within the city of Limerick which defied all Irish efforts to dislodge it. A strong castle and bridge were erected and Anglo-Norman settlers congregated here in great numbers. They established amicable relations with the inhabitants of the surrounding countryside and Irish names appeared amongst the names of the chief magistrates, even though these were generally of Anglo-Norman, Flemish, Italian and, later, English descent. Donnchadh Cairbreach O'Brien was the brother-in-law of William de Burgo. He derived his name from either Cairbreach Aova (now Kenry) where he was educated or from the adjective, *cairbreach*, the ruddy or rough-complexioned. He succeeded his brothers, Murtagh Dall and Conor Roe, as king of Thomond, but was a king with opposition as another brother, Murtagh Finn O'Brien, was also styled king of Thomond up to the time of his death in 1239. Donnchadh Cairbreach O'Brien seems to have anticipated the Anglo-Norman conquest at an early date, When Prince John landed at Waterford in 1185 Donnchadh Cairbreach was at hand to meet him. He paid homage to the English prince, acknowledged him as lord of Ireland; purchased the lands and lordship of Carrigogunnell for himself and his heirs forever, at an annual rent of £40, and sided with the Anglo-Normans in order to protect his territory. He succeeded Conor Roe as king of Thomond and was recognised as such by the Anglo-Normans. John gave him a grant of Thomond and declared that any other claimants, such as Donnchadh Cairbreach's brothers, were usurpers and enemies of the English crown. Donnchadh Cairbreach realised that he would eventually lose Limerick City to the Anglo-Normans and decided to move his residence and capital elsewhere. Between 1208 and 1216 he built what must have been the last royal *dún* in Europe in *Inis Cluain Rámh Fhada*, the island of the meadow of the long rowing, a place later known as Ennis Clonroad, and, eventually, Ennis. This was a shrewd and perceptive move and enabled his descendants to retain their kingdom until 1543 when Murrough the Tanist O'Brien transformed Thomond into an earldom under the surrender and regrant policy advocated by Henry VIII. Domhchadh Cairbreach O'Brien's move to Ennis ensured the survival of the O'Briens as kings and earls of Thomond, Viscounts Clare and Lords Inchiquin. Although an ally of the Anglo-Normans he occasionally warred against them. He attacked Limerick City in 1234 but later made peace with Henry III (1216-1272) in 1235 after he was defeated in battle by the justiciar, Maurice Fitzgerald, and his fellow Normans, Richard de Burgo, Hugh de Lacy, Walter de Ridelisford and John Cogan. Donnchadh Cairbreach O'Brien died in 1242, the last O'Brien to rule from Limerick.

Limerick and the other Viking settlements of Cork, Dublin, Waterford and Wexford were the only true towns in Gaelic Ireland at the time of the Anglo-Norman invasion. The Anglo-Normans built more towns and utilised these and

THE OLD HARBOUR AS IT LOOKED PRIOR TO WORK COMMENCING ON WELLESLEY BRIDGE IN 1824 -
Fitzgerald and Mc Gregor.

the existing ones as strongholds from which they could dominate the surrounding countryside. The 1197 charter awarded to Limerick (of which there is no official record) granted it the same privileges as Dublin had received in its grant in 1192. Inis Sibhtonn seems to have been renamed King's Island from the days of King John and became the base from which the present city developed. Prince John may have been residing at Laon, eighty-three miles to the north-east of Paris, on 18 December, 1197, when he is said to have granted a charter to Limerick. The MacCarthy of Desmond drove the Anglo-Normans out of the city in 1198 but they returned shortly afterwards. Donnchadh Cairbreach O'Brien captured the city in 1234 but Richard, Earl Marshall of England, took it after a four-day siege. William de Braose had received a grant of Limerick in

KING JOHN'S CASTLE, ALMOST A CENTURY AGO. Limerick City Museum.

1203 but King John regretted his magnanimity and tried to reclaim it. William insisted on his right to it, a right formally recognised in 1205. John regained it in 1206 but his dispute with William de Braose escalated. In 1210 he besieged William's castle in Meath; captured William's wife, son and daughter-in law; and had all three, "laden with cruel chains", sent to England where they were imprisoned in Windsor. King John landed at Crook, near Waterford, on 20 June; spent a little over nine weeks in Ireland; brought the de Braose lordship of Limerick to an end; drove the de Lacys out of Ulster and Meath; and, according to an English chronicler, received the homage of twenty Irish kings. During the reign of Henry III (1216-1272) there was a firm belief that King John had drawn up a charter concerning the observance of the laws and customs of England and had persuaded the Irish magnates to implement the same laws and customs in Ireland. This charter may have been drawn up when he held council in Dublin, during August, but no record of any such document now remains. By then Limerick and Tipperary was a county governed by a royal sheriff, one of the two Munsters mentioned by Gerald Cambrensis, the other being Thomond, the kingdom of Domhnall Mor O'Brien. Dublin had been shired by the 1190s, or earlier. The Anglo-Norman Munster, the later counties of Limerick and Tipperary, seems to have been shired in 1210 and was described as shired in 1211 and 1212; possessed separate shire courts as early as 1235; and had become distinctly separate shires, each with its own sheriff, between 1251 and 1254. Connacht became a shire in 1247. Meath and Kildare were constituted counties in 1297. Before that date the only recognised shires or counties were Connacht, Cork, Dublin, Kerry, Limerick, Louth, Roscommon, Tipperary and Waterford. Clare did not become a county until 1569 when Connacht was divided into Clare, Galway, Mayo, Roscommon and Sligo, a partition which left Clare and the North Liberties of Limerick City within the province of Connacht until 1660.

Limerick is an ancient city well-studied in the arts of war, according to its motto, *Urbs Antiqua Fuit Studiisque Asperrima Belli*. The city's coat-of-arms is represented by a gate-tower complete with portcullis, flanked by two towers, an apt depiction of the entrance into the city or the castle founded by King John to keep watch over Thomond and the O'Briens. Edward II (1298-1328) made grants available to enclose the suburbs and repair King John's Castle as the prevailing climate rendered additional military

LIMERICK COAT OF ARMS.
Shannon Development Photo Library.

defences necessary. Norman weaponry, the long sword, lance and longbow, coupled with the use of body armour, iron helmets and coats of mail (metal chains, rings or plates joined together) and the use of military strategy based on organised plans allowed the Anglo-Normans to conquer most of Ireland by the year 1250. Their Irish opponents relied on the axe, short sword, spear, javelin and sling-shots, disdained the use of protective clothing and fought their battles as individuals rather than team-players. The internecine warfare in which the Irish chieftains engaged left them at a major disadvantage when the Anglo-Normans advanced into Munster. As the Anglo-Normans settled into Limerick they introduced their own form of government, based on that of England, and gave the citizens of the city the same rights and privileges as those held by the inhabitants of Bristol and Dublin. The municipal privileges bestowed by the charter empowered the citizens and allowed them to form a corporation. Limerick benefited from the new order and as the population increased the boundaries were extended and the fortifications strengthened. In 1237 Henry III granted the customs of the city to the "good men of Limerick" to finance the extension and carry out the necessary work on the city's defences. This amounted to a tax on all goods sold in the Limerick market, butter, cheese, cloth, cattle, herrings, hides, hogs, honey, horses, iron, lead, oats, onions, salmon, salt, sheep, wheat, wine, wood, wool, and other wares.

Gold and silver ornaments, or even parts of such ornaments, hacked into pieces by the Vikings, formed our first currency. The first coins struck in Ireland were issued by the Vikings of Dublin in the late 900s. Brian Bóru's stepson, Sitric, Sithric Anlafsson or Silkenbeard, the Viking king of Dublin was commemorated on Hiberno-Norse coinage issued by Faeremin, a moneyer of Dublin, from about 1000 to 1035. John was created Lord of Ireland in 1172, Count of Mortain in 1189 and king of England in 1199. John may have had silver halfpennies, bearing his profile and name, struck during his first visit to Ireland in 1185. Another series of silver halfpennies and some farthings, bearing a representation of his face and the legend *Lord of Ireland*, were minted between 1190 and 1199, in Carrickfergus, Dublin, Kilkenny, Limerick and Waterford. The first Limerick mint appears to have come into operation between 1195 and 1199, possibly under the direction of Siward, the first recorded Limerick moneyer. King John tightened up the administration of

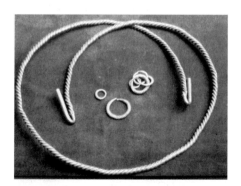

Gold torc and gold rings about 3,000 years old, made by twisting solid pieces of gold, to be seen in the Hunt Museum.

37

his Irish Lordship in 1200 by reserving to himself all Irish pleas regarding the Crown, the exchange and the mint. About five years later he redesigned the silver penny and specified the weight (22.5 grains) and silver content of each. These coins were minted at Dublin, Limerick and Waterford, primarily for overseas use and as payments for war service. Other coins, mainly halfpennies and farthings, were issued for normal trading purposes within each of the three cities. William Wace was the Limerick moneyer who issued penny, halfpenny and farthing coins between 1204 and 1211. During the reign of Henry III (1216-1272) the Norman conquerors of England were absorbed by the Angles and Saxons they had conquered and a new national identity was formed. The derogatory term, *Englishman*, which the Normans had applied to their conquered foes was borne by Norman,

A GOLD AND ENAMEL CROSS, ENGLISH, SIXTEENTH-CENTURY, IN THE HUNT MUSEUM.

Saxon and Angle alike. A similar process was underway in Ireland as some to the Anglo-Norman barons became more Irish than the Irish themselves. Coining operations recommenced in Dublin in 1251 and in 1252 a mint was established in Limerick to issue coinage on a regular basis. The Dublin mint closed in 1254 and the Limerick mint may have been shut down at the same time. During the reign of Edward I (1272-1307) the names of moneyers or mintmasters were no longer borne by the coins they struck. Limerick was burned in 1274, apparently by accident, while it was occupied by Richard de la Rokel, a former justiciar, and other magnates who were using it as a base from which to suppress the Irish. The city was rebuilt with a levy of twenty marks (£13.33) from each of the counties under English rule. In 1467 a temporary mint was opened in Limerick during the reign of Edward IV (1461-1483). Henry VI had been deposed in 1461; seized the English throne for a period of six months in 1470 but was, again, forced to abdicate; and had no coins minted in Ireland during the brief period of his restoration. Silver pennies seem to have been struck in Limerick as late as 1478 but it seems to have been closed before 1483 when the last coinage of Edward IV's reign was minted in Dublin and Drogheda. For a long time the Irish chieftains had been reluctant to adopt the use of coinage. When a monetary economy came into play with the *surrender and regrant policies* of Henry VIII (1509-1547) the chieftains benefited even further by turning their former clansmen and followers into coin-paying tenants. Henry VIII believed in central government with all of the organs of state under his own control, in London. It was during his reign that the decision to mint all Irish money in the English capital came into effect and a new title, *Hiberniae Rex*, king of Ireland, replaced *Dominus Hiberniae*, Lord of Ireland on all Irish coins from June 1541 onwards. Prior to this date the English kings were said to have held the temporal lordship of Ireland from the popes. A new act was passed recognising Henry VIII as King of Ireland in order to convince the Irish people that this widely-held belief was a fallacy. The Dublin mint opened in 1548 during the reign of Edward VI (1547-1553) but no Irish coinage was minted in this country during the reigns of Mary Tudor (1553-1558) or Elizabeth I (1558-1603).

The Black Book of Limerick records a number of financial transactions that took place between Hubert, a bishop of Limerick from 1223 to 1250, and a number of foreign bankers. In 1229 he borrowed money to meet papal taxation from Stephen Manetti, a member of the Florentine-Roman firm owned by Bernardo Rusticii, Andreas Millarius, Juvenalis Manetti, Mattheus Bonesalti and Maynerus Bellioci. A Roman banker, named Caranzone, arranged the loan which was repaid by 1237. The first "banknotes", however, seem to have been issued by goldsmiths during the reign of Elizabeth I (1558-1603). Because of their dealings in bullion and plate goldsmiths needed strongrooms to protect their stock against fire and theft. They were approached by others to hold coins, jewels, plate and other valuables within the safe custody of their strongrooms and issued receipts for these items. Eventually they accepted sums of money for safe-keeping, issued receipts known as either "notes" or "cash-notes" to whoever lodged the money, and, inadvertently, became bankers as these promissory notes passed from hand to hand. Moneylending developed as a separate trade from goldsmithing, however, wherever middlemen could introduce parties who needed money to those who were willing to lend it. In 1634 an Irish Act of

BANK POST BILL, ISSUED BY THOMAS AND WILLIAM ROCHE, AN EARLY BANKNOTE. *Limerick City Museum*

Parliament restricted usury, limited the legal rate of interest to ten per cent per annum and applied controls to the fees payable to brokers, clerks and solicitors. The first mention of bankers, as such, dates from 1709 when another Irish Act of Parliament stipulated that all notes issued by bankers, goldsmiths, merchants or traders should be "assignable or transferable by delivery or endorsement". The first record of a bank in the city dates back to 1789 when the *Bank of Limerick*, popularly known as *Maunsells' Bank*, was established. Thomas Maunsell (c.1732-1814) of Plassey was the son of Richard Maunsell, a mayor of the city in 1734. He seems to have been the senior partner in this enterprise, along with his brother Robert Maunsell (1745-1832) of Bank Place and his wife's brother-in-law Sir Matthew Blakiston (1760-1806), the son of a former mayor of London. The other partners, at various stages, were Robert Hedges Eyre Maunsell who was married to Elizabeth Dorothea, the daughter and co-heir of Thomas Maunsell, George Maunsell of Milford, Thomas Brock, John Kennedy and John Carleton, Junior. The bank was forced to close in 1820. Thomas and William Roche were two of the four sons, all bankers, of Stephen Roche, a wine-importer and butter exporter in the Limerick of 1769. Two of his sons became bankers in Cork and by 1799 Thomas and William were operating a provision business in Dominick Street, Limerick. They opened a bank in 1801; gradually took over the business of the *Bank of Limerick*, between 1809 and 1820; were amongst the few bankers to survive the disastrous year of 1820 when bank after bank failed; and curtailed their banking activities before selling their *Limerick Bank* to the new *Provincial Bank* which opened on 1 November, 1825. Ireland had prospered as an agricultural country after the outbreak of the Napoleonic war in 1803, Irish foodstuffs had been urgently needed to feed the population of Britain and grain prices had soared to record levels by 1812 as the English harvests of 1808 and 1810 had been exceptionally poor. Bankers had advanced credit to their clients as land prices soared but as Napoleon's power declined the English were able to import cheap continental grain and agricultural prices collapsed in Ireland. As land had been the principal security offered by creditors the banks were unable to recover their capital and bankruptcy proceedings followed, many of them coming to a head in 1820. In 1803 another *Limerick Bank* was opened by Michael Furnell who was high sheriff of Limerick in 1795, Henry Bevan of Camass, Bruff, and Mathias Woodsmason who may have been an experienced banker elsewhere before taking up residence at Ballyglashin, Newcastle. This bank was also known as *Furnell's Bank*; was forced into bankruptcy by 1806; but its creditors seem to have lost only a small proportion of their claims. George Evans Bruce was high sheriff of the county in 1800 and set up his own bank, *George Evans Bruce and Company*, when *Furnell's Bank* closed in 1806. His partners in this bank and in another banking firm, the *Charleville Bank*, in County Cork were Eyre Evans and George Bruce Evans. Both banks were dissolved, voluntarily, in

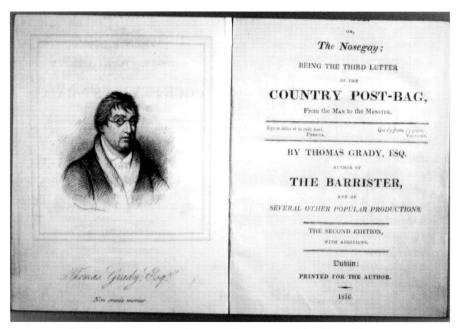

THE NOSEGAY, PUBLISHED BY THOMAS O'GRADY IN 1816. Limerick City Museum.

1820 and all creditors were paid in full. George Evans Bruce was viciously satirised in a satirical poem, *The Nosegay*, by Thomas "Spectacles" O'Grady. In 1810 Thomas "Spectacles" O'Grady borrowed £1,300 from the banker. George Evans Bruce demanded the money back in 1812 and it was repaid immediately. The two men quarrelled, George Evans Bruce circulated anonymous letters besmirching the name of his former creditor and the latter responded with a satirical poem that was savage, violent and venomous. George Evans Bruce tried to claim damages of £20,000 in court, was awarded £500 and six old pence (two-and-a-half new pence) and wound up without a penny of the money as Thomas "Spectacles" O'Grady left the county rather than pay damages to his foe.

The Tudor city was a prosperous place. Gerald, the earl of Kildare, held a parliament here in 1484, the year before Henry VII (1485-1509) came to the English throne. In 1495 the brotherhood of the Guild of Merchants was formed. Commercial jealousy between Limerick and Galway erupted into open hostility by 1524. In 1536 peace was restored with a formal treaty and by an injunction from Henry VIII (1509-1547) stating that he required a better demeanour from the men of Galway. Henry was declared king of Ireland in 1542. Alderman Sexten was his greatest proponent in Limerick, and in 1543 Sir Anthony St. Leger convened a parliament here in which many important acts were passed. The earl of Thomond and his followers swore fealty to the Crown when Lord-Deputy Sussex arrived to help him "suppress a revolt of some inferior branches of the O'Brien family against their chief" towards the end of Queen Mary's reign (1553-1558)

Fr. David Woulfe, Apostolic Commissary in Ireland from 1561, was persuaded, by Hugh O'Donnell, to give his allegiance to Queen Elizabeth. Despite his pledge, he was imprisoned in Dublin Castle by Sir Henry Sydney until he escaped in July 1572 after an incarceration of five years. He sailed for Spain in September, 1573. In 1568 and 1574 he prepared two reports on his homeland for the benefits of the Spanish ambassador and King Philip of Spain. The 1574 *Description of Ireland* begins with;

> Touching the City of Limerick. Limerick is stronger and more beautiful than all the other cities of Ireland, well walled with stout walls of hewn marble, and is an island city in the middle of that rapid Shannon river, and there is no entrance except by stone bridges, one of the two of which has 14 arches, and the other 8 ... for the most part the houses are of square stone of black marble and built in the form of towers or fortresses. The suburb of the city is even better walled ... and there are ten towers or bulwarks, most beautiful and strong about it, which allow no one to come near the wall.

The walls extended round a circuit of about three miles. Despite the many wars that devastated the whole of the surrounding province Limerick maintained the most unshaken loyalty to Elizabeth I. Sir Henry Sydney, lord deputy of Ireland visited here in 1567, 1569 and in 1576. He stated that he was received with greater magnificence than he had hitherto experienced in Ireland. In 1579 Sir William Pelham arrived here as lord deputy. The mayor appeared before him attended by 1,000 well-armed citizens. The city militia amounted to 800 men in 1584, double that of Cork and a third more than that of Waterford, making Limerick the most important city in Ireland, next to Dublin. During the Earl of Desmond's rebellion Limerick became the headquarters of the English army. The gates of the walled city, starting with the Englishtown and travelling clockwise, were Thomond Gate, Thomond Bridge Gate, Island Gate, St. Peter Cell Gate, Abbey North or Little Island Gate, Gaol Lane Gate, Fish Lane Gate, Bow Lane Gate, Castle Water Gate and New Gate. The gates of the Irishtown, starting at Baal's Bridge, were Baal's Bridge South Gate, East Water Gate, St. John's Gate, Mungret Gate and West Water Gate.

The Spanish wine trade sparked off intense rivalry between the merchants of Limerick and Galway. The Galway traders held a virtual monopoly on this business but were unable to prevent the Limerick men from competing. Limerick exported the products, and especially corn, of the rich neighbouring districts known then as Kennory and Conelogh. Payne states that they were called "The gardens of the land for the varietie and great plentie of venison, fish and foule than elsewhere in Ireland, although in every place there is great store".

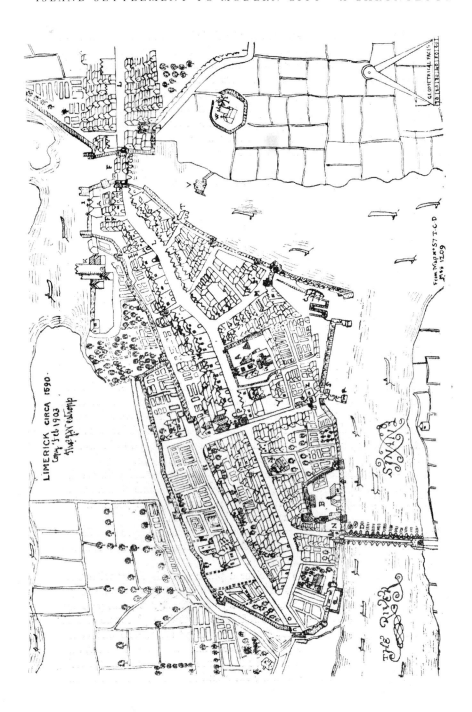

LIMERICK CITY 1590. RECONSTRUCTION FROM ORIGINAL MAP BY THOMAS J. WESTROPP IN 1903.

Travellers were usually impressed with the town's natural advantages. William Body wrote to Thomas Cromwell in 1536 that it was "a wonderous prosperous city" standing environed by the River Shannon, and might be called "Little London for the situation and the plenty". Stanihurst admired the navigable properties of the Shannon which made it possible for a ship of 200 tons burden to sail right up to the quays sixty miles from the sea. As in Galway the buildings were fine; Stanihurst calls them "sumptuous and substantial", but, again like Galway, Limerick suffered at the end of the century. Despite its strategic position the city's defences were in poor state of repair with "its cannon resting on rotten wooden frames" by 1588, the year of the Spanish Armada. When Sir John Davies saw it in 1606 it was still "a town of castles, compassed with the fairest walls that ever I saw", but the plenty which made Body compare it to London was no longer there, "the fair structures", contained nothing but "sluttishness and poverty within".

The merchants of the city sometimes sent their goods via Waterford during the mid-1500s. One cargo sent by Nicholas Wolf of Lymbrick, a "native merchant" contained 300 linen cloths, £3; twelve marten skins £2; six otter skins, 60p; and 200 sheepfells, £1.33. The towns of Munster supplied the majority of animal hides exported. In 1578 the shoemakers of Limerick were licensed to tan "as well for the maintenance of their trade as for the benefit of their neighbours and town dwellers". John Stacboll and James Creagh of Limerick are mentioned as business partners in the patent rolls "concerning a certain carvell laden with wines to the number of 6 score butts", while in another account the mayor and corporation complained to Lord Deputy Bellingham that a Limerick boat "laden with wines" had been wrecked on the Wexford coast and its goods plundered by the inhabitants. As relations worsened between England and Spain in the latter half of the sixteenth century the government of the day kept a watchful eye on ships trading in Spain. *The State Papers* contain numerous references to the wine trade as merchants were frequently consulted and examined about the preparations they had observed along the Spanish coast, especially the Andalusian coast. On 27 September, 1575, Queen Elizabeth granted the Corporation of Limerick certain privileges, one of which was "that no ship coming within the river there do sell or discharge any munitions, shot, powder, wines or other wares to any other than to the said corporation".

Limerick Corporation came into existence by prescription and charter, its authority was confirmed and regulated by statute, and its first documentary grant of municipal privileges was reputedly made in 1197. The corporation's governing charter dating from 1609 was granted by James I. This constituted the city a county of itself with the exception of the king's castle, the county court-house and the jail. It conferred an exclusive admiralty jurisdiction, both civil and criminal, over so much of the Shannon as extended three miles north-east of the

GILT SILVER ALTAR BELL DECORATED WITH THE FIGURE OF ST. JEROME, ITALIAN, SIXTEENTH-CENTURY, IN THE HUNT MUSEUM

city to the main sea, with all its creeks, banks and rivulets within those limits; constituted the mayor, recorder and four of the aldermen annually elected, justices of the peace for the county of the city; and incorporated a society of merchants of the staple with the privileges of the merchants of the Staple of Dublin. The corporation according to this charter, other charters had been issued in 1292, 1399, 1413, 1429, 1486, 1552, 1574, and 1582, consisted of a mayor, two sheriffs, and an indefinite number of aldermen, burgesses, and freemen, aided by a recorder, four charter justices, a town clerk (who was also clerk of the crown and of the peace of the county of the city), chamberlain, common speaker, water bailiff (an office abolished in 1823), sword bearer, high constable, petty constables, sergeants-at-mace, weigh-master, crane-master, and "other inferior" officers. James II granted a new charter which was later set aside and the constitution continued unaltered until 1823. *The Limerick Regulation Act* of that year remodelled the powers of the corporation. Numerous incorporated trading companies or guilds were established under various charters but by 1837, although these companies still existed, they were not recognised as component parts of the corporation, nor did they appear to have exercised any corporate rights. The guild of merchants, incorporated by James I, became extinct but was revived in 1823. Its members never met, nor was any attempt made to enforce its charter as its objects were effectually accomplished by the Chamber of Commerce. In 1837 the corporation revenues were derived from rents of houses and lands in the city and Liberties, the fishery of the salmon weir, tolls, customs (the most profitable source of income that year), and the

THE EIGHTEENTH-CENTURY RIVER FACADE OF THE CUSTOM HOUSE, HOME OF THE HUNT MUSEUM

cleansing of streets in the old city. This produced a gross income of between £4,000 and £5,000 per annum in the 1830s. Between 1890 to 1931 the corporation built a total of 297 houses. Their public housing development schemes between 1931 and 1940 led to the erection of 822 dwellings, starting with 454 houses in St. Mary's Park and the others in Janesboro, O'Dwyer Villas and Killalee. During the 1940s 1,137 houses were provided in Kileely and Prospect but even this figure was surpassed by the completion of 1,751 dwellings in Ballynanty Beg, Ballinacurra-Weston, Garryowen, Assumpta Park, Rathbane and the inner-city scheme at Carey's Road. Most of the public housing development between 1961 and 1971 concentrated on the south side of the city, Green Hill, Tankfield, St. John's, the upper section of Carey's Road and the beginning of the Kennedy Park - Keyes Park complex at Galvone. Carew Park, Glasgow Park, O'Malley Park, other parts of South Hill, and the inner-city developments at De Valera Park, Watergate and Vizes Court have all taken place since 1971. After 1973 there was a major change as most of the development took place on the north side of the city, starting with Moyross and continuing through Ballygrennan and Thomondgate, back into the city with Island Road, Lelia Place and Fitzgerald Place. The corporation is also responsible for the fire-fighting service, water supply, drainage, public lighting, maintenance of existing roads, construction of new roads, provision of car-parking facilities at Arthur's Quay, Bank Place, Charlotte Quay, Dominick Street, Denmark Street, Francis

Street, Michael Street, Pike's Bow and John's Square, and the introduction of disc parking in 1984.

The mayoralty of Limerick was an office said to have been first held by Adam Sarvant in 1197-1198. This office and those of the sheriffs, recorder and town-clerk were elected annually by the common council on the second Monday after 24 June, and the four charter justices, by the same body, on the second Monday after 29 September. The chamberlain was elected from among the burgesses for life, or during pleasure, by the mayor, sheriffs and recorder. The aldermen were elected for life among the burgesses by the common council; the title, however, was an honorary distinction, usually conferred on a person who has served in the office of mayor. The common speaker was elected every two years, under the provisions of the 1823 Act, by the body of freemen assembled on the first Tuesday after 24 June, in the Court of D'Oyer Hundred, and had to be approved by the common council before he could be sworn into office; the other officers were appointed respectively by the common council, the mayor, and the sheriffs. The mayor was a justice of the peace within the county of the city, and *ex officio* a magistrate for the county at large according to Samuel Lewis in 1837. He was also admiral of the Shannon, and, with the recorder and alderman, had very extensive magisterial and judicial powers connected with the exclusive admiralty given by the charter of 1609, and was empowered to appoint all the officers of a court of admiralty, a court which had fallen into disuse by then. The mayor was also a judge in local courts and was named first in the commission with the judges at the assizes for the county of the city; and was a coroner within the county of the city and parts of the Shannon comprised within the admiralty jurisdiction, and clerk of the markets. The other magistrates were the recorder, four charter justices and six additional justices appointed by the lord-lieutenant under the act of 1823. There have been many changes since the foundation of the Republic of Ireland but the mayoral office has continued although many of its functions have altered and other offices associated with it have been abolished. The biggest change of all was between 1962 and 1964 when Frances Condell held the mayoral office for two terms, the first woman to do so since the office was inaugurated 765 years before.

The freedom of Limerick was obtained by birth, for the eldest son, or marriage with any daughter, of a freeman, also by apprenticeship to a freeman within the city, and by gift of the corporation: the admissions of freemen were made by the common council, subject to the approbation of the Court of D'Oyer Hundred. This court was comprised of the entire body of freemen, and a certified minute of all proceedings at the meetings of the common council had to be transmitted by the town-clerk to the common speaker who presided over the court, for its approval. The word oyer means an assize or a hearing in a law-court. The Court of D'Oyer Hundred had ceased to function by the 1750s but

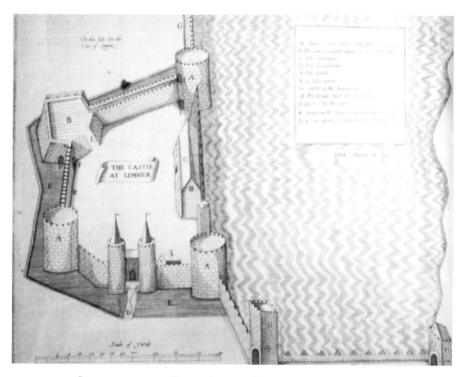

SEVENTEENTH-CENTURY PLAN OF CASTLE AT LIMERICK. Limerick City Museum

was revived in 1823. Issac Butt was made an honorary freeman on 1 January, 1877. On 14 July, 1880, Charles Stewart Parnell received the same honour. Amongst those who received the freedom of the city were Cardinal Logue in 1894, Thomas J. Clarke in 1889, Maude Gonne in 1900, Andrew Carnegie in 1903, Douglas Hyde in 1909, Mrs. Thomas Clarke, Eoin MacNeill and Eamon De Valera in 1918, Seán T. O Ceallaigh in 1948, John Fitzgerald Kennedy in 1963, Dr. Kenneth David Kaunda in 1964, Right Rev. Robert Wyse-Jackson in 1970, Pope John Paul II in 1979 and Willliam Jefferson Clinton in 1998.

Limerick City returned two representatives to the Irish Parliament from its earliest convocations until the Union, after which it sent one member to the Imperial Parliament. In 1831 the city again sent two representatives to Parliament, under an Act passed under William IV. In that year there were about 2,000 freeholders of the county of the city, making up a total of 2,413 electors. Under William's Act the voting franchise was extended to £10 householders, and to £20 and £10 leaseholders for the respective terms of 14 and 20 years; the non-resident freeman, except within seven miles, was disenfranchised; and the £2 freeholders retained the privilege only for life. The number of electors on 14 February, 1837, was 3,186. Of these 912 were freeholders, 14 were rent-chargers, 34 were leaseholders, 1946 were £10 householders and 280 freemen:

with the sheriffs acting as the returning officers. Until 1899 the right to vote was restricted to rate-paying occupiers or owners of property. Married women, of thirty years or over, received the vote in 1918 but it was not until 1935 that every citizen, of twenty-one years or over, became entitled to vote, and this age was reduced to eighteen in recent times.

Two accidental fires in 1618 and 1620 led to considerable improvement in the construction of buildings and the undertaking of major public works. The reign of King James I (1603-1625) was a tranquil one for the city; a quiet prosperity prevailed. Luke Gernon wrote, in 1620, that the lower town was surrounded by a wall a mile in compass, on which three men might walk abreast. The quay wall, which extended from the town wall into the middle of the river and was made for a defensive harbour for the shipping was about 200 paces in length. It was actually a double wall. "There is within it a long gallery arched overhead, and with windows most pleasant to walk in, and above that a terrace to walk upon with fair battlements; at the end of it there is a round tower with two or three chambers, one above the other, and a battlement above". In 1636 Lord Deputy Wentworth was splendidly entertained by the mayor for nine days and he presented the corporation with a valuable silver-gilt cup on his departure.

The Confederate Irish army laid a boom of tree trunks linked with iron across the Shannon, in order to prevent ships from bringing provisions upriver to the Water Gate of the city, when they marched against Limerick in 1642, under the command of Lord Ikerrin, Lord Muskerry and General Barry. Contemporary accounts of the period make no reference, whatsoever, to this boom. The citizens of the city welcomed them by throwing the gates open

*CURRAGHGOWER FALLS WITH KING JOHN'S CASTLE IN THE BACKGROUND. **Limerick City Museum.***

although the 200-man garrison in the castle resisted until they were forced to surrender after a stubborn defence. Later on the Confederates used a 32-pounder cannon captured within the city to reduce castles around the county. The fortifications were repaired and strengthened by the magistrates who also sent representatives to the Confederation of Kilkenny.

Stoney Thursday Corner was named after an incident, in 1646, in which the Mayor, John FitzThomas Bourke, was almost stoned to death on this site when he attempted to proclaim the details of the pacification that had been concluded between the Earl of Ormonde and the Confederation of Kilkenny. Shortly afterwards, the Supreme Council headed by the papal nuncio, Cardinal Rinuccini, moved into the city to encourage the Confederate forces who were besieging the Parliamentarians at Bunratty Castle, County Clare. In 1650 Rinuccini's party deprived the Marquess of Ormond, the man who had secured Limerick for Charles I, of all power. After Ormond's departure the earl of Castlehaven persuaded the magistrates to let him defend the city against Ireton's forces who were marching to attack it.

The Cromwellian siege of Limerick commenced in the spring of 1651 and was protracted until the approach of winter. Major-General Hugh O'Neill, the defender of Clonmel, was governor of the besieged city, while General Henry Ireton, Oliver Cromwell's son-in-law, commanded the Parliamentarian army. The Cromwellian forces had prepared for the siege in advance; ships had ferried tents, beds, arms, ammunition, cannon and provisions up to the Shannon; garrisons were placed in the castles of Kilmallock and Castleconnell; outposts were located at various strategic points, including a fort that stood in the middle of the Shannon, on the Lax Weir; Henry Ireton had made himself the master of O'Brien's Bridge and Killaloe, by treachery; while an attempt to make the Shannon fordable by diverting the water was later abandoned by his men.

Famine, misery, and death made life in the besieged city miserable for inhabitants and attackers alike. The attempts of the Confederation to relieve Limerick were defeated, although a sally by Hugh O'Neill nearly proved fatal to the Cromwellians. Eventually the inhabitants of Limerick were compelled to turn out all "useless persons" to prevent them from spreading the plague which then raged amongst them. Ireton whipped these involuntary refugees back to the besieged city, and hanged some of them to deter others from trying to pass through his lines. As the death toll rose within the city dissension broke out amongst the besieged as to the propriety of capitulating. Fennel, the man suspected of having betrayed the pass at Killaloe to Ireton, had somehow managed to be placed in charge of John's Gate which he threatened to give up to the Parliamentarians if the garrison would not surrender. Two hundred Cromwellian soldiers were admitted to the Irishtown, by Fennel, to garrison another fort called Price's Mill. Soon afterwards the East Gate was delivered up to Ireton's forces by some officers in favour of capitulation. This was a crucial move as the East Gate separated the Irishtown from the Englishtown and its possession placed the Cromwellians in a strong position. This position was further strengthened when Ireton's bombardment of King John's Castle, from Thomond Bridge, made a breach in the castle wall which was secured by twenty dragoons supported by infantry.

HENRY IRETON CONDEMNING BISHOP TERENCE O'BRIEN TO DEATH, A NINETEENTH-CENTURY DEPICTION OF THE SCENE. **Limerick City Musuem.**

The city surrendered. Hugh O'Neill met with Henry Ireton to negotiate terms. Twenty four people were excluded by name from the benefit of this treaty; 2,500 soldiers were allowed to march out unarmed; those willing to reside in the city were promised protection of life and property while a similar promise was made to those who wanted to move elsewhere; and the city, castle and places of strength were surrendered to the Cromwellians on 29 October, 1651, two days after the articles of surrender were signed.

Five thousand people died in the course of the siege. Ireton's council of officers demanded, and received, a pardon for Hugh O'Neill, one of the twenty-four excluded from the benefits of the treaty. Ireton wanted to hang him but facing the near-mutiny of his officers had little choice but to let him go. Bishop O'Dwyer was also pardoned but was believed to have made a private deal with the Cromwellians for his own safety. The other twenty two were executed, mainly for their active roles in the defence of Limerick. These were Major-General Purcell; Sir Geoffrey Galway; Lieutenant-Colonel Lacy; Captain George Woulfe; Captain-Lieutenant Sexton; Terence O'Brien, Bishop of Emly; John Quin, a Dominican friar; Captain Laurence Walsh, a priest; Francis Woulfe, a friar; Philip Dwyer, a priest; Alderman Dominick Fanning; Alderman Thomas Stritch; Alderman Jordan Roche; Burgess Edmond Roche; Sir Richard Everard; Doctor Daniel O'Higgin; Maurice Baggot of Baggotstown; Geoffrey Barron; a Welsh soldier named Evans and three other people including a deserter from the Cromwellian army. Ireton did not savour his victory for long. He died on 26 November 1651, of the plague or of a heavy 'flu or pneumonia which developed during his stay in Clarecastle, County Clare.

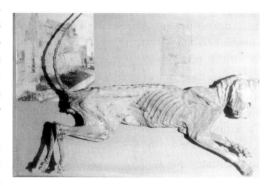

IRETON'S CAT. Limerick City Museum.

After the surrender, the city was left with 4,000 men still capable of bearing arms. The emblems of royalty were removed, the magistrates displaced, and for five years the city was subjected to a military government. Under Cromwellian rule house-rents were collected not only from the Irish inhabitants of Limerick, but from their own soldiers and adherents. Under the Act passed in 1653, English adventurers, officers and soldiers had been allowed to buy forfeited houses within the city and county. In the account books of this period, house rents were seen to fall off and abatements were made as families were transplanted out of the city; doors were built to keep intruders off the deserted streets; and as damaged houses collapsed, their timbers were salvaged and sold off. The Cromwellian government repaired the old castle for £661.40 and demolished some of the surrounding houses in order to secure it against attack. During Ireton's siege the great salmon weir, the Lax Weir, was damaged. This too was repaired but in September 1655, a "flood weare" destroyed the "great ffishing weare" and its tenant was granted an abatement in compensation. In 1653 a charter was granted giving the citizens of this city the same privileges and franchises as those enjoyed by the citizens of Bristol. In 1656 municipal government was restored with the election of a mayor and twelve English aldermen. Sir Ralph Wilson declared in favour of the king when he was governor of Limerick at the time of the Restoration. He was succeeded by the Earl of Orrery.

The Penal Laws were not enforced too stringently, within the city, during the vice-royalty of Lord Berkeley (1669-1672). A Catholic, John Halpin, was elected mayor in September 1672, but was deposed after four weeks when he refused to take the required oath of office. A fanatical Protestant, the Earl of Orrery, was appointed governor of Limerick and president of Munster soon after the Restoration. He was responsible for terminating the more tolerant Earl of Ormond's appointment to the vice-royalty in 1669, and in 1672 he had Lord Berkeley removed from the same office. In 1671 he banned the Catholic clergy from saying Mass in the cities of Cork and Limerick. The discovery of the Popish Plot in England, in 1678, gave the Earl of Orrery an opportunity to issue a proclamation banning all Catholics from the city, as "multitudes of loose Irish papists" had moved into the city during the previous three months. Despite issuing this proclamation Orrery confessed to the Earl of Ormonde that it was unlikely to have any effect, as any attempt to implement such legislation would fill all the prisons, drive many from their homes, send unemployment soaring, and destroy the economy. Many of the Catholic merchants had moved to Ennis as a temporary measure during the worst excesses of this period. James I (1603-1625) issued new coinage from the London mint between 1603 and 1607 and was the first of the English monarchs to decide on the use of a uniform currency throughout his kingdoms of Great Britain and Ireland. The lords justices in Dublin needed coinage during the troubled reign of Charles I (1625-1649) and issued an emergency currency made out to silver plate in 1642, 1643, 1646, and 1648, some of which was known as Ormonde money, after the lord lieutenant of Ireland who was appointed in 1643, the Earl of Ormonde. The 1646 issue was called weight money. The Catholic Confederates of Kilkenny issued their own currency, blacksmiths' money, in 1642 and 1643 for the same reason, a shortage of coinage. As the war between Parliament and Crown raged throughout Ireland the besieged Parliamentary forces in Bandon, Cork, Kinsale and Youghal issued their own currency made from crudely-struck copper and cut plate or counterstamped foreign coins.

During the Commonwealth era (1649-1660) the merchants of the old cities and new towns issued a large number of copper tokens, mainly pennies, from 1653 onwards. When James II (1685-1691) came to Ireland in 1689 he financed his Irish campaign by issuing token coins made out of base metals, brass, pewter and latten, an alloy of copper and zinc used in the manufacture of cannon, bells, monumental brasses and church

GUNMONEY, TWO HALF-CROWNS OF 1690.
Limerick City Museum.

GUNMONEY, A HALF-PENNY AND ONE SHILLING ISSUED IN 1691. Limerick City Museum.

articles and scrap metal. These coins were known as brass money; were called gunmoney in later times; and were minted in Dublin and Limerick. William of Orange captured the Dublin mint soon after the battle of the Boyne on 1 July, 1690. Limerick continued to mint its own gunmoney into 1691. In 1826, during the reign of George IV (1820-1830), Irish coinage was officially withdrawn from circulation and replaced with imperial coinage. New Irish coinage was minted at the Royal Mint, London, for the independent Irish Free State in 1928, a practice that continues into the present day. Traders' tokens were struck in the principal ports and towns of Ireland between 1653 and 1697, due mainly to a general shortage of small coins. In 1680 a new regal halfpenny was issued by the lord lieutenant, Sir Thomas Armstrong, and the traders' tokens were declared illegal. Between 1653 and 1679 coin tokens were issued in Limerick by *City of Limerick, Change and Charity* (1658), *The Paschal Lamb* of *Limerick Butchers* (1679), Anthony Bartlett, merchant (no date), John Bell, merchant (no date), John Bennet, merchant (1663 and 1668), Edward Clarke (1670) Rowland Creagh, merchant (no date), *B.G., near Key Lane* (1668), Thomas Linch (1679), Thomas Marten, merchant (1669), Richard Pearce, apothecary (1668), William Rimpland, chandler (1669) and Ed. Wight (1667).

One of Sean Marrinan's last articles mentioned that Edward Wight, came from Guildford, Surrey, as a soldier in Ireton's army; was sheriff in 1676, became mayor in 1694 and 1711; was married three times, to daughters of the Hoare, Bindon and Hawkesworth families; and died in 1723. *The Paschal Lamb* was the emblem of the Limerick butchers as late as 1731. An Anthony Bartless *(sic)* was a merchant in *Middle Ward*, on the east side, in 1659. Anthony Bartlett was mayor in 1680 and was described by Thomas Dineley as "Captain Anthony Bartlett a citizen who can neither write nor read". Edward Clarke was the name of the mayor in 1675 and of a sheriff in 1682. John Bell was a tenant of Lord Orrery in 1679. John Bennet was an alderman in 1659, a merchant in *Middle Ward*, on the west side, and his name appeared on the *Corporation Rent Rolls* in 1674, 1677 and 1678. Richard Pearce, a Quaker merchant, received a consignment of tobacco from Antigua in 1673. Thomas Marten occupied a house, valued at forty pounds, in St. Mary's Parish, in 1654; carried out the directives of the *Poll Money Ordinance* in 1660; and was one of the sheriffs in 1663 when he had "the roof of the great store house" in King John's Castle repaired. William Rimpland issued two halfpenny tokens, one in 1669 and the other in 1679. Another token was

issued by a *B.G. of Limerick* in 1668. *Near Key Lane* appeared on the reverse side of the token. A token with *Clare* on one side and *Limerick* on the other may have been issued in 1660, by the Cromwellian Commonwealth then occupying the city.

GENERAL GINKEL. (1630-1703) WAS CREATED BARON OF AUGHRIM AND EARL OF ATHLONE IN 1692.
Limerick City Museum

Dr. James Dowley, or Duley, was appointed Vicar Apostolic in 1657 although he did not take up office until 1669. In 1676 he became Catholic bishop of Limerick. In 1678, he surrendered himself to the authorities. He was neither imprisoned or transported but was released and kept under surveillance. In 1680 he appeared in court. Four years later, in 1684, he was still working in his diocese despite being old and infirm. As Catholic fortunes declined many of the new Protestant settlers and planters thrived. John Frend, a Cromwellian captain, was one of many Cromwellian officers who acquired a considerable amount of confiscated land in the county. In 1858 Caleb Powell described John's descendant, Ben Frend of Boskell, as having an iron leg which was "the softest part of him".

The Earl of Orrery was instructed to endeavour to procure "good English and Dutch merchants" to inhabit the city - good in this case meant of the right persuasion and politics. It was hoped that this influx of businessmen would cause

the city to flourish with trade. Orrery also restored the banished merchants of Limerick to their freedom and privileges, on their entering into recognisance's to keep the peace. The city prospered under his rule. The inland trade increased so rapidly under his instruction that the tolls of the gates were let for upwards of £300 per annum in 1672. In the same year, the mayor and citizens were able to perambulate dry-shod outside the walls of Englishtown as the waters of the Shannon fell to an unprecedented level during a considerable drought. The following year a great storm and high tide caused great damage to the city. Thomas Dineley described Limerick in 1680;

> It is one of the fairest cities of the Province of Munster upon the River Shannon, distinguished thus, the English Town and the Irish Town. The English Town is an island and hath a wall distinct; in this is kept the main guard and is seen the King's Castle. The Thomond Gate and the Balls Bridge Gate are the two chiefest gates thereof. That part of the city going by the name of the Irish Town is also walled in. Here is seen the Citadel; the chiefest gates of the Irish Town are the St. John's Gate and the Mongrett Gate.

The accession of James II (1685-1689) reversed the religious bias of the corporation in favour of the Catholic community.

The first Williamite siege took place soon after the battle of the Boyne when the French and Irish forces regrouped here and used the city as a major rallying point. The occupying armies spoke disparagingly of old and decaying

*SIEGE OF LIMERICK, A DEPICTION OF **1690**. Limerick City Museum.*

fortifications which could be knocked down with roasted apples, although the Williamite accounts treated the fortifications more respectfully. The Jacobites strengthened the defences; a trench with a covered way was constructed outside the walls; redoubts were erected; and suburban dwellings demolished to prevent besiegers using them. King William had expected the city to surrender by the time he reached Caherconlish on 7 August 1690. He had left his heavy siege artillery in Dublin and had brought only his light field guns with him. His siege train was despatched from Dublin. In the early hours of 11 August the Williamites saw "a great light in the air and heard a strange rumbling noise". Patrick Sarsfield had crossed the Shannon and destroyed the siege train at Ballyneety. The 20,000 besiegers were hampered by the loss of their heavier guns and battering ram whereas the city's occupants had an abundance of the munitions of war and were able to obtain supplies of every kind from Connaught, and by sea, where the French fleet rode undisturbed.

The Brazen Head was the name of a young red-haired woman beheaded in the fighting of 26 August, 1690, when King William's Brandenburg regiment, Saxon and Dutch mercenaries, made an almost suicidal frontal attack on the city walls near the Black Battery where they managed to get into the Irishtown through a gap in the south wall near today's St. John's Hospital. Despite heavy losses they almost succeeded in reaching Baal's Bridge. The women of Limerick fought alongside their men and managed to repel the invaders killing 500 of them near John's Mount, now John Street. It was during this encounter that the red-haired woman was killed. Some accounts say she was involved in the fighting while others state that she was merely an innocent bystander. She died near the principal inn which was named in her honour *The Brazen Head*. Simon Kent rebuilt the original inn at 23 John Street in 1794 and had a commemorative plaque placed on the buildings facade between the first floor windows. This plaque was removed to O'Connell Street and re-inserted outside another building in the 1960s. The Williamites battered their way into the city on two other occasions but were driven out each time by the Jacobites. William was forced to raise the siege and withdraw towards Waterford and England. He left Limerick to the combined Irish and French Jacobite army of 14,000 infantry and 2,500 cavalry under the command of General Boiseleau, the Duke of Berwick and other distinguished leaders, including the Earl of Tyrconnell who had established his vice-regal court here after the battle of the Boyne on 12 July 1690. The Earl of Tyrconnell and the French troops went to France after the siege, leaving Patrick Sarsfield in charge of the city until he returned, the following year, with the French commander, St. Ruth, but no French soldiery.

The second Williamite siege started in August 1691. This time General Ginkel invested the city in William's name. After the disastrous battle of Aughrim, Limerick became the last major Jacobite stronghold to hold out

PATRICK SARSFIELD. Limerick City Museum

against William. The siege became a protracted and sanguinary affair as French officers urged the Irish leaders to continue the struggle with promises of aid from Louis XIV. Thomond Bridge was the scene of one of Limerick's bloodiest encounters when 850 of its defenders were trapped outside the walls because the gates had been closed too quickly. 600 were slain, 150 were drowned and 100 were taken prisoner. When the Earl of Tyrconnell died Patrick Sarsfield had assumed control. After the slaughter on Thomond Bridge he sued for peace as the French reinforcements he had expected had failed to arrive. With a Scottish general named Wauchope he arranged an interview with General Ginkel to propose a three-day ceasefire prior to signing a treaty. That evening General Ginkel entertained Limerick's most prominent citizens to dinner and the following day both sides exchanged hostages.

The Treaty of Limerick was arranged after a long and angry debate to finalise the terms. Patrick Sarsfield, Lord Galmoyle, Colonel Nicholas Purcell, Colonel Nicholas Cusack, Sir Toby Butler, Colonel Garret Dillon and Colonel John Browne were chosen to act as commissioners for the Jacobites. General Ginkel acted as his own commissioner but called all of his officers above the grade of brigadier-general to his assistance. On 1 October, 1691, the lords-

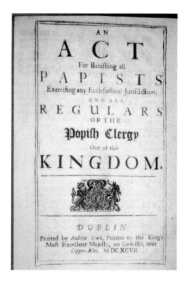
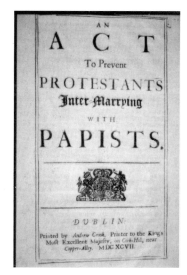

*PENAL LAWS AND ACTS OF PARLIAMENT, AFTER THE FALL OF LIMERICK. **Limerick City Museum.***

justices, Coningsby and Porter, arrived. On 3 October, 1691, this historic treaty was signed. Two days later French reinforcements arrived with fresh troops and 30,000 stands of arms. Patrick Sarsfield was urged to continue the war but he insisted on abiding by the terms of the treaty, a treaty which was ratified by William of Orange but later repudiated by the Irish parliament. The Irish Jacobite soldiers were allowed to march out of the city with full military honours. Nineteen thousand of them embarked for France, to found the Irish Brigade, while three thousand joined the Williamite army. Limerick became known as the "City of the Broken Treaty" because the terms of the treaty were repudiated almost as soon as the last shipload of Irish soldiers sailed away. *Remember Limerick* became the battle-cry of the Irish Brigade as they swept all before them on the battlefields of Europe. Patrick Sarsfield, the Earl of Lucan, was killed at the Battle of Landen in 1693, fighting for France. His last words are said to have been, "Would to God this was shed for Ireland". *The Wild Geese*, a word that late became synonymous with mercenary, was coined by ships' captains to describe their illegal cargoes of young recruits travelling abroad to join the Irish brigades of France and Spain. Between 1691 and the time of the French Revolution, over 100,000 left their native country to serve in the armies of Europe.

After the siege the entire city was a scene of desolation. The inhabitants had been compelled to quit their dwellings by the bombardment, only to return and find their effects destroyed. While everyone was engaged in repairing their losses, the poorer by erecting small huts under the walls, the richer by redecorating their houses, and the soldiers by restoring and enlarging the fortifications, a new and unthought of casualty nearly involved the whole in a second destruction. In 1693 one of the towers on the quay suddenly fell, and 250 barrels of gunpowder which it contained blew up with a tremendous explosion; 240 people were crushed to death or dreadfully maimed, some being struck dead by stones which fell a mile from town.

In 1716 two Dutch Jansenist monks travelled to Ireland. Their ship dropped anchor, for the first time since leaving Maselansluijs, at Scattery Island at "1 o'clock in the afternoon". All ships were then obliged "to undergo search" and theirs had to remain in the Scattery Roads for between one to two hours while this was done. In this instance the search was very brief and the ship arrived into Limerick "at abut 6 o'clock in the evening". They were met by a merchant named Kruijskerk, who acted as interpreter, and were brought to meet the upper-burgomaster (the mayor) on 2 August. They later commented on his staff of office, a white stick of about six feet in length, which served as a symbol of his jurisdiction.

On this day, Sunday, we went to church to hear the Divine Service in this Irish city. There was a large congregation. A large crowd of persons was gathered outside the church, awaiting the time of the Service - there were two during the morning, at 8 o'clock and at 10 o'clock. The Service [being] ended, the church also was closed. A large number of beggars were sitting along the road to the church, asking a small donation from the churchgoers. This class of persons is much more numerous in this country than I have ever seen in Braband.

The city of Lemrik is very strong by nature and has known many fortifications during the period prior to King William the Third. But when this king conquered Britain he had to besiege and fire on this city - which is why it became so dreadfully devastated. When the city had been captured the king ordered that all fortifications, and the castle on the river around the city, should be destroyed, and that all the cannon, and everything that might be used to offer resistance, should be removed.

The city of Lemrik is divided into two parts by the river, with a stone bridge over it which divides the Irish city from Lemrik. At night those two parts of the city are shut off from each other by means of an internal gate so that each part is inaccessible from the other. It is said that the reason for this is that in the Irish city there are mainly Catholics and that by this means they can be kept in check. If they should consider revolting they would not succeed in that because by this means all power has been taken from them.

There is but one long street in the city, running from one end of it to the other. In this street are situated the Exchange and the City Hall, which are the most beautiful buildings of the whole city but do not bear comparison with [those of]the

Netherland. Apart from this street, the other streets are in very poor and decayed condition and do not merit the title of city streets.

*PENAL LAWS AND ACTS OF PARLIAMENT, AFTER THE FALL OF LIMERICK. **Limerick City Museum.***

The Penal Laws passed by William's Irish Parliament ordered all Catholic clergy to depart from his kingdom by 1 May, 1698. They were forbidden to return and heavy penalties were introduced to prevent the populace from harbouring priests. After 29 December 1697 burials were forbidden in any suppressed monastery, abbey or convent not used for the Protestant liturgy. Catholics were barred from the legal profession as Catholic solicitors were considered "common disturbers" engaged in evading the law to secure the landed properties of their fellow-Catholics for their rightful owners rather than the Protestant usurpers. Protestant heiresses had to receive special permission to marry Catholics while Protestant men who married reputed Catholics without such permission were not allowed to act as guardians, executors, sit in the House of Commons or hold any civil or military office unless they could prove that they had converted their wives to Protestantism within a year of their marriage. If the son of a Catholic became a Protestant, the father could not sell or mortgage his estate or dispose of any portion of it by will; nor could a Catholic father become his own child's guardian if that child, no matter how young, had become a Protestant. Catholics were rendered incapable of purchasing landed property, or rents, or profits arising out of land. They were not allowed to hold leases of more that thirty-one years. In such cases the reserved rents had to be one third of the improved annual value but any Protestant who discovered a flaw in the agreement became entitled to the lease. A Catholic was not allowed to inherit from a Protestant, and if he did not have a Protestant heir to inherit his lands they had to be divided equally amongst his sons. Catholics were also completely debarred from taking part in social or political life, while defects in the administration of the law in favour of Catholics was usually rectified by new Acts. The Marquess of Winchester and the Earl of Galway visited the city on a tour of inspection as lords justices in 1698.

William Of Orange never opposed the anti-Catholic laws introduced after the treaty of Ryswick in 1697. With peace restored between England and France, the Irish Parliament revised the treaty of Limerick to their own satisfaction. After William's death in 1702, Anne, the second daughter of James II, succeeded to the English throne. No Roman Catholic strangers were allowed to reside in the city or suburbs under an act passed in 1703. The same act stated that the Catholic inhabitants of the city would be expelled from it unless they gave sufficient securities for their allegiance. These restrictions were removed in 1724. During the Scottish rebellion in 1745 similar restrictions were used, but no symptom of disaffection was discovered. Later in the eighteenth century the penal code was relaxed. Catholics were allowed to possess property under favourable terms and invest in land. They were allowed to take fifty-year leases on bogland in 1771, and if the bog was too deep to sustain a house foundation they were allowed to take an acre of ground for this purpose, on condition that it should not be within a mile of any city or town. Catholics were allowed to inherit and take a 999-year lease of property under an act passed in 1778 which also repealed the earlier act giving the entire property of a Catholic to his eldest

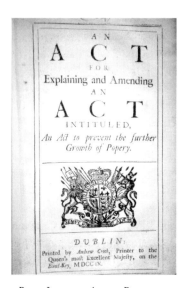
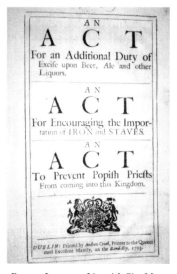

PENAL LAWS AND ACTS OF PARLIAMENT, AFTER THE FALL OF LIMERICK. **Limerick City Museum.**

son in the event of the son becoming a Protestant. The 1778 act also repealed another act under which Catholic priests and schoolmasters were liable to prosecution and transportation.

Toxeth Roche was the leader of the Orange faction who ruled Limerick City after 1691. This group was so corrupt that sixty years later Parliament declared them unfit to govern, and all of their illegal acts were declared void. George Roche may have been a relation of Toxeth's but this has never been proved. George became mayor in 1702; his son, David, was mayor in 1749; and his grandson, another David, married Frances Maunsell of Limerick. In 1760 the population of Limerick was 32,196. The two main inns in 1790 were Taylor's New Inn in Irishtown and the Black Swan at Thomondgate. The county infirmary was opened by Sylvester O'Halloran and Giles Vandeleur, two noted surgeons of the day, as a four-bed hospital in 1759. It was located in three small houses on Little Island and was conducted as a charity. Other people soon became involved in the project and additional finance was required for expansion. The county hospital developed from the infirmary but used the former title to benefit from an act in favour of county hospitals. Edmond Sexton Pery conveyed some ground, with the ruins of a former workhouse on it, in St. Francis Abbey, to the trustees, Charles Smyth and Dean Hoare, at the yearly rent of one peppercorn in 1765. Lady Hartstonge contributed heavily to the erection of a new hospital[†] capable of holding upwards of forty beds. Sylvester O'Halloran was retained as the officially appointed surgeon: he had given his services free in the infirmary; but Giles Vandeleur did not live long enough to see the new hospital, as he had died within sixteen months of opening the infirmary.

The stage coach appears to have operated as a summer only service between Dublin and Limerick from 1751 to 1756. It left the Hog in Armour Inn, James Street, Dublin at 7.00 a.m. on Mondays and returned on Saturdays. From 1772 onwards the stage departed from Francis Jenkinson's, 7 Bolton Street, Dublin on Thursdays and from Limerick on Mondays. Francis Jenkinson referred to his coach service as the Limerick Stage Coach from 1783 onwards but reduced his trips to once weekly in each direction from 1787. His vehicle was described as an elegant post coach capable of carrying four inside and two outside passengers in 1794. The Limerick-Dublin Mail Coach went into competition with the Limerick Stage Coach in 1794. Between then and 1806 the mail coach operated six days of the week while its rival did the same journey only three times a week. After 1806, Sundays excepted, the service became a daily one. The two-day Dublin Stage Coach was inaugurated in 1815, while a Caravan for Passengers ran between the two cities in 1824 covering the entire journey in 30 hours. Tierney's Caravan had a terminus at Patrick Coleman's, Francis Street, and another caravan operated from Limerick's mail coach office in George's

---

[†]later known as St. John's

Street. Both caravans had offices in Ennis, the former in Chapel Lane, the latter in Church Street. Stage waggons owned by Andrew Buchanan of Limerick competed for business with those of Foster and Osborne of Dublin in 1784. These waggons were used for transporting second-class passengers such as poorer merchants, traders and craftsmen. Foster and Osborne went into partnership with Benjamin Meredith of Limerick but by the end of 1784 the three had closed down, leaving the market to Andrew Buchanan. During the mid 1830s the competing mail and stage coaches were able to complete the journey between Limerick and Dublin in about fourteen hours. By 1849 the railroad had arrived and the trip could be done in seven hours and twenty minutes.

LIMERICK MAIL COACH BOOKING FORM OF 1837. Limerick City Library.

The Ennis Fly Coach was first linked to Dublin through the Galway-Dublin route rather than through Limerick. The Limerick-Ennis stage coach operated from 1809 while William Bourne's Limerick-Ennis mail coach service commenced officially on 5 July 1815 although it was listed in *Watson's Almanack* in 1813. This became part of the Bianconi network when the Bianconi coaches spread throughout Munster and most of Ireland in the 1820s, 1830s and 1840s. By then Limerick was connected with Cork (from 1815), Waterford (from 1819) and all the major towns and cities. Charles Bianconi operated the Limerick-Tralee run, by stage coach until 1853; and by mail car until 1866.

Charles Bianconi (1786-1875) was born in northern Italy and apprenticed to a print-maker who took him to Dublin. When his apprenticeship ended in 1804 he continued his education through the offices of two friends, Fr. Theobald Mathew and Edmond Ignatius Rice. In 1809 he opened a shop in Clonmel selling prints and mirrors before he started speculating in gold, reselling guineas purchased from the peasantry to the government. He ran his first jaunting car from Clonmel to Cahir in 1815 and by the end of that year had linked Clonmel to Limerick. By 1834 he had acquired the Limerick-Galway mail coach and several other Limerick-linked enterprises such as the Limerick-Killarney car (1839-1853), the Limerick-Tipperary car (1851-1861), the Limerick-Ennis mail car (1852-1865), the Limerick-Ennis day car (1854-1865) and the Limerick-Tralee car which was established in the 1830s. In later years he purchased shares in the railway companies with whom he refused to compete. Instead he used his coaches to connect with the rail services until an accident in 1865 persuaded him to retire. On doing so he sold off his interests, mainly to his former employees, on generous terms.

PETER O'BRIEN'S WINE STORES,

18, THOMAS-STREET, LIMERICK,

his day forwarded to *Mrs Butter Firgrove*

per *Morning & evening stage Coaches*

te at avenue sale carefully packed

covered Hampers; the cording sealed on *their* only knot, and in

ll coopered, taped, and sealed on both ends. The seal is " *Peter O'Brien*

ue delivery. *Carriage prepaid in Limerick { Sherry*"

;	Wine, and Description	Impression and Color of Wax on Cork.

PETER O'BRIEN'S WINE STORES WERE LOCATED AT 18 THOMAS STREET. PETER O'BRIEN (1799 - 1855) WAS A GRANDNEPHEW OF WILLIAM ROCHE OF LIMERICK AND A BROTHER OF JOHN O'BRIEN (1794 - 1855) WHO WAS A MEMBER OF PARLIAMENT FOR LIMERICK FROM 1842 TO 1852. ON 14 NOVEMBER, 1854, PETER O'BRIEN ISSUED A DELIVERY NOTE TO MRS. BUTLER OF FIRGROVE, BUNRATTY, COUNTY CLARE, FOR NINETEEN BOTTLES OF GOLDEN SHERRY. THIS WAS FORWARDED ON THE SAME DAY, IN TWO SEPARATE CONSIGNMENTS. THIRTEEN BOTTLES WERE DESPATCHED ON THE MORNING COACH AND THE OTHER SIX WERE SENT ON THE EVENING COACH. EACH CONSIGNMENT WAS PACKED IN A COVERED HAMPER AND THE INDIVIDUAL BOTTLES AND SINGLE KNOT ON THE CORDAGE OF EACH HAMPER WAS SEALED WITH RED WAX BEARING THE WORDS Peter O'Brien Sherry. THE DELIVERY NOTE ALSO RECOMMENDED THAT THE BOTTLES BE ALLOWED TO REST IN FRESH SAWDUST, IN A CELLAR OF EVEN TEMPERATURE. PETER O'BRIEN WAS THE UNCLE OF JOHN'S SON, THE MORE FAMOUS PETER "THE PACKER" O'BRIEN (1842 - 1914). HIS NEPHEW EARNED NOTORIETY AND HIS NICKNAME WHEN HE 'PACKED THE JURIES' TO THE DETRIMENT OF LAND LEAGUE DEFENDENTS IN 1881 AND 1882, AS COUNSEL FOR THE CROWN.

The first aerial flight from Limerick took place on Thursday, 27 April, 1786, when Richard Crosbie (1755-c.1824) made an ascent, by balloon, from the House of Industry, on a south-east by east wind, which brought him down near Ballygirreen, outside Newmarket on Fergus, County Clare. In 1849 John Hampton ascended from Marshall's Yard, Cecil Street, in a balloon named the

Erin-go-Bragh which had been inflated by the Limerick Gas Consumers Company. Two Limerick men, Hampden William Russell and a Mr. Townsend accompanied him. The three landed safely at Rathlahine, near Shannon, but were thrown from their light two wheeled carriage as they returned to Limerick, by road. James Leslie Allen of Limerick set out from Wales on 17 April, 1912 in a fifty horse power Bleriot monoplane. His companion, Denys Corbett-Wilson of Kilkenny, reached County Wexford safely in a similar machine. They had taken off together, but James Leslie Allen was never seen again.

The Catholic Emancipation Act was passed in 1829. This was celebrated with a procession through the city on 5 July, 1830, in which every sector of the community took part, regardless of class or creed. For the first time since the Jacobite forces left Limerick in 1691 Catholic clergy appeared on the streets wearing surplices, soutanes, stoles and birettas. The participants assembled at the Exchange where the various bodies were marshalled into order, and marched through the main streets to a second assembly point, at Bank Place, where the town clerk read out the proclamation. The military led the parade, followed by members of the corporation, the Freemason's lodges, the Chamber of Commerce and both Protestant and Catholic clergymen.

The old harbour was located upriver from Sarsfield Bridge at the junction of the Abbey and Shannon rivers from which it extended downstream for 1600 yards. By the 1750s it had become a roadstead, rather than a harbour, where

THE SHANNON, IN FORMER TIMES. *Limerick City Museum.*

ships could ride at anchor until low tide left them lying aground on the rocky river-bottom. This situation led to a spate of harbour construction from that period onwards which resulted in the erection of quays named after their founders, Meade, Harvey, Russell, Spaight, Kelly and Arthur. The Inland Steam Navigation Company opened up the Shannon communication from here with Athlone, Banagher, Portumna, Killaloe and Kilrush. They opened a terminus which was linked with the east coast in 1804. Another entrepreneur, James Patterson, went into shipping in 1812. By 1817 he owned one of the first steamboats, *Lady of the Shannon*, to ply regularly between Limerick and Kilrush. In the 1820s two boats operated this route twice weekly "on days uncertain".

The Shannon River was, and still is, Limerick's most important natural resource. The city, later embodied in the corporation, claimed an exclusive right to all fishing from here to Scattery Island from the days of the Vikings, and developed as a port despite being over sixty miles from the sea. In 1837 navigation was "obstructed and intricate, with insufficient water for large vessels" in the upper reaches of the channel. Samuel Lewis noted that;

> no funds are applied to the maintenance of the navigation, which is almost entirely neglected: ships may discharge ballast in any part without restriction, and the proprietors of adjoining lands may create any obstruction they please. At each side of the narrow arm of the Shannon that encircles the English town are several quays accessible only to boats; and at Merchants' Quay is the Long Dock, where the turf and fish boats unload. From the custom-house, at the mouth of the Abbey River, various detached quays, erected by private individuals, extend along the united channel, but they are in very bad condition; the ground around them is rugged and hard, so that vessels lying there are frequently damaged ... the Chamber of Commerce, consisting of opulent and most respectable merchants, has supreme interest in the navigation of the port, and from its funds has been defrayed the great portion of the expense that has been incurred by whatever improvements have been made, although it has no right or control over the river. The commissioners appointed by Act of Parliament, in 1823, have power to levy certain taxes for the erection of the Wellesley Bridge, and of docks to accommodate vessels frequenting the port.

The port of Limerick was revitalised by commercial interests intent on making the city a major maritime port. In 1822 the Limerick Chamber of Commerce, mayor and corporation decided that a new bridge and wet dock were essential if Limerick was to expand. A civil engineer, employed by the government to survey the Shannon, was persuaded to help in 1822. His name was John Grantham. He submitted his report with plans, drawings and estimates for a new bridge and wet dock, on suitable sites, in May 1822. On 17 June 1823 *An Act for the Erection of a bridge across the river Shannon and of a Floating Dock to*

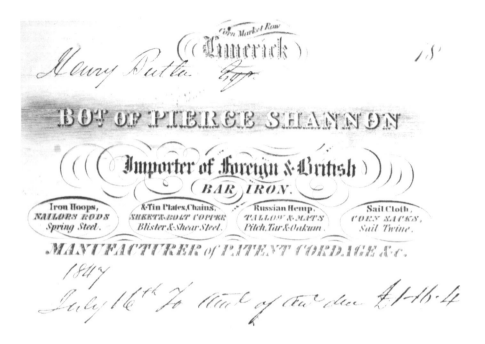

PIERCE SHANNON WAS AN IMPORTER OF FOREIGN AND BRITISH BAR IRON IN 1847. HIS PREMISES WAS IN CORN MARKET ROW AND HE WAS ALSO A MANUFACTURER OF PATENT CORDAGE (FOR THE RIGGING OF SAILING SHIPS), A SHIPS' CHANDLER AND A SUPPLIER OF COPPER, IRON AND STEEL GOODS.

accommodate sharp vessels frequenting the port of Limerick was passed. The Wellesley/Sarsfield bridge was built first but because there were insufficient funds left to finance the rest of the project, the wet dock, pier, quays, gates, walls and other works were not constructed for over twenty years. The Limerick Bridge Commissioners were empowered, by act of parliament in 1834, to borrow up to £200,000 to compensate mill-owners at Corbally and Curraghour; to make compulsory purchases of private quays and areas necessary for the proposed development; and to levy a charge on imported coal. In the 1830s agricultural produce, corn, provisions and butter were exported to London, Liverpool, Bristol and Glasgow from here, as this was the main shipping point for Kerry, Tipperary and Clare, as well as the county of Limerick. In 1835 the customs paid amounted to £146,222.89. Exports for the year included beef, pork, butter, bacon; lard, wheat, barley, oats, flour, oatmeal, eggs, hams, tongues, spirits, porter, ale, flax, linen, wool, feathers and salmon. During that year 51 vessels entered inwards from foreign ports and on 5 January, 1836, there were 71 vessels of 5,008 tons belonging to the Port of Limerick. The chief imports in 1835 were timber, coal, iron, flax-seed, tallow, pitch, tar, hoops, staves, wine and fruit.

Cannibalism saved the captain and crew of a Limerick ship from death by starvation in 1835. The *Francis Spaight* had sailed for St. John's, New Brunswick, on 25 November, 1835, when it was upended by strong gales during a snowstorm. Three of the crew of eighteen were drowned, two of these being Ben Cusack and "Griffin, our first mate"; provisions were washed away; water fouled; and only the cargo of timber kept the wrecked ship afloat until eleven survivors were rescued by the brig *Agenora* on 23 December. Patrick O'Brien had worked on the Limerick docks before joining the crew of the *Francis Spaight*. On 18 December 1835 the remaining crewmen of the ill-fated ship realised that the only way they might survive their ordeal was by eating human flesh. They decided to draw lots in order to select who would die. Fifteen-year-old Patrick O'Brien lost. He was killed and eaten by his shipmates. Three more of the crew shared his fate before the others were rescued. The captain and crew were later tried for murder, and acquitted, after their return to Limerick. This incident was commemorated in a ballad, *The Sorrowful Fate of O'Brien*, part of which is as follows;

> ... A bandage o'er O'Brien's eyes they quickly then did tie
> For the second lot that was pulled up said O'Brien was to die.
>
> He said unto his comrade boys: 'Now let my mother know
> The cruel death I did sustain, when you to Limerick go'.
> Then John O'Gorman he was called to bleed him in the vein
> Twice he tried to take his blood, but it was all in vain.
>
> Our captain cries: 'Cheer up my boys, this work will never so;
> O'Gorman you must cut his throat, or else you will die too'
> The Trembling cook, he took the knife, which sore did him confound,
> He cut his throat and drank his blood as it flowed from the wound.

Francis Spaight was the main Limerick agent involved in the timber and emigrant trades, a successful merchant, town councillor, magistrate and owner of the craft on which Pat O'Brien was killed. When a public collection was held for the survivors and relatives of those who died aboard the *Francis Spaight* he contributed £10. Emigration, particularly to Canada, was a major business in the 1830s and later. Limerick ships brought a steady stream of emigrants to the Gulf of St. Lawerence and usually returned to their home port with cargoes of timber. Cost was a major factor in

*TOKENS ISSUED BY STEIN BROWN AND COMPANY, A LOCAL DISTILLERY. **Limerick City Museum**.*

selecting a Canadian passage - a steerage passenger could travel from Limerick to Quebec for between £2.10 to £2.25 whereas the trip to New York cost from £3.25 to £3.50. In 1831 emigrants were advised to take 4 stone of oatmeal; 4 stone of cutlings for gruel; 4 stone of biscuits; 1/2 stone of sugar; 1/2 lb. of tea; 4 stone of butter; 20 stone of potatoes; "a few dozen eggs, which should be well greased to exclude the air, and consequently preserve them fresh" ; and a quart or two of whiskey for emergencies on the voyage. Each stone consisted of fourteen pounds weight. On 23 June, 1841, 300 vessels were waiting for the ice to break up in the St. Lawerence River before sailing for Canada from here.

The constabulary, or peace preservation police, consisted of a chief magistrate, one chief officer of the second class, 49 men and four horses in 1836. Of these 37 men were stationed in the city barracks, and the remainder in the Liberties. Their maintenance amounted to £1,852.07 for the year ending on 1 June 1836, two-thirds of which was paid from the Consolidated fund and the balance by Grand Jury presentment. This force was occasionally employed beyond the limits of the civil jurisdiction. In 1836 the peace preservation force and the county constabulary were amalgamated into a centralised police force under an inspector general. From 20 May 1867 they were known as the Royal Irish Constabulary. Their main role is fulfilled today by the Gardaí Síochána, who were established in 1922, as Guardians of the Peace.

The Great Famine forced the mayor, E.F.G. Ryan, to lead a deputation to Dublin on 23 March 1846 in order to urge the Relief Commission to provide the city with relief works before the population resorted to violence. General Edward Pine Coffin, of Devon, was appointed deputy commissary of the Limerick depot for the supply and distribution of food. He estimated that four million people would have to be fed during May, June and July of 1846 before the new crop of potatoes would be fit to eat. At that stage no one anticipated Black '47 or even dreamed that the dreaded potato blight would reappear in July 1846. In June of that year government supplies of Indian corn, at less than half of one new penny a pound, were exhausted, and the British Treasury refused to supply any more as their depots closed down. By the time supplies were resumed in February 1847 it was too late. Despite the desperate situation in which the people found themselves, the Limerick docks were kept busy as cereals, livestock and agricultural products were shipped out of the famine-stricken country. It was no wonder the Irish people refer to this episode in history as the Great Hunger rather than the Great Famine. Certain foods were never as plentiful but it usually went to pay the rent. On 5 August, 1846, a group of labourers tore up a road they had just laid when they were told their employment had come to an end. On another occasion the military officer commanding the city complained that his troops were "harassed off their legs by daily calls" on their services to protect stores and depots.

The English mail reached the city between 12.00 noon and 1.00 p.m., instead of in the evening, during William Monsell's tenure as Postmaster General. During his term of office he extended the telegraph system throughout Ireland. William got into trouble in the House of Commons for exceeding the Irish Postal estimates by spending money in Ireland out of the General Post Office (England) fund. He was selected for Grand Jury service by Caleb Powell in 1858. Caleb, himself was unlucky in politics. Although he served his constituents fairly, the Catholics disliked him because of his religion and the Protestants because of his policy.

The export and import of grain was one of the most important functions of the harbour. In the 1890s Bannatyne's Mill (later Ranks) employed a special

LIMERICK STEAMSHIP COMPANY, POSTERS ADVERTISING TRIPS TO KILKEE AND ELSEWHERE.
Limerick City Museum.

floating grain elevator to discharge large cargoes. The author of *the Cape Horn Breed* whose fully-rigged ship, *British Isles*, brought a cargo of grain from Tacoma in 1909 was impressed enough to write; "The cargo was discharged by shore labour with an up-to-date labour-saving technique which was proof of the progressive spirit of the local flour millers, who imported large quantities of grain from overseas, and sold flour, pollard and bran, not only throughout Ireland, but also for export to Britain and the Continent of Europe". His remarks about the city are interesting. "The berth resembled a promenade rather than a wharf, as there was a bandstand and gardens, and many people strolling to and from along the river bank which formed one side of the dock. The city of Limerick, with its castle and cathedral, its cobbled streets, and busy market place where cattle and pigs are sold directly by the farmers, its bacon factories, butter-factories and flour mills, and its people light-hearted and witty, and friendly to strangers, was a pleasant place in springtime when we arrived there on 18th April 1909".

The Limerick Steamship Company dated from 1893 but its roots were in the London & Limerick Steamship Company dating from the 1850s. The Limerick Steamship Company served the western and south-western ports of Ireland for six decades, trading mainly to the U.K. and near continent with general goods, livestock, coal and fertilisers. At one time they had "puffers" on the estuary trade and large seagoing vessels on world-wide trading. During World War II The Limerick Steamship Company was appointed with the Wexford Steamship Co. and Palgrave Murphys as managers of the new Irish Shipping Ltd. In addition to their own seven vessels they were assigned the *Irish Popular*, the *Irish Pine* and the *Irish Oak*. *The Irish Pine* was torpedoed in the Atlantic in 1942 with the loss of all thirty-three hands. *The Irish Oak* was torpedoed in 1943. Of their own vessels the *Maigue* and the *Rynanna* were both lost in January, 1940. In September of the same year, the *Luimneach* was sunk by U-boat gunfire. The *Clonlara* was torpedoed in August, 1941, in Biscay. February, 1943, saw the loss of the *Kyleclare* with all eighteen hands. After the war the company built up its fleet again and the familiar red and white banded funnels were seen again in Liverpool, Rotterdam, Antwerp and the western ports of Ireland. In May 1969 the Limerick Steamship Company amalgamated with the Palgrave Murphys to form Hibernian Transport. It was an unfortunate move. By the end of 1970 the new company was in liquidation and a colourful chapter of Limerick port history was closed. Fortunately an enthusiastic local marine historian, Dick Scott, has recorded the full story of the *Limerick Steamship Company*.

The cargo throughput in Limerick did not vary greatly up to the late 1960s. It was based entirely on the wet dock and quays at Limerick with an occasional grain vessel lightened at Beagh Castle anchorage. The most common cargoes were grain, loose timber, coal, fertilisers, petroleum and general cargoes. Three-hundred-and-fifty independent casual dockers busied themselves sorting and cessing timber, charging recklessly about with generals on handcarts and even bagging coal in the hold. "Car men" with their horse drawn drays transported most of the cargoes. Loose timber covered seven or eight acres of the docks and often stretched along the quays as well. Oil tanker movements were confined to daylight hours

Limerick Market Trustees Seal, 1852.
Limerick City Museum

and the greatest attraction for the curious onlookers was the swinging of partly laden 10,000 ton grain vessels supervised by the late Captain Carlo Hanrahan with whistle and booming voice. The Limerick Steamship Company collapsed following an unwise partnership when packaging revolutionised the traditional handling of timber. With a huge excess of casual dockers it was feared that restrictive practices would drive away the remaining trade. Good sense prevailed and a successful docks rationalisation scheme was introduced by the Harbour Commissioners resulting in a slimmed down stevedoring company with equipment and practices suitable for the changing times.

Since the 1960s, with the increasing size of vessels, the attention of the Harbour Commissioners was diverted downstream where the estuary offered the

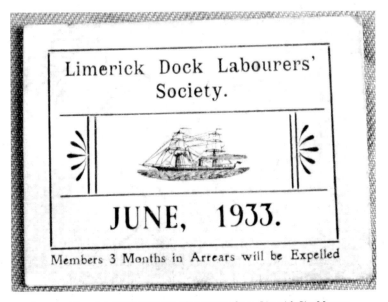

Limerick Dock Labourers' Society Membership Card. Limerick City Museum

greatest development potential. Various physical and economic surveys were undertaken to ascertain the potential of the estuary and the infrastructure required. The opening of a tanker terminal at Foynes and the provision of an oil jetty in Shannon are amongst the major developments that have since occurred in the estuary. Possibly the greatest breakthrough in the history of the port since the building of the wet dock was the establishment of the Alumina Extraction Plant at Aughinish. This was a major international industry importing bauxite in 60,000-ton vessels; receiving fuel oil and liquid caustic in tankers up to 30,000 tons deadweight and exporting alumina in many classes of vessels. The first bauxite vessel arrived in November 1982. Before this plant came into operation construction had begun on the giant electricity generating station at Moneypoint. This came onstream in 1985 and immediately doubled the size of the largest vessel handled in the Shannon to 150,000 tons deadweight. In 1962 the largest vessel visiting the Shannon was just over 9,000 tons deadweight and throughput was 0.43 million tonnes. In 1988 the largest vessel was 150,000 tons deadweight and throughput had increased to 5.55 million tonnes. Thus in a quarter of a century the size of vessel has increased sixteenfold and the volume of cargo twelvefold while investment had been in the region of two billion pounds. The throughput through the harbour was 6.925 million tons in 1993 and is expected to be well in excess of ten million tons by 2,000 AD.

The river pilots contribution to the development of Limerick port cannot be overestimated. Pilots boarded from yawls, usually ketch-rigged, or currachs, which were known as canoes, until motor boats came into use. The western pilot division was based in Cappa, County Clare, opposite Scattery Island and the eastern division maintained a base on Cain's Island opposite Bunratty. Until World War II erupted the western pilots usually brought vessels only as far as Grass Island where they relinquished control to the eastern pilots. Michael Joyce, squarerigger, pilot, harbour commissioner, alderman, member of Parliament, mayor of Limerick, president of the U.K. Pilots Association, and a founder and first chairman of Garryowen Rugby Club, was the most remarkable of the Shannon pilots. He became involved in politics and was elected to the Corporation in 1899. The following year he was elected M.P. for Limerick for the Irish Parliamentary Party and retained the seat until 1918. His nautical background was valued highly in Westminster and he was one of the principal architects of the *Pilotage Act of 1913* which still governs pilotage in Ireland. Michael was shipwrecked four times. The last occasion was while he was an M.P. travelling on the *S.S. Leinster* when she was torpedoed in the Irish Sea in 1918. His marine background enabled him to take charge of a lifeboat. He died at his home, the Moorings, O'Connell Avenue, Limerick in 1941 in his 90th year.

Limerick lace was once one of the city's most famous products. An Oxford man, Charles Walker, arrived in Ireland in 1824. He purchased a store at Mount

LIMERICK LACE SCARF. Limerick City Museum.

Kennett and by 1829 had established a lace-factory there. Twenty-four young girls whom he had brought over from England worked as instructors for the 300 children and young women employed at weekly wages ranging from 5 pence to 25 pence to produce run and tambour lace. His produce was sold through Henning's of London, initially, until he opened his own store there at a later stage. By 1837 his lace was known as Irish Blonde, and up to 400 young women were employed in its manufacture. By 1840 he had formed a partnership with Samuel Lambert. He died in 1843 but his company continued. In 1851 the firm, under the name of Lambert and Bury, won a prize medal at the Great Exhibition of the Industry of All Nations in London. After Walker's death business continued to flourish under the title of Lambert and Bury, and at one point employed up to 900 young women. William Lloyd established a lace-factory in Clare Street in 1836. Within a year he was employing 250 young women and exporting lace to London. When Queen Victoria married Prince Albert of Saxe-Coburg and Gotha on 10 February, 1840, she did not wear Limerick Lace, although she had been presented with a shawl made by the lace-makers of the city. In 1853 up to 1,500 people were employed as lace-makers in Limerick City. Co-incidentally the only lace-factory still operating today is run by the Good Shepherd Convent in Clare Street. In 1914 Limerick Lace was manufactured at Mrs. Vere O'Brien's Lace School and Depot at No. 48 O'Connell Street, which was managed by a Miss Dunne. At the same time as the lace industry was being developed, 100 boys were employed in a muslin-factory in the Abbey parish.

MASONIC MEMBERSHIP LIST OF 1844. LIMERICK CITY MUSEUM.

In 1844 J. G. Kohl published an account of the city in *Ireland, Scotland and England*, a record of his tour throughout all three countries. He was a German traveller who seemed to suffer from an excess of Anglomania and his account of Limerick confused the Englishtown with Newtownpery. His opinions of Ireland seemed to have been formed before he started writing and most of his observations seem to have been slotted within the narrow framework of preconceived perspectives:-

Limerick is the third city in Ireland, with a population of 75,000. Dublin, the first, contains 270,000, and Cork, the second, 110,000.

The trade of Limerick, like that of most Irish cities, has increased in an astonishing degree. The exports have trebled since 1820, and in 1841 the customs alone produced £246,000, or about 1,700,000 Prussian dollars. The inhabitants are, in consequence, full of hope that their port, hitherto a third class one, may soon be raised to the second class.

In the new parts of the town, the effects of this improving commerce are plain enough to be seen; the streets are broad and imposing, and the houses large and well built. St. George Street may vie with Sackville Street in Dublin. St. George is an English saint, and the whole of this new quarter is called the English town. Galway and many other Irish cities are divided, in the same way, into and English and Irish town. The Irish town is generally full of dirt, disorder and decay; the English quarter, on the other hand, reminds one of the better parts of London. The inhabitants of the two quarters live in a sort of constant opposition to one another .... It is the English that improve the navigation of the Shannon, urge the draining of the bogs, and gradually drive the Irish elves and fairies into the sea; it is the English who enrich the Irish towns with clean, comfortable, and civilised quarters; it is the English who constitute the soul and pith of the British power, and it is to them that the Irish owe it, if they are able to participate in the wide-spread commerce of Great Britain, and to share in all the opportunities and advantages that stand open to a British subject .... Nothing, however, is to be found in Limerick more beautiful that the "Limerick lasses" who are as much celebrated in Ireland as the "Lancashire witches" are in England .... It was arm-in-arm with a descendant from a royal race, a Mr. O'Rourke, that I sallied forth to see the town .... It was on a Saturday evening, and the pawnbrokers' shops were full of bustle. The poor people were redeeming their Sunday clothes, that they might look gay on the morrow .... On Monday their bit of finery would have to wander back to the money-lender, and the remainder of the week would be spent in rags and privation. Thousands of the poor Irish live thus....

Limerick has many fine buildings and public institutions, but all of modern erection, and just like what a traveller may see in other towns in Ireland and England.

John Daly (1846-1916) was an old Fenian and Irish Republican Brotherhood leader. On 11 April, 1884, he was arrested in Birkenhead and charged with carrying explosives. While on remand in Windsor Green Prison, Birmingham, he corresponded with his old friend Michael Hogan, the Bard of

THE DEAD FENIAN CHIEF.

JOHN DALY.
(MAYOR OF LIMERICK, 1899, 1900, 1901.)

City Printing Co. Limerick

JOHN DALY, THE FENIAN WHO REVIVED THE ANCIENT CUSTOM OF 'FASTING UPON THE ENEMY'. HIS HUNGER-STRIKE INSPIRED THE SUFFRAGETTES AND EARLY SINN FEINERS TO FOLLOW HIS EXAMPLE TWENTY YEARS LATER. Limerick City Museum.

Thomond. He was sentenced to life imprisonment but was released after serving twelve and a half years in jail, where he had become the first modern political prisoner to use the hunger strike weapon against the British. In 1899 he was elected mayor of Limerick and retained mayoral office for three consecutive terms, 1899,1900 and 1901. He died on 30 June, 1916, almost two months after the execution of his nephew, Ned.

The tradesmen at the turn of the century included auctioneers, bootmakers, bellowmakers, brassfounders, basket-makers, blacksmiths, brush-makers, cage-makers, candlemakers, car-makers, coachmen, coffin-makers, chandlers, crockery repairers, clock-menders, coopers, carpenters, dyers, dairy men, dockers, fiddlers, furniture-makers, fishermen, glaziers, grave diggers, labourers, lime-burners, lace-makers, last-makers, millwrights, nailers, pipe-makers, pavers, pipers, rag gatherers, snuff grinders, stonemasons, tinmen, thatchers, tailors, varnishers, weavers, wheelwrights, whip-makers, weight-masters, and wool card-makers.

Jewish history does not date back very far in Limerick. Bobby (Abraham) Genese died on 30 May, 1847. He was buried in a Christian cemetery but later exhumed and re-interred in a Jewish cemetery at Ballybough, Dublin. The 1861 census listed only one Jew living in the city while the 1871 census listed two in the county borough. By 1881 this figure had risen to four in the county borough. Lithuanian Jews arrived in Ireland in 1878. These were quiet reserved people who traded mainly in books and pictures. They formed an acceptable, but not integral, part of Limerick's retail trade. A few of them were wholesalers who supplied their co-religionists with the necessary trade goods. An anti-Jewish demonstration occurred on Easter Sunday, 1884. A hostile group of Limerick people surrounded the house of Lieb Siev after his maid-servant complained of

MEDAL OF ARCHCONFRATERNITY 1899 Limerick City Museum.

the cruel way in which she had seen him slaughter fowl on Holy Thursday. She had not realised that animals had to be killed in ritual fashion before their meat could be considered fit for consumption. Lieb Siev's windows were broken with stones and his daughter was injured. Two of the riot's ringleaders were sentenced to a month's imprisonment each, with hard labour. People tried to avoid paying petty debts to the Jews by instigating other incidents. Life became intolerable for the small Jewish community, and many of them moved to Cork in May, 1884. A few returned to Limerick, later on. The incidents continued. Two Jewish families were beaten up in August, 1892, and the house of Moses Leone was damaged by stone-throwing on 24 November, 1896. There were 130 Jews living in the city in 1896. From 1897 until 1904 they lived in peace with their neighbours. Most of Limerick's Lithuanian Jews had settled in Collooney Street by the 1890's. They held prayer meetings in a private house in Emmet Place, initially, and later moved to No. 18 Collooney Street, until they eventually opened a synagogue at 63 Collooney Street. On 14 August, 1888, Rev. Dr. Hermann Adler, Delegate Chief Rabbi, addressed the Limerick congregation as there were eight families living in the city at that time. By 1 December, 1892, there were ninety in the congregation. On 17 February 1902, the Jews bought a site in Newcastle, Kilmurry Parish, from William Nunan for £150. This was used as a Jewish cemetery.

The Limerick Confraternity was founded by the Redemptorist Fathers soon after their full development as a community in Mount St. Alphonsus, in 1867. They spent the last three days of 1867 celebrating a solemn *triduum* to Our Lady of Perpetual Succour, and on New Year's Day, 1868, they opened a mission for men and boys. When this mission ended, 8,000 men had received communion and 14,000 boys had been confirmed. The confraternity was founded and directed by Fr. Bridgett, who laid the foundations of a movement which dominated the religious and social life of Limerick for well over a century, earning it a reputation as a city of nothing but churches and "piety upon piety". Year after year, street by street, and house by house, the male members of the Limerick Confraternity trooped off to their meetings. Attendance was compulsory, excuses were checked and recorded by two officers of the association; social pressure was exerted to boost attendance but non-membership was tolerated, though not quite approved, amongst one's Catholic peers. By 1880 the Confraternity had 4,200 members. This figure had climbed to 7,000 by 1918, and the movement continued to flourish into the early 1960s.

Fr. John Creagh was born at Thomondgate on 19 August, 1870. He was educated by the Christian Brothers and the Redemptorists, in Limerick and in England, before his ordination on 1 September, 1895. He taught history at Teignmouth, England, and at Clonard, Belfast, before returning to Limerick where he was director of the Holy Family Confraternity in 1904. On 11 January, 1904, he delivered a sermon from the pulpit of the Redemptorist Church castigating the Jews of Limerick. He indicted their business methods, accused them of shedding Christian blood, and stated that they would "kidnap and slay Christian children" if they dared. This tirade was probably sparked off by a type of hire-purchase system operated by the business people of the city in which weekly payments were collected from various debtors within the locality. Fr. Creagh held the small Jewish enclave in Colooney Street responsible for this state of affairs. In fact, the few Jewish dealers involved in this *gombeenism* formed only a small percentage of the business community which was more than predominantly Christian. John Creagh wanted to start a credit union but could

A GERMAN STONEWARE TANKARD,
SIXTEENTH-CENTURY,
IN THE HUNT MUSEUM

not afford to antagonise either the Catholic or Protestant merchants whose business practices were identical to those of some of the Jewish community. The Jews, however, were few in number and by attacking them John Creagh knew that there would be little risk of reprisal. The Jewish community was insulted, assaulted and threatened after Fr. Creagh's sermon, according to a report of the Rabbi, Rev. Elias Bere Levin, on 18 January, 1904. Worse was to come. Fr. Creagh preached a second sermon, in which he urged Catholics "not to deal with the Jews" after he had further maligned them. This sermon may have been inspired by the expulsion of Redemptorist priests from France, an incident for which Fr. Creagh held the Jews responsible. The Limerick Pogrom was an economic boycott waged against Limerick's small Jewish community for two years. Life was made intolerable for them. Rabbi Levin and some of his flock were assaulted, their businesses boycotted, their livelihoods destroyed, and they were subjected to abuse and slander. They were never given a chance to defend themselves or place their case before the public. The Protestants of Limerick tried to support the Jews throughout this troubled period, but their sponsorship only deepened the animosity of the Redemptorists and the Confraternity of the Holy Family. Eventually the Jewish community were forced into asking the Protestants to desist, thus depriving themselves of essential funds and allies, in the hope that the Catholics would attempt a reconciliation. Despite this gesture the boycott continued. Standish O'Grady (1832-1915) wrote on 23 April that "it is difficult to believe that the priests and the Bishop of Limerick could not put an end to it if they tried ... These Limerick Jews seem to be a very harmless body, neither money-lenders nor extortioners; just traders trading in clothes, and selling the same at no more profit that is permitted". Arthur Griffith (1872-1922) supported Fr. Creagh in the *United Irishman*, demanding freedom for the Irish peasant from the international moneylenders (the Jews). He was reprimanded by Frederick Ryan, co-editor of *Dana*, who wrote that Irishmen who were claiming freedom for themselves could ill afford to refuse it to others. Dr. Bunbury, the Church of Ireland Bishop of Limerick, spoke to the Church of Ireland Synod. He defended the Jews, claiming that they charged no more than the other shopkeepers in the city. His speech was condemned at a special meeting of the corporation, in which the mayor, Michael Donnelly, denied that the Jews had been subjected to violence.

John Raleigh, a fifteen-year-old youth, was sentenced to one month's imprisonment, without hard labour, for assaulting Rabbi Elias Bere Levin, with a thrown stone, on 4 April, 1904. In court, Raleigh was defended by an anti-Semitic solicitor, Nash, who stated that as far as he was concerned, any reported assaults on the Jews were just fabrications by which the Jews hoped to enrich themselves. The resident magistrate, Hickson, said it was quite clear that Raleigh was guilty of the charges. It was not his first time to cause trouble or to annoy the Jews, and although he, and several other children, had been involved in

A CALVARY CHARGE, BY THE SCOTS GRAYS, CLEARED THE CITY STREETS OF LAND LEAGUERS, IN OCTOBER, 1881. THE EARLIER LAND LEAGUE WAS HEAVILY INFLUENCED BY THE OLDER, MORE VIOLENT, AGRARIAN SOCIETIES SUCH AS THE DEFENDERS, ROCKITES, TERRRY ALTS AND WHITEBOYS. IT WAS SUPPRESSED ON 18 OCTOBER, 1881. THE MORE EXTREME LADIES' LAND LEAGUE CONTINUED TO AGITATE ON BEHALF OF THEIR MALE COLLEAGUES UNTIL 18 AUGUST, 1882, THE DAY AFTER CHARLES STEWART PARNELL FOUNDED THE IRISH NATIONAL LAND LEAGUE - **The Illustrated London News.**

various incidents concerning the Jews, it was obvious that other parties should bear the responsibility for such actions. Raleigh served his sentence in Mountjoy jail. He was released in May and received a hero's welcome on returning to Limerick. He was carried home, shoulder high, from the railway station by enthusiastic supporters who also presented him with a silver watch and chain. John Raleigh was an authentic hero during the War of Independence, later became a successful businessman in the building industry and died in Castletroy, about 1970. Rabbi Elias Bere Levin (1862- 1936) had settled in the city in 1882 where he was appointed reader and *shochet* to the single congregation placed under the jurisdiction of the Chief Rabbi.

The Collooney Street outrage is another term used to describe the *pogrom* which is usually defined as an organised massacre or the preaching which culminates in such an event. Fr. John Creagh left Limerick in May, 1906. He worked as a missionary in the Philippines, New South Wales, Western Australia and New Zealand. He returned to Australia where he was appointed rector of the Redemptorist House in Perth from 1914 to 1916. He was vicar-apostolic of the Kimberleys from 1916 to 1923, and from 1923 to 1925 he was acting parish priest of Bunbury. From 1926 to 1930 he was in Pennant Hills and after that he was stationed at Waratah and Wellington, New Zealand, where he died in the Lewisham Hospital on 24 January, 1947. He was buried at Karori. Controversy followed him even after he had left Limerick. When a white stock drover, Jackie Parks, was accused of murdering an Aboriginal stockboy, Fr. Creagh attended Parks's trial in Perth to give evidence. He claimed that it had long been the practice, amongst drovers, to fire a charge of buckshot at the stockboys' legs to encourage them to work if they were slacking off. His seven years in the Kimberleys were described by a friend, Sr. Ignatius, as "lonely, poor and frustrated". She also referred to his flashing temper but admitted that he could be very kind.

The Jewish surnames of Limerick between 1847 and 1938 were Arinon, Blonde, Clein, Cropman, Fine, Genese, Gewurtz, Ginsberg, Goldberg, Gould, Graff, Greenfield, Jaffe, Jerome, Kaitcher, Leone, Levin, Moizel (Miessel), Sandler, Siev, Tobin, Toohey and Weinronk.

The Wolfe Tone Club was a legal front organisation for the illegal Irish Republican Brotherhood. On 25 January, 1914, the club organised a meeting in the Athenaeum Hall in Cecil Street to recruit members for the Irish Volunteer Movement. Padraig Pearse and Roger Casement addressed the large audience, out of which practically every man enlisted. On Whit Sunday, 23 May, 1915, volunteers from Dublin, Cork and Tipperary marched through the streets of the city with their Limerick comrades, led by men such as Padraig Pearse, Tom Clarke, Willie Pearse, Liam Mellows, Tomás McCurtin, Eamon de Valera, Terence McSwiney, George Clancy, Ned Daly and Seán McDermott. World

EDWARD DALY.
The Limerick City Museum.

War I was in progress, so the marchers had to suffer a barrage of insults from the soldiers and the "separation women" of the city whose husbands had enlisted in the British Army. (Wolfe Tone Street is now the name of Collooney Street). Séan Heuston took first place in Ireland at The Great Southern and Western Railway *Company's* examination of 1908. He worked as a railway clerk in Limerick until he was recalled to Dublin in 1913. While there, he worked in Kingsbridge Station, in the traffic manager's office, while his spare time was devoted to the organising of Fianna Eireann. He was a captain in D Company, First Battalion Dublin Brigade. During Easter Week he commanded the occupation and defence of the Mendicity institute on Dublin's South Quays. On 8 May, 1916, he was executed by firing squad in Kilmainham Jail. Kingsbridge Station later had its name changed to Heuston Station in his honour. Commandant Edward 'Ned' Daly (1891-1916), John Daly's nephew, was the youngest child and the only boy in a family of ten children. He was born in Frederick Street, (now O'Curry Street) and was educated in the Presentation Convent, Sexton Street, the Christian Brothers' School in Roxboro Road and Leamy's School, an academy for commercial training. His father, an old Fenian, died in 1896. His sister, Kathleen, was married to Tom Clarke, the first signatory of *The Proclamation.* In 1907 Ned emigrated to Glasgow but returned because of ill-health, and took up a clerical post with Francis Spaight and Sons Ltd. In 1912 he left Limerick for Dublin where he worked for Brooks Thomas and Company Ltd. At the time of the 1916 Rising he was on the staff of a wholesale chemist's on Westmoreland Street, May Roberts and Company Ltd. On Easter Monday, 1916, he commanded the First Battalion of the Dublin Brigade and was in charge of the Four Courts Garrison. He was court-martialled, sentenced to death and executed in the big yard of Kilmainham Jail, on the morning of 4 May, 1916. He was buried in Arbour Hill with the executed leaders of the Easter Rebellion. His sisters continued to support the nationalist struggle. Their home, Ardeevin, on the Ennis Road, was wrecked by the British Forces on the night of 9 April, 1921. Three of Ned Daly's colleagues were luckier, insofar as they escaped execution. Thomas McInerney, of 10 Lock Quay, Sean Nestor of 25 Edward Street and James Quigley, of 3 Garryowen Cottages, were interned in Frongoch, an internment camp in North Wales, in the aftermath of the 1916 rising. This particular establishment held over 1800 Republican prisoners and became known as the University of Revolution as many of the prisoners became prominent leaders in the War of Independence.

Robert Byrne was one of Limerick's earliest casualties during the War of Independence. He was jailed on an arms charge, and instigated a riot in Limerick Prison when his campaign to get political status for himself and his fellow prisoners failed. This riot was followed by a hunger strike in which several prisoners participated. Bobby, as he was called by his friends, was removed to the Limerick Union Hospital when he became ill. A rescue attempt by the I.R.A. succeeded, but Bobby was wounded in the process and died, after escaping, on the evening of 6 April, 1919. His removal to St. John's Cathedral on 8 April was attended by an estimated crowd of 10,000 people. This alarmed the authorities to such an extent that Limerick was declared a special military area the following day. Within days the Limerick Soviet came into existence. During the War of Independence an I.R.A. unit under the command of Michael Hartney captured two detectives, near the People's Park, on the night of 15 August, 1920. John

FUNERAL OF ROBERT BYRNE.

TOM CLARKE'S LETTERHEAD.

McInerney, from Carey's Road, was a member of the I.R.A. unit. This event sent the Crown forces on a rampage through Carey's Road and other parts of the city. R.I.C. and military personnel raided the homes and work-places of suspected Sinn Fein sympathisers. In High Street the home and stores of the Foley brothers were emptied with volleys of rifle-fire, and several other places were burned throughout the city including the home and business premises of Matthew Griffin, a Sinn Fein member of the Corporation. Clare Street was the scene of an abortive ambush in April, 1920. An informer leaked details of I.R.A. plans to the authorities. As the men of C Company of the I.R.A. took up their positions the British Army encircled them. The commandant of the I.R.A. unit ordered his men to retreat across the canal, by boat, as lorry loads of soldiers had cordoned off the bridges. The Welch Fusiliers went on a rampage through the city in April, 1920. Armed with bayonets, revolvers and entrenching tools they ran amok in the streets and raided houses, bars and cinemas. They attacked and beat up the citizens who retaliated with a barrage of bottles stones and anything else they could lay their hands on. Other troops came to their rescue by firing indiscriminately on the people. A publican named Dwyer was shot dead behind his own counter in Roches Street, while a cinema usherette, Miss Johnson, was killed as she was returning home from the Coliseum Cinema where she worked. Organised labour supported Sinn Fein's nationalist aspirations. At 11.30 p.m. on Sunday, 13 April, the Limerick Trades and Labour Council called for a complete work stoppage commencing the following Monday morning, 14 April, 1919. Proclamations were printed calling on workers to declare a cessation of all work from 5.00 a.m. on that Monday morning, as a protest against British government plans to place them under military law. A special strike committee was set up to oversee the general strike, print and issue their own money, publish their own proclamations, draft their own permits, and control food prices. Two other committees handled propaganda and the issue of permits. The former group produced a citizens' newssheet and prepared daily reports for the many foreign correspondents who had gathered in the city to report on a proposed trans-Atlantic aeroplane flight which a Major Woods had intended to undertake. The permits committee, which was staffed by four city councillors, issued permits allowing people to carry out essential works, maintain selected services, make necessary sales or purchases, and, despite the closure of all businesses, inconvenience the citizens as little as possible while making the city intolerable for the military. On 19 April the Limerick Chamber of Commerce demanded the abolition of martial law, strange partners for the Limerick Trades and Labour Council. Martial law was rescinded on 26 April, 1919, and the strike committee ordered everyone back to work.

The Black and Tans were given this derogatory title by Christopher O'Sullivan, proprietor and editor of *The Limerick Echo* when he described the "strange type of individual wearing the black cap and tunic of the Royal Irish Constabulary and khaki trousers of the British soldier" with whom he had travelled in a train from Limerick Junction to Limerick City. He later remarked, in a leading article, that "this puny creature resembled something one would

FRAMED NOTES ISSUED BY LIMERICK STRIKE COMMITTEE IN 1919. Limerick City Museum.

associate with the Scarteen Hunt (the Black and Tans) of Pallasgreen judging by his strange attire". Mike Nono, the Ennis comedian, perpetuated this nick-name shortly afterwards from the stage of Limerick's Theatre Royal when he used Christopher O'Sullivan's quip to describe the new occupying force set up by the British. The Black and Tans were the masters of Limerick by April, 1921. They operated a curfew, banned the holding of fairs, markets or auctions within an eight-mile radius of the General Post Office, cordoned off the streets whenever they wished, searched, arrested and brutalised the population, ransacked, looted and wrecked the homes and business premises of suspected I.R.A. or Sinn Fein sympathisers, and indulged in orgies of destruction whenever they were attacked, frustrated, drunk or annoyed. They were considered "the sweepings of the English jails", discharged ex-servicemen fit for little else but the terrorising of a civilian population. Cecil O'Donovan, seventeen-years-old, and his fourteen-year-old brother, Aidan, were shot dead by Black and Tans as they walked through the fields at Blackwater on 20 February, 1921. They had been accompanied by their cousins, Thomas and Benjamin O'Donovan, who had managed to escape when the Black and Tans had opened fire. None of the four youths had any paramilitary connections, nor were they associated with Sinn Fein or Fianna Eireann.

George Clancy (1879-1921) was a native of Grange. Better known as Seoirse he was a teacher, an Irish speaker, and organiser of both the Irish Volunteers and the Gaelic League, a leader of the anti-conscription campaign and a collector of the Dáil Éreann Loan. In January, 1921, he was elected mayor of Limerick. At 1.30 a.m. on Monday morning, 7 March, 1921, he went downstairs to answer a loud hammering on the door of his home. "It's all right Moll" he reassured his wife, "it's only a raid". Moll Clancy glimpsed three men at the door. They were tall, wore goggles, had caps pulled low over their foreheads and their coat collars were turned up, concealing their faces. She overheard the ensuing conversation. "Are you Clancy?" "Yes, I am". "Come out here then, we want you," "What for?", "Come outside", "No, I won't", said George as he stepped back into the hallway opening the front door wider. "Then take that!", one of the men shouted and he started shooting at George. Moll rushed forward and threw herself between her husband and his assassins. She was too late. George was fatally wounded and she was shot in the hand. This shooting was one of several such killings on that night, later known as the night of the Curfew Murders.

The Curfew Murders on the night of 6-7 March, 1921, were believed to have been perpetrated by a group of British intelligence officers variously known as the Cairo Gang or the Murder Gang. This group had first come together in Cairo, hence the former name, but they had been reassembled in Ireland to carry out a series of raids, searches and assassinations at the behest of Sir Henry

LIMERICK CORPORATION CHEQUE, SIGNED BY GEORGE CLANCY, MICHAEL O' CALLAGHAN AND PATRICK FLYNN.
Limerick City Museum.

Wilson. Michael Collins suspected that the British were "shooting by roster" when seventeen Irishmen were murdered in October, 1920. On the morning of Sunday, 21 November, 1920 his special counter-intelligence unit shot fourteen of these special agents dead. Despite the Collin's coup on Bloody Sunday the undercover war was continued by the English. A notorious ex-convict and rapist, Captain Nathan, was the ringleader of Wilson's murder gang in Limerick. He is generally believed to have been responsible for the Curfew Murders, and was definitely involved in the murder of Denis O'Donovan in Castleconnell. During the Spanish Civil War (1936-1939) he was killed fighting on the Republican side with Bela Kun and Frank Ryan (1902-1944). Michael O'Callaghan was mayor of Limerick in 1920. His grandfather, Eugene O'Callaghan, once proposed a motion urging the repeal of the Union at a corporation meeting in 1843. Michael had continued in the family's nationalist tradition. He was a member of Sinn Fein, a Volunteer officer and a member of the Gaelic League. He was shot at 1.00 a.m. on the morning of 7 March, 1921, by two men whose descriptions matched those of two of George Clancy's killers. Like George he was murdered in the presence of his wife. She later refused to attend the inquiry into his, Michael's, death and was elected in the "Partition Election" of May 1921. During this general election 124 Sinn Fein and four Independent candidates were returned for the Southern Ireland Parliament while the Northern Ireland Parliament returned forty Unionist, six Nationalist and six Sinn Fein candidates. Clancy's Strand and O'Callaghans's Strand are named after the two murdered

GEORGE CLANCY. Limerick City Museum.

mayors. Joseph O'Donoghue of Ballinacargy, County Westmeath, was also slain on the same night. At 11.40 p.m. on the night of 6 March 1921, he was taken from the Lyddy home at Tig na Fáinne, Janesboro, by twelve R.I.C. men under the command of a Detective Leech. His body was discovered on Janesboro Avenue the following morning.

James Casey was one of Kevin Hannan's great local heroes, one all but forgotten today. In March, 1921, Councillor James Casey acted as deputy mayor after the murder of George Clancy. He made all of the arrangements for the burials of George Clancy, Michael O'Callaghan and Joseph O'Donoghue ignoring the military authorities who ordered that no undue ostentation or speech-making take place and delivered an impassioned graveside oration. He acted as mayor until Stephen O'Mara (1885-1926) was elected mayor. Stephen's brother, James O'Mara (1873-1948), a prominent businessman, was a member of the Irish parliamentary Party until 1907. He supported the Irish Volunteers and Sinn Féin; was returned to the first Dáil Éireann on 21 January, 1919, as Sinn Féin member for Limerick and became Dáil Éireann's principal fundraiser in the United States of America, having been sent there by Eamon de Valera. He acted as a trustee for the Dáil funds until he resigned from that body in May, 1921, following a policy disagreement with Eamon de Valera. Stephen O'Mara replaced his brother as trustee of the Dáil funds. Patrick Quinlan stepped down as mayor in 1935 after the passing of the Limerick City Management Act. He was replaced by James Casey for the duration. In 1935 and 1936 James Casey was elected mayor for the first time although he had been acting mayor in 1921 and early 1935.

Whites Lane, near the junction of John Street, Broad Street and Mungret Street was the scene of a shoot-out on Friday, 8 April, 1921, when a group of I.R.A. men were almost surprised by six R.I.C. men who emerged suddenly from a public-house. Two R.I.C. men and two civilians were wounded, another civilian was killed and the I.R.A. commandant, Dundon, was wounded slightly. A few minutes before this incident a Black and Tan constable, Wiggins, was shot dead when his patrol stumbled across an I.R.A. unit as they were about to disband in the vicinity of Church Street and Palmerstown. Three of the I.R.A. men, Dundon, Downey and McGrath found shelter in an unoccupied house located between the homes of two R.I.C. sergeants on Lelia Street, while Jack Madigan's home on the same street was wrecked by the police, who spent most of that night raiding Sinn Fein and suspected Sinn Fein homes. A

THOMAS KEANE, EXECUTED IN LIMERICK ON 4 JUNE, 1921. HE WAS A LIEUTENANT IN C. COMPANY, 2ND BATTALION I.R.A.. Limerick City Museum.

proclamation ordered everyone to remain indoors by 2.00 p.m. on the following day, Saturday, 9 April, 1921, when General Cameron led a motorised convoy on official reprisals within the city. He supervised the bombing of Tommy McInerney's public house, Nos. 9 and 10 Lock Quay, and the shop and residence of a Mrs. Nealon in John Street. Mrs. Nealon was the aunt of Henry Meany, an I.R.A. activist. Tommy McInerney was the transport officer of the Mid Limerick Brigade of the I.R.A. On 21 April, 1916, Tommy had driven off Ballykissane Pier, Kerry, while conveying people to meet Roger Casement. His three passengers drowned, but Tommy survived. Henry Clancy was one of three I.R.A. men captured in Ballysimon on Sunday, 1 May, 1921. On their way into the city he jumped from the Crossley tender in which he was being transported only to be riddled with bullets as he regained his footing. Ironically he had survived the worst days of World War I with the Warwickshire Regiment only to die fighting the army he had once served in . The Black and Tans refused to allow all but five mourners to accompany his funeral procession. They attacked the cortege and

BOTTOM DOG, ISSUED ON 25 MAY 1918.
Limerick City Museum.

drove the sympathisers away. Michael Downey, one of the mourners, was shot as he crossed the Fair Green, and the priest officiating at the Clancy funeral had to leave it hurriedly to administer the last rites. Thomas Keane, who was captured with Henry Clancy, was executed in the New Barrack on 4 June 1921.

The truce between the I.R.A. and the British Army came into effect on 9 July, 1921. Ernie O'Malley, commander of the Second Southern Division, decided to avail of the peace to acquire explosives and other material in London. He spent November and December in London "with a Limerick officer, Johnny Raleigh" and they bought surplus war stock which was being auctioned off by the British Disposal Board. The pair purchased prismatic compasses, range-finders, prismatic glasses, wireless sets and other equipment from the board, bought three tons of an explosive base from a chemical factory and were amazed at the ease with which they could bribe the staff in both places. John Raleigh and Ernie O'Malley cut expenses to a minimum and practically starved themselves in order to spend everything on arms and supplies. They dealt with professional gun-runners in the East End, masqueraded as Ulster Volunteers on occasion and met with the Irish Delegation in Hans Place.

Eamon de Valera was in Strand House, now Jury's Hotel on the Ennis Road, Limerick, on Monday night, 5 December 1921. At 2.15 a.m. on Tuesday, 6 December, 1921, the Anglo-Irish Treaty was signed in London and was later approved in Dail Eireann by a vote of 64 to 57 on 7 January, 1922. On that Monday night Eamon de Valera said; "This is a separate nation and never till the end of time will they [the English] get from this nation allegiance to their rulers". He cautioned his listeners against optimism. The following day he returned to Dublin. Early in 1922 the Black and Tans and the Auxiliaries left Limerick, and the new Free State. The Royal Irish Constabulary force was disbanded and the new Garda Siochana was established. The uncrowned harp was now the new

Bought of **NESTOR BROS.**

(Partners :—Alexander Nestor, Henry Nestor).

▣ FANCY TOBACCONISTS ▣

IMPORTERS OF HAVANA, MANILLA & INDIAN CIGARS.

For Pipes, Cigarettes, Walking Sticks, &c., see our Prices.

Telephone No. 96.

NESTOR BROTHERS WERE TOBACCONISTS AND IMPORTERS OF MANILLA AND INDIAN CIGARS IN 1938 AND 1939. ON 1 OCTOBER, TWO POUNDS OF FLAKE TOBACCO WERE SOLD FOR £2.07 AND ONE DOZEN BOXES OF SWAN MATCHES FOR SEVEN AND A HALF PENCE. THE FIRM WAS LOCATED AT 33 O'CONNELL STREET.

national emblem. Civil war soon broke out. The Mid Limerick Brigade should have moved in to occupy the posts evacuated by the British, but the general headquarters of the Free State suspected that Liam Forde, the Mid-Limerick Brigade commandant, might not recognise their authority. Michael Brennan, Commandant of the First Western Division, was asked to move into Limerick with his own men to occupy barracks buildings vacated by the departing British military and police. Soon, three entirely different forces occupied the city which, as in former times, commanded the Shannon and the entry to the south and west of Ireland. These groups consisted of Brennan's Claremen who favoured the Treaty, the men of the Mid-Limerick Brigade who disagreed with Forde's views but resented the presence of the Claremen as a slur upon their loyalty to the Free State, and anti-Treaty forces who had moved into the city and set up posts of their own on 6 March, 1922. Shortly afterwards both Free State forces

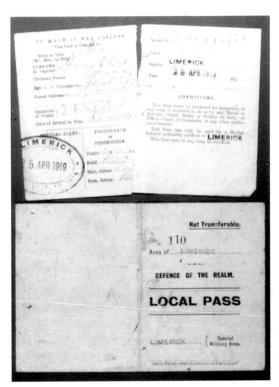

BRITISH MILITARY PASSES. Limerick City Museum.

93

17 FRANCIS STREET,
(Opposite Town Hall)

Limerick, 193

M *Cone Blackpool*

DR. TO # M. MURPHY.

VULCANIZING SERVICES.

C. H. DAVIS. PRINTER, LIMERICK

M. MURPHY ADVERTISED HIS VULCANIZING SERVICES AT 17 FRANCIS STREET, OPPOSITE TOWN HALL, IN THE 1930S. IN THE 1850S VULCANIZATION WAS DESCRIBED AS A NEW METHOD OF TREATING INDIAN RUBBER. BY WHICH ITS VALUABLE PROPERTIES WERE GREATLY INCREASED, AND SOME NEW ONES BESTOWED UPON IT . VULCANISED INDIA RUBBER WAS THE MATERIAL USED IN WASHERS, FIRE-HOSE TUBES, ELASTIC BANDS, TROUSER-STRAPS, SURGICAL BANDAGES, RAILWAY-CARRAIGE BUFFERS AND MANY OTHER ARTICLES UNTIL THE ADVENT OF PLASTIC.

withdrew from Limerick in an acceptable compromise drafted by Liam Lynch and Oscar Traynor and confirmed by General Eoin O'Duffy. A small occupying garrison, responsible to Liam Lynch, was left to hold the city. War erupted on 28 June, 1922. General Michael Brennan believed that "the Civil War turned on Limerick". Liam Lynch controlled most of the south and west with the exception of parts of Limerick, Clare and south Galway. He reinforced Limerick in the belief that the opposing Free State forces were stronger, or as strong, as his own, and was afraid to move men to Dublin in case Limerick would fall. He tried to neutralise his opponents, Brennan and O'Hannigan, by drafting agreements to prevent either side attacking the other, and actually persuaded Donnchadha O'Hannigan to sign such an agreement on 4 July, 1922. General Dermot MacManus revoked this agreement, personally, the following day. He had travelled from Dublin to Limerick, posing as a tramp, to tell Liam Lynch that neither Brennan nor O'Hannigan had authority to enter into negotiations. But on 7 July MacManus, though "absolutely disapproving" of any such agreement, wrote that he would allow one signed by Lynch and Brennan to stand, leaving the city in an uneasy state of truce. Brennan observed these terms until he sent Lynch a polite note ending the truce on 11 July. By 5.00 p.m. that day the Free State troops had taken up new positions. Brennan had entered into negotiations while he was waiting for arms to arrive. The bluffing was over. The Civil War had started in earnest. As the Free State troops took up their positions one of their number was shot.

William Street became a battle zone by 7.00 p.m. on 11 July, 1922, when the Free State forces opened fire on the Republican garrison holding the Ordnance Barracks. On Sunday, 16 July, Seamus Hogan, the man who had delivered the necessary arms to Brennan, reported that his men were running short of ammunition during an attack they were making on the Strand Barracks which was held by the Republicans. There was heavy street fighting in the city on 18 July when the Republicans tried to take full control before Free State reinforcements arrived. On Wednesday, 19 July, the Free State army set up an 18-pounder gun on Arthur's Quay to bombard the Strand Barrack. The barracks eventually fell but some of its defenders managed to escape. The Castle Barrack was captured by the Free State Army on Thursday 20 July. On Friday, 21 July, 1922, the Republican forces abandoned the city to the victorious Free State army. By then the area around what is now Sarsfield Barrack, Little Jerusalem, Wolfe Tone Street, Lord Edward Street, St. Joseph Street and Bowman Street,

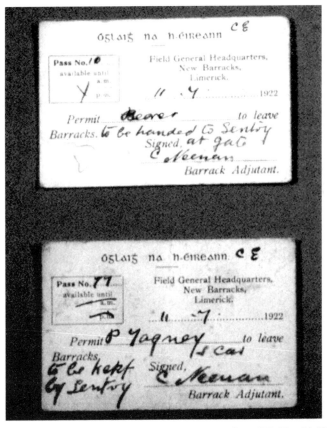

MILITARY PASSES ISSUED BY I.R.A. IRREGULARS IN THE NEW BARRACKS, JULY 1922, Limerick City Museum

had become a no-man's-land. Limerick prison had been designed to hold 120 prisoners a century before. By 6 November, 1922, it contained 800, with up to twelve prisoners each in cells meant to contain only one person. While the Republican men were in prison or on the run with the various guerrilla units, many of the day-to-day details were managed by their womenfolk in the *Cumann 'na mBan*. Two of the most active of these women in the city were Madge Daly and Nurse Guthrie, who were involved in numerous escape plots. The Civil War ended in May 1923. De Valera and Fianna Fail remained outside the Dail until 1927. In March 1932 Fianna Fail secured 70 seats in a general election, thus putting the men who had opposed the Treaty effectively in government. Roches Stores was looted during the "Troubles". One man, a prominent citizen in later life, was seen wheeling a rack of men's clothes towards his own premises, a drapery. In another incident, between the time the Republicans left a certain barracks and the Free State Army moved in, a motor car abandoned in the barracks' yard was moved into a nearby premises. Soon after the end of the Civil War this "liberated" vehicle appeared on the streets of the city as a taxi.

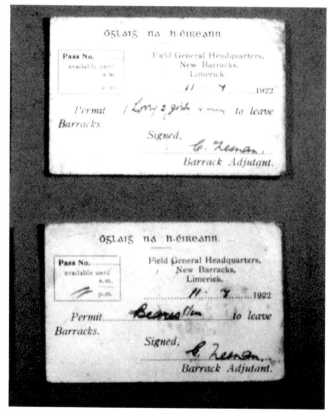

MILITARY PASSES ISSUED BY I.R.A. IRREGULARS IN THE NEW BARRACKS, JULY 1922, Limerick City Museum

KING'S ISLAND CAN BE SEEN QUITE CLEARLY IN THE BACKGROUND. HENRY STREET, PART OF O'CONNELL STREET, PATRICK STREET AND RUTLAND STREET ARE VISIBLE IN THE FOREGROUND. **Shannon Development Photo Library**

Limerick:
The Englishtown and King's Island

The Englishtown is the oldest part of the city and occupies the southern end of King's Island, a tract formed by the Shannon, here divided into two streams, of which the narrower and more rapid was once called *An Ghabal Beag*, the small fork and, later, the Abbey River. Both are tidal, with tides of over fourteen feet. The term, Englishtown, came into use as the original inhabitants who were unwilling, or unable, to assimilate English culture, customs and language were squeezed out by the invading Anglo-Normans. This was the earliest part of the city to be walled in, first by Vikings, secondly by Anglo-Normans. The island's natural features, the surrounding water and the dependable water supply ensured the security of its inhabitants. By 1450 the surrounding countryside was in a state of unrest due to the prevailing power of the "Irish enemy and English rebels". The loyal, but beleaguered, citizens of the Englishtown survived because supply ships, protected by Henry VI (1422-1455), brought the provisions they needed, sometimes from as far away as France.

The Fortifications, which had included the Englishtown alone, were extended to enclose part of the ground on the southern bank of the river between 1450 and 1495. Richard Stanihurst wrote in 1577; "The town is planted in an island, which plot in old time, before the building of the city was stored with grass ... yet the river is so navigable, as a ship of 200 tons may sail to the quay of the city [which was both] sumptuous and substantial". In an old map of the city, displayed in the Hunt Collection, the part of the island on which the Englishtown was located is shown as being completely walled in and surrounded by water. A moat or secondary channel of water separated the town from the upper two-thirds or so of the island. This map can be dated to some time before 1611 as it pre-dates the building of the bastion in King John's Castle. Another fortification is shown on the west side of the island, north of St. Munchin's Church as well as a tower-house on the east bank of the Abbey River, in Corbally.

The Island Road separates the Englishtown from the rest of King's Island and runs almost parallel with the remains and route of the old town walls. The Island Gate stood at the northern end of the road, near Verdant Place; a sallyport can still be seen close to the ruins of St. Saviour's Dominican Friary; Little Island Gate once spanned the roadway at St. Ann's Court; Bonfields or Abbey Gate stood at the junction of Bishop Street and Meat Market Lane; Gaol Lane Gate was located between Gaol Lane and Long Lane; and the Hemlin or Fish Gate was situated at the O'Doherty Terrace end of Fish Lane. These ancient gateways stood in the Englishtown walls and monitored the comings and goings of citizens and strangers between the Englishtown and the rest of the island. The Quay Gate was at the southern end of Bridge Street and the Creagh Gate was at the lower end of Creagh Lane, both of them overlooking the Abbey River. The Shannon River could be overseen from the Bow Lane Gate which was located on the lower steps leading from the new civic offices to St. Augustine Place; a sallyport is visible in the riverside curtain wall of King Johns's Castle; and the gate on Thomond Bridge guarded the entry into the city from Thomond.

Lee Estate and Assumpta Park lie to the east of the Island Road which leads into St. Ita's Street. St. Munchin's Street and St. Senan's Street lead off eastwards and Oliver Plunkett Street leads off westward from St. Ita's Street which is crossed, further northwards, by St. Columcille Street and St. Brendan's Street. St. Patrick's Avenue is off St. Ita's Street, between St. Senan's Street and St. Columcille Street, and St. Bridget's Avenue is likewise, between St. Columcille Street and St. Brendan's Street. There are sports grounds to the north of Verdant Place, west of St. Ita's Street and an old military cemetery lies north-west of the junction between Island View Terrace, St. Ita's Street and Island Road. The oldest parts of this ancient city can be found within the walls of the Englishtown.

African Wars like the Ashantee Campaign of 1873 resulted in medals being struck for Limerick Heroes such as W.H. Maunsell. Limerick City Museum.

The Military Cemetery is located beyond the walls and appears to date from about 1856, as that is the date inscribed above the adjoining gate-house which controls access to the cemetery. This was the last house on Island Road until St. Mary's Park, in St. Mary's Parish, was built in 1935, with several new streets all named after Irish saints. This cemetery appears to have been reserved for the burial of soldiers and ex-soldiers who had no apparent family links with the city and county. One exception, however, has relatives buried in the Quaker cemetery at Ballinacurra. Being a soldier, his beliefs would have been at odds with their pacifism. Quartermaster Sergeant Langrise and his wife, Annie, buried a child of one year and nine months here in 1871. There are about sixty burials in the cemetery, including that of a Sergeant George Willies who died in 1864 and Edward Joyce, a member of the 20th Hussars "who entered into rest" on 13 October, 1883, aged twenty. Thirty-seven members of the Royal Welch Fusiliers are also buried here. Maureen Sparling, the Limerick poetess and writer, lives in the former gate-house which could easily be renamed King's Island Cottage to commemorate her book, *Tales from King's Island Cottage* (1995). She has published four books of poetry *Echoes of Old Limerick* (1991), *Happy Moments* (1993), *Reflections of Life* (1994) and *Ripples in the Sand* (1997).

ST. MARY'S CATHEDRAL. Shannon Development Photo Library.

The Cathedral Church of St. Mary the Virgin was built on a hill overlooking the island and facing into the River Shannon. Limerick became an episcopal city mainly because it was the centre of Dalcassian power since the days of Brian Bóru and its first Bishop, Gilbert, was the papal legate who presided over the synod of Rathbreasail in 1111. Gilbert resigned his bishopric in 1140 and the Limerick diocese featured in Cardinal John Papiro's list of 1152. St. Mary's Cathedral is the oldest surviving building still serving its original purpose. 1168 is the date generally accepted as the date of its foundation, although Rev. J. Dowd believed 1172 to be a likelier choice. Other sources trace its beginnings to a period between 1180 to 1190 or to 1192. An earlier St. Mary's may have been located elsewhere in 1111 and relocated here on the orders of Domhnall Mór O Brien.

Domhnall Mór is said to have founded the church more familiarly known as St. Mary's Cathedral on the site of his former palace, some time before 1192-1194. According to tradition this can be proved from a document granting lands at Mungret to "Brictus, Bishop of Limerick, and to his successors, and to the clergy of St. Mary's of Luimneach" which was witnessed by Matthew,

Archbishop of Cashel. As Mathew Henry did not become Archbishop of Cashel until 1192 this updated land grant mentioning St. Mary's clergy dates from 1192 to the time of Domhnall Mor's death in 1194. The western front of the Cathedral is traditionally regarded as the oldest part of the entire building. Brian Hodkinson, during archaelogical excavations, examined the bottom of a trench near the western doorway. He found no noteworthy features in the pre-church layers at the bottom of the trench. He did discover, however, the remains of fifteen burials which were interspersed with shards of Rouen-ware. This would suggest that the western front was of late thirteenth-century date. Brian Hodkinson also excavated a trench that had been dug outside the northern transept. This intersected an earlier pre-church retaining wall that ran from north to south. He tentatively interpreted this as one side of an entrance-way to a sunken featured structure similar to those found at King John's Castle. Both the northern and southern transepts were remodelled and shortened, probably in late medieval times.

The Thingmount, or *Thing-Mote*, a Viking council chamber and court of justice, is believed to have been one of the earliest recorded buildings on the site of St. Mary's Cathedral. There is no evidence to support this assumption, only a widely held local belief. Pagan temples dedicated to Thor and Freya stood close beside the *Thingmount*, making this area the civic and religious centre of Viking Limerick until the O'Briens deserted their other capitals to establish a royal

The Arthur Crucifix - Limerick City Museum   *The O'Dea Crozier - Limerick City Museum*

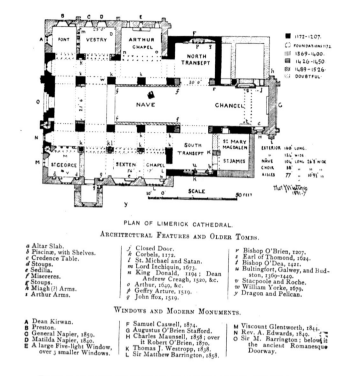

PLAN OF LIMERICK CATHEDRAL.

ARCHITECTURAL FEATURES AND OLDER TOMBS.

a Altar Slab.
b Piscinæ, with Shelves.
c Credence Table.
d Stoups.
e Sedilia.
f Misereres.
g Stoups.
h Miagh (?) Arms.
i Arthur Arms.

j Closed Door.
k Corbels, 1172.
l St. Michael and Satan.
m Lord Inchiquin, 1673.
n King Donald, 1194 ; Dean Andrew Creagh, 1520, &c.
o Arthur, 1649, &c.
p Geffry Arture, 1519.
q John ffox, 1519.

r Bishop O'Brien, 1207.
s Earl of Thomond, 1624.
t Bishop O'Dea, 1421.
u Bultingfort, Galwey, and Budston, 1369-1449.
v Stacpoole and Roche.
w William Yorke, 1679.
y Dragon and Pelican.

WINDOWS AND MODERN MONUMENTS.

A Dean Kirwan.
B Preston.
C General Napier, 1859.
D Matilda Napier, 1840.
E A large Five-light Window, over 3 smaller Windows.

F Samuel Caswell, 1874.
G Augustus O'Brien Stafford.
H Charles Maunsell, 1858 ; over it Robert O'Brien, 1870.
K Thomas J. Westropp, 1838.
L Sir Matthew Barrington, 1858.

M Viscount Glentworth, 1844.
N Rev. A. Edwards, 1849.
O Sir M. Barrington ; below it the ancient Romanesque Doorway.

FLOOR PLAN OF ST. MARY'S CATHEDRAL IN THE 1890S. T.J. Westropp.

residence where the cathedral now stands. The original Christian church may not have been cruciform in design but developed from subsequent rebuilding, modification and renovation over a period of time. Brian de Breffny believed otherwise and wrote that the original floor plan was cruciform with an aisled nave, a short chancel not much deeper than the transepts, and was strongly influenced by the Cistercians. The aisles had arches, no vaulted bays and simple diaphragm walls which supported the roof. Construction of the original building was completed in 1207. Brian de Breffny believed this took place between 1180-1195 while T.J. Westropp thought that the nave, side aisles, transepts and choir assumed the shape of a Latin cross between 1172-1207. Between 1891-1897 T.J. Westropp traced the development and growth of St. Mary's over the centuries. His floor plan shows the cathedral's main architectural features and their locations. The great Romanesque doorway in the western face is flanked at either angle by projecting buttresses. The impressive main entrance is now open only on formal occasions. The usual entry today is through a porch on the southern side. The western doorway was partly sculptured under Bishop O'Dea's episcopate, "not in a spirit of vain glory, but in order that others hereafter should imitate the memorials of their piety". Tradition claims that this was once the original entrance to the O'Brien palace and it was "restored" in the nineteenth century. A stone staircase leading to the tower and monks' walks is located in the wall south of the Romanesque doorway. The chancel was built, or enlarged, by Donoh O'Brien, bishop of Limerick and a member of the royal house of Thomond, in 1207. His name, Donoh, is inscribed over an escutcheon bearing a chevron between three lions, on a small slab of stone positioned high above the doorway on the north wall. He also established a chapter consisting of dean, archdeacon, precenter, treasurer, and six canons. He died in 1209. The present chancel dates from the fifteenth century, as do a number of the chapels which were added to the aisles, and one added to the south transept. James and Edmond Harold were responsible for decorating or enlarging the chancel in 1529. This part of St. Mary's was almost destroyed by cannon fire from the great battery at Corbally during the siege of 1691. The present east window was installed in 1860 and replaced a much larger one which was not in keeping with the style of St. Mary's. Most of the windows are later insertions modelled on fifteenth-century styles. King Domhnall Mor O'Brien's coffin lid is encased in black marble at the base of the Earls of Thomond memorial on the northern wall. This oblong stone, less that five feet long, is the oldest monument in the cathedral. It is narrower at one end and bears the O'Brien arms, three rudely carved lions and a Celtic cross, and is ornamented by a border with ancient Irish characters. In 1997 a burial chamber containing three skeletons, possibly dating from the eighteenth century, was found a few feet away. The Earls of Thomond memorial occupies all of a large Gothic arch in the north wall. It consists of three tiers of black marble with side columns and divisions of grey and pink marble and composite pillars of Limerick marble. An effigy of Donough, Fourth Earl of Thomond, who died on 5 September, 1624, lies on the lowest tier or shelf. The next shelf contains the effigy of his wife, Elizabeth Fitzgerald, second daughter of Gerald, Eleventh Earl of Kildare. Both effigies are damaged as the tomb was "defaced in ye time of ye late rebellion of Ireland", by the Cromwellians. It was repaired by Henry (1618-1691), the Seventh Earl of Thomond, mistakenly identified as the "second Earl" on the inscription, in 1678. Little else remains of the original tomb. Horses were stabled in the cathedral during the Cromwellian occupation of the city. Account books of the time recorded a payment of £6.91 to "Cap. John Ffreind for horse guard kept in ye church in Limericke". St. Mary's was wantonly vandalised during this period by the soldiery. The high altar, reredos and surrounds demonstrate the continuity of O'Brien patronage. The translated inscription reads "To God be the praise. By means of this work the O'Brien family give thanks to God for the founder and benefactors of this church. To God be the praise. Erected in 1907". Michael Pearse, the stonemason who executed the reredos and stone surrounds, was the father of Patrick and Willie Pearse, architects of the 1916 Rising. Willie Pearse (1881-1916) worked as a stonecutter here for a few years. Three decapitated skeletons were found under the sanctuary floor when the cathedral was being renovated, between 1989 and 1997. This report was incorrect. The skulls simply rolled off the vault table after the bodies decomposed - there was was no evidence of decapitation. An extensive restoration programme was initiated as part of the city's preparation for the tercentenary of the siege in 1991. Work on the exterior of the building was completed in 1993 and the excavation and re-laying of the floors, in order to install underfloor central heating, was continued into late 1996.

The original pre-Reformation high altar is over thirteen feet long, two feet and nine inches wide, nine inches thick and weighs more than three tons. It was

THE EARL OF THOMOND'S MEMORIAL, HAS DOMHNALL MOR O'BRIEN'S COFFIN-LID AT ITS BASE.
Limerick City Museum.

dragged out of the cathedral by Cromwellian horsemen and the edges were chipped by hitting off the pillars while it was being removed. This stone *mensa* or altar was dumped in the cathedral grounds but was discovered in 1962 and placed in the south transept for safe-keeping. It was returned to its original position in the chancel in 1997. Five crosses are engraved into the altar which was carved from a single limestone block. The pale blue frontal on the altar was woven by Anglican nuns in Dublin and is based on designs from the eighth-century *Book of Kells*. Bishop Cornelius O'Dea was connected to the O'Briens by fosterage. When he died in 1426 he was buried under a monument of black marble adorned with a recumbent effigy of the robed and mitred bishop which has long since vanished. Part of his monument still survives, beneath that of Bishop Adam's, on the south wall of the chancel. Cornelius O'Dea founded a library in what is now the Chapter Room (over the Chapel of St. George) which was completely destroyed in 1691. Bishop Bernard Adams (1566-1625) was born in Middlesex; educated in Trinity College, Oxford, where he became a fellow in 1588; and was nominated bishop of Limerick by King James I in 1603. He was consecrated in this role in 1604, and was also bishop of Kilfenora from 1606 to 1617. His inscription - in Latin and English, contains the following;

... sufficient God did give me, which I spent;

I little borrowed, and as little spent;
I left them whom I loved enough in store,
Increased this Bishopric - relieved the poore...

The credence table dates from the thirteenth century. The black oak *misericords*, or choir stalls, were carved between 1480 and 1500, possibly out of oak from Cratloe Woods. Sitting was prohibited in the early church but the clergy were allowed to support themselves by leaning upon staffs or crutches placed under their arm-pits. This concession led to the introduction of the *Misericordia* or act of mercy which resulted in seats designed to tip up vertically revealing a shallow ledge, three or four inches deep, on the underside upon which the clerical posterior could be rested while the occupant of the choir stall appeared to be standing rather than sitting. There are twenty-three of these fifteenth-century misericords in St. Mary's. The decoration is mainly on the underside of each seat, and the carved motifs include depictions of human and animal figures as well as those of legendary and imaginary creatures. These pieces of furniture are unique insofar as they are the only medieval examples of their kind preserved in Ireland. They have been placed in the chapel of St. Nicholas in recent times.

MISERICORDS, IN ST. MARY'S CATHEDRAL.
Limerick City Museum.

The choir screen was designed by Conor O'Brien of Foynes. His niece, Brigid, posed as a model for the two angels carved on it. Conor was at sea when the screen was installed in 1921. In his absence the builder erected it back to front, a mistake that was corrected in 1997 when it was dismantled and placed in front of the newly-created Lady Chapel. Conor O'Brien (1880-1952) was an author, architect, voyager, yachtsman and nationalist gun-runner. He designed his own yacht, *Saoirse*, sailed her round the world and was the first man to display the Irish tricolour in many foreign ports. The screen was built to commemorate Edmund Pery, Viscount Glentworth, who was killed in World War I, and his sister, Lady Victoria Brady.

The nave has four plain pointed arches resting on massive piers, over which run "monks' walks" or lintelled passages through the walls and windows. The unbroken vault of the roof over the nave and choir is an unusual feature while the ground level rises by three feet and six inches in a series of seven steps from the Romanesque doorway to the east window. Thomas Arthur and his wife Johanna Morrough built the eastern end of the nave, and installed a window, in 1410. The oak beams in the roof came from Cratloe Woods and five chandeliers hang from the barrel-vaulted roof. Four are quite similar in size. Three of these larger ones were made by Daniel Crosbie of Dublin and were presented to the cathedral by Limerick Corporation in 1759. Another was found in a dump by Edward Coulter, an art collector, who restored it before presenting it to St. Mary's. An older chandelier hangs in the sanctuary. The Samuel Barrington memorial, dating from 1693 can be found in the nave where there is also a bust of Robert Maunsell on the south-western pillar. The north transept dates from 1360. In 1860 some of the stonework around the five-light window was renovated and a few years later it was filled with stained glass as a memorial to Samuel Caswell, who died in 1874. Three Canadian sisters, Jessie "Ruby" Michie, Helen Rowland Wilson and Gladys Skellaton Cleeve restored the transept of the Chapel of the Holy Spirit during the early twentieth century. The leper squint derived its name from its use. Lepers were not allowed into the medieval churches but were permitted to hear Mass and receive Communion through openings like this. Part of the organ now obstructs the view of the squint. John Ffox, the Prior of the Holy Cross, died on 28 August, 1518. His mural slab is located beneath the leper squint. Geoffrey Archer, the fifth recorded cathedral treasurer, died in 1519. He is commemorated with a stone slab set into a triple-arched sedillia (a wall-seat used for those celebrating mass) recess, upon the bottom of which a decorative cross is inscribed. The Harold tablet was originally placed elsewhere but moved here during later renovations. Haraldr Sigtryggsson is remembered in history as Aralt Mac Sitric, Harold son of Sitric, and was the Viking king of Limerick. He died in 940 and seems to have been the progenitor of the Harold or Harrold families. William Harold was mayor of the city in 1498 and 1505, Robert in 1512, Nicholas in 1516 and 1517, James in 1525, Edmond in 1531, James in 1544, Nicholas in 1566, and Thomas in 1574. The Caen-stone pulpit at the corner of the north transept and the chancel was erected by *Foster of London* in memory of Archdeacon Maunsell who died in 1860.

The south transept may have been the Lady Chapel in the late twelfth-century cathedral. The arch corbels date from 1420 and the west pier is built against the old arcade. This transept, with the chapels along the south aisle, was extensively repaired by the Galweys, Sextens and others about 1489. Anne Westropp restored this transept and rebuilt its five-light window some time around 1862, while the Barringtons restored the chapels along the south aisle in 1866. It was restored again in 1962 and re-dedicated as the Chapel of St. James and St. Mary Magdalene. The Westropp memorial, a triple arcade, depicting the *Agony in the Garden, the Entombment,* and the *Resurrection,* was erected by Anne

NORTH SIDE OF CHOIR, PRIOR TO RENOVATIONS IN ST. MARY'S CATHEDRAL. Limerick City Museum.

Westropp in memory of her son Thomas Johnson Westropp, who died in 1839. His middle name was mis-spelled and the incorrect date of his death was given on the carved inscription of this ornate monument, which was crafted by James Redfern of London and displayed at the International Exhibition of 1862. His body was supposedly brought home to Cheltenham for burial. He died in Madiera, but on his mother's death the chest was opened and found to contain no human remains. The cross on the wall beneath the Westropp memorial is the original cross of consecration of the chapel. The mural tablet on the wall at the entrance lists family tombstones of the Arthurs, 1439 and 1729, Creaghs, 1632, Fannings, 1634, and Rices, 1709 and 1924. The sedilia in the south wall consists of a triple recess with trefoil arches resting on four slender spiral-fluted shafts. It dates from about 1400 and was erected by John Budstone, or Budston, bailiff of the city in 1401. The Galwey-Bultingfort-Stritch monument is a low cinquefoil arch resting on octagonal piers, two on each side, with an angular hood. This was erected by Edmond Galwey, and his grandfather, Richard Bultingfort, both of whom died in 1414. Richard Bultingfort, or Bullingfort, may have derived his name from a place of that name in Hertfordshire. He married Catherine Roche by whom he had a daughter, Margaret, who married Geoffrey Galwey, and a son John, who succeeded to some of his estate. Richard owned several tenements in the city and suburbs, one near the Tholsel, one near St. Mary's cemetery, one near Thomond Bridge, a large selection of silver plate, and other property in Cork. He appears to have been a typical hard-working, God-fearing, church-loving medieval burgess, respected by his peers and loved by his wife, family, friends and servants. He was mayor of Limerick in 1357, 1367, 1376, 1380, 1386 and 1390. Between 1369 and 1405 he helped bishops Peter Creagh and Cornelius O'Dea to restore a large section of the cathedral and, at some undefined date, allowed Nicholas Stritch a right of burial in the same tomb.

Murrough the Burner O'Brien (1614-1674), the Sixth Baron and First Earl of Inchiquin was a talented survivor, one of Ireland's greatest generals, a political opportunist and the most hated man in the country. The morning after his burial, in 1674, the citizens of Limerick stormed into St. Mary's Cathedral, removed his body and threw it into the Shannon. Two centuries later his empty coffin was found in the north aisle. His unoccupied grave was marked only by the letter "I" cut into the pavement. The Arthur Chapel, the burial place of the Arthur family, is also known as the Chapel of St. Nicholas and St. Catherine. In 1439 Catherine, the widow of Nicholas Arthur, was buried beside her husband "in the ancestral monument near the altar of St. Catherine". At one stage King Domhnall's coffin lid and the pre-Reformation altar were stored here. The tendency to use this chapel as a store or display area continued into 1998 as the black oak *misericords* are now on exhibition here. The curious corbelling evident in the Arthur Chapel and the clumsy way in which it was

ST. MARY'S CATHEDRAL. *Limerick City Museum.*

built against the north transept has led some people to suggest that this chapel probably incorporates part of the O'Brien palace within its fabric. The Arthur surname is of Viking or Norse origin and was associated with Limerick long before the arrival of the Anglo-Normans. Thomas Fitz-Arthur was mayor of Limerick in 1218 and his son, Nicholas Fitz-Thomas was elected in 1241. Both used the Norman variant of their surname and other bearers of the Arthur name held the mayoral office fifty-six times between 1365 and 1635.

T.J. Westropp wrote that the chapels appeared to have been built without any intention of having the levels or shapes of their windows conforming with those of the adjoining fabric. John Jebb (1775-1833) became bishop of Limerick in 1823. He was a native of Drogheda and is commemorated in the white marble statue of a seated bishop, which was executed by E.H. Baily of the Royal Academy, London, in 1836. Andrew Creagh was Dean of St. Mary's, twice, first

St. Mary's Graveyard, with the city in the
background.
Shannon Development Photo Library.

in 1505 until he was deprived of his living for some reason now unknown. He was reinstated after receiving the king's pardon. In 1543 he resigned and was succeeded by Andrew Stritche. The stone slab marking his grave is on the western side of the chapel near that of Thomas FitzDavid Creagh who died in June 1497. Thomas's wife is also commemorated on the slab, as well as his son, Peter Creagh, who died in May 1546. William Fraser (1700-1753) was buried here. He was the only son of his namesake who served as a captain in Schomberg's Company in 1689-1691. After the surrender of the city William, Senior, married Mara Lloyd of Drumsallagh and continued to live in Limerick. William, Junior, is buried on the east-side of the vestry. Anne Fanning died in 1634. Her memorial slab bears two coats of arms. One of the two two-light windows was installed by the widow of James Fitzgerald Bannatyne, the other by the clergy of the diocese in memory of Rev. James Dowd. The vestry is also known as the O'Brien Chapel, the Napier Chapel or St. Mark's Chapel. Murrough the Burner was reputedly buried in its north-western corner but it may only have been his memorial slab which was placed here, as T.J. Westropp stated that he was buried in the north aisle. The chapel is generally considered to be the fifteenth-century burial place of the O'Brien family. Its vaulted ceiling is considered one of its more interesting features. The long prayer desk was constructed out of fifteenth-century black oak removed from Listowel Church. Sir Arthur Vickers presented the timber to St. Mary's and a local craftsman completed the desk. The heraldic carvings may date from the fifteenth century. Sir Arthur Vickers was Ulster king of arms and in charge of the Irish crown jewels when Edward VII visited Ireland in 1908. Sir Arthur became the scapegoat to cover someone else when he was unable to produce the jewels. His

A STAINED GLASS REPRESENTATION OF AN ANGEL BLOWING A TRUMPET, ENGLISH, FOURTHEENTH-CENTURY, IN THE HUNT MUSEUM

keys to the vaults in Dublin Castle had mysteriously disappeared and he was dismissed from his post. The Duke of Tyrconnell, Richard Talbot, became Lord Lieutenant of Ireland under James II, the first Catholic viceroy appointed in over a century. He died in Limerick in 1691 and tradition relates that he was buried secretly, at night, under the west wall of the vestry. The baptistry, with its ancient font, is the burial place of Catherine Plunket. Her husband, Walter, was appointed a commissioner of the Limerick mint by King James II in 1689. She died in 1752. Her graveslab is on the floor, as is that of Piers O'Morony of Cloonenagh, County Clare, who died in 1723. He was a landowner in Killard, west Clare, in 1659, and was married to Margaret Creagh. This chapel is now used as an office and the Angel at Prayer outside it was originally at the head of the Cleeve grave in the cathedral grounds. The south aisle contains the only perpendicular order window in the cathedral. It was donated by Croker Barrington and depicts the *Talents*, the *Good Samaritan* and the *Husbandman*. The light stained-glass window, at the western end, was donated by the Rev. Arthur Williams in memory of his wife, Isabella (1822-1849). The newest window in the cathedral is located in the Jebb Chapel, a stained-glass window executed by the Harry Clarke Studio. The south aisle formed three of the cathedral's thirteen chapels during the fifteenth century. It was laid out as a great hall in medieval times but later served the bishops of Limerick as a consistory court, a court in which they presided over the administration of ecclesiastical law within the diocese of Limerick. The cathedral shop is located within this area. The *Crucifixion* carving set into the central pillar of this aisle has been dated to the tenth century. The choir room was originally erected as a chapel, dedicated to St. Mary Magdalene, by John Budstone some time about 1400. Until the south transept was rededicated in 1962 the choir room had still been known as the Chapels of St. Mary Magdalene and St. James and the plain Gothic arches of the conjoined chapels remain closed in its western wall. These two chapels were considered by some to be the first structural alterations and were carried out under the episcopate of Stephen de Valle (or Wall) between 1360 and 1369. During the siege of 1691 the chapels were damaged. In 1866 the choir room was restored. St. George's Chapel, or the Pery Chapel, contains the Glentworth memorials which include two windows dedicated to Edmond Viscount Glentworth in the south wall, and the Hartstonge family memorials in memory of Elizabeth Hartstonge who died in 1663 and Henry Hartstonge (1789-1834), Viscount Glentworth, son of the first, and father of the second, Earl of Limerick. The recumbent effigy is dedicated to Edmond Henry, Lord Glentworth (1809-1844), Viscount Limerick, Baron Glentworth of Mallow and Baron Foxford of Stackpole Court in County Clare.

The cathedral organ was presented by Bishop Adams in 1626. It has been rebuilt and added to throughout the years. Lawtons of Aberdeen carried out a major overhaul and added the solo organ and a new console in 1913. It was cleaned and overhauled in 1958 and electrical action and a new console were added in 1966. The square tower, located over the western facade of the church, is 120 feet high. Access to it, and to the "monks' walk", is through a stone staircase in the buttress at the south-western corner. A narrow worn staircase in the eastern wall of the tower, and over the arch which supports it, gives access to the bell-ringers' room. The outer door on the south side of this room allows entry to the battlements, from which an excellent view of the city and the county to the south can be obtained. Entry to the northern battlements can be obtained through another door at the top of the staircase.

The bell chamber is reached by a steep window staircase. Tradition relates how the friars carried off thirteen silver bells which they concealed in the Abbey River at the time of the Reformation. The hiding-place of these bells was forgotten over the centuries. Another folk tale says that the bells were stolen from an Italian church during political disturbances. Their founder searched Europe for them and his quest finally extended to Ireland. As he sailed up the Shannon he recognised the familiar chime of his long sought bells, only to drop dead before he could reclaim them. A peal of eight bells is the poetic expression used by campanologists, or bell-ringers, to describe the eight bells installed in the bell-tower. In 1673 six bells were presented to the cathedral by William Yorke. Two more, cast by Tobias Covey, were added in 1703. Later on, three new bells were cast, two in 1829 and one in 1859. Bells were also recast in 1703, 1873,1907, 1930 and 1938. The ropes attached to the bells average an overall length of forty feet with a tail of thirteen feet six inches. The chief campanologist of St. Mary's is called the captain of the bells. William Yorke was three times mayor of the seventeenth-century city, in 1673, 1674 and 1678. He died in 1679 and his black marble memorial can be seen on the western side of a pillar on the north side of the nave. William Perdue, the craftsman whose family cast the bells, died in 1673. His memorial may have been on the floor of the main aisle, near the west door. William Everard Gardiner Hewson, Ballyengland, was the son of John Hewson of Castle Hewson. He was a keen campanologist who rang the changes in many English cathedrals, as well as Irish. He was responsible for re-

THE CASHEL BELL, A CAST BRONZE BELL DECORATED WITH AN IRISH RINGED CROSS AND FOUND IN 1859 IN CASHEL, CO. TIPPERARY. ONCE PART OF THE COLLECTION OF LORD DUNRAVEN, AND NOW IN THE HUNT MUSEUM.

casting and re-hanging five of the bells. He died, nearby, in Barrington's Hospital, and is buried in the cathedral grounds. The 1914-1918 war memorial was erected in memory of the men of Thomond who perished in that war, especially those whose names were inscribed on the wall tablet inside the south-western doorway. The 1939-1945 war memorial was erected by the parents of those whose names are inscribed on the roll of honour. Many Irish families have had a tradition of service in the British Army. Limerick's imperial past can be traced through the memorials of her dead in St. Mary's Cathedral. Limerick men served in their own, and other regiments, throughout the world, in France, Egypt, Palestine, South Africa, India, the East Indies, Spain, Afghanistan, Turkey, The Crimea, the Americas and wherever the English flag was flown. Some of the battles in which they fought have passed into history. The regiments in which they served formed the backbone of the British Army. These included the Royal Munster Fusiliers, the Connaught Rangers, the Coldstream Guards, the Inniskillings, the Prince of Wales' Own West Yorkshire Regiment, the King's Light Infantry, the Prince of Wales' Dragoon Guards, the North Gloucestershire Regiment of Foot, and many more whose names can be found on the floor and walls of St. Mary's. The Royal Navy also features in the cathedral's memorials as well as some brief references to those who served in the

WORLD WAR I MEMORIAL IN ST. MARY'S
CATHEDRAL. Limerick City Museum.

fledgling Royal Air Force. The roster of officers included Bannatynes, Campbells, Crokers, Gabbets, Glentworths, Glosters, Ievers, Lloyds, MacAdams, Maunsells, Napiers, O'Briens, Powers, Russells, Shaws, Summerfields and Wallers, Limerick's nineteenth-century elite.

St. Mary's Cathedral contains many architectural features, too numerous for individual mention. In this account only the more prominent memorials are mentioned but there are several more worth looking at. The cathedral's silver plate is rarely put on public display as bank-vaults are now the only places in which such treasures can be considered safe. During the Cromwellian occupation General Ireton lived in a house in the cathedral grounds and James Craven was paid £5 "for mending and setting up the clocke in Mary's church" with materials valued at £15.77. During renovations in 1893-1895 the western porch was removed; "Iretons House" and "Galwey's Castle" were demolished with other old houses; and the chapels of the south aisle were re-roofed. The episcopal see of Limerick was founded by St. Munchin but little mention was made of it until after the Vikings converted to Christianity. One of them, Gille or Gilbert, was consecrated by the Archbishop of Canterbury and governed the see until 1140. The charter of Domhnall Mór O'Brien refers to the bishops of the diocese as *lumnicenses* or *lumnicani*. They lost some of their see to the bishops of Killaloe and Emly until Gerald Le Mareschal recovered it for them in 1284. By the time of the Reformation the property was extensive and valuable, but was afterwards so much diminished by grants to the Fitzgerald family that the see of Ardfert and Aghadoe was added to it in 1660.

Dean Talbot of St. Mary's wrote extensively on the history and monuments of St. Mary's. The epilogue to his *The Monuments of St. Mary's Cathedral, Limerick* (1976) is worth repeating. It terminated with a thought and a prayer for both the living and the dead;

> We salute them, one and all: the founder, King Donal Mór O'Brien, kneeling at the altar: Edward the Bruce praying before he marched to Faughart to disaster and to death: Cardinal Rinuccini, joining in a solemn *Te Deum*, receiving the English standards captured by Owen Roe O'Neill at Benburb: General Ireton asking forgiveness for his own misdeeds and those of his father-in-law, Oliver Cromwell: Terence O'Brien, Bishop of Emly, listening to his death sentence pronounced by court martial in the cathedral: Patrick Sarsfield singing a hymn of thanksgiving for the victory which his famous 'ride' brought on reaching Ballyneety, and not long afterwards, praying for guidance as he led the 'Flight of the Wild Geese' to the continent, and so to the unlucky, lonesome Tyrconnell and the anti-clerical Murrough O'Brien (Murrough of the Burnings): to the Scottish historian Thomas Carlyle, who, so overpowered by emotion, whispered 'That lovely big dark brown edifice'; and then to more modern times, that Englishman, William Thackeray, as he entered the shrine exclaimed (God help him) 'The old cathedral, a barbarous old turreted 14th century building'. And so we salute them all ... pilgrims travelling to eternity.

The churchyard contains many interesting tombstones and memorials with epitaphs ranging from the eloquent to the prosaic. Charles Graves, bishop of Limerick, is remembered with a Celtic cross inscribed with the symbols of the *Paschal Lamb* and the *Four Evangelists*. His epitaph was written in Latin by R. G. Tyrrel (later vice provost of Dublin University); in Irish by Douglas Hyde (President of Ireland 1938-1945); and in English by A.P. Graves (author of *Father O'Flynn*). The Croker arms can be found on a stone slab inserted in the churchyard wall at the southern end of the old Exchange wall. William John Shaw died on 2 December, 1869. He is remembered with a cenotaph erected by the pig buyers of Limerick and his employees, inscribed twice to ensure its benefactors' generosity was not overlooked. South of the cathedral's south-western doorway is another Victorian "masterpiece", the block-like tomb of James Butler Boyd. Katie (Cis) Smyth (1897-1995) is commemorated on a stone tablet set into the garden wall to the south-west, off the path leading towards the south porch;

The kiss of the sun for pardon
The song of the bird for mirth
One is nearer God's heart in a garden
Than any place else on earth
in fond memory of
Katie (Cis) Smyth 1897- 1995
who as a labour of great love for
this cathedral at the age of 97 yrs
still tended this flower bed
having done so for more than fifty years.

In the late 1980s a decision was taken to embark upon a restoration project for the cathedral, one of many such projects that have been undertaken over the centuries. Work commenced on making the entire building weather-proof in 1990. Many sections of the extensive roof were reslated and all of the walkways and valleys were re-lined with copper; the exterior stonework was newly pointed; and the interior walls were stripped of their plaster to enable them to dry out. This part of the project took almost a year to complete and despite the obvious disruption daily church services

THE FLIGHT INTO EGYPT, AS CARVED AND PAINTED IN FIFTEENTH-CENTURY FLANDERS, AND NOW ON DISPLAY IN THE HUNT MUSEUM.

continued uninterrupted. After a "resting period" of a few years work recommenced on the interior of the building, in October, 1996. The entire ground floor was excavated in the course of which a number of vaults were discovered and many bones unearthed. The remains of several medieval walls were found in the choir area and, in order to avoid disturbing them, the plans for that area were altered. The excavated floor was filled; a damp-proof course was installed; several miles of piping, for new under-floor central heating, were put in place; and new tiles and limestone slabs completed the floor.

In the process of restoration and renovation some important items were relocated. Lord Limerick's limestone screen was moved ten metres eastward and nearer to the high altar; the misericords were transferred to the Jebb Chapel; the pre-Reformation limestone altar was moved from the St. James Chapel to replace the high altar at the eastern end of the cathedral; and a new, raised chancel was constructed in the former location of the choir. The old pews were discarded and new chairs purchased, part of the on-going work to make St. Mary's Cathedral a more comfortable building while restoring its ancient fabric. Much has been done but much remains to be done and funds have to be raised to pay for the work which has just been finished. Funds were raised mainly on a local level to date, with the people and firms of Limerick being extraordinarily generous. Limerick Corporation and Limerick County Council were, and continue to be, sources of enormous help and encouragement.

The interior walls have to be completed and several more projected internal and essential alterations have yet to be made to St. Mary's Cathedral.

St. Mary's Cathedral and Nicholas Street. Limerick City Museum.

The cathedral is, to state the obvious, one of the most important medieval buildings, not alone in Limerick but in the entire country, and it deserves the financial support of the state as well as the willing help which has been demonstrated at local level. With the growing tourism industry in the region St. Mary's Cathedral will become more important. Today, civic and ecumenical services, as well as choral and orchestral concerts, pageants and plays, are held in the cathedral throughout the year, contributing to the wider community of the city.

The pedestrian entrance from Merchants' Quay was constructed by Limerick Civic Trust in co-operation with FÁS in 1991. It was officially opened by Judge Kevin O'Higgins during the mayoralty of the late Jim Kemmy, and leads upwards to the magnificent west doorway of the cathedral. The Exchange wall forms part of the eastern boundary of St. Mary's Church. This facade of hewn stone with its seven blocked-in Tuscan columns linked by a handsome balustrade faces Nicholas Street, although the rest of the building has been demolished and now forms part of the churchyard. The Exchange was erected as a local administrative centre in 1673, was rebuilt in 1702 and 1778, and eventually fell into disuse when the Town Hall was opened in Rutland Street in 1846. The Nail, a brass table standing on a short pillar, was set up in the Exchange by Robert Smith, Mayor of Limerick, in 1685, at his own expense. His name was engraved on it and the saying to *pay on the nail* seems to have been associated with this type of brass table or scales which were used throughout Ireland, England, Scotland and Wales. Robert Smith is believed to have engraved his name on it with his own hand. After the closure of the Exchange it was moved to the Town Hall and is now in the Limerick Museum.

The Blue School is remembered by means of a plaque on the northern wall of that part of the cathedral where it was housed. It took its name, the Blue School or the Blue Coat Hospital, from the blue and yellow uniforms worn by its pupils. Rev. J. Moore founded the school in 1717 and bequeathed some property in Dublin for its support. In 1724 Mrs. Alice Craven conveyed her house on the corner of Nicholas Street and Bow Lane to the dean and chapter for the same purpose, a school in which boys were taught a trade while they sang in the cathedral choir. The school supported fifteen boys. It fell into decay in 1748 but was revived by the bishop and dean in 1772. The building in which it was contained is situated on the corner of St. Augustine Place and Nicholas Street.

George Alexander Osborne (1806 - 1893) was born in Limerick, the son of an organist and vicar-choral of St. Mary's Cathedral. He emigrated to Brussels in 1824, adopted music as a profession and became a music instructor to the eldest son of the Prince of Orange. George Alexander Osborne almost died in the Belgian Revolution of 1830 and fled to Paris in 1831. Here he met Auber, Berlioz, Cherubini, Chopin, Ernst, Heller and Liszt, and became a well known pianist and composer of light musical pieces and chamber-music. He moved to London in 1844 and made his living as a teacher up to the time of his death.

St. Augustine Place was once known as Bow Lane. It extends from Nicholas Street to Merchants' Quay, finishing in a series of broad steps at City Hall and derives its name from an Augustinian foundation which was granted to Edmund Sexton in 1610 as "the house, site, etc., of the abbey, friary, hospital or cell of the B.V. Mary and St. Edward, king and martyr, otherwise Holy Cross, in Limerick". (This was actually located on Sir Harry's Mall so this street seems to have been misnamed). The Crutched Friars, Augustinian Friars, Austin Friars or the Order of Hermits of St. Augustine seem to have been introduced into Ireland about 1259. These friars were a branch of the Augustinian Canons, an older order that had received papal recognition two centuries earlier and had a fervent patron in Domhnall Mór O'Brien who founded a convent for Augustinian nuns, Peter's Cell.

Timothy Collopy (died in 1810 or 1811) was born in the city, apprenticed to a baker and served Mass in the Augustinian church in Creagh Lane. Fr. Walsh, an Augustinian priest, discovered Timothy's artistic talents and raised enough

LIMERICK SILVERSMITHS WERE RENOWNED FOR THE QUALITY OF THEIR WORKMANSHIP, ESPECIALLY IN THE PERIOD 1725 TO 1846. THOSE RECORDED DURING THAT PERIOD WERE ADAM AND JONATHAN BUCK, COLLINS BREHON, GEORGE BRUSH, ROBERT BRADFORD, THOMAS BURKE, CALEB COLBECK, JOHN COLLUM, PATRICK CONNELL, HENRY DOWNES, MAURICE, GARRETT AND WILLIAM FITZGERALD, JOHN GLOSTER, JOHN HILL, JOSEPH AND SAMUEL JOHNS, GEORGE HALLORAN, JOHN HACKETT, DANIEL LYSAGHT, JOHN LAING, DONALD MECGYLLYSAGHTA, GEORGE AND W.D. MOORE, THOMAS O'CARRYD, GILLADUFFE O'COWLTAYN, ROBERT O'SHAUGHNESSY, EDWARD PARKER, JOHN PURCELL, FRANCIS PHIPPS, SAMUEL PURDON, JAMES, JOHN, GEORGE AND JOSEPH ROBINSON, ROBERT AND H. SMITH, JOHN STRITCH (OR STRIT), R. WALLACE, MATTHEW, JOHN AND T. WALSH AND WILLIAM WARD. THE SAUCE BOAT, CUP AND SPOON WERE MANUFACTURED IN THE CITY

money from his wealthier parishioners to send the young man to Rome where he studied art. He returned to Limerick as an accomplished portrait painter, held exhibitions of his works in Dublin in 1777 and 1780, and relocated to London in 1783.

Merchants' Quay was once the only quay fronting on the Long Dock. It was located near the site on which the Vikings are reputed to have first landed. It contained an old custom house which burned down in 1747 and was the area in which the merchants congregated to await their ships and cargoes and conduct business. The Quay or Great Quay was the original name of this quay which had been constructed about 1500 and could accommodate vessels capable of discharging 200 tons or more. This was the quay described by Richard Stanihurst in 1577. In the 1680s it had an entrance that was one hundred feet across and was guarded by two towers, the taller of which was to the south. It possessed a quay wall that extended 600 feet westwards from Quay Lane Gate, built in two levels, the upper one of which acted as a promenade and had a large open area on the landward side for the loading or unloading of cargoes. The principal exports to England, France, Holland, Italy, Spain and the Mediterranean ports were ale, bacon, barley, beans, beef, butter, live cattle, corn, feathers, frieze (coarse woollen cloth), fish (including salmon), hides (of cattle, deer, goats and otter), horses, malt, oats, ore (silver and lead from Tipperary

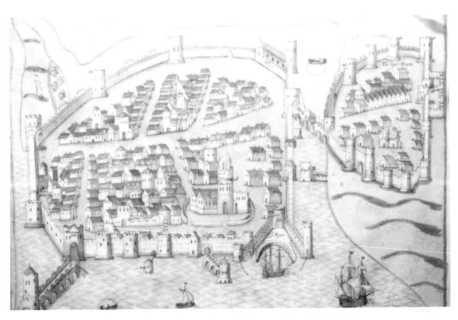

1633 MAP OF LIMERICK FROM PACATA HIBERNIA. Limerick City Museum.

mines), peas, pipestaves, rapeseed, tallow, timber, wool and wool-fells. The principal imports in the 1680s were coffee, deal boards of Norwegian origin, English hops, iron, lemons, madder (a red dye), oranges, West Indian sugar, pottery (from Buckley, Devon and Staffordshire), salt, sheep and tobacco.

The Potato Market was built on the site of the medieval Long Dock in 1843, by the Reformed Corporation. It was restored by Limerick Civic Trust during the 1980s. It has failed to become a general market area; but has become a successful venue for some public events, especially those using marquees, such as the recent food festival.

The Sylvester O'Halloran Footbridge is named after the distinguished surgeon, historian, antiquarian, patriot and genius who was born in Caherdavin in 1728, educated in London, Leyden and Paris, practised in his native city, and died in his house near St. Mary's Cathedral in 1807. As a surgeon Sylvester O'Halloran specialised in brain and eye surgery, developing a new method of

THE SYLVESTER O'HALLORAN FOOTBRIDGE, WITH MATHEW BRIDGE AND BARRINGTONS HOSPITAL IN THE BACKGROUND. **Shannon Development Photo Library.**

treating cataracts, in the latter half of the eighteenth century. In 1774 he wrote *A General History of Ireland*. Six years later he became an honorary member of the newly-formed Dublin College of Surgeons. His *A History of Ireland* was published in 1803, but did not find favour with the establishment as it contained too many details which the Anglo-Irish ascendancy would rather had been forgotten. His brother, Fr. Joseph Ignatius O'Halloran, a Jesuit priest, was successively professor of rhetoric, philosophy, and divinity in Bordeaux, before returning to Ireland. Dr. Sylvester O'Halloran was buried in the family vault in Kilteely grave-yard in 1807 but he has not been forgotten. In 1987 the new footbridge over the Abbey River was named after him. This bridge may be entered through the Potato Market leading onto a pleasant riverside walk behind the Custom House and Sarsfield House, and finishing on Arthur's Quay.

The Curragour Falls, or Curraghgower Falls, derive their place-name from a derivative of *Corach Dhobhair*, the moving, eddying or whirling water, *Cora Dhobhair*, the water weir, or *Carraig Dhobhair*, the rock of the water. An inquisition of 1615 mentions:-

> Two mills called the Kings Mills under one roof in the west part of the city walls betwixt the said city weir and the rock called Corrogower upon the R. Shannon, near the King's Castle of Limerick.

This inquisition appears to support *Carraig Dhobhair*, the rock of the water, as being the original name. The Curraghgower Mill was located on the falls, in the middle of the river. It was acquired by James Fisher who went into partnership with Larry Quinlivan, setting up a company known as Fisher and Quinlivan. The mill was destroyed by a fire in 1850 and the site fell into ruin and was abandoned.

The Lax Weir can trace its name back to the Viking occupation of the city as the Scandanavian word for salmon, *lax*, still survives more than eleven centuries later. The weir itself may have been built by the Vikings but the site in which it is located may have been utilised by prehistoric man over 4000 years ago. Ancient man has long been associated with river fords such as this and has used canoes on the Shannon from about 4,800 BC [A dugout - canoe, found in the mudflats, near the mouth of the Maigue river in 1996, has been radiocarbon-dated to that time]. This great stone weir extended across the river from the old mill at Corbally to the church at Parteen, was the largest stone weir in the country, being approximately 1,500 feet in length, and consisted of a number of stone piers, each about thirty feet long, divided by spaces that varied from abut fifteen to forty feet. There was a large gap, about fifty feet across, in the centre of the weir to allow fish upriver to breed. These gaps were common in weirs from time immemorial, occassion-

SILVER COIN OF THE GREEK CITY OF SYRACUSE IN SOUTHERN ITALY, 2500 YEARS OLD, REVERED SINCE THE THIRTEENTH-CENTURY AS ONE OF THE BIBLICAL '30 PIECES OF SILVER'. FOUND BY JOHN HUNT IN A MIXED BASKET OF ITEMS, AND NOW IN THE HUNT MUSEUM.

ally were narrowed, even closed, by greedy weir owners and had to be protected by law in late Georgian and Victorian times. The gap in the Lax Weir was known at different times as the King's Gap or the Queen's Gap. The Electricity Supply Board closed this weir and erected a new one, Thomond Weir, downriver, in the mid-1930s.

The watch-tower on St. Thomas's Island is said to have been built by the Anglo-Norman inhabitants of the city. The lower section is the fabric of an old castle; and the narrow window slits and corbelled bartizan are part of the original structure. It has been modified, restyled and "modernised" over the centuries and was used as a guard-house to protect the fisheries into the 1800s. The watch-tower was known as Caslaun-na-Corran, the castle of the weir, and was used as a banquet-hall by the mayor and Common Council who came here to claim and eat the salmon, their legal dues or perquisites from the fishery. According to folklore prevalent amongst the fishermen, the Dominican Order built a retreat house on St. Thomas's Island and had another in Rossbrien. There is no documentary evidence to support the idea of either foundation other than the tradition of the fishermen which is repeated in *Dominicans in Limerick 1227-1977* (1977).

The Irish knew this place as *Cora na mBradán*, the salmon weir, and the Weir Castle was remembered as *Caisleán na Corann*. Fisheries in tidal waters were vested in the Crown from the time of the Norman invasion. In 1200 King John granted William De Braose Limerick's "appurtenances in waters and mills, in fish ponds and fisheries". In 1215 John agreed to pay the bishop of Limerick and his successors £10 annually, forever, as the church had a prior claim on the mill-seats and fisheries of Limerick. Maurice Fitzgerald, as justiciary of Ireland, gave a three-year-lease to the citizens of Limerick for the sum of £66.66 in 1247. The lease expired but succeeding lord lieutenants refused to accept a surrender of the lease even though the corporation was unable to pay the rent. The matter came to a head in 1274 and in 1282 Edward I gave the weir to Robert De St. Edmund. Robert, like the corporation, was unable to meet the rent. In 1308 Edward II granted the Lax Weir to David, bishop of Killaloe, for a rent of £10.66, but he had returned it to the corporation by 1312. The rent was not paid from 1317 to 1320. During the reign of Richard II (1377-1399), Patrick Fox held the weir on condition that the profits were used for repairing the city. The corporation got possession of the weir in 1414, and later got a separate grant of the fishery. After the Cromwellian siege in 1651, Robert Pawsey, Robert Playstead and Joshua Bennett leased the weir for £165 a year. After the Restoration, Charles II (1660-1685) granted the weir and fishery to Sir George Preston in 1662. He soon found himself in dispute with the corporation, who let the fishery to Sir William King and Gerald Fitzgerald for £160 a year. The corporation eventually bought out Preston's interest, but the entire affair cost them £1200 between purchase, court costs and legal fees, in 1685. In 1719 a company was formed by George Roche, John Vincent, John Higgins, Rowley Colepoys, Francis Sargent, David Davis and David Bindon which took a one hundred year lease from the corporation at an annual rent of £325. This expired in 1818. The fishery was leased to the firm of McAdam and Little who were obliged to surrender it soon after they had rebuilt the weir with cut-stone and erected twelve piers. In 1834 Poole Gabbett leased the fishery for £300 a year. In 1885 the corporation sold their interest in the Lax Weir to Alexander Bannatyne in the Landed Estates Court for £5,050.

BRONZE FIGURE OF A HAWK-GOD HORUS, EGYPTIAN, ABOUT 3200 YEARS OLD, NOW IN THE HUNT MUSEUM

Bannatyne sold his interest to the Lax Weir Company a syndicate from London who also operated three draft nets at the railway bridge (named the Shannon Bridge or Clare Railway Bridge), a snap net between the weir and Thomond Bridge and six draft nets on the Lower Shannon. When Poole Gabbett leased the fishery in 1834 he received a ninety-nine-year lease. This lease expired in 1933 and the Electricity Supply Board acquired the Lax Weir Fishery. By then the Hydro-electric Scheme had been in operation for six years, the water levels and flow had been altered, and the Electricity Supply Board had acquired or abolished all the old privileges associated with the weir.

The Abbey Fishermen fished in the Shannon River from time immemorial. They claimed in the law courts that the Lax Weir was built by the Dominican friars in the eleventh century [although the order was not founded until 1217]. They divided the river, between Doonass and Barrington's Pier, into sections known locally as *enuires. Enuire* may be a derivative of the Middle English or Anglo-French term, *en eure*, or the Old French, *en euvre*, meaning in use or in practice, the latter being a term that could date back to the days of King John (1199-1216). The fishermen were never officially recognised as a trade guild but they banded together into an association which was mutually advantageous. They made rules and regulations to control this fishery, allotted one *enuire* to every fishermen's team of four, fishing from two boats or cots known as *brochawns,* and distributed the enuires by lottery, allowing each team to fish their respective *enuires* from 10.00 a.m. in the morning until 10.00 a.m. the following day. An account of these *enuires* by John Clancy of the Strand, an old Abbey fisherman, was published by R. Herbert in the *North Munster Antiquarian Journal,* in 1947:-

The first *Enuire* is called *Doonass* and stretches from St. Senan's Well on the Clare side to the Waterworks on the Limerick side ... The second *Enuire* is called Barnaluinge ... adjoining the Mount Shannon estate ... The third *Enuire* is *Geentass* ... centre-ways from Mount Shannon wood ... The fourth *Enuire* is called the *Poulnalauns* ... above Castletroy. The fifth *Enuire* is called *Bunabha* ... at the mouth of the Mulcaire river ...

The sixth *Enuire* is called the *Cut* or *Dam*, from the time the old Board of Works cut the bed of the river here in order to take the pressure of water from the Limerick lands. It runs from the *Cut* to mid-stream opposite Castletroy. On the Limerick side of the river are [the draws known as] *Slune, Drominayne, Faill Drominseoirse, Paddy and Feebeg*. On the Clare shore are *Poulderidheen, Clogheen, Faillmor, Doolin and Mulqueeny*. This comes in from the tail of the cut or dam on the Clare shore to mid-stream at the Castletroy falls.

The seventh *Enuire* is called *Taunymhor*, extending from below Castletroy Falls down to Shanny's pub on the Clare shore. The draws are *Traghknock* and *Tawnyhmor*. On the Limerick shore the draws are *Snamicau*, or the *Scour of the fall*, the *Lower Hole, Lugnahaille*.

The eighth *Enuire* is called the *Heights of Dromin Beg*. It extends from Shanny's pub to the old Plassy Bridge. From the Clare shore to mid-stream the draws are *The North Flat, Keadine, Tarraunthomais*. The draws on the Limerick shore are *The South Flat, The Bull Dogs*, which lie in the vicinity of Plassy, and *Skittogue* (from the lower islands to Plassy).

The ninth *Enuire* is *Cragarach* or *Rough Bottom*, extending from Plassy Bridge to the Canal boat stake. The draws on the Limerick shore are *Tulleragh, Cullough*, and *Cragarach*. On the Clare side the draws are *Ardan Crohoo*, or crooked height, *The Hills* and *Hollows*.

The tenth *Enuire* is *Lugshinnell*. It lies below the third small bridge on the Plassy

BEAUTIFULLY DECORATED AND COLOURED FLAKE AXEHEAD, IRISH, ABOUT 4,000 YEARS OLD, IN THE HUNT MUSEUM.

bank and continues to the old Limerick waterworks pumping station on the Plassy banks. The draws are *Dromroe, Blister, and Jones's Hole*, which finishes the Rhebogue water intake works. Dromroe comes in below the third Bridge at Plassy and until you reach the fourth bridge, to mid-stream.

The eleventh *Enuire* is called *Bealanauna*, from below Rhebogue waterworks to well below the mouth of the old canal. This was fished from one shore to the other and it all went by the above name.

The twelfth *Enuire* is called *Callagh Beolain* or *Carraig* for short (?). It lies between the island of Lanarone down to the old salmon weir at Corbally. The draws are as follows on the Limerick shore to mid-stream, *Swan Drop*, above the S.E. point of Lanarone. There are also some lamprey eel beds here; *The Middle Draw*, between the centre of Lanarone and the Limerick shore. On the Clare shore are *Ahaun*, at the cut carried out by the Board of Works to drain the water off the Limerick lands. Below this point the draw *Davy* comes in. It lies on the tail of Lanarone, on the north side of it. Also from the tail of Lanarone runs *Feebib* for 100 yards till it embraces *Ail Shura* running from the shore connecting Clare with Limerick (?). It lies in the vicinity of the lands of Gleanncorraidhe. Then comes *Shura*, the *Kiln Heights, Finnoe*, the *Upper Neck, Poulahurradh*, to the *Athlunkard Bridge* on the Clare shore. On the Limerick shore the draws are *Shore Goulach* and *Outer Goulach*, on to the Bridge.

From below the bridge the draws are *Soughmor*, on the Limerick shore to mid-stream down to the mill dam. On the Clare shore the draws are *Glasa Crubeen, Lugnafearna*, to mid-stream of the dam on the Clare shore.

Below the dam the draws are, *The Monk, Garraidhe, Dubhnalawn*, which lies from the upper point of St. Thomas' Island to Corbally dam. On the other side of the island are *Lugbrawn* or the *Quarry Hole*, which winds up in the back of the lax weir.

Below the weir the draws are *Garbh, Caim, Liggaun, Traghoo, Lawdromatho*, all on the Clare shore.

From Parteen Creek to the Railway Bridge on the Limerick shore the draws are *Aumanick, Amoor*, the *Roinn, Drominmhor, Caulahass, Dromin Garbh, Dromin Bhuidhe*.

Below the Railway Bridge on the Limerick shore the draws are *Bealacnahown* (at the mouth of the Abbey River), Tearnacraobha, Craobh. On the Thomondgate side the draws are *Ail, Charity, Dromatho, Poulacrobh*, and the *Cashel Draft*, which is now taken up by the ESB salmon weir.

Below Thomond Weir to the falls of Curragour was formerly called Enuire, because it was a common fishery. The draws are *Achullagh*, below Thomond Bridge on the Clare shore; *Tarrauncaum* and the *Middle Ardauns. Leganeira, Beal* or the mouth of the falls. Below Curragour lies *Shaungour* or *Traghgower*, also *Teannainnaluinge*, which comes in from Sarsfield Bridge to the Lansdowne Factory. There is finally *Leenthawn*, which runs to the lands of Old Church at Barrington's Pier.

TOLLS TOKEN, FOR ATHLUNKARD BRIDGE. Limerick City Museum.

City Hall moved to its present location in 1990, a site not far from where the Viking Thingmount reputedly sheltered Limerick's first local authority over a millennium ago. The former city gaol occupied this site until it was demolished in 1988 but most of its front facade has been retained and incorporated within

THE OLD CITY GAOL, ON THE SITE NOW OCCUPIED BY CITY HALL, IN THE 1980S. Shannon Development Photo Library.

the fabric of the modern civic offices, facing onto Crosbie Row and some steps leading downwards from St. Augustine Place to Merchants' Quay. The city gaol was built in an area known as Dean's Close in 1813 and was described by Samuel Lewis as a gloomy quadrangular edifice with which the old county gaol, located in Mary Street, had been united. It was visited by Elizabeth Fry, the prison reformer, in 1827 and seems to have been remarkably "well regulated, orderly, and clean" in the 1830s. Public hangings took place in front of the jail which had been designed with a stage, or drop, in front to facilitate spectators. The large window facing onto Crosbie Row, named after Dean Crosbie, was the "drop" through which many an unfortunate went to his or her death. Both city and county prisoners were kept in the city jail in 1821. Before its eventual demolition the building served as Geary's sweet-factory. There is a riverside promenade extending northwards behind the civic offices. The entry is to the left of the main door.

The County Court-house, on Merchant's Quay, still serves its original purpose. It was designed by two local architects, Nicholas and William Hannan, and was completed at a cost of £12,000 in 1810. It replaced an older county court-house which had been erected in 1732 on the site of the ancient Franciscan abbey. The present structure is a quadrangular building with a portico supported by four tall pillars which was designed to contain civil and criminal courts, jury-rooms and other offices concerned with the dispensation of justice. A new city court-house was built when City Hall was constructed.

THE COUNTY-COURT HOUSE. Limerick City Museum.

St. Francis Abbey was founded before 1279, the year a Franciscan of Limerick, Br. Malachy, was postulated to the see of Tuam. He was rejected by Pope Honorious IV in 1286. The exact date of its foundation is unknown, but T.J. Westropp suggested that it could have been founded by Donnchadh Cairbreach O'Brien before 1241 or by William Fion de Burgo, who had died by 1287. He also gave a third date and founder, 1350, by Mary, Countess of Desmond, which has been disproved by the 1279 appointment. This first Franciscan friary was located between Sheep Street and Sir Harry's Mall, north-east of Jail Lane. It was known as St. Francis Abbey, and even though its buildings have all long since disappeared, it is still remembered in local names like those of the Abbey River, Chapel Lane and St. Francis' Abbey Lane. Fion de Burgo, Thomas de Clare and Richard de Clare were buried here. St. Francis Abbey stood outside the city walls to the east. After the Reformation its lands were parcelled out and many of its buildings put to secular use. The church, dormitory, cloister and hall were demolished, only buildings useful to a farmer were retained. The choir was turned into a court-house and Edmond Sexten received a grant of the property in 1543. He kept the friars here as his tenants until 1548. The Franciscan Order was re-established elsewhere in the town in 1615 and a chapter was held there in 1629. On 23 June, 1636, all but one of the Sexten tenements in St. Francis Abbey, Richard Coyne's, were burned. The friars returned to the area for a while in 1687 but were forced to leave soon afterwards, in 1691. The old county hospital was built on its site in 1765. The Franciscans erected a well-built spacious chapel in Newgate Lane where they remained until they moved to Henry Street where they had "an elegant structure in progress" in 1827. Edmond Sexten was mayor of Limerick in 1535. His grandson, and namesake, managed to get legal title to freedom from rates and taxes on St. Francis Abbey in 1603. In 1609 a grant of King James I certified that the former choir was suitable for holding assizes and sessions for the county, as a result of which Edmond Sexten enjoyed two votes in the corporation, and the mayor and corporation were obliged to present him with the first salmon taken in the sea weir each year.

BRIDGE STREET, WITHIN LIVING MEMORY,
Limerick City Museum

Bridge Street was once known as Quay Lane but derives its present place-name from a "new" bridge extended across the Abbey River in 1762.

Quay Lane was mentioned by the playwright, John O'Keefe, in his *Recollections* which were published in 1826: "I knew Mr. Ferrar of Limerick, a printer, bookseller and author; he wrote an excellent *History of Limerick* which a few years ago I read with pleasure. His little shop was at the corner of Quay Lane. Ferrar was very deaf, yet had a cheerful, animated countenance, thin, and of middle size".

THE COLLEEN BAWN, A STAFFORDSHIRE FIGURINE. Limerick City Museum.

The City Court-house, or the Gerald Griffin Memorial School, is supposedly located on the site of the Augustinian abbey founded by the O'Briens during the thirteenth century. The City Court-house was built on the same site in Quay Lane or Bridge Street in 1640. This was later replaced by the present edifice erected between 1763 and 1765 at a cost of £700. The Quay Lane facade of this structure follows the curve of the street. The most spectacular of the cases tried here was that of John Scanlan who was executed on 20 March, 1820, for the murder of the Colleen Bawn. Fr. Brahan, the Catholic parish priest of St. Mary's Parish, bought the old court-house for £200 on 3 September 1845. The Christian Brothers spent £500 on renovating the building before opening it as a school on 2 February, 1846. Initially four brothers taught 560 pupils in this converted court-house in which Gerald Griffin had witnessed the trials of John Scanlon and Stephen Sullivan for the murder of Ellen Hanley, the *Colleen Bawn*.

The Mathew Bridge was originally known as the New Bridge and connected Englishtown with Newtownpery. It consisted of three irregular arches erected at a cost of £1,800 in 1762. There were two lamp-posts set opposite each other, in the centre of the bridge, which were used as impromptu gallows in 1798. In 1844 John Duggan was awarded the contract for a new bridge which was officially opened in June 1846. This was designed by W.H. Owen and named after Fr. Theobald Mathew (1790-1861), the Capuchin friar who launched a national temperance movement at about the same time as Daniel O'Connell was urging the repeal of the Union. Fr. Mathew was known as the Apostle of Temperance and is said to have obtained 180,000 disciples in Limerick in 1846 (the population of city and county in 1831 was 248,201).

Andrew Cherry (1762-1812), songwriter, dramatist, playwright, comic actor and wit was born in what is now the post office in Bridge Street. *The Dear Little*

Shamrock of Ireland was his best known song and he is also remembered for a letter he wrote to a former manager;

> Sir- I am not so great a fool as you take me for! I have been bitten once by you, and I will never give you an opportunity of making two bites of
>
> A. Cherry.

Crosbie Row is also known as Cherry Place to commemorate this famous city wit.

Nicholas Street, previously High Street, derives its name from a fourth-century archbishop in Asia Minor, St. Nicholas of Myra, the saint popularly known as Santa Claus. He was a popular patron saint with the Anglo-Normans and was commemorated in the name of a now-vanished medieval parish church on the site of the later Thomond Cinema, now Styx.

Newgate Lane leads towards the side entrance of City Hall and derives its name from one of the old city gates. The City Brewery, near the Golden Mills, was located in Newgate Lane, between the Old City Jail and King John's Castle. This was also known as the Newgate Brewery and was one of the earliest established in the city to make beer for public, rather that private, consumption. It was founded, and owned, by the Fitt family in 1739. Ale, pale ale and porter were brewed here in 1866. Danish ale was one of the city's earliest products as the Vikings were the first Limerickmen to brew beer - a custom which had originated in the Middle East five thousand years before. Water was often unsafe to drink, but the sterilising effects of fermentation in the beer-making process rendered it safe. Over the intervening

FIFTEENTH-CENTURY PANEL PAINTING OF SAINTS SEBASTIAN, NICHOLAS OF MYRA AND ANTHONY OF EGYPT, TEMPERA ON GOLD GROUND, GERMANY, IN THE HUNT MUSEUM.

centuries weak, or "small" beer, was consumed as drink and most beer was home brewed until its manufacture became a commercial proposition during the eighteenth century.

St. Mary's Court was originally known as Doctor Hall's Alms Houses. In 1761, under the terms of his will, "the present neat and convenient edifice was erected, which contains apartments for thirteen men and twelve women, who receive each five pounds a-year, school rooms, with apartments for the teacher, and a chapel, where the clergymen of the Established Church celebrates divine service twice a week". The buildings were restored in the mid 1970s.

Exchange Street derives its name from the old exchange, the remaining wall of which faces the entry to Nicholas Street.

St. Peter's Street, the entrance to which is on the opposite side of Nicholas Street to that of St. Augustine Place, leads into Bishop Street and derives its name from an ancient nunnery built by Domhnall Mór O'Brien for the canonesses of St. Augustine in 1171, Peter's Cell. The foundation was dedicated to St. Peter and was encompassed by the north-eastern walls enclosing the fortified Englishtown. Peter's Cell survived as an area name despite the disappearance of the nunnery and the walls. The Augustinian Convent of Killone, in County Clare, became the mother-house of Peter's Cell after 1189. The Peter's Cell Theatre was established some time before 1760 when some entre-

A STONE HEAD, PETER'S CELL, Limerick City Museum

preneur converted part of the ruined convent into a playhouse complete with a stage, boxes, a pit, one gallery, and a few dressing rooms. Spranger Barry, manager of two theatres, one in Dublin, the other in Cork, instituted a regular summer season here in 1760. Seats cost fifteen pence for the boxes, ten pence in the pits and five pence in the gallery. Audience participation was a feature of the performances as the Limerick bucks and dandies vied with each other, even by walking onstage, to display their finery. Fruit-sellers sold peaches at one fifth of a penny each (one old half penny), an unusual refreshment for that time and place. This theatre was still in use as late as April, 1770.

THE EXCHANGE, FROM A DRAWING OF 1786. J. FERRAR.

King John's Castle is said to have been built on the orders of that monarch to keep watch over Thomond and the O'Briens. It may have been erected as early as 1185 and is similar in style to one built in Framlingham, Suffolk, in 1190. The castle may have been completed by 1200 as a reference was made to its bawn in that year. It was mentioned in 1202 and castle repairs were noted in 1207, 1212, 1216 and 1227. The bishop of Limerick complained about the fortress encroaching on church lands in 1216. Other repairs were recorded in 1272, 1326, 1417, 1423, and throughout the centuries. On 3 August 1988, Michael Noonan, Minister for Defence, outlined an international tourist development scheme for the entire area, including the castle.

The castle is said to have been built without a keep but major archaeological excavations carried out between 1989 and 1995 revealed the presence of a large structure now known as the banquet-hall. The layout plan of the castle consisted of a powerful curtain wall with towers surrounding a roughly rectangular enclosure, an idea much favoured by the Anglo-Normans during the thirteenth-century and used in other royal castles like those established in Dublin, Roscommon and Kilkenny. The bottom of the walls was curved to deflect missiles dropped from the battlements outwards, round towers jutted out from the walls to enable archers to catch enemies in a cross-fire and prevent them from undermining the walls, and the entire structure was encircled with a moat fed by the River Shannon. The inner bailey of the castle contained the great hall, kitchen, private rooms, chapel and stables, most of which were removed to make way for a military barracks at a later stage. In 1935 Limerick Corporation breached the walls and erected twenty-two houses in the castle courtyard. Some of the children reared in these houses knew every nook and cranny of their castle home. They were aware of the existence of the 'banquet-hall' and several of them had gained entry to part of it from the sallyport on the western side. Their former homes and the last of ten barracks' buildings have been demolished since 1989. An interpretative centre was built on the site of the east wall and was opened to the public in 1991.

The gatehouse faces north-north-west and is protected by two flanking towers. A temporary iron grill is set into the centre of each tower's wooden floor, and a moveable glass skylight is situated in the middle of either roof, reminders

A BANQUET-HALL, OR ANCIENT KEEP, EMERGING DURING ARCHAEOLOGICAL EXCAVATIONS AT KING JOHN'S CASTLE. Shannon Development Photo Library.

of the castle's imperial military past when munitions had to be supplied to gun-crews on the roofs. Stone steps leading up to the pointed doorway replace a drawbridge, but the slots in the stonework through which a portcullis descended can still be seen. A murder-hole, in this case a long narrow slit now covered by a large flagstone, protects the original entrance between the two D-shaped flanking towers.

The north-western tower, the one nearest to Thomond Bridge, is the oldest of the three remaining towers while the two D-shaped flankers may be of a later date, possibly the thirteenth century. The marks of Ginkel's bombardment of 1691 can still be seen on its facade, especially where brickwork was inserted to replace damaged stone. All of the towers had their roofs removed to accommodate artillery as methods of warfare changed, and the south-eastern tower was demolished and replaced with a new bastion which could accommodate "five or six pieces of ordnance" in 1611. The roofs of the north-western and the north-eastern towers are slightly conical as their floor levels were raised when the area was converted into an armoury. In 1988 only the base floor of this north-eastern tower remained and it was kept closed to the public. The third tower to the south-west was also closed, but the walls by the river and the gatehouse are still intact although the battlements were demolished at the end of the eighteenth century. King John's Castle dominated Limerick for over 700 years. It was neglected under the rule of King John's son, Henry III, who succeeded to the throne at nine years of age in 1216 and ruled until 1272. In 1224 the king's goods in Limerick were scarcely worth eighteen pence, yet in 1226 it was the only castle in Ireland which was not fortified against the king. It was then defended by Richard de Burgh, its constable, one of an uninterrupted line of such incumbents who held that post, stretching from the appointment of Godfrey Roche, or de Rupe, in 1216 and finishing with the death of Viscount Gort in 1942. The Earl of Desmond's followers took the castle in 1332 but were unable to hold it against the Crown forces. The O'Briens and MacNamaras captured the castle in 1369 but lost it soon afterwards. In 1417 Henry V (1413-1422) granted monies for repairs, while his successor gave the charge of the castle to the mayor and citizens of Limerick on the condition that it should be kept in repair. Fr. Woulfe compiled a report, in 1574, on the city;

> There is a castle in the said city built by John son of King Henry II and for many years it was disused, and the houses and roof of said castle in ruins, and a part of the wall is already down, but with little expense it can be repaired, and it is in a most beautiful place above the city which it can keep in check, although the people of that city have been always loyal to the Princes of England ... Artillery. Limerick has none save two very small pieces, and no other munitions of war save a few arquebuses, bows and crossbows. I may truly affirm that in all the city there is not half a pipe of powder for the artillery.

The castle remained in a state of disrepair until the end of the sixteenth century. Its condition was noted in 1585 and it would have been unable to resist attack in 1588 if any ships of the Spanish Armada had sailed into the pool of Limerick. Sir George Carew, Lord President of Munster, ordered its restoration

KING JOHN'S CASTLE IN THE LATE 1980S, WITH THOMOND BRIDGE TO THE LEFT.
Shannon Development Photo Library

in 1600. Sir Josias Bodley fulfilled his instructions over the succeeding years. The building was modified and its defences strengthened. Two tower bases and the curtain wall were reinforced, a long storehouse was erected by the riverside wall, and a large bastion complete with sallyport was built in 1611. A 1633 map of the castle shows the bastion, three round towers that "beare ordinance", a drawbridge over the moat, or ditches, and fortifications on either end of Thomond Bridge. Lord Muskery forced the city to surrender to his Confederate Irish forces in 1642. Captain George Courtenay resisted and defended King John's Castle with sixty of his own men, twenty-eight warders and one hundred others until the Confederates bombarded his position from St. Mary's Cathedral, breached his walls with cannon and ignited mines. The position was reversed when General Ireton forced the Confederate garrison to surrender to the Cromwellian forces in 1651. He had bombarded the castle from the foot of Thomond Bridge and succeeded in breaching its walls. During the war between the two kings the castle was held by the Jacobites. Patrick Sarsfield surrendered King John's Castle to the Williamites under Ginkel in 1691.

The castle barracks was built within the walls of the castle in 1751 and was capable of accommodating four hundred men. Over the eighteenth and nineteenth centuries the buildings were altered and renovated to cater for the military. The angle-towers were reduced in height and reinforced to bear heavy guns, while the flanking gate-towers lost their rectangular projections. Limerick's motto describes its history very accurately: *Urbs Antiqua Fuit Studiisque Asperrima Belli*, an ancient city well-studied in the arts of war. The city arms are represented by a gate-tower complete with portcullis, flanked by two towers, an apt depiction of the entrance into the castle of the city.

Limerick Museum is now located in a replica of an eighteenth-century store that was built in the winter of 1997 and 1998. Limerick Museum first opened to the public in 1916 occupying part of the City Library in Pery Square, with the librarian of the day acting as curator. In 1974, pressure for library space caused the museum to be dismantled and the exhibits to be put in storage. In 1977 the curator was appointed, and in 1979 the museum reopened in John's Square, occupying two of the newly-restored houses.

In 1977, the collection consisted of about 5,000 objects. It now has about 30,000 objects. The museum collects all kinds of objects which illustrate the past of Limerick City and the MidWest region in general. The main themes in the collection are: Archaeology of the Mid-West from the Middle Stone Age, c. 6,000 B.C. to the medieval period.

THE LIMERICK CITY MUSEUM WAS BASED IN THIS BUILDING ON JOHN'S SQUARE UNTIL 1998.
Shannon Development Photo Library

History of Limerick Corporation, including city charters from Cromwell and Charles II, the civic sword granted by Elizabeth I in 1575, the city maces made by the Limerick silversmith, John Robinson, in 1739, the mayoral chair made by J.P. Lynch in 1897 and the famous Nail from the City Exchange.

Limerick silver of the 18th and early 19th century - the largest collection of Irish provincial silver anywhere.

Limerick lace - many fine examples of this craft which began in the city in 1829.

Local crafts and commerce, including furniture, clocks and watches, gunmaking, and the famous Limerick gloves, which were sold packed in a walnut shell as a demonstration of their fineness.

The Nail, Limerick City Museum.

Limerick printed books and newspapers of the 18th and 19th centuries.

Currency circulating in Ireland from Viking times, including medieval Limerick minted silver coins of King John and King Edward IV, gunmoney struck in Limerick during the sieges of 1690 and 1691, Limerick merchants tokens of the 17th, 18th and 19th centuries, and banknotes of Limerick private banks of the early 19th century.

Local aspects of Irish nationalist movements from 1798, including the Repeal Association, William Smith O'Brien, the Fenian Rising, Land League - Home Rule, the Irish Volunteers, 1916, the War of Independence and the Civil War. Also in this section is a display on Limerick as a garrison city and local involvement in the British Army, particularly the Royal Munster Fusiliers.

Labour history, including the unique Limerick Guild ceremonial aprons, and the Limerick Soviet of April, 1919.

Maps of Limerick from the 16th century.

Local topographical prints, paintings and old photographs

A very large collection of old postcards of Limerick city and county, and Co. Clare.

Temporary exhibitions, both visiting and from the museums own collection, are a regular feature of the museums displays. Among those held to date are:
Treasures of Thomond
Irish Wildlife
Limerick Silver

150 Years of Irish Railways
Labour in Irish History
The Limerick Soviet
Irish Folklife
Geology of the Mid-West
Limerick Harbour
Mid-West Patchwork
Australia 1788-1988
Irish Medals
The Munster Fusiliers and World War I
Woodturning
The Archaeology of Lough Gur
The Spanish Armada
The Circus in Limerick
Kings in Conflict (1690-91 Siege Tercentenary)
Food and Limerick

1916 MEDALS, **Limerick City Museum**

The Limerick Silver exhibition won the Irish Museums Trust Temporary Exhibition award, 1981.

The Kings in Conflict exhibition won the first Gulbenkian Irish Museums award in 1992 against competition such as the National Museum's Gold exhibition, Trinity College's 400 exhibition, Tralee's Geraldine Experience and the Ulster Folk and Transport Museum.

The premises at John's Square was always recognised as a temporary location. The new premises at Castle Lane will allow the museum to display a larger selection from the collection, and the location, beside King John's Castle, should greatly increase visitor numbers, particularly overseas tourists.

Limerick Museum is one of eight professionally staffed local authority museums in the Republic. Collectively these museums have received national recognition in the Cultural Institutions Act 1997, which allows for them to become designated museums for the collection of archeological material (which since 1994 is state property, collectable only by the National Museum). Their importance is also recognised by the Heritage Council, whose policy is to encourage their development and the establishment of museums by other local authorities. The Heritage Council has grant aided these museums since 1992 with the provision of computer hardware and software and staff to computerise the museum catalogues.

The Curator, Larry Walsh, has an M.A. in archaeology, U.C.D. He worked on various archeological excavations 1972-1977, including Wood Quay, Dublin. He became the curator of Limerick Museum in 1977, a position he holds at the time of writing. He is a Consultant editor and co-editor, *Old Limerick Journal*, 1989-1997. (Currently editor). His publications include numerous articles in local history journals, *Treasures of Thomond* (1980), *Limerick Silver* (1981), *Reflections on Munster Railways* (1984), *Historic Limerick* (1984), and *Limerick in Old Postcards*, co-authored with Jim Kemmy (1997).

Castle Street leads westwards towards Thomond Bridge. It derives its name from King John's Castle on its southern side, and contains some remnants of the town wall, a toll-house and several other notable buildings on its northern flank.

Thomond Bridge may have been erected as early as 1185 to lead from King John's Castle, in the Englishtown, to Thomondgate, on the Clare side of the Shannon. Like the castle, the bridge was reputedly built on the orders of King John and erected for £30. Other accounts state that a bridge was built in 1210. The real date hardly matters as this first structure collapsed about 1292, drowning eighty men. William de Prene became "Carpenter of the King's houses and castles in Ireland" in 1284 at the rate of five new pence a day for his sustenance, with an allowance of £2 a year for his robes. By 1290 he had been appointed "Keeper of the King's works in Ireland" - one of the highest

THE OLDER THOMOND BRIDGE AS IT LOOKED IN THE EARLY *1800S*. THIS WAS A BRIDGE THAT DATED FROM THE *1290S* AND WAS MODIFIED, REPAIRED AND REBUILT OVER A PERIOD OF *550 YEARS*. *Fitzgerald and Mc Gregor.*

administrative positions a skilled craftsman could reach during the late thirteenth century. He was arrested in 1292 and charged with stealing £3 worth of nails from Roscommon Castle and selling them in Dublin, taking £20 in wages due to others, embezzling £300 by falsifying the accounts of workmen he employed, and of causing the deaths of eighty men who drowned when Thomond Bridge collapsed. He was dismissed from the King's service and imprisoned until he could find pledges for £200.

Thomond Bridge was rebuilt with fourteen arches of unequal size which were turned on wicker-wick, the marks of which Samuel Lewis noted in 1837. In 1790 Charles Etienne Coquebert de Montbret, appointed French consul to Dublin by Louis XVI in 1789, noted that this bridge of fourteen arches, all different, was astonishingly flat and solid. One of the disadvantages of using the bridge was that it was often covered by the waters of the River Shannon, and despite the fact that it was subsequently widened, the surface level was never raised. Gate-towers controlled access to both ends of the bridge until Limerick was no longer a walled city. The present Thomond Bridge was designed by James and George Pain. Its foundation-stone was laid in 1836, although work on it did not commence until 1838. It is a plain strong structure, somewhat out of keeping with the rather ornate gothic-style toll-house designed and built for it on the city side, opposite the castle. The commemorative plaque states that work on the bridge was completed in 1840.

Shawn-a-Scoob, John of the Brooms, an industrious broom-maker from Cratloe Woods, used to sell his merchandise in the city markets. Tradition relates how the Limerick burghers were unable to select their first mayor and eventually decided to appoint to the office the first man to cross Thomond Bridge on a certain morning. To his surprise Shawn-a-Scoob was given the office. Some time elapsed before his worried wife came looking for him, only to discover him living in the lap of luxury and, apparently, unable to recognise her. "Shawn, Shawn", she cried, "Don't you know me?" "Get home out of that, woman", he replied, "sure I don't even know myself".

St. Munchin's College celebrated the bicentenary of its foundation in 1996. It was founded as a seminary for the Roman Catholic diocese of Limerick in 1796. The Catholic Emancipation Act became law on 13 April, 1829, but many of the penal laws against Catholicism had been eased long before that date. A relief act of 1782 allowed Catholics to open schools and a movement to establish colleges for young men had started by 1783. Bishop Denis Conway (1779-1796) became the first major benefactor of St. Munchin's College by leaving a bequest of £420. The seminary was first located in Palmerstown, on 29 September, 1796, at the corner with Old Francis Street, on the southern side of Mungret Street. It was transferred to Newgate Lane on 21 March, 1797, moved to a house in Peter's

Cell in 1800, and in 1809 was moved to Park House which was purchased by Bishop Young in that year for £1,800. The seminary was known as the "new college" when it was transferred to Park. It was housed in a new building which was erected in the grounds, near the entrance, and existed until 1830, when students were drafted to Waterford, Carlow and Maynooth (building removed in 1864). Bishop Charles Touhy (1815-1828) closed the seminary and gave the premises to the Christian Brothers.

St. Munchin's College and Mercantile Seminary opened on 1 October, 1853, at No. 1 Lower Hartstonge Street under the patronage of Bishop John Ryan (1828-1864). Just over five years later the bishop decided that the college should not be under the control of the diocesan clergy and he closed it down on 26 February, 1859. Four Jesuits arrived into the city on 16 February and took charge of St. Munchin's College on 10 March, at the instigation of the bishop. They opened it as a day school and by September, 1862, the college was being conducted in two locations, Hartstonge Street and the Crescent. Bishop George Butler (1864-1886) placed St. Munchin's College under the care of the diocesan clergy in 1867 and the curriculum was expanded to prepare young men for business, the civil service and the professions. The college was transferred to Mungret College and opened there on 23 September, 1880. Public funds had been used to open Mungret as an agricultural college and Bishop Butler had been very discreet in making no allusion to the fact that it was now doubling as a seminary. No mention of seminarians was made in a prospectus issued in 1882 and St. Munchin's College remained under the supervision of the Jesuits up to the time of his death, on 3 February, 1886.

Dr. E.T. O'Dwyer.
Limerick City Museum.

Soon after his appointment to the episcopate, Bishop Edward Thomas O'Dwyer (1886-1917) gave notice of his intention to move his seminarians out of Mungret. In September of 1886 six of them left to continue their studies in Maynooth. Others went to Maynooth in September, 1887, and in December, 1887, he announced that he would re-open St. Munchin's College in Lord Limerick's former residence at Henry Street. By the end of 1887 Mungret College had undergone major renovation; a large college complex had been put in place; accommodation for one hundred students had been added; and the college was on the verge of achieving university status. The bishop's decision to place the seminary under diocesan control once again was a major blow. St.

Munchin's College opened as the Limerick Diocesan College at 105 Henry Street on 9 January 1888. The Jesuits acquired the ownership of Mungret College in 1892 and by 1898 the conflict between themselves and the bishop had become quite bitter. Corbally House was built by Pierce Shannon, an ironmonger and ships' chandler whose ships sailed to Russia and the Baltic Sea, about 1824. He died in 1844 and his house became the residence of the Catholic bishops of Limerick from 1867 to 1956. Patrick J. Sheahan designed the new St. Munchin's College when it was decided to transfer the expanded school and seminary to Corbally during the episcopate of Henry Murphy (1958-1973). The foundation stone of the new complex was laid on 28 April, 1960. The Henry Street building closed in June 1962, and 285 students entered the new college on 10 September, 1962, even though some on the buildings had not been completed. The college had been firmly established as a secondary school by 1920 and its prospectus in 1996 describes it as a Catholic diocesan secondary school under the patronage of the Catholic bishop. As early as 1853 no distinction was made between the subjects taught to the future priests and laymen of the diocese.

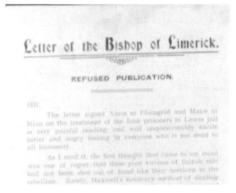

ADDRESS OF BISHOP O'DWYER OF LIMERICK ON THE POLITICAL SITUATION IN IRELAND WAS CENSORED BY THE BRITISH AUTHORITIES. Limerick City Museum.

Fr. Joseph Bourke was mentioned by Canon Begley in 1938 as the president of the diocesan college for a number of years. Canon Begley's history records how Joseph Bourke served as the administrator of Cratloe until he was transferred to St. Patrick's Parish in 1889. In 1890 Joseph Bourke was appointed parish priest of Askeaton, where he died on 19 May, 1892. This remarkable prelate seems to have alienated many of his colleagues by writing an open letter to the Bishop and clergy of the Diocese of Limerick in 1881. He had it printed, privately and distributed it throughout the Diocese. He outlined his grievances, writing from Mungret College, on 1 September, 1881;

> Rev. Dear Sir,
>   I beg to enclose a short statement regarding the Crescent School in Limerick, a School that had been established and conducted by me for so many years by my personal efforts and resources, and *at my sole personal risk without collection, subscription, or security* from the Diocese of Limerick, Some Rev. Gentlemen have stated and *circulated* the falsehood that the school belongs not to

me but to the Diocese... In the year 1868 and towards the end of that year, in conjuction with another Clergyman of the Diocese, I took the house at the Crescent in which the School is held, and prepared to open a *boarding and day-school* without assistance from anybody, with *our own resources*, and at our own *personal* risk. The Lord Bishop of the Diocese gave his consent to the proposal, and the School was opened in the beginning of 1869. Six months after the opening the other Clergyman withdrew from the enterprise and took with him *all* the money he had invested in it, leaving me the *sole* responsibility of the new Boarding School charged with £120 a year in rent and rates, and as might be supposed, for new furniture and fixtures deeply in debt. These difficulties I had to face. I looked for neither collection nor subscription from the Diocese. I depended on my *own* resources, and with God's blessing the School became a success.

Fr. Joseph Bourke was approached by a 'Venerable Dignitary of the Diocese' in 1873 and was asked to make his school over to the bishop as a diocesan institution. He informed the man in question that he had intended to leave the school to the diocese when he severed his links with education. Joseph Bourke, at the other's request, committed the details of his proposal to paper. This was an unfortunate move as other diocesan clergymen used this statement to take control of an educational establishment that had become known as the diocesan seminary but was actually Joseph Bourke's personal property.

When the Crescent School had been working for nearly 12 years, the College at Mungret offered. Being situated outside the city and having a good tract of land about it, I thought it would prove a boon for the education of the Diocese. I took it on my sole responsibility, as I undertook the Crescent School 12 years before, the Lord Bishop giving his consent... Last year the first of Mungret College was a comparative success, the Number of Students, all Boarders, varying between 40 and 50, while the Crescent School considerably. The large outlay on Mungret, with its working expenses, and the loss I sustained at the Crescent School proved too much for *my resources*. I found myself deeply in debt, and unable to open the College of Mungret for the coming year.

Being in debt, what more *natural* what more *just*, than that I should realise my assets in both Schools, the Crescent and Mungret, for both of which I contracted those debts? For I don't ask, much less claim, *any right to continue to teach*, and both places are able to pay their liabilities *without* help from *any* quarter: help would be necessary *only* if they had to be worked on. Then both places are in my *sole* name, one since last year, the other for the past 12 years; the rent and rates of both have been paid by me up to *last rent day; every penny* due for both establishments is chargeable to me.

The paper Joseph Bourke signed in 1873 was a statement of purpose and was not a transfer of property. Fr. Joseph Bourke offered to hand the school over to his bishop in 1874 and 1877, because of overwork, but his offers were declined. The bishop never asked him to conduct an audit or submit accounts because neither he, the diocese or diocesan clergy had contributed towards the upkeep of his school or schools. Joseph Bourke worried about his reputation and good name as some clergymen 'from imperfect knowledge' had circulated rumours about him, queried his accounting and believed he had used diocesan money to fund his schools. His booklet, *A Letter Addressed to the Lord Bishop and the Clergy of the Diocese of Limerick* (1881), was the only way in which Joseph Bourke could defend himself.

Fr. John McEnery (1796-1841) was educated in St. Munchin's Seminary at Park House. Ordained in 1819 he was appointed chaplain to the Cary family, Torquay, England, in 1822. He spent the remainder of his life there, near the underground chambers known as Kent's Cavern, devoting his spare time to palaeontology, the study of fossils. Rev. John McEnery was the first to discover the remains of the prehistoric sabre-toothed tiger in Britain. Many museums were enriched with his finds and his own collection was acquired by the British Museum after his death. His epitaph summed up his career; "Mr. McEnery was the pioneer of systematic observation in Kent's Hole and other Caverns in this neighbourhood, the sagacious and reverent observer of the works in nature of Him whose is the earth and the fullness thereof". He was buried in Torre churchyard.

The North Munster Masonic Centre on Castle Street is the first premises to be owned by the Freemasons in the Limerick region since the foundation of the first lodge in Limerick in 1732. The new centre is located adjacent to the Bishop's Palace, in Castle Street, in a part of a building that may have served some congregational or episcopal purpose in the not so distant past. It was later used as a public hall, St. Munchin's Parochial Hall, and served as a meeting place for boy scouts and, for most of the last fifteen years, a store for the Civic Trust. The Freemasons of Limerick intend to install a museum and library, together with various function rooms, and catering facilities, which will also be available for use by local community groups. Work on the new building had commenced at the time of writing. Their charitable ethos leads them into donating to local charities and they have recently provided Alzheimer Society centres in the Republic with nine special ambulances, of which one was presented to the day-care centre in Limerick, in November, 1996. The Freemasons also make donations from time to time to local charities.

The Freemasons, as an organisation, base their teachings on events dating back to the days of King Solomon and the building of the Temple of Jerusalem. History links them with the fraternal associations of free stonemasons, the craftsmen who built Europe's greatest castles and churches during the Middle Ages. The stonemasons who survived the Black Death (1348-1349) held annual assemblies, the first "lodges", safeguarded their jobs, gave charity to their members in need, established rules to govern their relations with others, set up a controlled rank structure of three degrees, entered apprentice, fellow craft and master mason, to maintain work standards, and seem to have developed a passion for secrecy after parliament outlawed their assemblies in 1425. Henry VIII seized church property after he severed relationships with Rome and confiscated the assets of Catholic institutions, brotherhoods, fraternities and guilds.

GOLDEN BOWL BY JOSEPH JOHNS, BEARING THE ARMS OF GEORGE FREND, FREEMASON, 1761. Limerick City Museum.

The Grand Lodge of Ireland is located in Dublin. It presides over the thirty-two counties and is the second oldest in the world. It was founded in 1725, eight years after the establishment of its English counterpart. Belief in a supreme being is the main prerequisite for membership and Protestants and Catholics alike, along with other denominations, joined the Freemasons. The Papacy declared its opposition to Freemasonry in 1751, and while these Papal Bulls were ignored, some Catholics withdrew from membership when the ban began to be more rigidly enforced, probably for political reasons, from 1799 onwards. Others left the society soon after Catholic emancipation was granted. The Freemasons resembled the later chambers of commerce by providing the professional and business communities of major towns and cities with a social *milieu* in which to meet. Newcomers to an area, especially if they had been initiated as members elsewhere, found membership a definite advantage. The Freemasons are non-political and non-sectarian in outlook and have a distinct charitable ethos but they were virtually "demonised" as religious prejudice was harnessed as a political weapon in the 1830s and 1840s. The Orange Society was established after the Protestant Peep-O'-Day Boys and the Catholic Defenders fought a pitched battle at the Diamond, County Armagh, on 21 September, 1795. Unfortunately this new body modelled its organisation on that of the Freemasons, utilising a lodge system similar to that of the Masonic Order, and so became confused in the public mind with the Freemasons, whereas there is no real connection at all.

Antient Union lodge No. 13 was consecrated in Limerick on 22 November, 1732, but the only records now available are from 1793 onwards. Many of the accounts refer to the feasts or meetings on one or other of the St. John's days. On 24 June, 1794, the lodge met and marched in procession to St. John's Church for divine service. A similar procession took place on 27 December, 1801;-

> .... being the Festival of St. John the members attended by a numerous and most respectable number of visiting brethren, proceeded to the Cathedral Church where an excellent sermon on the duties of Freemasonry was preached by the Rev. Brother Dr. Maunsell. After Divine Service they marched through the City agreeable to ancient custom. At half an hour past five they sat down to an excellent dinner.

On 6 July 1802, the lodge decided to present Rev. William Butler O'Dell with a gold medal as a token of appreciation for a sermon he had written and published for their charitable fund. During the mid-1800s the Freemasons held an annual ball to raise funds for the Masonic Orphan Institute. This was a major event in Limerick's social calendar; was usually attended by up to 300 guests; was held in the ballroom of the Philosophical and Literary Society in the Commercial Buildings, Rutland Street, and merited a full report in local newspapers, like the *Limerick Chronicle*. In January, 1803, the Freemasons decided "to procure a proper place for the meeting of this body" as Ancient Union Lodge No. 13 and later lodges had no regular meeting place. On 1 February of the same year the lodge met at the Royal Coffee House. On 7 August, 1804, the lodge had removed to the Mercantile Coffee House. Richard Franklin, one of the members, suggested that future meetings be moved to the house of W. Collopy, the proprietor of the Royal Coffee House, on 6 August, 1805. By 1819 the lodge room was located in Moriarty's Hotel; had been transferred to Supple's Hotel, in Thomas Street, by 1 May, 1821; and had been returned to Moriarty's Hotel, by 3 September, 1822. In the meantime the membership

DECANTER AND GLASSES, ONCE OWNED BY THE EDEN MASONIC LODGE. Limerick City Museum.

of the Freemasons within the city had been augmented by the foundation of Eden Lodge which had originally been established as Lodge No. 271 in 1756. This lodge changed its warrant and number to Lodge No. 73 in 1843. It was during this period that it was decided that control of the six lodges meeting in the Limerick region should be based in Limerick rather than Cork, as had been the case since 1732. The Provincial Grand Lodge of North Munster was created in June, 1842, and Michael Furnell, a past master of Antient Lodge No. 13 , became the first provincial grandmaster. In 1844 the six lodges were recorded as The Union Lodge No. 13., Limerick, The Eden Lodge No. 73, Limerick, Emerald Lodge No. 49, Charleville, Masonic Lodge No. 107, Kilrush, Masonic Lodge No. 60, Ennis, and St. Jame's Lodge No. 208, Nenagh. In 1846 Triune Lodge No. 333 was established and Excelsior Lodge No. 268 was established in 1873. All of the lodges in the region operated independently of each other under the guidance of the Provincial Grand Lodge of North Munster which has jurisdiction over the city and county of Limerick, the counties of Clare and Tipperary and the northern part of County Kerry. The Freemasons of Lodge 13 met at 92 George Street on 24 December, 1840. In January. 1841, they convened at Cruises Hotel, the property of Edward Cruise (1802-1887). It was decided to look for a suitable building in which a masonic hall be incorporated. On 24 March, 1841, a committee report suggested that the lodge take a portion of the Northumberland Buildings "lately occupied by Mr. Nash". A new masonic hall was opened in Henry Street, in time for the next meeting, on 22 May, 1841. Lodge 13 and lodge 271, the only two lodges meeting in the city at that time seem to have met under the one roof for some time prior to 26 December, 1842. The master of the lodge suggested at that meeting;

> That a communication be made to Lodge 271 on the advantage that each lodge would derive from opening a door of communication between their lodge rooms and having the apartments of each common to both lodges.

This arrangement seems to have fallen apart by 6 March, 1844, as the entire lodge had "to consider the propriety of removing from our present Lodge rooms". On 9 March the lodge decided to move and by 13 May, 1844, the lodge rooms had been relocated to 97 George Street. The North Munster Provincial Grand Lodge listed its officers, who were elected each June and December, into the late 1880s, on 27 December, 1846. It read like a *Who's Who* of Thomond's commercial and landowning social elite. Michael Furnell was the provincial grand master; The O'Gorman, an uncle of James Patrick The O'Gorman Mahon (1800-1891), was the provincial grand registrar; Henry Watson was the provincial senior grand warden; Edward Crips Villiers was the provincial junior grand warden; and the two provincial grand chaplains were Rev. William Eyre Massey and Rev. John Locke. The other officers included the high sheriff, William H. Barrington, Samuel Dickson, John Southwell Brown, Jonathan

Bruce, William Massey, William Williams, John Gleeson, Joseph Myles, James Pain, Thomas Jervis, Sir William A Chatterton, Colonel Charles Smyth Vereker, James Dempster, Frederick Saville, John O'Grady, The O'Gorman Mahon, J. C. Donnellan, Thomas Wright, John Crips, George Furnell, H.W. Smith, Richard Wallace, James D. Goggin, William Runalagh and R. Benson.

In September of 1852 members of Lodge No. 13 resumed their search for new quarters; considered renting the back office of "Brother Dartnell", for fifteen pounds a year, but found it too small; met in the hall of Eden Lodge in October; and the Union Lodge met at the Freemason's Hall in Upper Cecil Street in January, 1853. John Bassett leased rooms at 37 George Street to Antient Lodge No. 13, at thirty pounds per annum, from 18 March, 1854, to the following August. From then, until the following January, the Antient Lodge shared the lodge rooms of Lodge 73. Patrick M. Lynch, of Lynch's Hotel, Bedford Row, leased the large upper room of his house to Lodge No. 13 on 4 January, 1855.

Lord Dunboyne of Knappogue Castle served as the provincial grand master of North Munster from 1866 to 1881. The secretary of Antient Union Lodge No. 13 complained of "the extreme inconvenience of the present rooms at Lynch's Hotel and the want of accommodation and attention", on 28 May,

J.P. NEWSOM & COMPANY AT 20 AND 21 WILLIAM STREET WERE IRONMAKERS, HOUSE FURNISHERS, PLUMBERS AND BUILDERS' PROVIDERS INTO MODERN TIMES. WHEN THE FREEMASONS RENOVATED THE MASONIC HALL IN THE CRESCENT, BETWEEN 8 DECEMBER, 1909, AND 24 FEBRUARY, 1910, THE MATERIALS, ELECTRICIANS, PLUMBERS AND URINALS WERE SUPLIED BY NEWSOMS.

1856, and Brother Trousdell, of Lodge 73, offered temporary accommodation to his fellow-Freemasons. Antient Union Lodge No. 13 leased rooms at 39 Thomas Street, from a Mrs. O'Halloran, on 3 July, 1856. The lodge returned to the former lodge rooms at 97 George Street, part of the Limerick Institution premises, on 3 October, 1863. The lodge leased rooms in the Masonic Hall, from the Masonic Hall Company, from 30 December, 1870, to 31 March, 1877. This hall was located in Glentworth Street; was known as the Havergal Hall at a later stage; became the Lyric Theatre; and its site is used as a car park at the time of writing. The Provincial Grand Lodge, on behalf of the lodges meeting in Limerick, took a lease of the building at 6 Richmond Place (now The Crescent), on 13 March, 1880. The first meeting was held here on 26 June, 1880, and this property continued to be leased until 1972 when the Freemasons moved to 97 O'Connell Street. In 1987 the Provincial Grand Lodge considered the acquisition of new lodge rooms and after some initial difficulties in acquiring title to the site on Castle Street it was eventually purchased in 1995. Considerable help was received from Jim Kemmy who instigated a meeting with representatives of FÁS and this, in due course, led to the Freemasons sponsoring a FÁS community youth training project for the construction of the centre, starting in January 1998. There are six lodges under the jurisdiction of the Provincial Grand Lodge of North Munster, Lodge No. 13 (Limerick), Lodge No. 73 (Limerick), Lodge No. 268 (Limerick), Lodge No. 201 (Nenagh),Lodge No. 333 (Limerick) and, meeting in Roscrea, Lodge No. 311 (Templemore).

The Bishop's Palace, in Church Street, with its gable wall backing on to Castle Street, may have been designed by Francis Bindon (1698-1765), the architect

THE BISHOP'S PALACE. Limerick City Museum.

who pioneered palladian-style Irish architecture, although the Civic Trust dates it back to the seventeenth century and claim it is the oldest standing domestic dwelling in the city. The Civic Trust bought the building in 1986 when it was in ruin and it was opened in 1990, after restoration, as the society's permanent base. This was the official residence of the Church of Ireland bishops of Limerick until they moved to Henry Street in 1784. Its most famous resident was, or is, the *Bishop's Lady*, Limerick's most famous ghost, immortalised in the Bard of Thomond's poem, *Drunken Thady and the Bishop's Lady.* In 1732 the former episcopal residence was in use as a pub, *The Three Tuns.* There were only four carriages in use around the city between 1740 and 1750. These were "the Bishop's, the Dean's, and one other clergyman's and one neighbouring gentleman's". By 1776, with the growth of Newtownpery, there were 183 four-wheeled carriages in the district.

The Limerick Civic Trust was inaugurated at a public meeting on 17 February, 1983, Ireland's first civic trust, although others had long since been established throughout England, Scotland and Wales. The trust exists to aid the social and economic regeneration of the Limerick communities and has identified the need for action in three ways; to strengthen community awareness through its programme of activities; to create a better understanding of the area through information, advice and education; and to assist the economic life of the area through the provision of work schemes, by the re-use of redundant historic buildings and derelict sites. The projected plans for the revitalisation of Limerick's inner city have been spearheaded by the Limerick Civic Trust, Shannon Development, Limerick Corporation, and the Government.

J.F.T. Loveday kept a diary of his tour through England, Wales, Ireland and Scotland in 1732. While researching other travel material, Brian Ó Dálaigh, found the following account of Loveday's trip through Limerick;

> Sunday 18 [June 1732]. Limerick is encompassed by the Shannon, the chief river of Ireland, which divides its stream and embraces it. The city is divided into 2 parts, the English and the Irish town. The walls seem to be of different ages; on part of them [is] a very fine and exceedingly wide walk; great vessels, says Boate may come up to the very walls. Limerick chiefly consists of one street, of no great width and is for the most part stone building. St. Munchin's and St. John's [are] the only churches besides the cathedral. In the chancel of the former, which was heretofore the cathedral, found by St. Munchin, the first bishop of Limerick, is a monument for Bishop Smith's lady just south of the altar; the bishop was buried here since, but as yet there is no epitaph for him. Smith built a house hard by, which Bishop Burscough, his immediate successor, rents of his executors, for the palace these many years has been leased out and is now the sign of the 3 Tuns. St. Mary's, the

cathedral, is a large ancient pile, its pillars large and inelegant. As usual here, in the church are galleries and pews, the pulpit standing at the upper end before the altar. North of the altar is a very large and stately monument, erected for an earl of Thomond and his lady, his effigy defaced. Opposite to it on the south side is the recumbent effigy on a raised tomb (which is of much later date and has an inscription on it) of Bishop Corneilius O Dea, who resigned his bishopric in 1426 and died in 1434. It is alabaster and the people are continually cutting of it for the bloody flux. The hymns only were chanted here, both M and E. A parish sit in the choir, whose church stood where the hospital is now. The dean will not suffer them to contribute anything towards the repair of the cathedral. Mr. Bendon, the present dean, his revenue near £400 per annum; the bishop's £1800 per annum. In the vestry which is also used for a chapter house, is a Latin inscription in old Irish capitals inserted in the wall and there are other gravestones. No monument for any bishop, but the above mentioned, though Ware informs us that more were buried here. The vicar's choral have no houses but others have built upon their ground and pay them ground rent. There is no library here now. The barracks are at the ruined castle.

Church Street derives its name from St. Munchin's Church, towards its northern end.

St. Munchin's Church of Ireland Church was erected in 1827 almost on the same site as an older edifice said to have been built in 561. Tradition claims that the older structure was burnt by the Vikings. This was borne out by a stratum of ashes discovered when the foundations of the present building were being built. The ancient parish church of St. Munchin may have served as a cathedral long before St. Mary's was built. Despite all of the renovations and re-buildings over successive centuries one of the unique features of this church, as late as the nineteenth century, was its retention of an episcopal throne, a link predating Domhnall Mór

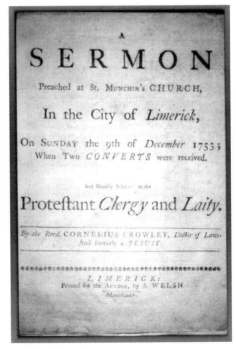

LIMERICK PRINTING. SERMON PREACHED AT ST. MUNCHIN'S CHURCH TO CELEBRATE THE CONVERSION OF TWO INDIVIDUALS IN 1754. Limerick City Museum.

St. Munchin's Church of Ireland Church, a view from John's Castle. Limerick City Museum.

O'Brien's foundation. St. Munchin is supposed to be buried in the churchyard. The church was disused, neglected and vandalised until recently. Carved memorials had been ripped from the tombs, the graveyard was badly littered, the church roof was in poor condition, holed in places, and the entrance and windows were sealed off. St. Munchin's was restored by the Civic Trust over a six month period. On 13 March, 1989, the renovated structure was leased to the Island Theatre Company by the Civic Trust but an exclusion clause in the lease prohibits its use for public performances. The present church, designed by the Pain brothers and erected for £1,460 in 1827, is a handsome edifice with a square tower embattled and crowned with pinnacles. St. Munchin's is also the burial ground of the Smyths, Lord Gort's family. St. Munchin, or St. Mainchín, an early bishop, is said to have been the nephew of Bloid, king of Thomond, and a disciple of St. Patrick, who asked him to convert the inhabitants of Connacht to Christianity. He had a hermitage at Kilmunchen, in Mungret, and is generally accepted as the first bishop of Limerick, although this may be wishful thinking on the part of early chroniclers. He was the patron saint of the O'Donovans and as the Vikings converted to Christianity they accepted the patron of their mentors as their own. His association with Mungret may have been transferred to the city by folk memory or folklore. Mythology claims that when the local people refused to help Munchin build his church he laid a curse upon them to the effect that strangers would flourish while the natives perished. This same story is also told of Ennis and may have been brought there by Limerick traders who settled in the Clare town during Cromwellian times. St. Munchin was also an abbot of Mungret. He died towards the end of the fifth century, and his feast is celebrated on 2 January.

The Villier's Alms Houses, and schools, were endowed by Mrs. Hannah Villiers in her will which was established in the court of King's Bench in 1815. In 1826 an Elizabethan style building, designed by the Pain brothers, was erected in the bishop's garden by Mrs. Villiers' trustees. The structure "consists of a centre and two projecting wings, the former being surrounded by a cupola; it contains apartments for twelve poor widows, each of whom receives £24 Irish per annum; and there are two school-rooms". Despite some modernisation the building remains basically unchanged. The garden wall in front of the alms houses is part of the old city wall.

The Parade extends southwards from Church Street to where Nicholas Street joins Convent Street, opposite the "new" entrance to King John's Castle. It derives its name from its former use as a military parade ground. Methodism was introduced into the city by Robert Swindells who preached his first sermon here in 1748 or 1749. Soon afterwards John Wesley visited him. They formed the Methodist Society of Ireland and rented the old church of St. Francis's Abbey, where the Methodists remained until they spent £600 on erecting "a handsome edifice near the city court-house". In 1812 they built a new Wesleyan Chapel in George's Street, but in 1815 a religious controversy split the congregation in two. The Wesleyan Methodists kept possession of the George's Street preaching house and the Primitive Wesleyan Methodists retained the old one. The dispute arose concerning the expediency of the original group's preachers administering the sacraments of Baptism and the Lord's Supper.

THE SALLYPORT, IN THE GROUNDS OF ST. MARY'S CONVENT. Limerick City Museum.

Convent Street derives its name from St. Mary's Convent which has been located here since 1812. Three Franciscan nuns moved into a house near the ruins of the Dominican friary in that year, added a chapel, choir and cells, and built a school for the children of the neighbourhood. Two of the nuns returned to Dublin in 1816, but another three arrived from Galway shortly afterwards. The Franciscan or Poor Clare convent was dissolved in 1831. The Sisters of Mercy moved into Limerick in 1838 and occupied the convent building, which was only a fraction of its present size and fronting on to Island Road rather than Bishop Street. Their school is built on the site of an earlier nunnery, Peter's Cell.

St. Saviour's Dominican Friary may have been founded by Donnchadh Cairbreach O'Brien in 1227 on land donated by the English king. Edward I made a grant in 1285 in which he mentioned the affection he bore for the friars of Limerick whose house, he claimed, was founded by his own ancestor. Donnchadh Cairbreach was buried here in 1242. In 1462 the earl of Desmond, James, was buried in the rebuilt priory. It was suppressed in 1541. The Dominican friars owned fishing-rights in a salmon-weir, St. Thomas's Island and some land at Monabrahir, near Parteen, which were granted to the earl of Desmond on 7 June, 1543. He returned these properties to the friars during the

THE DOMINICAN FRIARY RUINS IN THE GROUNDS OF ST. MARY'S CONVENT. Limerick City Museum.

reign of Mary Tudor (1553-1558). Robert Ansley received a grant of the friary in 1589 and it later passed into the possession of James Gould, who owned it at the time of his death in 1600. In 1644 Pope Vincent X established a university in St. Saviour's for the Catholic Confederation. Only one wall and some fifteenth-century, and later, carvings survive. The latter have been placed in two grottoes.

In 1837 "a nunnery had been established; attached is a large school for girls, who are gratuitously instructed by the ladies of the convent".

The Gerald Griffin Memorial School, formerly the City Court-House.
Shannon Development Photo Library.

Gerald Griffin (1803-1840) was born in a house that stood on the corner of Old Dominic Street and Love Lane on 12 December 1803. His family moved out of the city to Fairy Lawn in 1810, until his parents eventually decided to emigrate to Pennsylvania. Gerald was reared in Adare and Pallaskenry, the ninth son of a large family. Originally he had intended to study medicine and had been left, with two sisters and a brother, to the care of an older brother who was a doctor in Pallaskenry. He moved to Limerick where he worked as a reporter and helped in the formation of a dramatic society before moving to London in 1823. John Banim (1798-1842) encouraged him to write and he worked as a reporter, book reviewer, parliamentary reporter and translator. The publication of *Holland Tide* established his literary reputation in 1827. This was followed by *Tales of the Munster Festivals* and in 1829 he published *The Collegians* which was based on the *Colleen Bawn's* story. At the height of his fame he burned his manuscripts and joined the Christian Brothers. From 1825 he had been troubled by rheumatism and recurrent illness. He succumbed to typhus in Cork on 12 June, 1840.

George's Quay is named after George III (1760-1820) who came to the English throne at the age of twenty-two. It is called Barrington's Mall by many Limerick people.

Robert Graves (1895-1985) patronised the Lock Bar, on the western end of George's Quay, during the War of Independence. Folklore claims that he visited the pub in Black-and-Tan uniform, but this is most unlikely as he was an officer in the Third Battalion of the Royal Welch Fusiliers. He was stationed in Limerick during January and February of 1919. His grandfather had been bishop of Limerick and his father, Alfred Perceval Graves (1846-1931), was a well-known collector and writer of songs. Alfred Perceval Graves wrote several books, *Songs of Killarney* (1873), *Irish Songs and Ballads* (1880), *Songs of Old Ireland* (1883), and *Father O'Flynn and other Irish Lyrics* (1889). Robert Graves was actually born in Wimbledon on 24 July, 1895, but always described himself as an Irishman. In his autobiography *Goodbye to All That* (1929), he wrote of being garrisoned in the city which looked like a war-ravaged town. He knew it was a Sinn Fein stronghold but assumed that his regiment, the Royal Welch, were in control. He spoke of an antique dealer named O'Reilly who knew his grandfather well and recounted a conversation with the former detailing how the birth-rate was falling, no one was building new houses and everyone was dying of drink. He refused to search houses for concealed rifles as he was an Irishman whose family had long been associated with the city and he had no intention of getting involved in Irish politics. He played his last game of rugby here, in January, 1919, and he, and his military team mates, were trounced by a local team.

Robert Graves was a poet and became a professor of English literature at Cairo University in 1926. He is best known for his historical novels *I, Claudius* (1934) *Claudius the God, Sergeant Lamb of the Ninth, Count Belisarius, Wife to Mr. Milton, Proceed, Sergeant Lamb, The Golden Fleece, They Hanged My Saintly Billy* and *The Isles of Unwisdom.* He compiled a dictionary of Greek mythology, *The Greek Myths,* examined or researched early Christianity in *The Nazerene Gospel Restored,* and explored the poetic impulse in *The White Goddess.*

Barrington's Hospital was endowed by Joseph Barrington in 1829, a date commemorated in the carved lettering above its main door. The Barrington family, Sir Joseph Barrington and his sons, Matthew, Daniel, Croker and Samuel, spent £10,000, on the construction of this large edifice on George's Quay. The Barringtons have been associated with the city since Francis Barrington arrived from England in the 1640s. Samuel Barrington survived the Williamite siege of 1691. He was a clock-maker who died in 1693 and was buried in St. Mary's Cathedral. His epitaph reads; "Little Samuell Barinton that great undertaker of famous cittis clock and chime maker..." Joseph Barrington was an enterprising man with a philanthropic flair. He was disliked by Caleb Powell, who described him as a "pewterer dwelling in a very small shop" who had "rais'd himself to eminence" and acquired extensive landed property in Limerick. Joseph owned,

BARRINGTON'S HOSPITAL
and City of Limerick Infirmary
GEORGE'S QUAY, LIMERICK

FOR SALE BY PUBLIC TENDER
BY DIRECTION OF THE HIGH COURT

Conn Shanahan & Co. Ltd., M.I.A.V.I., 5 Cecil St., Limerick
Telephone 061-45337/43957

BARRINGTON'S HOSPITAL. A BROCHURE ADVERTISING THE SALE OF THIS VENERABLE INSTITUTION IN 1989.
Limerick City Museum.

amongst other possessions, a pewter works under the sign of the *Copper Globes* on Charlotte Quay. Ironically, soon after Caleb Powell wrote that description of Joseph in 1858, Powell's ownership of Clonshavoy passed into Barrington hands. Joseph became a baronet in 1831, the year after he had founded Barrington's hospital. His first cousin, William Canter of Ballyvarra, was a skilful bone-setter. Joseph died in 1846. Sir Matthew Barrington was a solicitor with practices in Limerick and Dublin. He was Crown prosecutor in Munster during a very disturbed period that included the Special Commission held at Limerick in 1848. His son, William H. Barrington, was a grand juror selected by Caleb Powell in 1858. Matthew is best re-membered as the instigator of the Barrington's Mont De Pieta or pawnshop.

Barrington's *Mont De Pieta* was the first of eight such establishments opened in Ireland in 1837. It operated as a type of pawnshop in which an interest rate of less than two new pence to the pound was charged, and there was no

BARRINGTON'S MONT DE PIETA. TOKENS.
Limerick City Museum

charge for the ticket of pledged articles. In 1840 it made a profit of £1,357 which was used to fund Barrington's Hospital. By 1841 the *Montes De Pietas*, or *Mons Pietas*, had started to lose money. By 1843 only three remained in the country and the last one, in Portadown, closed at the end of that year. The Franciscans of Perugia founded the first *Mont De Pieta* in 1461. The idea proved so successful that Pope Leo X had to issue a bill in their defence in 1515 to silence the vested banking interests who had objected to religious orders getting involved in financial affairs.

Sir Fitzwilliam Barrington lived in Glenstal House as a child. He returned to Limerick for the closure of Barrington's Hospital, of which he had been honorary secretary, on Wednesday, 30 March, 1988. Part of Barrington's Hospital is still serving its original purpose. There is a modern sign on the eastern end of the large complex indicating that Barrington's Hospital and Medical Centre is operating on parts of the first and second floors. The Dyslexic Support Centre is located on the ground floor at the western end of the building. Some of the former hospital now serves as a hostel and Barrington's Lodge advertises guest accommodation and car-parking facilities near Baal's Bridge. The original hospital had been built in this location to service the slums of the Irishtown and Englishtown during the 1820s and 1830s. It served the entire area and the expanding city as a general hospital and specialised in the care of children, having several wards for boys and girls.

Doctor Thomas Arthur (1593-1674) was born in the city, was educated in Bordeaux and received his medical training in Paris and Rheims. He was a Catholic who returned to his native city to practice medicine. Thomas Arthur was driven out of the city in 1641 but returned during the Cromwellian siege. He treated Colonel Henry Ingoldsby's scorbutic fever, for which he received a fee of five pounds, and earned a fortune from his patients that he invested in the purchase of confiscated lands. He left an account of his own life and a notebook detailing the fees and accounts of his cases between 1619 and 1666.

Mary Street derives its name from the cathedral and extends from Baal's Bridge to Nicholas Street. Behind Barrington's Hospital plasterwork bears the legend *Saint Mary's Prize Band 1885* and an adjoining hall has a tablet stating that it was built in 1922. On the opposite site of the street is a small terrace with a stone tablet on one house proclaiming that these houses were built for the "working classes"

The Tholsel was founded in 1449. This was the city's earliest town hall, or court, and later served as a jail. The jail was four storeys high, with a plain facade close to the street and was completed by 1750 to serve as the County Gaol.

THE THOLSEL, IN MARY STREET, FROM A DRAWING BY T. RYAN. Limerick City Museum.

When John Howard, the prison reformer, visited here in 1788 he pointed out various defects which probably resulted in the erection of a newer county gaol. The building, still known as the Thosel, was used for other purposes after its closure as a prison. In 1837 it was the chief civil court with the mayor and sheriffs presiding as judges, assisted by the recorder, when present, as assessor, and the town clerk as prothonotary. This court was held under the Charter of Henry V, which gave pleas, real and personal, to any amount arising within the county of the city. The court sat every Wednesday. The process was either by attachment against goods, action against the person, or the issuing of a writ to summons someone who was in hiding. The Tholsel was demolished in 1936, but a small portion of the structure remains behind the former shop of the same name.

Fanning's Castle, in the grounds of the Art College, backing on to Mary Street, is a late-sixteenth or early-seventeenth century house built by a merchant of that name. It was the home of Dominick Fanning, the mayor of Limerick executed by the Cromwellians for his part in the defence of the city in 1651. Thirty years later, in 1681, it was occupied by another mayor, Francis Whitamore, and tradition relates how Patrick Sarsfield stayed here during the Williamite siege. The windows are unusually large for a fortified residence. Another building was added to the original fabric at a later stage.

Athlunkard Street derives its name from *Áth an Longphuirt*, the ford of the encampment or fortress, a townland on the Clare side of the Shannon. The street finishes at O'Dwyer Bridge but the roadway continues northwards as Corbally Road and crosses the Shannon River at Athlunkard Bridge, near the site 'of an ancient ford. An early Viking settlement is believed to have been in the immediate vicinity of the original fording place, not far from the *longphort* of the O'Briens. This was discovered when a pipeline associated with the proposed Limerick Main Drainage Scheme was to have been driven through an earthworks near the Lax Weir. Athlunkard Street developed after the demolition of the old city walls in 1760, part of the general clearance that presaged the building of Newtownpery. Salvaged material from the demolished walls and buildings was used to build the quays. Athlunkard Street itself was built in 1824.

The O'Dwyer Bridge was erected in 1931 to replace Park Bridge, a lofty bridge of five irregular arches which had been built in 1835 to replace "a mean structure". This bridge was dedicated to the Catholic bishop of Limerick, Dr. E.T. O'Dwyer. The Athlunkard Boat Club is located on its north-western end, behind an old iron gate. The wrought-iron ornamental gates at the entrance to

*ATHLUNKARD STREET IN THE 1980S WITH ST. MARY'S CHURCH TO THE RIGHT AND ST. MARY'S CATHEDRAL IN THE BACKGROUND. **Shannon Development Photo Library.***

the Athlunkard Boat Club were part of a set that originally stood at the entrance to Todd's Bow, William Street. Archibald Murray, of William Todd and Company, presented one set to the club in 1901. The other set was acquired by the Gubbins family in Castleconnell. The gates had been manufactured by Bethells' foundry works at Watergate and contain adorning copperwork motifs popular in the Celtic Renaissance style of the period, Treaty Stones, coats-of-arms, spinning-wheels, round towers, Maids of Erin and figures of Henry Grattan.

Rev. Edward Thomas O'Dwyer (1842-1917) was consecrated Bishop of Limerick on 29 June 1886. He once stood on Issac Butt's platform when he sought election but on another occasion he told the Irish Party that their public policy was stupid and he claimed that the Plan of Campaign was morally wrong. In 1915 he condemned English attempts to recruit Irishmen into the ranks during World War I. On 17 May, 1916, he wrote to General J.G. Maxwell, Commander-in-Chief of the British Forces in Ireland who had asked him to remove two of his clergy, Fr. Tom Wall and Fr. Michael Hayes " to such employment as will prevent them having intercourse with the people", as General Maxwell considered them "a dangerous menace to the peace and safety of the realm". The Bishop replied that he did not "see in them any justification for disciplinary action" on his part as "they are both excellent priests, who hold strong national views, but I do not know they have violated any law, civil or ecclesiastical". He continued to castigate Maxwell for "altogether your regime has been one of the worst and blackest chapters in the history of the misgovernment of the country". He was a staunch nationalist although he disapproved of the Easter Rising; "Was I to condemn them! Even if their rebellion was not justifiable theo-logically ... in my humble judgement there is deep down in the heart of Ireland the sacred fire of nationality". Edward Thomas O'Dwyer never bowed to public opinion. On 19 August, 1917, he died at home after returning from his summer holidays in Kilkee. He was seventy-five years old.

St. Mary's Catholic Church was erected on the Sluice or Little Island between 1746 and 1749. It was

ST. MARY'S CHURCH, SOON AFTER CONSTRUCTION.
Limerick City Museum.

cruciform in design, without external decoration, and contained a handsome altar donated by a merchant, John Kelly, in 1760. This church was demolished when the newer church, designed by Messrs. Ashlin and Coleman, Dublin, and erected by Messrs. Maguire and Shortt, Dublin, was opened on 31 July, 1932. The foundations of the older structure remain, forming an attractive feature within the garden.

The Cell of St. Mary House, or Priory, was located on the bank of the Abbey River, on King's Island, east of Baal's Bridge.

Bourke's House, on Athlunkard Street, was also known as Castle Friary because Franciscan friars lived here from 1732 to 1766. This is not a typical Irish tower-house although the machicolation proves that it was built as a fortified structure. Note that what is seen on the street is the inside of the original wall. A Gothic-style drinking fountain was inserted in the stone facade of this late medieval dwelling in 1860. This was a presentation to the people of Limerick by the Malcolmson family, founders of the Limerick Shipping Company. The inscription reads, "Protect what is erected for your benefit". The fountain no longer serves its original purpose.

John Ferrar, the grandson of a Williamite cavalry officer and a descendant of Nicholas Ferrar who founded the Little Gidding Community, published a short sketch of Limerick's history in 1766. He established *The Limerick Chronicle* in 1768, and in 1787 produced a substantially enlarged version of his history. Denis Fitzgerald Mahony

BOURKE'S HOUSE IS BELIEVED TO HAVE BEEN BUILT BY DOMHNALL MOR O'BRIEN AFTER HE HAD GIVEN HIS PALACE TO THE CHURCH. IT DERIVES ITS NAME FROM ANOTHER OWNER, JOHN BOURKE, A CATHOLIC ALDERMAN OF THE 1650S AND WAS USED AS A FRANCISCAN FRIARY IN PENAL TIMES, FROM ABOUT 1730 TO 1780. THE ORIGINAL MEDIEVAL HOUSE EXTENDED INTO WHAT IS NOW ATHLUNKARD STREET BUT ONLY THE WALL OF ITS NORTHERN GABLE REMAINED AFTER THE STREET WAS BUILT. THE INTERNAL PART OF THE WALL FACES INTO THE STREET.

(1773-1840) was a part owner of *The Limerick Chronicle*. He lived in the Tontine Buildings on Sir Harry's Mall and was a successful stockbroker, alderman, magistrate and philanthropist. His son, Andrew Watson Mahony (1817-1839) was drowned on the *Night of the Big Wind* , 6 January, 1839, when the schooner *Undine* was swamped in the Shannon.

Sir Harry's Mall derived its name from Sir Henry "Harry" Hartstonge, who lived near Baal's Bridge, and was married to Lucy Pery, the sister of Edmund Sexton Pery. He reclaimed the foreshore on which the mall was built. The Sandmall was another name for Sir Harry's Mall as the sand dredged from the rivers was stored here. The sand from which most of the older parts of the city

SIR HARRY'S MALL, NOW BUT A MEMORY. **Shannon Development Photo Library.**

was built had been washed into the river-bed from the catchment areas of the Shannon, Mulcair, Newport and Clare rivers. It was deposited in several places along the Shannon's bed but the three most important locations were where the Mulcair river entered the Shannon, the deep waters below Plassey Bridge, and between the Lax Weir and the Island Point. The sandmen used an ugly but versatile craft, known as a sand barge, or cut, to recover and transport the sand. This was thirty feet long by five wide sloped fore and aft; had a small jib; a hand-winch in the stern for raising dredges filled with sand from the river bottom; could be loaded from the gunwale by one man, but needed a crew of two; carried ropes, anchors, grapnels and a *skeef*, a wooden bailer; and was powered and steered from the stern, over which a heavy sweep was set in a socket. The sandmen of the Parish carried on their arduous, often hazardous trade, from the earliest days of the city's foundation. The quantities of sand required for the building of the Shannon Scheme caused commercial sand quarries to be opened in Limerick and it was this competition that put them out of business.

The Northern Relief Road resulted in a major archaeological survey being conducted along the length of the proposed site all the way from Sir Harry's Mall to Bishop's Palace. The piling for the new bridge had to be moved from the original site suggested as in the process of examining the immediate area a medieval graveyard was discovered, one of which no record has been found at the time of writing. Celie O'Rahilly, the city archaeologist, Flo Hurley, Ken Hanley, Brian Hodkinson, Fiona Reilly, Bernie Doherty and Ken Wiggins have made several interesting discoveries along the route of the roadway. The skeletons found at Sir Harry's Mall were standard Christian burials from early Christian times, positioned east-west, head to the west, (facing the east). Sir Harry's Mall, once occupied by the Barry, Brosnan, Clancy, Flanagan, Golden, Griffin, Guina, Hayes, Hickey, Kelly, Killeen, Mulcahy, O'Brien, O'Doherty, O'Donovan, O'Halloran, O'Mahony, Purtill, Sheehan and Sweeney families, had been built, unknowingly, over the dead of an earlier era.

A total of 470 remains were discovered in the excavated cemetery of St. Francis Abbey. An examination of 150 seventeenth-century skeletons revealed that rickets and spina-bifida were prevalent and some of those buried here were victims of the sieges, as their skeletons bore marks of violent deaths, musket balls being found in one skull, several others being shattered. Most corpses were buried in shrouds, as shroud pins were regularly found. A few were buried in coffins; and a lead coffin was discovered in one spot, presumably that of Oliver Lombard, a Corkman who had requested burial here. The graveyard extends under the houses in Long Lane, as the residents have often found human bones while carrying out repairs or renovations. Only a portion of the original Abbey of St. Francis was found and no trace was discovered of the priory of the Fratres Cruciferi or Crouched Friars, which was believed to have stood on Sir Harry's Mall some time prior to 1216. Several kilns, a seventeenth-century chamber-pot (made in Germany), sixteenth-century coins, parts of the town wall and the base of a column from St. Francis Abbey were found in the course of the archaeological excavation.

The Jim Kemmy Bridge is the designated name of the new bridge over the Abbey River. This is being constructed at the time of writing and Dr. Edward M. Walsh referred to it at the launch of *The Old Limerick Journal*, in Jury's Hotel on the Ennis Road, on 20 July, 1998. This was his last action as President of Limerick University, the launch of the thirty-fourth edition of *The Old Limerick Journal.*

The Old Limerick Journal is a major source for local historians and its continued publication is the most fitting memorial for men like Jim Kemmy, Kevin Hannan, Willie 'Whack' Gleeson and Seamus Ó Cinnéide.

POSTER FOR A BARRINGTON'S HOSPITAL FUNCTION, IN GARRYOWEN, 1895.
Limerick City Museum.

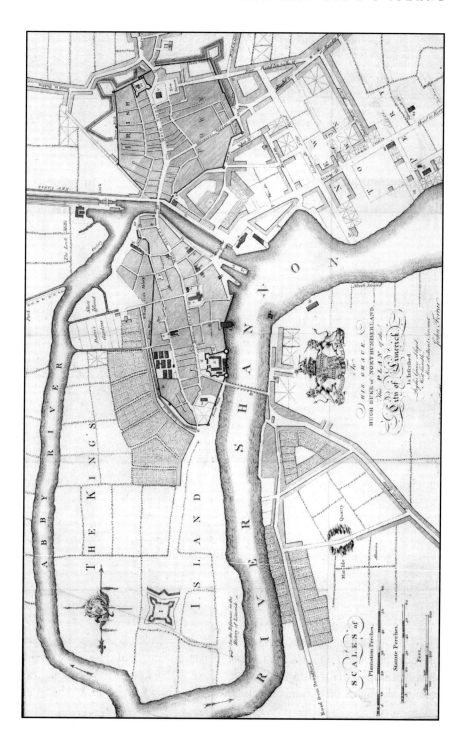

Limerick: The Irishtown

The Irishtown came into existence as the Anglo-Norman invaders of the old city forced the earlier inhabitants out of their island homes, across to the opposite bank of the Abbey River. This second settlement dates back to the days of King John. The streets were wider and some of the houses more modern but it became part of the walled city even though it retained a separate identity. From about 1320 the fortifications were extended to enclose the Irishtown, work that was completed with the erection of John's Gate in 1495. In 1654 only one Irishtown landlord, Christopher Sexton, was considered to be acting in "English interests", as the others, landlords and tenants alike, were classed as "Irish papists". When the old city walls were knocked in the mid-1700s Mungret Street and John's Square became elite residential areas. The development of Newtownpery led to the downgrading of the Irishtown. Formerly fashionable houses were turned into tenements, the more prosperous inhabitants moved away, and even today some sites remain cleared, but undeveloped, some for over sixty years. Urban renewal schemes have halted the decline in recent years. Older historic buildings have been restored, and the people of the area are more aware of their heritage.

Baal's Bridge or Ball's Bridge was built about 1340. This was a bridge of four

OLD BAAL'S BRIDGE. Limerick City Museum.

arches with a range of houses on one side. Folklore, however, speaks of a much earlier bridge that owed its name and construction to Baal, a Singland man who was converted to Christianity by St. Patrick, nine centuries before. The original fourteenth century Baal's Bridge was replaced by a single-arch structure built in 1831 by the Limerick Navigation Company, at a cost of £3,000, as the older bridge interrupted the communication between the canal and the tide-water of the river. The name may be a derivation of *Droichead Maol*, the bald bridge, meaning a bridge without parapets, or a corruption of Boyle's Bridge, part of a grant made to the earl of Shannon whose family name was Boyle. It was known as the Tide Bridge in Elizabethan times; was "disgraced by a row of houses" as late as 1827; and the silversmiths of Limerick used a version of the City Arms as their hallmark, or mark of origin device. It was taken down in November, 1830, and replaced with the present structure, designed by the Pain brothers, the following November.

The Irishtown Walls, travelling clockwise from Baal's Bridge and Lock Quay, were guarded by the East Water Gate, Cromwell's Tower, a sallyport, Black Battery, Devil's Tower, Cogan's Tower, John's Gate, Mungret Gate and West Water Gate.

Balls Bridge.

BAAL'S BRIDGE, ALMOST A CENTURY AGO. Limerick City Museum.

East Water Gate was located on the junction of Old Clare Street and Curry Lane. Clare Street and Old Clare Street derived their names from John Fitzgibbon (1749-1802) who was created Viscount and Earl of Clare in 1795 and who helped Lord Castlereagh (1769-1822) to have the Act of Union passed. In 1849 there was an auxiliary workhouse for female paupers in Curry Lane. Twenty-seven of these women were killed in a stampede from this building as a false alarm of its being on fire frightened the inmates. The remnants of some sixteenth-century houses are still retained within the fabric of houses and walls in Curry Lane and the adjoining area, especially Broad Street.

Broad Street may simply mean the

THE EARL OF CLARE, BLACK JACK FITZGIBBON. Limerick City Museum.

wide street and seems to have been used as a place-name from about 1750 onwards. It extends southwards from Baal's Bridge before converging into a Y-shaped street pattern similar to an early seventeenth-century one in Ennis. Mungret Street and John's Street form the arms of the Y with Grattan Street extending eastwards from John's Street, almost from the junction.

Cromwell's Tower may derive its name from one of the Cromwell family who were associated with County Limerick for at least three centuries before the advent of Oliver Cromwell. Isolde Cromwell held the lands of Ballygodan, near Herbertstown, in 1325, and James Cromwell was mayor of Limerick in 1598.

The Sallyport and Cogan's Tower can still be discerned in the remaining part of the east wall which stretches from the junction of Old Clare Street and O'Sullivan's Place to the corner of New Road and St. Lelia Street. The recent urban renewal has ensured that the remains of the sallyport, the D-shaped base of Cogan's Tower and the rampart behind the town wall will be preserved for future generations. The rampart itself was built of earth between the sieges of 1690 and 1691 in order to strengthen the walls. A new estate and a pub named The Sallyport now occupy part of the ancient site behind the wall.

The Citadel was the Irishtown's main fortification. It was not shown on the 1590 map of the city in the Hardiman collection, Trinity College, Dublin, but can be dated to either the early or middle years of the seventeenth century. In 1690 it was the scene of a heroic Jacobite defence, the battle of the Breach, which was fought nearby inside the site of the Devil's Battery or the Black Battery. The gate-building, or sallyport, of the original stronghold has been incorporated into the structure of St. John's Hospital, as have parts of the old city walls.

ENTRANCE TO ST. JOHN'S HOSPITAL.

THE CITADEL. Limerick City Museum.

Other parts of the city walls and some remains of the famous battery can still be seen within the hospital grounds. The Citadel remained in use as a military barracks until 1752. St. John's Gate was located on the main roadway, nearby, but no trace of it now remains. The Artillery Barracks in the Irishtown was adapted for 6 officers, 194 men, and 104 horses with an hospital for 35 patients in 1837. (This is a reference Lewis made to the Mulgrave Street Hospital which was built in 1804).

St. John's Hospital, or the Fever Hospital of St. John's, was originally known as the Fever and Lock Hospital, John Street. In 1781 Lady Hartstonge obtained the use of the old St. John's Barracks. She set up two or three beds, and the hospital developed from this meagre beginning. The old buildings were demolished in 1787 and a new structure, from which the present building evolved was built on the site. The new entrance building was officially opened by Michael Noonan, T.D., Minister for Health, in December 1996. A commemorative tablet, behind the reception desk, is inscribed:

> The hospital was founded in 1780 by Lady Lucy Hartstonge who at her own expense fitted out the old Guard House of the Citadel to cater for patients. The little Company of Mary, founded by Mary Potter in 1877, began its association with the hospital in 1888. Since then the Little Company of Mary Sisters have tended the sick with "maternal care"
>
> These two sections of the original stone walls have been exposed to mark the hospital's origins and history.
>
> December 1996

Lady Hartstonge died in 1793 but the work she had started continued. Dr.

St. John's Hospital, at the turn of the last century . Limerick City Museum.

Sylvester O'Halloran was a visiting surgeon here, up to 1806 Dr. Samuel Crump (1767-1796) died of typhus he contracted from a patient, the foundress's husband, Sir Henry Hartstonge, died in 1796 and the Rev. Averill Hill succeeded the Hartstonges as the hospital's chief patron. Bishop E.T.O'Dwyer tried to evict the Little Company of Mary sisters from the hospital in 1891 and 1897 but eventually allowed them to remain. St. John's was the first fever hospital, founded as such, in the old British Empire.

Garryowen Road derives its name from *Garrdha Eoin*, Owen's garden, Owen or Eoin being a hibernicisation of John. The John in question was St. John and his garden was the garth or precinct of the original St. John's Church. This was more extensive than the site now enclosed by the walls around the old Protestant church and was known as St. John's Acre in 1659.

Mungret Street derived its name from Mungret Gate, the gateway which guarded the entry into the city from the Mungret direction. The large market areas of the 1500s, 1600s and 1700s seem to have been located in the vicinity of John's Gate and Mungret Gate, where several major roads converged on the walled city. *Slighe Dhala Meic Umhoir,* the road of Dala, son of Umhoir, linked Limerick with Tara in prehistoric times and during the medieval period one could pass through these gates and travel to Cork and Dublin or to nearer places like Adare, Kilmallock or Mungret. One had to pass through the Irishtown and

Garryowen.

*GARRYOWEN, AT THE TURN OF THE LAST CENTURY. **Limerick City Museum.***

Englishtown, over Baal's Bridge and Thomond Bridge, before travelling on to Ennis or Galway.

Séan Ó Tuama an Ghrinn (1706 or 1708-1775) was a hospitable publican in Croom and Limerick City, as well as a poet who earned himself the sobriquet of *an Ghrinn*, the wit or humorous. In his heyday he presided over many assemblies of his fellow-poets in Limerick and Croom. He kept a tavern at Mungret Gate, but also organised a gathering of his fellow-poets, or *filí*, at Croom to commemorate the death of one of their number, Séan Clarach MacDomhnaill (1681-1754). These poets formed their own court of poetry and became known as the Maigue Poets, named after the river that flows through Croom. This body continued to meet at intervals over the succeeding years. These poets enjoyed life, wine, women and song. They were savage satirists, wrote Jacobite songs, mourned lost wars, loves and possessions, composed verses on every subject under the sun, and, according to folklore and the most popular theorising, the verse form, the Limerick, is named after them.

The Limerick is described as a nonsense verse in a five-line stanza, said to have originated from an eighteenth-century ale-house chorus or refrain, *Will You Come Up to Limerick*. Limericks are characterised by the most outrageous puns and simple but fantastic rhyming;

CERTIFICATE OF MEMBERSHIP, HELD BY A MEMBER OF THE CONFRATERNITY OF THE HOLY FAMILY, ST. JOHN'S CATHEDRAL. Limerick City Museum.

The Limerick packs laughs anatomical
In to space that's quite economical.
But the best ones I've seen
So seldom are clean
And the clean ones so seldom are comical

The humour can vary from subtle wit to the coarsest of crude earthiness. No subject seems to have escaped the Limerick composer's attention, and the verse has been handled, and mishandled, by various poets, would-be-poets, entertainers and satirists, over the centuries.

The Irish Brigade are also supposed to have been adept in the composition of Limericks. This form of poetry is as popular today as it may have been during the seventeenth century when, according to tradition, Jacobite soldiers amused themselves with nonsense verses as the city of Limerick lay under siege. After the treaty of Limerick these men of the Irish Brigade were dispersed throughout Europe, and further afield, as mercenary soldiers, the Wild Geese. They took their verse-form with them;

The Limerick form is complex
Its contents run chiefly to sex.
It burgeons with vergeons
And masculine urgeons
And swarms with erotic effects.

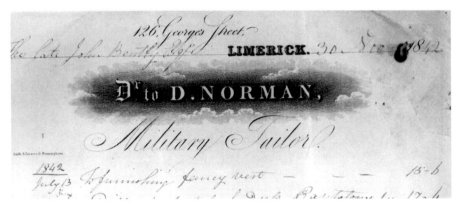

D. Norman was a military tailor at 126 George's Street in 1842. Limerick City was an important military centre in nineteenth century Ireland.

Séan Ó Tuama devoted most of his attention to poetry but was also extremely concerned about the encroachment of the English language. During his lifetime English replaced Irish as the everyday language in areas that had been Irish-speaking in his youth. His open-handed hospitality eventually ruined him, as he kept open house and entertained many penniless *filí*. James Clarence Mangan (1803-1849) translated some of the work of the Maigue poets into English, including Séan Ó Tuama's lament as an inn-keeper, and Aindrias MacCraith's reply;

I sell the best brandy and sherry
to make my good customers merry,
But at times their finances
Run short as it chances
And then I feel very sad, very.

MacCraith thought that this Limerick was aimed at himself and rejoined with;

O Tuomy! You boast yourself handy

At selling good ale and bright brandy,
But the fact is your liquor
Makes everyone sicker,
I tell you that, I your friend, Andy.

Séan Ó Tuama died in 1775 and was buried in the old churchyard of Croom.

Garryowen, *Garraí* or *Gardín Eoghain*, Owen's garden was a favourite resort of the citizens from the mid-eighteenth century until well into the nineteenth century. The original Garryowen was located outside the city walls east of the Citadel. The Garryowen Boys were the sons of Limerick's wealthy merchants who formed a gang of that name. They specialised in smashing street lamps, rattling door knockers and baiting the night watchmen. Their exploits were celebrated in the Bard of Thomond's *Drunken Thady and the Bishop's Lady* and in *Garryowen in Glory*, another epic work written by an unknown poet. Harry O'Brien and Johnny O'Connell were the ring leaders of this wild bunch.

For Johnny Connell, the dreaded man,
With his wild-raking Garryowen clan,
Cleared the streets and smashed each lamp,
And made the watchmen all decamp!

THE GARRYOWEN BREWERY FOUNDATION STONE GIVES
DETAILS OF ITS ESTABLISHMENT IN 1780.
Limerick City Museum.

Johnny later became a prominent member of the city's business community and donated a site at Baker Place to the Dominicans who erected their church on it. He lent them £500, at no interest, in order to pay debts on their new church. The Earl of Limerick leased the ground to the order. Johnny's father, John O'Connell, founded a brewery in 1780 on a site between Green Hill Road and Mulgrave Street. This closed down in 1881. The inscribed foundation-stone from the old brewery is in the Limerick Museum but the site itself was built over, in succeeding years, with rows of houses, Grattan Villas, 1899, Garryowen Villas, 1897; Geraldine Villas, 1899; and Fairview Terrace in 1905. Soldiers from the Strand and Artillery barracks occupied these houses. The nearby Sarsfield Avenue was the first local housing venture carried out by the Irish Free State. Johnny O'Connell was buried in Donoghmore graveyard.

Garryowen in Glory was set to music, with a rousing martial air and was 'exported' to America during the American Revolution of the 1770s. It was played by the First New York Regiment on the march to Quebec in 1775; became the original regimental march of the First Battalion (83rd foot) Royal Ulster Rifles; and was played by the 28th Gloucestershire Regiment on the field of Waterloo. The 18th Royal Irish Rifles and the 18th Foot also adopted *Garryowen in Glory* as their regimental march, as did the 69th New York Regiment, the Fighting 69th, during the 1860s. The Sioux Indians called it *Devil's Music* because it was played by the Seventh U.S. Cavalry who also had the words *Garry Owen* inscribed on their regimental shield. Several Limerick men were killed at the Battle of the Little Big Horn in 1876 when General Custer was defeated by Chief Sitting Bull.

The Garryowen Kick was described by Des Harty as a ploy, also known as the *up and under*, which originated with Limerick's famous Garryowen Rugby Football Club. The Garryowen R.F.C. has played in Australia, New Zealand and South Africa as well as in interprovincial championship games, Munster Senior Cup, Musgrave Cup, Munster Shield and Charity Cup matches. They lost their grounds, *Under The Tower*, after the liquidation of the Limerick Markets and they played the last game on their home ground, a Munster final, against University College Cork in 1937.

The Markets' Field was the cradle of the Gaelic Athletic Association long before they moved to their main grounds on the Ennis Road. In September 1888 the first great Gaelic sports were held here under the rules of the G.A.A. and I.C.A.

Greyhound Racing is held in the Markets' Field on Monday, Thursday and Saturday nights. The greyhound was originally bred as a hunting dog and was known as a *mílchu* to the ancient Irish. This was a term applied to all hunting hounds whether they were greyhounds, wolfhounds, or any other breed used for that purpose. A ninth-century book, *Cormac's Glossary*, mentioned how greyhounds, and coursing contests, could be found at every *aonach*, or fair. The ninth-century record is the earliest written account of greyhounds. Tradition folklore and legend associate them with the *Fianna* and other mythical and legendary figures of an earlier time. The greyhound stadium in the Markets' Field is under the auspices of *Bord na gCon*, The Irish Greyhound Board, which has its office in 104 Henry Street.

St. Laurence's Church was located near the old county hospital on what is now Mulgrave Street. By 1827 Fitzgerald could find no vestige of it.

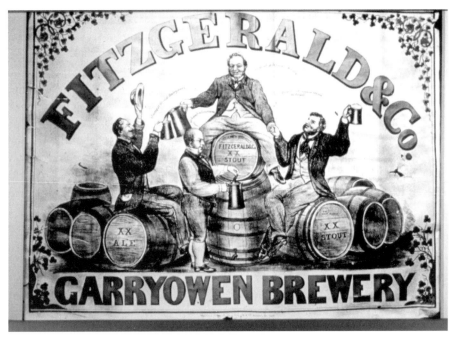

*FITZGERALD'S GARRYOWEN BREWERY ADVERTISED THEIR BUSINESS WITH POSTERS SUCH AS THIS. THE VIKINGS INTRODUCED THE ART OF BREWING BEER TO THE CITY. **Limerick City Museum.***

Garryowen Porter had to compete for business with the Guinness Brewery in the 1870s. On 15 October, 1872, John Cronin proposed at a meeting of the guardians of the Limerick Union that "the resolution ordering that Guinness's porter be supplied to the house be rescinded" as Garryowen porter could be supplied instead. His proposal was seconded by the mayor, John Watson Mahony, who stated that the "Garryowen porter was supplied to the lunatic asylum for a long time past and not a single complaint was made against it." Alderman Myles supported the motion and quoted a Dr. Cameron, who had certified that the local product was unadulterated and good. Lord Clarina objected to this motion on the grounds that they, the guardians, "were not there to protect local trade, but to protect the poor and the rate-payers. They were aware that Guinness's was the best porter in the world and he believed that the medical officers were in favour of continuing it in the hospital". The original motion was carried at the meeting, but it is doubtful if it was ever implemented.

Porter, or stout, was first brewed in 1722 by Ralph Harwood in London. Roasted barley gave it its distinctive dark colouring, and its name was derived from the London porters with whom it had soon become a popular beverage.

Thaddeus O'Malley (1796-1877) was born in Garryowen. He became a Catholic priest in 1819, worked in an American parish until 1827 and then returned to Ireland. He was opposed to Daniel O'Connell and published a series of letters on the advantages of the Poor Law which divided Ireland into 130 unions or administrative districts, centred on market towns or cities where union houses, meaning work houses, were built. He also favoured a system of national education that brought him into conflict with Archbishop John MacHale (1791-1881) of Tuam. The government appointed him rector of the Catholic University of Malta but he was dismissed when he proved unwilling to submit to Protestant laymen in matters of ecclesiastical interest. He returned to Ireland in 1845, started two newspapers, *The Social Economist* and *The Federalist* in support of his views and tried to heal the rift between the O'Connell Party and Young Ireland. He retired from public life when he failed to achieve his ambitions and lived as a recluse in Dublin for over twenty years. He came out of retirement in 1870 to support the Home Rule Movement but fell foul of his superiors when he wrote a book, *Harmony in Religion*, which advocated reforms in the Catholic Church. In 1873 he wrote a pamphlet, *Home Rule on the Basis of Federalism*, which went into several editions. He is buried in Glasnevin Cemetery, Dublin.

Seán South (1930-1957), of Garryowen, was a fervent Catholic who established a branch of *Maria Duce* in the city during the early 1950s. He is best remembered in song and in story, as a Republican hero killed during an abortive paramilitary raid on an R.U.C. barracks, at Brookeborough, County Fermanagh. Lord mayors, county and urban councillors, city corporation members and Catholic clergy from all over Ireland extended sympathy to his family and friends at the time of his funeral. During his brief paramilitary career Seán South, or Sabhat, had visited many of the R.U.C. barracks along the border to assess their armaments. In Brookeborough he had seen only pistols and sten-guns in the R.U.C. arsenal, which was on open display, so he did not realise that a bren-gun was kept in the married quarters, upstairs. Seán advised his comrades to use a county council lorry, which sten-gun bullets would not penetrate, for their raid. As the truck pulled up opposite the barracks the sergeant realised what was happening and opened fire with the bren-gun, the bullets of which "tore through the truck as if it were made of paper." Seán South's last words were, "They've got a bren-gun", as its bullets literally cut him in two. Several of the Republicans were wounded. Fergal O'Hanlon bled to death from a wound in his thigh, but some of his companions were luckier and received competent medical treatment.

LAND LEAGUE DEMONSTRATIONS, SUCH AS THIS ONE IN NOVEMBER, 1880, EXPRESSED THE TENANT- FARMERS'
DISCONTENT. THE SOCIETY WAS FORMED IN 1879 AND ITS PRIMARY AIM WAS TO SECURE THE THREE F'S, FAIR
RENT, FAIR SALE, AND FIXITY OF TENURE. **The Graphic.**

Maria Duce was a right-wing Catholic association founded by Fr. Denis Fahey of the Holy Ghost Missionary Order in the early 1930s and Seán South was one of its most active members in the city. He wrote under a series of pen names, was anti-Protestant, anti-Jewish, anti-Communist, anti-Socialist and anti-cinema,and equated Irish nationalism with Roman Catholicism. If he had been imprisoned, rather than killed, it may have altered his outlook, as a prison term either makes or breaks a Republican. Seán South received his initial military training legally as a member of the Local Defence Force and its auxiliary branch, Forsaí Cosanta Áitiuil, which replaced it after the Emergency.

Hay and Straw Markets were held on Wednesdays and Saturdays in 1837. The large wheat market had sheds all around its enclosure and the butter market, a spacious and lofty building, was opened daily throughout the year. There were two potato markets, one in the Englishtown, the other in the Irishtown, as well as two meat markets, plentifully supplied with butchers' meat and poultry, but the supply of fish and vegetables was often deficient. The smaller of these markets, called the Northumberland Buildings, had attached to it large apartments for public buildings, a bazaar, and commercial chambers. Four annual fairs were held in the city on Easter Tuesday, 4 July, 4 August and 12 December. The August Fair carried a curious privilege as no person could be

MARKET DAY 1910, WITH CORNMARKET ROW IN BACKGROUND. STEREO-TRAVEL CO., CORONA, NEW YORK

arrested in the city or Liberties on a process issued out of the Tholsel Court for fifteen days after it.

The Lane names of the Irishtown are all but forgotten as so many of these old thoroughfares have disappeared over the years with their histories unrecorded. The following list includes only their names, not their locations: Scabby Lane, Mass Lane, Scott's Lane, Bushy Lane, Goat's Lane, William's Lane, Ball Alley Lane, Monaghan Lane, Father Quin Lane, Sheehy Lane, Garvey's Lane, Black Bull Lane, Town Wall Lane, Jones's Lane, Magdalen Lane, Moloney Lane, Curry Lane, Barrack Lane, Hatter's Lane, Pencil's Alley, Purcell's Alley, Joshua's Lane, Moore's Lane, Repeal Alley, Forker's Lane and White Wine Lane.

John's Square is a three sided "square" facing St. John's churchyard. It dates back to 1751, prior to the formation of Newtownpery, and was one of the city's earliest Georgian developments. John Purdon of Tinerana may have been the entrepreneur who thought up John's Square, but Davis Ducart is generally believed to have been its architect. The houses were sold for £630 each, and proved to be a popular investment with county families such as the Perys, Vere

*JOHN'S SQUARE, AT THE TURN OF THE LAST CENTURY - **Limerick City Museum.***

Hunts and Monsells who purchased townhouses here in which they could while away the winter months. The square was restored in the 1970s. Two of the restored houses still contain part of the Limerick Museum, founded in 1916, which was transferred here in 1979.

The Former Church of Ireland Rectory, number three, is easily identified because of its elaborate doorway, with composite pillars and a fanlight, which was modelled on these doorways favoured by the builders of Newtownpery. Canon Frederick Langbridge (1849-1922), a former rector of St. John's Parish, lived here. His daughter, Rosamund, was the authoress of three novels, *The Flame and the Flood* (1908), *Land of the Ever Young* (1920) and the *Green Banks of Shannon* (1929).

St. John's Church of Ireland Church stands on the site of an earlier one dating from about 1200. Thomas Dineley sketched the older building in 1680. A Latin-inscribed plaque in the churchyard wall makes only a passing reference to the damage caused by the Williamite sieges as it reads in translation; "John Forde being mayor and promoter of this work the parishioners of St. John of the Holy Cross after the havoc of the war procured the building of these walls of the cemetery at their own expense AD 1693. John Paterson, vicar; Edward Uncles and Robert Kemp, churchwardens; and John Barry, Sculptor." In 1843 John Norris Russell laid a stone to commemorate repairs to the older church. The present structure was built in 1851 and 1852. It was consecrated on 24 June, 1852, during J. N. Russell's term of office as sheriff. This was designed in the popular round-arched Anglo-Norman style church architecture of the period by Joseph Welland (1798-1860). The church fell into disuse in the early 1970s and was handed over to Limerick Corporation in 1975. . A folk tale of the area claims that Brian Merriman may have been buried here. Even though this story has been discounted by some Limerick historians it would have made economic sense. Brian Merriman (c.1747-1805)

St. John's Church of Ireland Church, built within the city walls.

was a poet best remembered for his satirical *Cúirt an Mheán Oíche (The Midnight Court)*. He moved to Limerick City soon after his marriage in 1790; became a teacher of mathematics in a local school; and died at his home in Old Clare Street, on 29 July, 1805. His widow, Catherine, may have had him buried here, rather than in Feakle.

St. John's Roman Catholic Church was a commodious edifice built in the form of a cross and completed in 1753. Between 1856 and 1861 a new Gothic-Revival-style cathedral was erected to replace the old eighteenth-century one. Philip Charles Hardwick (1820-1890) was the architect responsible for this building. The design of the tower with its 296-foot high spire, however, was the work of two Limerick men, Maurice and S. Hennessy. The tower has a base of twenty four feet square, tapers into an octagonal spire at a height of 163 feet, and the 136 feet of the spire is composed of chiselled ashlar work. Limestone for the tower was quarried at the Rosbrien quarries and a local mason, named Frank Clohessy, topped the spire. A galvanised iron cross, seventeen feet high and weighing seven cwt. (784 pounds), was hoisted into position on Thursday, 27 September, 1882. There was a storm on the following Saturday night and just before eleven Mass on Sunday morning the cross and seventeen feet of solid masonry crashed to the ground with some pieces falling through the cathedral roof. A new cross was placed on the repaired spire on 3 August, 1883 and the height of the spire, from the base of the tower to the top of the cross, is 308 feet and 3 inches. The building was consecrated by Cardinal Logue in July, 1894.

The Arthur Crucifix was made to house a fragment of the true cross for Bishop Arthur in 1625. The maker, Phi Lyles (possibly Philip Lyles) seems to have had an earlier cross of about 1400 from which the figured plating on the stem was derived. Laurence Walsh wrote;

> The front of the cross bears repeated scenes of the *Nativity* and the *Flight into Egypt*, in Gothic style, out of keeping with a 1625 date. The technique of manufacture appears superficially to be repousse on thin plates which would be fixed to a wooden core, but the cross is actually formed of thick cast plates held by screws. The scenes on the cross are obscured by the seventeenth-century settings of the relic, in the form of a cross above, the figure of Christ, the skull and crossbones and

ST. JOHN'S CATHEDRAL, IN THE EARLY 1950s.
Limerick City Museum.

the jewels. The settings of the jewels on the pedestal are identical to those on the O'Dea mitre, and could be products of the same workshop. The central setting of the pedestal front bears the Arms of France, ancient, which dates from the fourteenth of early fifteenth century. The craftsman appears to have had an early cross from which he made a mould, and re-used the jewel settings from it"

The Arthur Crucifix and the Arthur Chalice are now on display in the Hunt Museum, Custom House. *The Virgin and Child* statue was designed by Benzoni. The cathedral's stained-glass widows were installed in the apse by Dr. Butler, the bishop of Limerick, in 1867 and in the transepts by Thomas and Harriet O'Brien

St. John's Cathedral, showing the interior.
Limerick City Museum.

of South Hill, in 1881 to commemorate "their dear friend, Dr. George Butler".

Patrick Sarsfield (1644-1693), the product of a French military academy, commanded by virtue of his bloodline rather than his considerable ability as a soldier. The late Yann Philippe Mac Bradai explained to me how Patrick Sarsfield, Lord Lucan, was descended from the royal houses of both Ireland and England. Through Lady Margaret Butler, the grandmother of Rory O Moore (1641), he was related to the Boleyns and the Ormondes and was a cousin of Black Thomas Butler - the man Queen Elizabeth I called "My black husband", and by whom she was nebulously believed to have had an illegitimate son. Diana Spencer, the late wife of England's crown prince, Charles, was a descendant of Patrick

The Sarsfield Monument. Limerick City Museum.

Sarsfield's brother, William. Sarah Ferguson, the former wife of Prince Andrew, is a descendant of William Sarsfield's in-laws, the Monmouths. Both ladies are descended, illegitimately, from the house of Stuart. Patrick Sarsfield, like many other men of his time, was a Catholic in Ireland and a Protestant in England. He had a distinguished military career in England, Ireland and France. Today he is commemorated with a statue designed by John Lawlor of Dublin, cast in Young's London Art Foundry, and placed in the garden of St. John's presbytery in1881.

The Cathedral Fountain was erected in Cathedral Square by the Pery and Jubilee Committee in 1865. Iron goblets were attached to two of its spouts to provide on the spot drinking facilities for the public at large and help them to fill small containers easily, while larger vessels were filled at the other two spouts.

The Old Dispensary, in Lower Gerald Griffin Street, has been repaired and restored by the Jehovah's Witnesses who now use it as a kingdom hall for their local congregation. This large red-brick building is similar in design to other such structures erected in the late-nineteenth century. The Jehovah's Witnesses had a turbulent history in Ireland throughout the 1940s and 1950s. In 1956 a Limerick newspaper appealed to its readership to have nothing to do with the Witnesses or "their propaganda and to refuse firmly to enter into any discussions with them. Any copies of their publications which readers may have acquired should be destroyed immediately. So strongly does the church wish us to shun their evil doctrines that any Catholic who reads publications of the Society leaves himself open to excommunication". By May 1987 there were 2,661 Jehovah's Witnesses in Ireland.

Charles Etienne Coquebert De Montbret enjoyed his visit to Limerick in 1790, particularly the fresh salmon which fetched from two and a half new pence to five new pence a pound during the winter, but could be purchased for less than one new penny in the summer. Fish was procured from the Shannon by the inhabitants of west Clare and north Kerry who fished in, and off, the mouth of the river, and by the native fisherfolk of the city who fished for trout, eels, perch and pike. The corporation leased a salmon-fishery while, farther down-river, all kinds of shell and flat fish were caught along the neighbouring coasts. In May of each year numerous temporary causeways were formed several yards into the river on each side, by the poor, on which they fished with nets for eel-fry; the quantities taken were so great that each individual filled a couple of washing tubs with them at every tide. The corporation still claimed an exclusive right to all fishing from the city to Scattery Island. Limerick remained prone to flooding, and storms accompanied by high tides did great damage in 1698 and 1751. Charles Etienne enjoyed his visit here although he recorded that the city's upper class "eat and drink too much, wasting their time". He found the company convivial, claimed he had never met so many men of learning in such a short period, and was delighted to discover so many of them spoke French. While staying here he often visited Ralph Ousley's house where a collection of newspapers from all over the world, and a wide range of archaeological artefacts, were stored.

The Palmerstown Brewery was located in an area enclosed by Mungret Street, Palmerstown, Old Francis Street and Benson's Lane. After its demolition the site became a scrap-yard until the Seán Heuston housing scheme was built there. St. Mary's Park was used for the re-housing of people from the area uprooted during the slum clearances of the 1930s. Part of the old Palmerstown brewery site was later occupied by Newsom's Ltd. St. John's Brewery was located where St. John's Girls' School now stands while Miss Tucker's Brewery was situated in a building behind No. 5 North John's Square. In 1820 there were twenty tanneries and one pawnbroker in the city but by 1865 there were only two tanneries, over twenty pawnbrokers, and three breweries.

Chalk Sunday took its name from an old custom, no longer practised, of children putting chalk marks on the backs of bachelors who were unwed by the first Sunday in Lent. Clampett's Bow, a narrow laneway off John Street, was the scene of a minor siege on Chalk Sunday night, 2 March, 1879, when John Moran, his two daughters, and a man named Halloran resisted constabulary attempts to arrest them for an assault which was sparked off by a chalking incident.

Clay pipes were manufactured in Merrit's factory in Broad Street which employed over twenty Merrit relations in the process. Clay for the pipes was imported twice a year, in fifty-ton cargoes, from Liverpool.

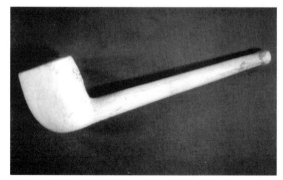

A CLAY PIPE MANUFACTURED BY KIVLIHAN OF LIMERICK.
Limerick City Museum.

The Fortifications were restored after the siege of 1691. For over sixty years afterwards the walls, defensive structures and gate-towers were kept in complete repair. A garrison and several companies of city militia maintained a strong army presence and every precaution of an important military station was observed. In 1760, Limerick was declared to be no longer a fortress, and the dismantling of its walls and other defences was immediately commenced and completed slowly by degrees, as the extension of the various improvements rendered necessary.

Troy's Lock is a short distance upstream from Lock Quay. The nearby hump-backed canal bridge had its pronounced shape flattened in recent times to allow modern vehicles to use it but the old walls were retained. Paddy's Hedge, a popular boreen used by courting couples, has almost vanished, but its route can still be discerned west of the ruined keeper's house.

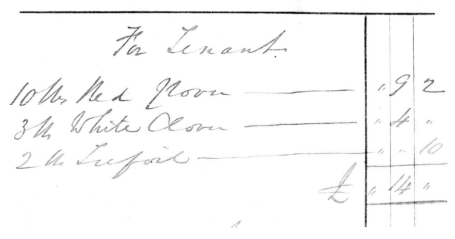

John Abraham and Sons were nurserymen, seedsmen and florists at 8 George Street, next door to Cruise's Hotel, in 1844.

The Canal Brewery was built on the north bank of the canal in 1814 by the firm Walker and Company of Cork, at a cost of £25,000. Despite its location it never prospered and closed after a brief period, some time after 1824.

Clare Street backed onto the walls of the Irishtown and derived its place-name from the notorious Black Jack Fitzgibbon (1749-1802), Earl of Clare, a lawyer and politician. He was born in Donnybrook, Dublin, and was the first native lord chancellor in almost one hundred years. Henry O'Sullivan, a tobacco merchant, constructed this street on the swampy lands of Mona Muckey, an anglicisation of *Móin na Muice*, the moor or common of the pigs. He dedicated his new street to Black Jack, or John, Fitzgibbon who was created Viscount and Earl of Clare in 1795.

The Annaghbeg Ford, over a mile above Athlunkard Bridge, may have been the earliest crossing point over the Shannon. As such, it would have been utilised by Vikings and Irish alike even though it was considered a rapid and dangerous ford. In 1690 the Williamites used it when its water level had dropped to its lowest point in years.

Athlunklard Bridge was designed by the Pain brothers. Work on the five large elliptic arches was started in 1826 and completed at a cost of £16,000 in 1830.

The Long Can owes its name to Joseph Lancaster, a London-born Quaker, who established a non-sectarian school here about 1806. In 1827 forty children of both sexes were educated in the Lancastrian School which was located behind what was the chapel of the Good Shepherd Convent in Clare Street. Mary Anne Walshe sold pigs' toes, *crubeens*, at one end of the Long Can for fifty years. She announced her retirement by closing the door of her premises and putting up a note, "no more toes" on her window.

The Good Shepherd Convent is built on the site of the old Lancastrian School. As school attendance figures dropped in Joseph Lancaster's school the building gradually fell into disrepair. In November 1821 the Christian Brothers purchased the building for £200, subject to a yearly rent of £20.37. They let part of their garden to Madame De Beligond, superioress of the Good Shepherd Convent, in 1858, at an annual rent of £10. When they left the building in 1888 they sold it to the nuns for £200. The Thomond Brewery, off old Clare Street,

CONVENT OF THE GOOD SHEPHERD, IN OTHER DAYS. Limerick City Museum.

was owned by the Stein family in 1865 and was one of three breweries still operative in the city in that year. It was sold in 1879 and demolished soon afterwards. The Good Shepherd nuns established a girls' reformatory on the site where young women who had become pregnant out of wedlock sometimes endured a harsh existence. The Good Shepherd Laundry was built on the Farrancroghy execution site on which public executions took place during the sixteenth and seventeenth centuries.

VIEW OF LIMERICK AND NEWTOWNPERY, IN 1786, FROM THE WATCH HOUSE ON THE NORTH STRAND. J. FERRAR.

Newtownpery

Newtownpery was developed by Edmond Sexton Pery and the independent citizens of the city in an attempt to break the stranglehold the Roche-Vereker-Smyth-Prendergast clique had acquired over the old municipality. In 1769 Christopher Colles drew up the blueprint for a new town which was brought into being at the instigation of the Pery family who had "more property than the whole of the Ancient and Loyal Corporation". South Prior's Land was their property and extended along the southern bank of the Shannon and the proposed urban development was concentrated in this region. The developers of the new town, called after Edmond Sexten Pery, the principal landowner, moved their businesses, services and residences outside the old municipal boundaries, where the corrupt clique were unable to operate. Two of the major factors that contributed to the growth of the new town were legislation enacted in 1759 lowering the rateable valuation on land outside the city walls, and, secondly, the way in which the citizens of Newtownpery manipulated St. Michael's Vestry in order to circumvent the jurisdiction of the corporation. The new town expanded rapidly. George's Quay was built in 1763. This was followed by the erection of the South Mall (now Charlotte's Quay) in 1766 and Sir Harry's Mall in 1767. The Custom House was erected in 1769 and the Assembly House went up in 1770. All of this earlier development took place on the fringes of the Pery properties, but as Newtownpery expanded new brick residences and shops radically changed the appearance of the city to an extent only equalled by Dublin during the eighteenth century. Maps and aerial photographs illustrate how neatly the broad straight streets cut across one another to form spacious blocks. From the air one can see noticeable differences in the streetscapes of the older and newer parts of the city. The more recent urban renewal, between 1989 and 1997, has complemented the Georgian streetscape. Even the new Shannon Bridge at the far end of Mallow Street slots into the eighteenth-century thoroughfare as if Davis Ducart or Francis Bindon had designed it for Edmond Sexton Pery.

Edmond Sexton Pery (1719-1806) spearheaded the Newtownpery development, the main growth of which was over his own land, when the city walls were demolished. He was a clear-sighted city planner, an astute businessman, and pioneered the Georgian architecture of which Limerick can be so proud. In 1768 he was speaker in the Irish House of Commons, but was raised to the peerage as Viscount Pery, Earl of Limerick, in 1786. His grandfather, Colonel Edward Pery, married Dympna, the daughter of Bartholomew Stacpoole who was a merchant, and recorder of Limerick in 1651 when he signed the capitulation of the city to Cromwell's forces. The present Earl of Limerick, Patrick Sexton Pery, is a businessman now resident in England. He attended the celebrations to commemorate the eighth centenary of the 1197 charter on Friday, 3 October, 1997, along with the lord mayors and mayors of eleven other cities, including those of Belfast, Derry and Dublin.

Denmark Street has been so-named since at least 1770 but as it was outside the walls of both the Englishtown and Irishtown it is unlikely to have had anything to do with the city's earliest settlers, the Danes. Queen Anne (1702-1714), the younger daughter of James II, succeeded to the throne when William III died, after falling from his horse, on 21 February, 1702. It is probably in memory of her husband, Prince George of Denmark, who died in 1708, that the street was named Denmark Street.

St. Michael's Catholic Church, in Denmark Street, opened on 29 September, 1781. Work on the building commenced in 1779. It was enlarged in 1805. This was a large edifice without any external ornamentation, with an adjoining house and garden for the clergymen. Daniel O'Connell held some of his rallies within this church and William Bardwell, the architect, designed a fifteenth-century-style wall memorial for St. Michael's in 1839. Edward Thomas O'Dwyer was the curate here in 1881. At a later stage in his career, when he became bishop of Limerick, he denied responsibility for the demolition of the older St. Michael's which was replaced with the present structure in the early 1880s. This last building was designed by M. Morris who, because of restricted space, was forced to conceal its facade in a small yard off Denmark Street.

Cornmarket Row derived its name from the market buildings which were built outside the walls of the old city. All of the row was demolished in January, 1998, to make way for a new complex. The market is inside the line of the walls, the buildings opposite outside.

The Record Printing Works, at No. 6 Cornmarket Row, published seditious material, *The Bottom Dog* and *The Factionist*, during the War of Independence. The proprietor was usually warned of impending R.I.C. raids by Sergeant McCarthy of Clare Street, who used to give three taps on the window pane

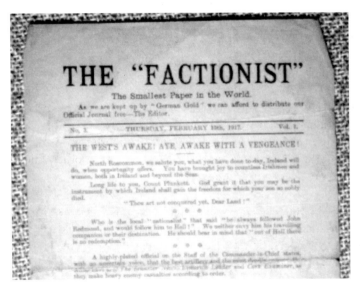

THE FACTIONIST, ISSUED ON 15 FEBRUARY, 1917.
Limerick City Museum.

nearest to the door of the premises. The late Jimmy Flynn had a wholesale hardware store in Cornmarket Row, one in which Tom O'Donnell, of Tom and Pashcal fame, worked.

The Mardyke took its name from a new quay Limerick corporation developed in 1715. Mardyke seems to be a derivative of the Anglo-Saxon term *mere*, a pool or lake, and dyke, an embankment, from the Old Norse of Middle English word *dik*. This includes the area known today as Charlotte Quay and Michael Street. Part of the old city wall can be seen in the Michael Street car-park while a considerable amount of old foundations was revealed, but covered again, during excavations near the north-eastern corner. Ten feet below the surface was a large stone wheel with a toothed edge which was part of an apparatus for drawing up water containers, a twelve-foot length of wooden conduit or piping, old weapons and cannon balls. These finds confirmed that there was a well in use on this site in 1691 when the city was under siege. The well may have been closed because of seepage from St. Michael's graveyard, a short distance away.

St. Michael's Church has been attributed to the Vikings, but it is more likely to have been an Anglo-Norman foundation as the latter people had a great veneration for St. Michael. This church was positioned on a division of the Abbey River, and maps of a later period show its location outside the West Water Gate. Henry Ireton saw this old church in 1651 although other accounts claim it was in ruin by then and had been dismantled before the Cromwellian siege to prevent the soldiery using it as a base from which to attack the West Water Gate. By 1654 the church had disappeared as the civil survey mentioned only a ruined castle and mill seat at *Beall na Corrie* (Ballinacurra), a few thatched cabins, the prior's mill near the churchyard and a few gardens. Today only the graveyard remains. Once again it is an island, this time in a sea of tarmacadam, and new buildings, within the Charlotte Quay area. This is a small neat recently-renovated graveyard containing mainly late-eighteenth century and nineteenth century tombstones, many of which show signs of repair. It is located on the western end of the car-park, near the Granary, and there are entrances to the east and west. Philip Roche was interred here but his memorial has disappeared, as have those of other prominent citizens of the past. The last burial took place here in 1945.

Davis Ducart , known also as Davis Duckart or Davis Duchart, seems to be of Franco-Italian origin. He was born Daviso de Arcort, possibly in Sardinia, and was an architect and engineer in the Sardinian service. His family are most likely to have lived in Italy, either in Piedmont or Sardinia, and he came to Ireland at some date now unknown. He was an engineer on the Newry-Lough Neagh canal, built between 1730 and 1741 and worked on the Tyrone and Boyne Navigation. He delivered a plan and estimate for Mayoralty House (later the Mercy Hospital) by 6 May, 1765, although it was not completed until 1773 and designed a Baroque-Palladian-style house, Kilshannig, County Cork, for Abraham Devonsher in 1765. He started work on what seems to have been the last Palladian-style house in Ireland, Castletown Cox, County Kilkenny, in 1767, for Michael Cox, Archbishop of Cashel. Davis Ducart may have arrived into Limerick at the invitation of Edmond Sexton Pery. He drew up the grid plan for the new town envisaged by his employer as leases of the Pery Estate refer to "a new plan devised by Davis Ducart in 1769". The actual blue print, however, seems to have been completed by Christopher Colles. Davis Ducart had property in Drumlea, County Tyrone; had some connection with canal work and collieries in the same county; and died in either 1784 or 1785. His exact role in the formation of Newtownpery has never been clearly defined, but, with Edmond Sexton Pery, he is generally credited as co-founder of Limerick's Georgian heritage. Newspaper advertising of 1769 extolling the virtues of Newtownpery could almost have been written by an auctioneer of today;

> An extensive view up and down the river, commanding a full prospect of many agreeable objects ... the county Clare mountains ... spacious basin ... shipping ... several Quays and the Pool ... in short the most elegant town residence in the Kingdom, or perhaps in the World, cannot boast such rural beauty or so fine a landscape, and the Variety is daily increasing.

THE FORMER CHURCH OF IRELAND RECTORY IN JOHN'S SQUARE.
Shannon Development Photo Library.

The once-fashionable districts of John's Square, Mungret Street and Quay Lane were gradually deserted by their former occupants. These people moved on to the elevated ground, parallel to the river, which was once known as the South Prior's Land before it became the property of the Pery family. It later became known as Newtownpery.

Christopher Colles (1735-1816) is mentioned in *Ferrar's Limerick Directory* of 1769, as an architect in Main Street, another name for High Street, now both Nicholas Street and Mary Street. Davis Ducart does not appear to have had any architectural of business office within the town. He may have availed of space granted to him by his clients as he appears to have had a roving way of life which meant that he carried only the most basic tools of his trade with him from place to place. Davis Ducart was probably extremely reliant on men such as Christopher Colles who had all the cumbersome equipment needed for the preparation of intricate blueprints, plans and architectural drawings requiring endless detail. This would support the theory that Davis Ducart acted as a consultant, suggested various styles or designs and then had a competent architect or draughtsman commit his (Ducart's) ideas to paper. He may have had an office in, or near, Cork - he would have needed it - as his name has been linked with several buildings in that region, but this is only a remote possibility. Christopher Colles was a native of Kilkenny and had been trained in mathematics, geography, engineering and natural philosophy. In 1761 he was associated with the River Nore Navigation Board and his father, Alderman William Colles, later entered into a contract, on 1 June, 1767, to build a canal from Maidenhall to Thomastown. William Colles owned mills and a marble works but died before he could complete his contract. Christopher Colles emigrated to America, soon afterwards. He advertised as a specialist in hydraulics, land surveying and canal building, and as a teacher of mathematics, in *The Pennsylvania Chronicle* of 26 August, 1771. He lived in Philadelphia for a while, before moving to New York, where he was resident in 1774. In 1769 Christopher Colles was the only architect listed in the Limerick directory of that year.

The Granary was built for "an enormous sum" after Philip Roche, son of John Roche, purchased a site on the Mardyke in 1787. Philip was a merchant prince,

THE GRANARY AND MICHAEL STREET DURING THE EARLY 1990s. Shannon Development Photo Library.

an adventurer, a major exporter of flax, cereals and seeds, and one of the most successful businessmen in the south of Ireland. He died in 1797 and was buried nearby in St. Michael's graveyard. His nephew, Thomas Kelly, rented the Granary to the customs authorities as a bonding warehouse for spirits, wines and tobaccos during the nineteenth century. The building remained in use as a bonding warehouse into the 1970s. In 1980 the Shannon Free Airport Development Company bought the Granary from Michael Harkin and re-developed it. Its original structure was retained intact. A concrete-framed office wing, a hanging garden and a water fountain were added, while the old edifice and the new were linked by a glass-enclosed service area which houses the main staircase. Within the old Granary two intermediate floors were removed and replaced with a single floor, the windows were renovated and the entire building was re-roofed. Today's Granary accommodates a range of services including the Limerick City Library and the Limerick Regional Archives.

ARTHUR QUAY PARK, BUILT ON WHAT WAS ONCE PART OF THE OLD CITY HARBOUR.
Shannon Development Photo Library.

The Limerick Regional Archives are located within the Granary. This office offers a comprehensive genealogical research service to people whose ancestors emigrated from either the city or county of Limerick. Copies of all extant pre-twentieth century church records, Roman Catholic, Church of Ireland, Presbyterian, Methodist and Quaker, are housed here. Land surveys from about 1830 to 1850 are used to place families accurately in the townland they lived in, while the 1901 Census is available to check if any members of the family remained in the area.

Rutland Street derives its name from Charles Manners (1754-1787), Fourth Earl of Rutland. He was appointed Lord Lieutenant of Ireland in 1784 and visited Limerick In 1785.

*VIEW OF RUTLAND STREET FROM ST. MARY'S CATHEDRAL, **Limerick City Museum.***

The Former City Hall was originally known as the Commercial Buildings, and was erected for £8,000 by the Mercantile Body (incorporated as the Chamber of Commerce in 1815) in 1805. Its building was funded by more than 100 shares of £65 each and it had one of the most spacious and elegant coffee rooms in Ireland, a large well supplied newsroom and apartments for those of the Chamber of Commerce. The Chamber moved to their present premises in O'Connell Street, in 1833 and their former premises was allowed to deteriorate, being used as a sugar store and printing house, until taken over by the Reformed Corporation in 1846.

The Limerick Chamber of Commerce was incorporated by Royal Charter in 1815 to protect the city's trade and control the pilotage of the Shannon River. Their funds were financed with fees paid by their members on the import and export of goods, while surplus money was used to promote Limerick's commercial interests, develop markets, aid manufacturers, improve navigation, maintain buoys to warn shipping of hazards, and pay for salvage services. Under an act passed in 1834 the president of the chamber of commerce, the mayor, and a commissioner of St. Michael's Parish were appointed as Limerick Bridge

Commissioners. In January 1983 the chamber of commerce minute books were transferred into the care of Dr. O'Mahony of the Mid West Archives, now the Limerick Regional Archives.

THE HUNT MUSEUM, IN RUTLAND STREET, Hunt Museum.

The Custom House is an elegant, Palladian-style building designed by Davis Ducart and finished under the superintendence of Christopher Colles in 1769, at a cost of £8,000. Work commenced on the building in 1765, under the direction of Davis Ducart and by 1769 the new custom house was a busy administrative centre of "His Majesty's Revenue". Customs' duties in 1775 amounted to £51,000 and a total of sixty-seven men, all customs personnel, were based here and on Scattery Island, Kilrush and Tarbert. This was a busy centre from the day it opened, with the comings and goings of the shipping men, boatmen, surveyors, tide-waiters (customs officers who had to wait or attend on the landing of goods), land carriage officers, riding surveyors and coast officers, all under the orders of a collector, the equivalent of today's collector-general. The original building consisted of a hewn-stone centre with two wings facing a small quay-side park where the Abbey River rejoins the Shannon, and replaced an older structure on Merchant's Quay which was described as a plain brick building supported with four rusticated pillars. The custom's duties in 1633 came to a total of £1,619.07, so Limerick could afford to build an imposing custom house from an early period. Such a building could also become a "legitimate target" in wartime. On 3 April, 1920, a group of I.R.A. men under the command of Joe O'Brien set fires in the Custom House in an attempt to set it ablaze. After

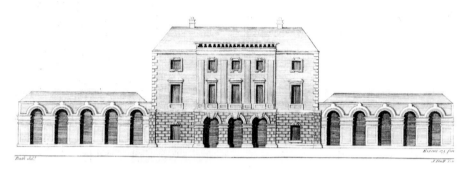

THE CUSTOM HOUSE, OVERLOOKING THE HARBOUR, 1786. J. FERRAR.

they left the premises, civilian and military fire brigades extinguished the flames. The building was located here because of its accessibility to the quays, particularly Merchant's Quay and the city's famous Long Dock. In 1997 the Hunt Museum transferred from its former base in Plassey House and was relocated in the Custom House.

The Hunt Museum is located within the restored and renovated Custom House and in an attractive new building with a matching stone facade. It

A BRONZE FIGURE OF A REARING HORSE, BY LEONARDO DA VINCI, OF THE ITALIAN RENAISSANCE. NOW IN THE HUNT MUSEUM.

contains a selection of items from the Bronze Age, Early Christian period, medieval times and later. It is meaningless to list any of the artefacts in the context of the whole collection but I could not resist doing so in relation to a few. These artefacts include cauldrons, stone axe-heads, Early Christian brooches, a damaged *Síle na gig*, medieval crucifix figures and pottery, the ninth-century Cashel Bell, Irish silver-work, and two glass chamber-pots, one with a lid, which survive from the end of the eighteenth century. These chamber-pots, a nineteenth-century decanter inscribed *"Cannock and Tait"*, and an incomplete drinking glass engraved with a crown and inscribed

An enamelled bronze plaque from thirteenth-century Limoges in France, showing Christ seated, with angels above. On display in the Hunt Museum.

> *"Lord/Arch/Bishop/of/Dublin/1715"*

are the only four items of Irish glass-ware in the museum. The drinking glass may have been made to celebrate the Jacobite defeat in 1715, while the engraved crown may have been a punning symbol based on the Archbishop of Dublin's name, William King. The O'Dea mitre and crozier were made by Thomas O'Carryd in 1418 for Bishop Cornelius O'Dea, bishop of Limerick. They are now on display here, by courtesy of the diocesan trustees, along with items that had been exhibited in Plassey House where the museum had been from 1978 to 1997. The Hunt family had been antique dealers and collectors on a grand scale. Photographs of their homes reveal how John Hunt, Senior, his wife, son and daughter lived with their collection. Eclectic is the only word that describes the way in which the exhibits are displayed; drawers open to reveal almost anything; the rooms are elegant eighteenth-century chambers with twentieth-century comfort; chairs and settees entice one to sit and relax while savouring a view of either the exhibits or nearby River Shannon; and there is a relaxed atmosphere in which one can browse at a leisurely pace. The shop and restaurant are located on the ground floor, on the riverside and there are lecture rooms in the basement and sub-basement. Tony Ryan, chairman of the board of the Hunt Museum, welcomed Frank McCourt onto the board on Monday, 8 December, 1997, stating that his presence would add "extra dimension to the skills of the existing board members".

John Hunt, Senior, was a noted historian, archaeologist, and collector. The Craggaunowen Project in County Clare was his brainchild, and is now an

Apollo - Genius of the Arts, a wooden figure representing all of the trades and activities of seventeenth-century Augsburg in Germany, possibly made for display in a Guild Hall. Now in the Hunt Museum.

important tourist asset. It is located on the shores of a small lake close to a large state forest, outside Kilkishen, and contains a restored tower house-cum-museum, Craggaunowen Castle, replicas of a *crannog*, ring-fort and a *fulacht fiadha* or cooking place, an authentic bronze age trackway and the reconstructed model of St. Brendan's boat in which Tim Severin sailed across the Atlantic.

A Viking Longship, or long boat, was about thirty metres in length; carried a crew of up to one hundred men; was propelled by sail and oar; and could achieve a speed of twenty knots, twenty nautical miles or just overy twenty-three miles an hour. A momument, representing a longships prow, is located next to the museum. It had originally stood in Rutland Street.

Sarsfield House is built on the site of Reuben Harvey's grain-stores and carrier-pigeon terminus. Reuben, the son of Joseph Massey Harvey of Cork, used the birds to communicate between Plassey Mill and his stores and granary in Francis Street. Carrier pigeons were also used by other merchants in the city to keep themselves informed of whatever ships and cargoes were approaching Limerick along the

Gertrude and John Hunt

Shannon, or from outside ports. Reuben Harvey refused to meet his workers' demands for payment for time spent travelling from the canal harbour to the Plassey Mill in his barges, and became one of the earliest city employers to face strike action. The dispute was never resolved and eventually led to the closure of his works. Another milling family, the Dempseys took over his stores and granary and operated their own business there. Their company was registered at London Bridge by 1840. They sold the Limerick site in 1970. Until then they were also the owners of the grounds behind Custom House. The income tax offices were originally located in the centre of O'Connell Street where they were raided by the I.R.A. on the night of 3 April, 1920, under the command of Davy Dundon. Staff were held up, offices ransacked, and mail was taken away for assessment by I.R.A. intelligence officers. The income tax authorities are now based in Sarsfield House.

Bank Place is located near Mathew Bridge, just around the corner form Rutland Street. It derived its name from Maunsell's Bank.

BANK PLACE, EN FETE, PRIOR TO 1928. Limerick City Museum.

Maunsell's Bank was founded by Robert Maunsell (1745-1832), his brother Thomas, and Sir Matthew Blackstone in 1789. Robert was born in Limerick and reared in India where he joined the Indian Civil Service. He became chief of the Council of Gangham and a member of the Supreme Council of Madras before retiring to Limerick where he established the banking firm of Maunsell and Company. When the bank, in Bank Place, failed in 1820, Robert had already withdrawn from it, with the fortune he had made in India still intact.

Bedford Row was named in honour of John Russell (1766-1839), 6th Duke of Bedford, who was Viceroy of Ireland in 1806. His third son, John Russell (1792 - 1878), was a Whig politician who supported Catholic Emancipation and succeeded Robert Peel as prime minister in 1846.

The Primitive Wesleyan Methodist Preaching House was founded in Bedford Row in 1821. This had been built in a Gothic style, with a handsome entrance, an elegant balustrade and apartments for the preacher. Next door to it was the Independent Meeting House. Both have long since closed but their locations can still be traced. The Grand Central Cinema was established in the former preaching house, at a later date.

The Old Maternity Hospital is located on the western corner of Bedford Row and Henry Street. Part of this fine building is now let to various businesses.

Patrick Street derives its name from Patrick Arthur, one of a famous Limerick family long associated with the city and seventeenth-century Ennis.

Cruise's Street derives its name from a famous hotel which was located at the point where the new street joins Patrick Street. This hostelry was known as The

CRUISE'S ROYAL HOTEL CHARGED COUNT DE LA POER THIRTY FIVE PENCE FOR A BEDROOM, MAID- SERVICE, BOOT CLEANING AND BREAKFAST ON THE MORNING OF HIS WEDDING DAY, 1 JUNE, 1881. HE HAD ARRIVED THE PREVIOUS NIGHT, 31 MAY, AND MARRIED MARY OLIVIA AUGUSTA MONSELL, THE DAUGHTER OF LORD EMILY OF TERVCE, THE FOLLOWIGN DAY, J.J. CLEARY WAS THEN THE OWNER OF THE HOTEL.

Royal Mail Coach Hotel, the Bianconi Coach Station or Cruise's Hotel. It was established in 1791 to cater for the expanding stage coach services of the day. In 1828 Prince Herman Ludwig Heinrich von Puckler-Muskav stayed here during his memorable trip to Limerick - in which he was mistaken for an illegitimate son of Napoleon Bonaparte. William Thackeray was a guest here in 1842. He described George's Street as a handsome one:

> with plenty of idlers, you may be sure, lolling in each portico; likewise you see numerous young officers, with very tight waists and absurd brass shell-epaulettes to their absurd little frock coats, walking the pavement - the dandies of the street .. the houses are bright red - the street is full and gay, carriages and cars in plenty go jingling by - dragoons in red are every now and then clattering up the street, and upon every car which passes with ladies in it you are sure (I don't know how it is) to see a pretty one ... After you get out of the Main Street the handsome part of town is at an end, and you suddenly find yourself in such a labyrinth of busy swarming poverty and squalid commerce as never was seen - no not in St. Giles's where Jew and Irishman side by side exhibit their genius for dirt. Here every house almost was half a ruin and swarming with people ...

An old picture of Cruise's Hotel shows a four-horse coach, with roof-passengers and postillions, outside the main entrance to the hotel, beside which an archway leading into the coaching yard could also be seen. In more recent times Seán Bourke, the man responsible for the "springing " of George Blake from an English prison, was a regular customer in the hotel's Round Bar. Seán died while on holiday in Kilkee and the manuscript he was working on has never been found.

GEORGE'S STREET, NOW O'CONNELL STREET, AT THE TURN OF THE LAST CENTURY. **Limerick City Museum.**

O'Connell Street was formerly known as George Street and commemorated George III (1738-1820), according to Maurice Lenihan (1811-1895). The king became insane in 1801, recovered, but lapsed into insanity, again, in 1810 and was unable to function effectively after 1811, his son ruling in his stead, as regent.

Furnell's Limerick Bank was located in a building close to the corner of O'Connell Street and William Street. It was founded by Michael "The Banker" Furnell in 1804 but failed a few years later. Michael was a descendant of Thomas Furnell who arrived into the county during the Confederate wars of the 1640s and established the Furnell name in Ballyclough and Cahirelly. George Evans Bruce founded another bank, Bruce's Bank, at No. 6, Rutland Street in 1806, which also failed, and closed, in 1820.

Roche's Stores was founded by Philip Roche in 1787. As a Catholic he was not permitted to buy land, but by purchasing the ground he required in the name of his friend and kinsman, Dr. Pery, the Church of Ireland bishop of Limerick, he acquired the sites on which he built his stores, a range of houses on the south side of Rutland Street, and another range of houses on the south side of Patrick Street. His religion was no bar to commercial success. He carried on an enormous trade with Holland in rape seed, flax and other materials and was a major supplier of government provisions until his death in 1797.

Alexander Brothers' Corner was once the local name for the corner of O'Connell Street and William Street. It derived its name from the grandsons of

O'CONNELL STREET IN THE 1950s. Limerick City Museum.

Edward Alexander, a prominent Quaker businessman, who had their grocery and ship-chandlery in this location. Edward Alexander opened the original shop in Barrington's Mall. He was succeeded by his son, William, who became involved in the corn business, ploughed his profits into the development of housing on the outskirts of the city and transferred the family business to a new location, the corner of George Street and William Street.

William Todd and Co. occupied about four-fifths of a large city block fronting O'Connell Street with William Street to the north and Thomas Street to the south. On Tuesday, 25 August, 1959, at 11.00 a.m., a fire was first noticed in the Todds' building. The building was in flames within the hour. By 12.30 the block was a blazing inferno and at 1.00 p.m. the army was called in to cordon off the area and assist the firemen. The Limerick Fire Brigade brought the fire under control with the help of the E.S.B. Fire Service, the Ranks Auxiliary Fire Service and outside fire brigades from Ennis, Shannon, Ardnacrusha, Charleville, Rathkeale, Tipperary, Cork and Fermoy. This was the biggest fire disaster in the city since the eight-acre site of MacMahon's timber yard was destroyed by flames in 1906. Todds', Burtons', Liptons', Goodwins' and Cesars' were completely gutted; Gaywear, Cromers' and Nicholas' were badly damaged; and Michael Gleeson's licensed premises and Jack Flanagan's were badly affected when Todd's collapsed across Little William Street.

The Augustinian Church is built on the site of an old theatre which the Augustinian prior purchased for £400 in 1822, although the Limerick Theatre building had originally cost the public £5,000 to construct. After purchasing it

*Augustinian Church, the old Entrance. **Limerick City Museum.***

the Augustinians spent £600 on improving it and the original structure remained in use as a church until 1939. The foundation stone of the present church was laid in March, 1939. Designed and built by two Dublin firms, respectively, Jones and Kelly and George Walsh and Sons, the Augustinian church cost £42,000 to erect. It can hold a congregation of 2,000 and was opened on 20 December, 1942. An inscribed stone on its facade draws attention to an adjoining stone, part of a lintel taken from a chapel the Augustinians had founded in Fish Lane in 1633. In 1778 the Augustinians erected a neat chapel in Creagh Lane where they stayed until 1823. In 1998 an eighteenth-century silver chalice was discovered in a cylinder at the back of a safe behind the main altar of the present church. It had been donated to the Augustinian Sisters in Dublin by Dame Alice Nagle in 1750, according to an engraved inscription.

The Royal George Hotel was once visited by Queen Victoria. Rev. Robert Wyse Jackson, former Church of Ireland bishop of Limerick wrote, in 1973, that;

> in its original form it fitted handsomely into the Georgian facade of O'Connell Street. The last function before it was demolished and rebuilt was one which I organised for the Archbishop of Canterbury, Dr. Ramsey, when he came to Limerick to dedicate a window in St. Mary's Cathedral to the memory of his kinsman, Major Stafford O'Brien of Cratloe.

O'Mahony's Bookshop was founded by John Patrick O'Mahony, as O'Mahony and Company Limited, in 1902. The original shop had a floor space of 450 square feet and sold books, stationery, souvenirs and religious supplies. In 1996 the entire building, with the exception of the facade, was gutted and converted into a retail area of over 10,000 square feet, with basement, and with two floors reserved overhead for office administration. O'Mahony and Company is now the oldest and largest independent bookselling operation in the country, having other shops in Ennis and Tralee.

William Roche's Hanging Gardens were one of the wonders of Limerick in the early 1800s after William Roche erected a series of store-houses behind his house in George's Street for £15,000, in 1808. The gardens were located over the vaulted store-houses, which were protected from the damp by flags cemented together, with channels of lead to draw the moisture away through tubes of the same metal concealed in the arches. The facade of these elevated terraced gardens, the highest of which was seventy feet above the street, was about two-hundred feet in length. The top terrace contained hot-houses in which grapes, pineapples, peaches and oranges were grown; vegetables and hardy fruit trees were produced on the middle terrace; while the lower terrace was turned over to flowers of every form, scent and hue. The government of the day leased the store-houses from William at a fine of £10,000 and at an annual rent of £300 in 1826, a rent which had increased to £500 per annum in 1837. The gardens extended from what is now No. 99 O'Connell Street as far as Henry Street.

The Transport Union Hall on O'Connell Street became the headquarters of the Mid Limerick Brigade of the I.R.A. during the War of Independence. This was "an open secret", as the I.R.A. presence within the building could not be kept from all of the workers who used the place for meetings and other activities. The I.R.A. quarters were located in the attic, access to which was through a cunningly-concealed trap door. In the event of a police or military raid on the premises a bell-push was used to sound an alarm which the I.R.A. staff would heed. Their usual shelter at such times, while the building was being searched by their enemies, was the roof-top, close to the adjoining building where the British Crown solicitor had his office.

The Limerick Chamber of Commerce premises was surveyed by the Irish Architectural Archive in 1984. Located at 96 O'Connell Street, this terraced house, comprising four storeys over a basement, dates from around 1800. The interior has been restored and renewed rather than renovated and many of the original internal features, woodwork and plaster work, are intact. About 1875 the front facade was re-faced in a plaster of lime and fine sand (stucco); the cast-iron balcony was inserted at first-floor level; the gate piers and cast-iron railings were built over the basement area; and the door screen was moved forward towards the front door to form an inside porch when the building was remodelled. The main reception rooms were, and still are, on the first floor. They are connected by the original pair of panelled doors, cleverly designed to slide laterally on castors into wall cavities on either side, creating a spacious opening between both rooms. The

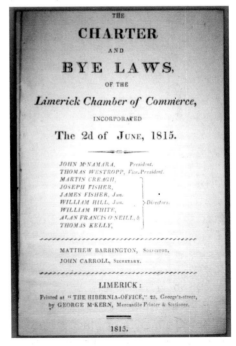

CHARTER AND BYE LAWS OF LIMERICK CHAMBER OF COMMERCE INCORPORATED, 2 JUNE, 1815.
Limerick City Museum

front room was originally the principal drawing room and contains a white statuary marble chimney piece, French-style casement windows, a distinctive plaster ceiling and two oil paintings, one of Sir Alexander Shaw (president of the Limerick Chamber of Commerce, 1899-1905) and another of Lord Monteagle (Member of Parliament for Limerick 1820-1832). The first floor rear room contains its original tripartite Wyatt window and a fine Irish breakfront bookcase of mahogany dating from circa 1830. The rear facade is virtually unaltered except for the addition of a ground-floor wing containing service rooms and toilets. The former coach-house has been modified to provide vehicular access to parking in the former garden which is now metalled over. A dovecote on the wall, facing the rear of the house, has been retained. The Limerick Chamber of Commerce has occupied this building since they left their former premises in Rutland Street over a century and a half ago. The organisation's proudest possession is a painting *The Chairing of Thomas Spring Rice* (1820) which was executed in oils by William Turner of London. This picture was last restored by James Gorry in 1945. The Limerick Harbour Commissioners had the ground floor of this building before their move to Pery Square.

The Belltable Arts Centre is located in a building now owned by the Arch Confraternity Credit Union who accept only a nominal rent from their tenants. The Gough family were the original owners during the last century. When one of the Gough daughters demonstrated that she might have enough talent for a career as an opera singer, her indulgent father, a prominent building contractor, had the Belltable erected in the garden. The acoustics were, and still are, excellent. It became the Coliseum Cinema from the silent-film era until its closure in the early 1950s. On occasion its patrons amused themselves by tossing *crubeens* (pigs' toes or trotters) from the balcony into the stalls. This former opera-house cum-cinema was opened as the Belltable Arts Centre on 21 April, 1981. Its small theatre is known as Peter's Cell, after an older theatre of the same name [Peter's Cell].

Thomas Blake (1894-1921) worked in Laird's Pharmacy on O'Connell Street. His knowledge of chemistry helped him to direct and assist in the manufacture of munitions and explosives. He lived at No. 1, St. Alphonsus Avenue, with his two brothers. All three were members of the Irish Volunteers. On Friday, 28 January, 1921, his bullet-riddled body was found on the city's Clyde Road, (now St. Alphonsus St.). His funeral took place the following Sunday at Shanavoher, Croom. The burial was marred by disturbances. The Crown forces attacked the mourners during the interment and another Volunteer, Paddy O'Halloran, died a few days later from injuries received at the funeral.

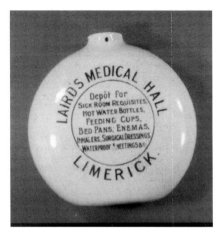

LAIRD'S MEDICAL HALL MANUFACTURED HOT WATER FLASKS (OR BOTTLES) SUCH AS THIS.
Limerick City Museum.

The Crescent was formerly known as Richmond Place and derived its name from Charles Lennox (1764-1819), Fourth Duke of Richmond. He was lord lieutenant of Ireland in 1807 and 1813 and died in Montreal, as governor-general of Canada. It was also called Richmond Crescent and is sometimes referred to as O'Connell Crescent, in honour of Daniel O'Connell (1775-1847)

The Daniel O'Connell Statue was erected in The Crescent during Dr. Thomas Kane's second term of office as mayor in 1857. Originally £1,040 had been subscribed to erect a statue of Viscount Fitzgibbon on this site, but when five members of the corporation objected, the idea was abandoned and the O'Connell monument, sculpted by John Hogan, was placed on its present site at a total cost of

O'Connell Statue, Limerick

THE O'CONNELL MONUMENT. Limerick City Museum.

211

£1,300. Daniel O'Connell (1775-1847), known as the Liberator, or the King of the Beggars, is generally credited with achieving religious freedom for the Catholic majority.

Crescent House was purchased from Richard Russell by the Jesuits, who also acquired the adjoining houses, in order to erect a new church dedicated to St. Aloysius on the site.

The Jesuit Church was dedicated to the Sacred Heart rather that to St. Aloysius on 27 January, 1869. The original plans may have been drafted by Charles Geoghegan, according to Charlotte Murphy, who credits William Corbett with the overall design of the church completed in 1868. The present facade dates from 1900.

CHURCH OF THE SACRED HEART. Limerick City Museum

Hobson's Choice is a phrase that found a second home in the city of Limerick. Timothy O'Brien of the Crescent was a large landowner with extensive properties in Limerick, Clare and Tipperary. He had two beautiful daughters, Emma and Mary Jane, both of whom were courted by a young man called Hobson, who was unable to decide on which sister to marry. He eventually married Emma. Both sisters died in 1907.

ST. JOSEPH'S CHURCH. Limerick City Museum.

St. Joseph's Church was designed by William Corbett, built by J.J. Ryan and Sons, and opened on 24 April, 1904. This church's greatest treasure is a chalice used by Cardinal Rinuccini when he celebrated the victory of Benburb (1646) in St. Mary's Cathedral.

O'Connell Avenue was once known as Military Road because soldiers stationed in the New Barracks, now Sarsfield Barracks, regularly paraded along this route, since at least 1798. The barracks was then virtually on the city outskirts and the garrison regularly marched into the older areas of Limerick via Military Road, The Crescent, O'Connell Street, Patrick Street and Rutland Street.

The Baptist Church was built in red brick with limestone dressings. It contained a fine lecture-room, several classrooms and other apartments, and could seat up to 300 people. P. Kennedy, 3 Military Road, was the builder, and the design was by George P. Beater of Dublin. While it was being constructed in 1894 it was estimated that the edifice would cost over £2,000 to complete.

William Street derives its name from William Russell, a local merchant. Ellen Street and Patrick Street were named after members of the Arthur family. Catherine Street was named after Catherine Unthank and Nicholas Street was called after the long-vanished church of St. Nicholas. In 1837 the city supported four newspapers, three published twice a week, and one weekly. Social gatherings were moved from the Assembly House which had been built for £4,000 in 1770 to Swinburne's Hotel and the Limerick Institution, formed in 1809, could boast of a library containing over 2,000 volumes. The linen and cotton Industry had declined by the 1830s despite the efforts of the Limerick Chamber of Commerce to halt the deterioration by erecting a new linen hall and holding a weekly market every Friday and Saturday. The adaptation of new designs did little to help the faltering market, so the problem was eventually turned over to the agricultural association. This body tried to promote the linen, woollen, cotton and other trades among the poor with a fund of £7,000 allocated to them by the association's board of directors in London. At the same time the glove trade was in trouble, and most of the "Limerick gloves" on sale were actually manufactured in Cork.

Baker Place derives its name from Richard Baker, the entrepreneur who built the houses here. The Tait Clock in Baker Place was erected as a tribute to Sir Peter Tait, a Scotsman, who pioneered the manufacture of ready-made clothing in an era when even army uniforms were all made by hand. In 1850 he introduced power-driven machinery and mass-production methods to the city. Within a few years his factory was producing uniforms for the entire British army. During the American Civil War, Limerick was an important maritime and

BAKER PLACE, ABOUT 1905 - Limerick City Museum

industrial centre which supplied both North and South with military uniforms. Uniforms for the British, American, European and other armies were manufactured here and helped Limerick to develop into a major city. Sir Peter Tait was mayor three times between 1866 and 1868. He lived in South Hill House. During his mayoralty in 1867, the 65-foot high clock tower designed by William Corbett, the city surveyor, was completed at a cost of £750. Today this four-faced clock is worked by electricity.

THE TAIT CLOCK COMMEMORATES SIR PETER TAIT, THREE TIMES MAYOR OF THE CITY.

The Tait Business Centre is a modern industrial development named after Limerick's most successful Victorian businessman, who would have appreciated such a memorial. Purpose-built factory units, workshops and offices are provided for small manufacturing and other related businesses.

St. Saviour's Dominican Church was designed by the Pain brothers soon after the friars moved from Fish Lane to Baker Place in 1815. A new chancel was built in 1863 and the main body of the church was considerably altered in 1870. In 1898 the Sacred Heart Chapel was erected as a

OUR LADY OF LIMERICK. STATUE IN THE DOMINICAN CHURCH.

memorial to Fr. Carbery, the prior. This chapel and that of St. Martin de Porres on the opposite side of the church were later joined by the Terence Albert O'Brien Memorial Chapel of 1982 with its modern stained-glass windows. Terence Albert O'Brien (1600-1651), Bishop of Emly, encouraged Irish resistance within the walls of the besieged city in 1651. At one stage the Cromwellians offered him £10,000 and safe passage to any country outside of the kingdom. He refused the bribe. Ireton excluded him from the amnesty and had him hanged. Terence Albert O'Brien was a master of sacred theology, an alumnus of the Limerick Convent of St. Saviour, and was elected prior of the Province of Ireland at Kilkenny in 1643. After the death of James O'Hurley in 1644 he was created bishop of Emly. *Our Lady of Limerick*, an oak statue of the *Madonna and Child* preserved in the Dominican Church, dates from the second quarter of the seventeenth century. The Dominicans believe that this life-sized statue and a silver-gilt chalice were given in 1640, as an act of reparation, by Patrick Sarsfield of Limerick and his wife, Eleanor White. This Patrick Sarsfield, not to be confused with his namesake, the Jacobite general, lost his rich lands around Shannon and Bunratty under the Act of Settlement in 1653 and was forced to start a new life in Burren and Corcomroe. Patrick was a nephew of Judge Dominic Sarsfield, the man who sentenced Sir John Bourke (c.1550-1607) to death for harbouring Catholic priests in Brittas Castle, and the statue was presented to the Dominicans because of Sir John Bourke's long association with their church. The *Madonna's* fifteen-decade silver rosary beads date from the late eighteenth or nineteenth century but her crown is modern.

PERY SQUARE LOOKING TOWARDS THE DOMINICAN CHURCH. **Shannon Development Photo Library.**

Pery Square derives its name from Edmund Sexton Pery (1719-1806) and leads off, in a north-easterly direction, towards Pery Street and Baker Place.

The Pery Square Tontine Buildings were completed in 1838. These are a notable example of Georgian architecture. The doorways, complete with fanlights, have supporting Doric columns on either side. The entire terrace is know as the Tontine Building.

The Carnegie Library building now houses the City Gallery of Art. The Romanesque-Celtic doorway and arches reflect the taste of a period which has since become known as the *Celtic Twilight*. The formation stone of the building, designed by George Sheridan was laid by the philantropist Andrew Carnegie, who donated £7,000 towards the building, for which he was granted the honorary freedom of the city. In 1916 the City Museum opened here, and the City Gallery was added in 1948. In 1979 the museum was relocated in John's Square, and in 1985 the library moved to the Granary in Michael Street allowing the Art Gallery to occupy the entire building. At the time of writing, the building is undergoing major renovations and extension.

CARNEGIE LIBRARY. Limerick City Library

The Cenotaph in Pery Square is a link with the city's military past. It is dedicated to the Limerick men who died in both World Wars, particularly the Munster Fusiliers. The Order of National Ex-Servicemen erected a small monument nearby to commemorate soldiers of the national army.

The People's Park, or New Park, is enclosed by iron railings on three sides. The earl of Limerick granted Pery Square and the surrounding grounds to the corporation on certain conditions. He gave them a 500-year lease when they agreed that no political

PEOPLE'S PARK AND THE SPRING RICE MEMORIAL. Limerick City Museum.

217

or religious meetings would be allowed in the free park, bands would not be allowed to play there on Sundays, and the corporation would make a new street extending from Mallow Street to the park. The People's Park was formally opened by Mayor Spaight on 20 August, 1877.

Thomas Spring Rice (1790-1866) is commemorated in the centre of the People's Park, where his statue is mounted on a Doric column designed by Alexander Nimmo in the early 1830s. Thomas Spring Rice coined the term West Briton. Richard Lalor Sheil (1791-1851), a lawyer and politician believed Thomas was a political schizophrenic:

> He sees the poor laws from the Shannon as he sees the Repeal from the Thames.
> He takes a Treasury view of the one, and a Mount Trenchard view of the other ...
> He designates himself as a West Briton. He does himself an injustice for he is more
> than English. All the mud of his native Shannon has not only been washed off by
> his ablutions in the Cam, but he comes more fresh and glossy from the academic
> water than those who at their birth were immersed in the classic stream.

Thomas Spring Rice was Chancellor of the Exchequer from 1835 to 1839 and was created Baron Monteagle of Brandon in 1840. The drinking fountain in the People's Park was erected by the employees of Russell's Mills.

PERY SQUARE. Limerick City Museum.

St. Michael's Church of Ireland Church was designed to blend with the surrounding architecture. It was consecrated in 1844 and replaced an older church, St. George's, on O'Connell Street, which was founded and endowed by the Pery family. This older edifice was opened on 14 June, 1789, and contained an east window which was "a beautiful antique of the thirteenth century, and was formerly in the old Franciscan Abbey". The height of the tower, which rises directly above the main doorway, was increased when the present building was reopened, after major renovations, on 18 November, 1877. The stained-glass windows, brass plaques, church fittings and furniture from the now-disused parish church of Kilkeady were sent here for storage, almost a century later.

Barrington Street derives its name from two members of the Barrington family who had invested money in the Tontine Company that built houses in Pery Square. Tontines were formed by public subscription during the eighteenth and early-nineteenth centuries. These were companies in which a limited number of people agreed to invest a certain sum of money each over a specified period. At the end of the designated time the company, called a tontine, would wind up its affairs and distribute all of its assets and monies amongst its surviving members. Only those who were alive at that stage participated in the share-out, as the next of kin of dead investors had no claim on the tontine. The tontine was called after its inventor, Lorenzo Tonti. It was a popular scheme with investors, who often designated their children as subscribers. Tontines became illegal in some countries as members often tried to "assist" nature with the "odd accident" or two in the hope of furthering their own claims.

The Limerick and Tipperary Branch of the Samaritans is located at 20 Barrington Street. It was founded in 1975 and was located in Cecil Street for its first eighteen years. In 1993 the branch moved to premises more suited to its needs at 20 Barrington Street, the official opening of which was performed by the then president of Ireland, Mary Robinson. During its twenty-five years of existence this branch has covered the city and county of Limerick, most of north Tipperary and a substantial part of south Tipperary.

Little Barrington Street was a minor street, leading from Barrington Street. Frank McCourt's grandmother lived here.

Frank McCourt's Book, *Angela's Ashes, a Memoir of a Childhood*, is the most explosive autobiography that this country has seen since Brendan Behan published *Borstal Boy* in 1958. Limerick people either love it or loathe it but few are indifferent. It is blackly humorous, laced with Limerick wit and has provoked a startled response in all who read it. Jim Kemmy loved and identified with *Angela's Ashes*, presented copies to various friends and acquaintances and marvelled at Frank McCourt's astonishing account. Kevin Hannan hated the book, thought it was a scurrilous attack on Limerick and its people and wanted to write a letter condemning the book and its author from his death-bed. Frank McCourt published *Angela's Ashes* in New York in 1996, won the Pulitizer Prize in 1997, and was appointed writer-in-residence by Limerick University later that year.

The Frank McCourt Trail is the name bestowed on the search for Frank McCourt's childhood haunts by avid fans and readers. Frank McCourt was born in New York but his parents returned to Ireland before he was five years old. The family lived near Toome, County Armagh, before moving to Limerick, the birthplace of his mother, Angela Sheehan. The McCourt's lived with Angela's mother until they acquired a furnished room on Windmill Street. They moved to Hartstonge Street after the death of young Oliver. Eugene McCourt died in Hartstonge Street, so the entire family moved again to Roden Street, on top of Barrack Hill. Frank's father went to England for a brief spell, lost contact with his family for months but returned to Limerick on learning of his wife's hospitalisation with pneumonia. He found his four sons living with their aunt in Windmill Street, waited for his wife to recover, and then returned to England, leaving Angela and his sons in Roden Street. Apart from this, and a later visit to Limerick, he seemed to vanish from their lives. At the age of eleven Frank McCourt was helping John Hannan to deliver coal. His elderly mentor was a great believer in education and Frank availed of his advice;

> School, Frankie, School. The Books, the books, the books. Get out of Limerick before your legs rot and your mind collapses entirely.

Angela McCourt and her children were evicted from Roden Street and went to live with her cousin in Rosbrien Road. Frank did not agree with the cousin and went to live with his uncle at 4 Little Barrington Street. He became a telegram boy on his fourteenth birthday and Angela and his brothers moved in with his uncle and himself. He augmented his income by writing letters to a moneylender's clients threatening to take legal action if they did not pay up. He had his first pint in South's of Newenham Street to celebrate a new job he had acquired with Eason's and he continued to work for both Eason's and the moneylender until the latter died. Frank McCourt emigrated to America at the age of nineteen.

Glentworth Street derives its name from Rev. William Cecil Pery who was created Baron Glentworth of Mallow in 1790.

THE GLENTWORTH GARAGE WORKS IN LOWER GLENTWORTH STREET WERE SOLE AGENTS FOR SUNBEAM, ROVER AND ALL PRINCIPAL ENGLISH AND AMERICAN CARS, COMMERCIAL VEHICLES, AGRICULTURAL TRACTORS AND LORRIES. IN JULY 1920 MRS. GLEESON OF TINERANA, KILLALOE, HAD HER CAR SERVICED THERE AND WAS CHARGED £3.45 FOR EIGHTEEN GALLONS OF PETROL RECEIVED ON THE 6TH, 13TH AND 24TH OF THAT MONTH.

The Glentworth Hotel was the home of James Pain (1779-1877), a noted architect, who, with his brother, George Richard Pain, studied architecture with John Nash. They later collaborated in the building and renovation of some of Ireland's finest houses. James eventually decided to live in Limerick while George continued to live in Cork.

The Limerick Savings Bank, "The Stone Jug", is a Doric-temple-style building with four fluted columns, designed by W. H. Owen soon after the Earl of Limerick leased land in Upper Glentworth Street to the bank in 1839. This was one of several banks established in the city in the opening decades of the nineteenth century. It was founded in 1820 to encourage and facilitate savings by the less affluent members of society, and in the year ending 25 December, 1823, a total of £17,000 was lodged.

*A TOKEN ISSUED BY UNTHANK AND COMPANY IN WILLIAM STREET. **Limerick City Museum.***

Catherine Street was named after Catherine Unthank, according to popular belief.

Trinity Church was built by Rev. Edward Newenham Hoare who collected funds for its erection in 1834. The building is occupied since the 1960s by the Mid-Western Health Board. In the early 1830s there were more than 3,000 Protestants living in St. Michael's Parish, with only St. George's private chapel for worship. Lord Limerick, at the time, was not willing to give the ground for a parish church, so the only way out of the difficulty was to erect a trustee church attached to a charitable institution. Rev. Hoare, curate of St. John's, raised £2,913 on three tours to England and Scotland in 1834, more than half the cost of the church with the Asylum for Blind Females to one side and the rectory to the other, both with access to the church gallery. The remainder of the money was collected by local subscription and the debt paid off by 1838. The chapel opened for worship on Sunday, 4 May 1834. St. Lawrence's Parish was attached to Trinity Church in 1842, and the chaplain became rector of St. Lawrence's Parish.

Hartstonge Street derives its name from Sir Henry Hartstonge who was a member of Parliament for the county from 1776 to 1789. He was the husband of Edmund Sexton Pery's sister, Lucy, and his family resided on this street. His niece, Mary Alice Ormsby, married Edmund Henry Pery on 29 January, 1783.

The Leamy Free Schools, in Hartstonge Street, were established by will of William Leamy, who in 1814 left £13,300 for the education of the children of the poor, especially those in the neighbourhood of Limerick. William Leamy, a native of Limerick, spent his life at sea. He made a large fortune, possibly from piracy on the high seas; and died on the island of Madeira. In 1841 the Court of Chancery in Ireland decided the way in which the endownment should be made. The Leamy pupils were to be taught gratuitously, and to receive a good English education, members of the Church of Ireland were to be instructed in the scriptures, and Roman Catholics in the Scripture lessons in the national school books. A sum of £3,940 was spent on the schools and site in Hartstonge Street while the interest on the £10,000 balance maintained the school. The school experienced some difficulties after it opened in 1844. It was well supported by the Protestant students, but rarely had more than twenty Catholic students. It closed for a few years in 1865. Reopening before 1874. In 1887 the Catholic bishop forbade Catholic children from attending the school. Bishop Dwyer, using the excuse that William Leamy may have died a Catholic, claimed that the school should be denominational rather than non-denominational, as most of the poor children were Catholic, stating:

I will never allow the Catholics of Limerick, while I am bishop, to attend a mixed school.

The bishop was opposed to multi-denominational education and dominated the educational field within the city. The dispute was resolved in April, 1894, when a new scheme for the school was drawn up. The Protestant community got a quarter of the school's assets and the remainder, including the property, was vested in the Catholic community. The Department of Education now administers the Leamy Endowment.

Mallow Street was named after Rev. William Cecil Pery who was created Baron Glentworth of Mallow in 1790.

The Baha'i Faith was founded by a Persian aristocrat, Baha'u'llah (1817-1892), who is regarded by his followers as the most recent in a long line of Messengers of God. The Baha'i faith was established in Limerick in the late 1960s. The community is small and members congregate in each others' homes for worship.

Parnell Street is named after Charles Stewart Parnell (1846-1891) who, it was alleged, made some very uncomplimentary remarks about his parliamentary colleagues on the platform of Limerick Railway Station according to a report in the *Freeman's Journal* of 1 August, 1879. These remarks were investigated by the *Limerick Reporter* and discovered to be fabrications which reflected Whig chagrin at the results of an Ennis by-election in which Parnell had ousted Lysaght Finegan. Charles Stewart Parnell wrote to Maurice Lenihan, editor of the *Limerick Reporter* on 5 August, 1879, to thank him for his "manly and common sense appreciation" of the situation. When Parnell died in 1891 his last words were "Kiss me, sweet wifie, and I will try to sleep a little," not "Let my love be given to my colleagues and to the Irish people".

This street was formerly known as Nelson Street to commemorate Admiral Horatio Nelson, who won the naval Battle of Trafalgar on 21 October, 1805. His last words, "Kiss me, Hardy", were addressed to his flag-captain who duly obliged. Nelson died towards the end of a battle which saw the victorious English capture nineteen French and Spanish line-of-battle ships and 20,000 prisoners.

Limerick Railway Station may have been designed by Sancton Wood (1814-1886), the English architect who designed Heuston Station (Dublin) and all the other railway stations stretching from Monasterevan to Limerick Junction. The Waterford and Limerick railway was the first Irish railway to receive parliamentary approval, although it was not the first line to open, as the Dublin and Kingstown line opened in 1834. The first train to run between Limerick and

CON COLBERT BUS AND RAIL STATION, A VICTORIAN STRUCTURE HONOURING A REPUBLICAN HERO.

Tipperary, connecting the cities of Dublin and Limerick, did so on 9 May 1848. The Limerick Railway Station opened in 1858. This is a spacious stone building with plenty of space for freight, buses and parking. Lavatories were first provided on some trains in 1872. This was a luxury third-class passengers were unable to avail of, but there were frequent and lengthy stops at almost every station. On 1 June, 1898, dining-cars were available on the Cork mail train. Michael Quin, a retired merchant who took a prominent part in civic affairs, was elected mayor in 1848. His mayoral medallion states; "Got possession of the Island Bank for the citizens. Railway communications opened 9th May between Dublin and Limerick." Robert E. Mitchell was the first superintendent of the Great Southern and Western Railway, which employed up to 600 men at a locomotive repair yards in Roxboro by the turn of the century.

Con Colbert (1896-1916) was born at Monalena, Castlemahon, and reared in Galeview House, Athea, from 1899 onwards. He was employed as a clerk at Limerick Railway Station which is now known as Con Colbert Station. He joined the Irish Republican Brotherhood, was a pioneer of Fianna Éireann and, after moving to Dublin, was a captain of F Company, Fourth Dublin Battalion. He served under Eamonn Ceannt (1881-1916) during Easter Week, commanded the garrisons at Watkins Brewery (Ardee Street), Jameson's Distillery (Bow Street) and took part in the fighting at Marrowbone Lane. He was executed on 8 May, 1916.

LIMERICK TOKEN ISSUED BY THOMAS LINCH IN 1670. Limerick City Museum.

Sexton Street derived its name from Edmund Sexton Pery in 1797. It was also known as Pery Street at one time. The Sexton Street area was once the seat of Limerick's mineral water industry. Wells were sunk to a depth of over fifty feet, at times, to extract bacteria-free mineral waters with a unique preservative quality. These mineral waters were utilised by the Limerick bacon factories and were responsible for the distinctive flavour and world-wide reputation of Limerick ham. The Russell family were involved in both the milling and bacon industries. Grain-stores built by John Norris Russell can still be seen in Limerick and Ennis. During the Civil War, July to August, 1922, O'Mara's Bacon factory and a large section of William Street were destroyed. On 1 September 1825 the Christian Brothers leased a half-acre site behind the Artillery Barracks, on Sexton Street, from Samuel Dixon at an annual rent of £15.75.

The Sexton Street Christian Brothers School had the foundation-stone of its monastery laid on 21 September, 1825. On 13 June the brothers left the diocesan college in Corbally and moved into their own new quarters. On 2 June, 1828, the foundation-stone of their school was laid and on 20 May 1829 the school opened. The erection of the monastery cost £859.81 and the school was built for £562.29. Between August, 1852, and April, 1853, the monastery was extended. The directors of the Waterford and Limerick Railway gave the brothers a site next to their monastery, which they enclosed with a boundary wall between 22 September, 1862, and March, 1863. Over the next few years two new wings were added to the school. In 1871 Br. Welsh bought an adjoining house, John Russell's, for £700. He later built St. Joseph's Male Orphanage on the Russell property.

Asiatic Cholera swept through Asia and Europe before it reached Ireland, and Limerick, in 1832. It was transmitted through poor sanitation, inefficient sewerage disposal, an unsafe water supply, contaminated food and a lack of personal hygiene. The city hospitals were unable to cope with all the casualties and the Christian Brothers allowed their schools to be used as cholera hospitals from May to October 1832.

Mulgrave Street commemorates Constantine Henry Phipps (1797-1863). He was the Second Earl Mulgrave, a Whig politician who supported the movement for Catholic Emancipation, and was lord lieutenant of Ireland from 1835 to 1839. In 1835 he visited Limerick to open the new Wellesley Bridge. The street runs from Newtown Mahon, on the outskirts of the Irishtown, in a south-westerly direction to connect with Blackboy Road, The Pike, Ballysimon Road and, intersects Childers Road before continuing as the N24 towards Waterford.

Brian Boru House was the childhood home of Kate O'Brien the novelist. Her grandfather, Tom O'Brien, had been evicted from his farm near Bruree, possibly because of an association with The Young Ireland Movement. He became a successful horse dealer and entered into a partnership with his sons, Michael, Tom and John. John lived abroad to oversee their English and European affairs while his two brothers lived in Limerick. Michael O'Brien built the ten-roomed Brian Boru House in the late 1870s had it embellished with low-relief limestone carvings of shamrocks and the O'Brien crest and had his own name and the date *A.D. 1880* inscribed on the gateway to the stable yard. Tom O'Brien married Catherine Thornhill of Kilfinnane in 1886 and brought her back to Brian Boru House which he now shared with Michael, their father and brother having died some time before, leaving the business to the two brothers. The couple had ten children, one of whom died in infancy, Michael Alphonsus. The eldest child, Mary, was born on 12 June, 1902. The census form of 1901 lists the other children and their ages, John (eleven years), Clare (eight), Annie (seven), Thomas (five), Kate (three), Patrick (one) and Michael (two months). In 1903 Kate O'Brien became a boarder in Laurel Hill, which was then presided over by Anne Blackett, who described herself as a "lady principal" in the census forms.

The Mulgrave Street Hospital was erected for £7,100, in 1811, on what was then called the New Cork Road. In 1827 Fitzgerald described it as the New County Hospital. Elizabeth Fry, the prison reformer, visited here with a Mr. Gurney and the Protestant bishop of Limerick and they were gratified with the good order, cleanliness and comfort of the hospital. The lower floor was occupied by the hall, board-room, surgery, kitchen and other apartments. Two upper floors contained ten wards for male patients and six for female patients. The building contained a resident surgeon and served the city and county until the 1950s, when the Regional Hospital opened at Dooradoyle. The Limerick School of Commerce then occupied the old infirmary.

The Harris Family are of Welsh ancestry and derive their name and descent from John Harris of Llanadog who married Anne Stephens in 1774. He moved his family to Ireland during the late 1700s and established a business in

SUGAR BOWL, MANUFACTURED BY JONATHAN BUCK. Limerick City Museum.

Waterford. He was succeeded by his sons, Richard, Tom and Henry. Richard Harris's tenth child, James, was born in Wexford. He broke with the family's Protestant tradition by marrying a Catholic, Anne Meehan, and moved to Limerick where he founded the Harris Mills, a flour and meal milling concern and bakery. Richard Harris, one of six children born to James and Anne, was described as an aristocratic businessman and under his guidance the firm prospered. At the turn of the century the Harris family had their principal business premises on William Street, a flour and meal mill, a number of Shannonside silos, a fleet of boats and a large bakery in Henry Street. Ivan and Billy Harris took over the business after their father retired. Ivan Harris married a local girl, Mildred Harty, and they started their married life in a large estate house on the North Circular Road. Richard St. John Harris is the fifth child of this marriage. He was born on 1 October, 1930.

Richard St. John Harris was reared in *Overdale*, a six-bedroom house on the Ennis Road. He joined Joan Littlewood's Theatre Workshop, London, in 1956 and made his acting debut in her production of Brendan Behan's *The Quare Fellow*, at Stratford. Later that year he appeared on stage in *A View from the Bridge*, in London. Between 1956 and 1958 he toured Russia and eastern Europe and appeared in some television plays. He had his first leading role on the London stage in 1959, with *The Ginger Man*. In 1958 he made his film debut with *Alive and Kicking*. This was followed by a series of parts in other films like *Shake Hands with the Devil* (1959), *A Terrible Beauty* (1960) *Mutiny on the Bounty* (1962), *Major Dundee* (1965), *A Man called Horse* (1969), *Cromwell* (1970), *The Wild Geese* (1978) and several others, the most famous of recent times being John B. Keane's *The Field*, in which he played the leading role. In 1968 he received the best actor accolade for his role in Camelot. Richard Harris recorded several songs in 1969, including *McArthur Park* was the producer of *Echoes of a Summer* in 1976, and received the Grammy Award for having presented the best spoken work for *Jonathon Livingston Seagull*.

Gerald Griffin Street was once known as Cornwallis Street, to honour Charles Cornwallis (1738-1805), First Marquis and Second Earl Cornwallis, a title to which he succeeded in 1762. He was a professional soldier; became joint vice-treasurer of Ireland in 1769; opposed the American rebels after taking up his command there in 1776; and surrendered his forces to General George Washington at Yorktown, on 19 October, 1781. He arrived in Ireland to quell the 1798 Rebellion; accepted the surrender of General Humbert in September, 1798; and was Commander-in-Chief and Lord Lieutenant of Ireland from 1798-1801. He was in favour of Catholic Emancipation and the Act of Union and resigned his Irish posts when the former was not granted at the time of the Act of Union. Charles Cornwallis is remembered in history as Butcher Cornwallis. This street was once the site of Tottenham Heaphy's Theatre, The New Theatre Royal. This was located at the south western corner of Gerald Griffin Street and Little Gerald Griffin Street which were then known as Cornwallis Street and Playhouse Lane. Heaphy built his theatre for £600 in 1770. It was eighty feet long by forty feet wide, awkwardly designed, and lacked a proper facade as the front part was used by a coach-builder, named Edward Gubbins, for both business and domestic purposes. In fact, access to the playhouse boxes was through Edward's kitchen and the entry to the pit was through Playhouse Lane. A site next to the Assembly house, at the eastern end of Charlotte's Quay, was given to Tottenham Heaphy, by Thomas Smyth, in August, 1774, but there is no record of this being used for theatrical purposes. In 1771 Tottenham Heaphy complained of counterfeit admission tickets, unruly audiences, backstage romeo's, heating, light, air-conditioning and maintenance. He often let his theatre to other entrepreneurs such as Richard Daly who leased it from him in 1781. Sir Vere Hunt of Curragh Chase formed the Limerick Theatrical Society with Major Alcock of 47th Regiment and Captain Trevor Lloyd Ashe, a skilled instrumentalist, on 17 January, 1785. The society then leased the Theatre Royal from Richard Daly who sub-let to them. In 1790 Sir Vere Hunt turned the ballroom of the Assembly House into a 'beautiful' theatre and established a touring theatrical group which operated with some success until a disagreement with his manager led to its closure. By then the city had a population of about 50,000. In 1858 Charles Dickens appeared on stage in Limerick to give a dramatised public reading. On 4 September a correspondent for the *Limerick Chronicle*, disappointed with the famous man's performance, acknowledged his ability as a writer but stated that as a "general reader we cannot give him

RICHARD WALLACE WAS A JEWELLER, WATCHMAKER, SILVERSMITH AND OPTICIAN AT 129 GEORGE STREET IN 1884.

unqualified praise, for though he undoubtedly possesses dramatic talents of a first rate order for personifying characters, yet he recited several passages of a descriptive nature in a sing-song, schoolboy style that was below par".

Henry Street derives its name from Edmund Henry Pery (1758-1844) who was created Viscount Limerick in 1800, Earl of Limerick in 1803 and Baron Foxford in 1815. He was a member of parliament for the city from 1786 to 1795.

The Church of St. Alphonsus Liguori and the adjoining residence were designed by Philip C. Hardwick, in Gothic-style, for the Redemptorist Fathers, who first arrived in Ireland in 1850. Known also as the Missionary Fathers of St. Alphonsus, they preached at a mission held in the old St. John's Church in 1851 and were invited back the following year to speak at St. Michael's. Dr. Ryan, the Catholic bishop of Limerick, gave them a foundation in 1853 and they opened a small oratory in Bank Place. In 1854 they acquired a large field in Courtbrack, at the top of Henry Street, where they erected a temporary chapel. They resided near it until they built their own residence, the foundation-stone of which was laid in August, 1856. The foundation stone of the church was laid on 30 May, 1858. Both buildings were constructed by a builder named Wallace, under the supervision of William Corbett. George Goldie (1828-1887) of London

LIMERICK BANKNOTE, ISSUED BY THE BANK OF LIMERICK. Limerick City Museum.

designed the high altar which was unveiled on Sunday, 15 October, 1865, although the tower was not completed until 1879. The chief building material is magnesium limestone, imported from France, with horizontal strips of pink granite used to enliven the facade. Clare and Sicilian marble were used in decorating the interior, the former in the columns supporting the apse arch, and the latter in the altar rail.

Hibernian House, at 105 Henry Street, is one of two adjoining mansions built for the Protestant bishop of Limerick (later Lord Glentworth) and his older brother, Viscount Pery. The craftsmen who worked on these buildings had also been employed to construct Glin Castle and included in their number a famous Georgian plasterer, Michael Stapleton. The two houses date from the 1780s and William Cecil Pery (1721-1794) was a resident of No. 104 in 1784. He was consecrated as a bishop of Killaloe in 1781, became bishop of Limerick three years later; and was created Baron Glentworth of Mallow in 1790. Edmund Sexton Pery (1719-1806), his brother, was created Viscount Pery of Newton Pery in 1785 and his son, Edmond Henry Pery, lived in the adjoining house, sometimes known as No. 105, Pery House or the Earl of Limerick's House, in 1813. This second house later became St. Munchin's College and the office of the Greyhound Racing Board is in the adjoining house, the former episcopal palace. Five other bishops occupied 104 Henry Street after William Cecil Pery, Thomas Barnard, Charles Warburton, John Jebb, Edmund Knox and Charles Graves.

Limerick Youth Service has its headquarters building at 5 Lower Glentworth Street, an information bureau and secretarial services at Sonas House, 35 O'Connell Street, a residential and outdoor pursuit centre in Lisselton, County

Kerry and maintains its youth resource centre at Henry Street. This last building, a former garage, has one entrance on the corner of Henry Street and Lower Glentworth Street. In January, 1998, President Mary McAleese presented gold awards to two members of the Limerick Youth Service, Catherine O'Neill of Southhill and Thomas Ryan of Moyross.

The Franciscan Church is a neo-classical building designed by William Corbett and erected by the firm of McCarthy and Guerin. The foundation-stone was laid on 28 May, 1876. It was extended and renovated in 1931. All traffic leaving the city by Sarsfield Bridge has to pass its facade.

Three Black and Tans were attacked on Henry Street, by a group of I.R.A. men on 22 June, 1920. Constable Oakley was shot dead and his two companions, E.T. Jones and H. Jones, disarmed. One of the I.R.A. men got rid of his revolver by dropping it into a nearby post office pillar-box, from which the I.R.A. recovered it the following morning.

The Presbyterian Church had its foundation-stone laid by the moderator, Rev. D.A. Taylor, on 16 October, 1899. Prior to then the Presbyterians had occupied a "commodious edifice of hewn stone" in Glentworth Street which they had erected about 1817. The earlier history of Limerick's Presbyterian congregation is rather vaguely detailed, but it is probable that some members of the Church of Scotland settled in the city about 1649. They rented the old chapel of the

THE PRESBYTERIAN CHURCH, BEFORE THE CONSTRUCTION OF THE SHANNON BRIDGE IN THE LATE 1980S. Shannon Development Photo Library.

Augustinian nunnery in Peter's Cell from Lord Milton until 1765, when they built the Dissenters Meeting House in Pump Lane, at the north end of the Englishtown. This building was considered "plain and handsome", with a house for the minister adjoining. Both were erected for £500. The Glentworth Street church proved to be too small. It was enlarged in 1829 and had a gallery added in 1846. When the present church and lecture hall was built, the old building was sold to George McKern & Sons Ltd., Printers, on 18 August, 1904. When the foundation-stone was laid a bottle was deposited at the right-hand corner, bearing the names of the ministers of the church from the reign of Charles I to October 1899, as well as a copy of the *Limerick Chronicle*, and current coins of the realm from a sovereign to a farthing. This building was erected for £8,000 and was opened on 3 October, 1901, by Prof. Heron D.D., moderator of the General Assembly. Constructed mainly of red brick, with dressings of Portland stone for the arches and windows, the first system of lighting used was gas lighting until, in 1915, electricity was installed. The most unusual feature was the church's lecture-hall which was located underneath the church. The Presbyterians now worship in a smaller church building, Christ Church, on O'Connell Street. Their former church was converted into legal offices but is now closed again. The new Jury's Inn is located behind the church.

The Great Hunger (1845-1847) is commemorated with a fountain and sculpture, *Broken Heart*, at the Mount Kennett end of Lower Mallow Street. This monument is located outside the new Jury's Inn and carries the following inscription:-

"Broken Heart"
Memorial to the victims of the Great Famine
(1845- 1849)
Commissioned by Gerry Barrett (Edward Holdings, Galway)

This memorial is to commemorate the thousands of people who used this site as a holding station in the famine of 1845 to 1849 prior to emigration to the New World never to return.

The memorial was designed by Ms. Marie Pizzuti and unveiled by his worship the mayor, Councillor K. O'Hanlon, on 21st May, 1997.

The census figures of 1841 and 1851 are termed as approximates only, as many census forms were never filled in or returned. Nevertheless these figures give some indication of the scale of the genocide inflicted on a helpless people. Landless labourers were virtually wiped out as a class. Others died of cholera, typhoid or relapsing fever. Many more were buried, their deaths unrecorded, their graves forgotten. Emigration took place on an unprecedented scale, as many landlords found it cheaper to send their former tenants abroad and other would-be emigrants managed to raise the "passage money", somehow, to take themselves and their families away from Ireland, many dying *en route* in the coffin ships. In 1841 Limerick, city and county, had a total population of 330,029 people. By 1851 the population had fallen to 262,132, as death and emigration had reduced the total by 67,897. Limerick City and the North Liberties, however, had an increase in population, from 49,593 to 57,854, an increase of 8,261, as people fled to the apparent safety of the city. The North Liberties contained a workhouse, had a population of 1,202 in 1841, and had increased its population to 4,406 by 1851.

Villier's Schools were founded soon after the will of Mrs. Hannah Villier was established in the Court of King's Bench on 12 December, 1815. Samuel Lewis reported that very large schools for males and females were being constructed in 1837. In 1866 Maurice Lenihan stated that £7,507.90 had been spent by Mrs. Villier's trustees on acquiring a site, building schoolhouses in Henry Street and Nicholas Street, and on the Villier's Alms Houses. There were 50 boys and 44 girls in attendance in the Henry Street school in 1866, but fewer attended the Nicholas Street School, which was run in connection with the National Board of Education. In more recent times, Villiers School's were relocated in the North Liberties, off the North Circular Road.

VILLIERS SCHOOLS, LATER THE SHANNON ARMS HOTEL, ON HENRY STREET. Limerick City Museum.

Collooney Street was named after an engagement in which the Limerick City Militia distinguished itself under the command of Colonel Vereker, on 5 September, 1798, some time after the English forces had run from the French in the "Races of Castlebar". City tradition claims that Vereker lied about his exploits and that the corporation supported his claim, turning his defeat into a triumph. In 1803 the military commandant of the city foiled a surprise attack by "those engaged in Emmett's conspiracy". The prompt and decisive measures he adopted prevented a revolution. Limerick remained a staunch garrison town. In 1821 symptoms of subordination in the Liberties led to a proclamation declaring the county to be in a state of disturbance, and to require an extraordinary establishment of police, which was accordingly sent. The Castle Barrack accommodated 17 officers and 270 non-commissioned officers and privates, with an hospital for twenty-nine patients in 1837. The new barrack at the western side of Collooney Street, behind the small Spellacy Square, was adapted for 37 officers, 714 infantry and cavalry, and 54 horses in 1837. It also contained an hospital for sixty patients and a recently-constructed six-cell military prison. Today the latter barrack is known as Sarsfield Barracks. At the start of the twentieth century these two barracks were still in use, as well as the Ordnance Barracks in Mulgrave Street (now Heiton's premises) and the Militia or Strand Barracks. Most of the officers lived in the Georgian houses in the Crescent or Clare Street. The various regiments were composed of Irish, English, Welsh and Scottish soldiers although the Welsh and Scottish regiments were never allowed to share the same barracks because of some long-rooted animosity between them. The Royal Irish Constabulary also maintained a heavy presence in the city at the turn of the century, with barracks at Edward Street, John Street, William Street, Mary Street, O'Curry Street (then known as Frederick Street), Mulgrave Street, Thomondgate, Caherdavin, Corbally, and on the outskirts of the city at Cratloe Castle, Castletroy, Mungret and Clarina. In the early nineteenth century the Revenue Police used the city as a headquarters with other stations located at Ennis, Gort and Cashel.

THE 1798 REBELLION WAS COMMEMORATED IN LIMERICK WITH A MEDAL STRUCK FOR THE MILITIAMEN 'HEROES OF COLOONY', SILVER FOR THE MEN, GOLD FOR THE OFFICERS. *Limerick City Museum.*

Spellacy Square is the smallest square in Limerick City. It derives its name from a member of the Spellacy family of Cratloe.

The Spellissy Surname has been described as a rare Thomond surname by Rev. Patrick Woulfe in *Sloinnte Gaedheal is Gall, Irish Names and Surnames* (1923). Variations of the name include Spellacy, Spelessy, Spillessy, and Spilacy. The name appears in Irish as *Ó Spealghusa, Ó Spilgheasa* and *Ó Speallassa* and has been translated as *Speal-ghusa*, scythe-choice or strong scythemen. P.J. Spellissy of Islington, London, and the late George Spellissy of Tiermaclane, County Clare, claim the Spellissys were descended from a man who "came in from the water", either through the Fergus Estuary, or through Miltown Malbay. Family tradition in Clare states that the name was originally *Spoleto* and that the family originated in the north of Italy. I have found nothing to corroborate this. The name is mainly found throughout counties Clare and Limerick, in Tiermaclane, Ennis, Kilmaley, Cratloe, Raheen Cross and Limerick City.

LAUREL HILL CONVENT, ABOUT 1902 OR 1903. Limerick City Museum.

The South Circular Road is described in the Pery leases as Boherglas, from *Bóthar Glas*, the green road, an apt name for such an area during the eighteenth century.

Laurel Hill Convent was founded in 1844 by Mother D'Hover, superioress of the Faithful Companions of Jesus, with the help of Br. J.P. Welsh of the Christian Brothers, who procured the site for her. One of this convent's most famous students, Kate O'Brien, was born in Mulgrave Street.

Kate O'Brien (1897-1974), novelist, playwright, journalist, critic, and travel-writer was educated in Laurel Hill before completing her education at University College, Dublin, in 1916. Kate belonged to the rich, educated, Limerick middle class but left Ireland to seek her fortune, as Ireland offered few opportunities for qualified women. Spain influenced her most. She worked there as a governess in 1922-1923, but lived for most of her life in England. Kate found employment successively as a teacher, a journalist, a writer, and, during the war years, with the Ministry of Information. She contracted a short-lived marriage and thereafter remained single. In this way she was atypical of many women of her time, who still saw no role for themselves apart from the traditional ones of wife and mother. In 1926 she wrote a play which was shown on the London stage for three months, *Distinguished Villa*. This was followed by *The Bridge*, another play, in 1927 and her book *Without My Cloak* in 1931. She won the Hawthornden Prize for *Without My Cloak* and followed this with *The Ante-Room* (1934), *Mary Lavelle* (1936), *The Schoolroom Window* (1937), *Farewell Spain* (1937), *Pray for the Wanderer* (1938), *The Land of Spices* (1941), *English Diaries and Journals* (1943), *The Last of Summer* (1943), *That Lady* (1946), *Teresa of Avila* (1951), *The Flower of May* (1953), *As Music and Splendour* (1958), *My Ireland* (1962) and *Presentation Parlour* (1963). Her exile was voluntary, as Kate "belonged to the world of writers and artists who traditionally are at home any place where they may live in peace and practise their art." She died in Faversham, Kent, on 13 August, 1974.

The Limerick Harbour Commissioners was a new title applied to the former Limerick Bridge Commissioners under an act passed in parliament on 9 July, 1847, which allowed them to borrow up to £50,000 for the construction of new harbour works, including a wet dock.

The Wet Dock, built of native limestone, covers an eight-acre area and was built for a total cost of £54,000, £39,000 for labour and £15,000 for materials. The foundation-stone was laid by Mayor John Bruce on 26 September, 1849, and the dock was formally opened by Earl St. Germans, Lord Lieutenant General and General Governor of Ireland, on 26 September, 1853. The depth of water within it is twenty feet at neap tide and twenty-five feet at spring tide. The entrance is seventy feet wide, and the dock measures 1,385 feet in length by a width of 463 feet. Between 6000-8000 tons of shipping can be accommodated here, while cranes are available for the discharging of cargoes. Other vessels of up to 600 tons can berth at the quays where there is a depth of up to sixteen feet of water at ordinary tides. Work on a repair dock began in December, 1867. On 17 February, 1868, there was a one-day strike. Despite labour unrest throughout the entire project the repair, or graving, dock was formally opened by Earl Spencer, the lord lieutenant, on 13 May, 1873. Despite modifications and renovations over the intervening period, the docks remain basically unchanged

The New Floating Docks, or Wet Dock, at the time of its official opening, Wednesday, 26 September, 1853. The Illustrated London News.

since Victorian times. The Harbour Commissioners still control the port and are responsible for the docks and the 3,300 feet length of quays. An article in the *Evening Press* on 17 December, 1987, referred to Captain John "Chalkie" White, a native of Cornwall, as the longest-serving master coming into the port. For the previous twenty-six years he had brought refined oil from Milford Haven and Stanlow, in England, to Limerick City. Despite his experience of the Shannon waters, which he knows extremely well, he would not negotiate the channel without the aid of a Shannon pilot.

Grain Elevator, once a common dockland sight. Limerick City Museum.

A Docker's Mass is celebrated in Dolan's Pub and Restaurant on the Dock Road in the last week of November each year. The tradition was observed by the previous owners, Malachy Cosgrave, Ger Fahy, John Halvey and Mrs Barry, and is now honoured by Michael and Valerie Dolan, who purchased the premises on 23 December, 1994. The dockers attend Mass in St. Joseph's Church on the customary morning and then return to the bar to commemorate their predecessors. In the early 1800s John Norris Russell, a timber merchant and shipbuilder, was a major developer in this area. He built a corn and maize mill here in 1810, fitted it with steam-powered engines in 1827, added a nine-storey high corn store in 1837, built a large corn store (now converted to modern apartments) in Ennis, acquired other mills at Corbally, Garryowen, Lock, Plassey and Askeaton and used his own fleet of ships operating from the nearby docks. The firm he founded was acquired by Ranks in 1930.

The Limerick Flour-Mills were extensive and mainly located within the city liberties in 1837, when upwards of 50,000 barrels of flour were ground annually. By the end of the nineteenth century Limerick had the largest flour-milling industry in the south of Ireland, and could be listed as one of the country's largest exporters of provincial harvests, and importers of foreign wheat, a role maintained by the flour-millers throughout the days of the Great Hunger. Limerick contained five large mills in 1913. Working conditions were brutal.

Dock Road, as it became derelict. Limerick City Museum.

The Bard of Thomond worked in a mill for three years and later said: "It was like three years penal servitude". People worked twelve hours a day on six days of the week. The grain had to be turned continuously, as a result of which workers continually toiled in dust and darkness, affecting their lungs. They were not permitted to take breaks, had to eat while they worked, and were not allowed to rest.

The Bannatynes' Building is one of several six-storied grain stores which still survive from the nineteenth century, when men like James Bannatyne, who made his fortune importing wheat from Montreal, dominated the commercial life of the city. This building was erected on a six foot deep concrete foundation which was laid in 1873 on a solid rock strata, thirteen to twenty-five feet below the

LIMERICK DOCKS AND DOCK ROAD IN THE EARLY 1990s. Shannon Development Photo Library.

surface of the ground. William Sydney Cox, the architect, designed the building to hold 300 tons of cereal in each of eight large bins extending from the basement to the top floor. Cereal was delivered to the ground floor, from where it was distributed throughout the store by machinery. Built by the firm of MacCarthy and Guerin in 1874, the Bannatynes' building is as impressive a structure today as it was then. A Victorian architectural report commented on the aspect of its blank windows; the appearance of part of the roof which was

239

broken up by gables and dormers; its length of 135 feet by a breadth of 60 feet; the materials used in its construction, limestone, rubble, masonry with chiselled limestone strings and dressings, white Scotch fire-brick in its external arches, and Killaloe slates on the roof; and the first floor and basement, vaulted and groined in brick, with cast iron pillars, and iron tonguing connecting the planking. A short distance away was the massive Ranks' complex, which dwarfed Bannatyne's building in size and was demolished by a controlled explosion, during the recent urban renewal. The facades of other vanished structures can also be seen nearby along the Dock Road. By 1989 the only grain store serving its original purpose, in the city, was O'Neill's Mill in Upper William Street.

The Sailors' Memorial is a tasteful modern monument located on the small jetty-cum-park which juts into the Shannon from Bishop's Quay, at the eastern

THE SAILORS' MEMORIAL ON RUSSELL'S QUAY.

side of the new Shannon Bridge. This consists of a cut-stone plinth with an old anchor embedded on one side and carries the following inscription: "In proud memory of merchant seamen from Limerick and the Shannon Estuary who were lost at sea in the course of duty. *Brat Dé ar a n-anamacha.*

The Dock Clock was designed by the harbour engineer, William J. Hall, and erected in 1880.

The Poor Man's Kilkee is the name bestowed on the small jetty-cum-park extending from Harvey's Quay into the Shannon. This was once part of the swivel bridge lock but is now used by the general public as a recreation area. Kilkee, on the west coast of Clare, was a popular vacation centre for the citizens of Limerick from the early nineteenth century onwards. Those who were unable to afford a seaside holiday had to be satisfied with the city's parks and public

BOATING AT SARSFIELD BRIDGE, WITH THE LIMERICK BOATING CLUB PREMISES IN THE FOREGROUND AND SHANNON ROWING CLUB PREMISES IN THE BACKGROUND. BOTH PREMISES ARE LOCATED ON WELLESLEY PIER, A CONSTRUCTION MORE POPULARLY KNOWN TODAY AS SHANNON ISLAND.
Shannon Development Photo Library.

places. The man-made island on which the boating clubs are located was constructed as a buttress to support the outer wall of the lock. The late Michael Clarke explained how a weir extended from this lock wall to the Clare side of the Shannon, parallel with the bridge, to retain water of a certain level within the basin. The demolition of this old weir and construction of car parks on the old quays deprived the city of what had been one of its greatest assets.

The Shannon Rowing Club was founded by Sir Peter Tait in 1868. It has a magnificent premises on Shannon Island, on the northern side of Sarsfield Bridge and was one of five boat clubs that competed in the City Regatta each year, into the 1960s

The Limerick Boat Club, founded in 1870, has its premises on Shannon Island, on the southern side of the dissecting Sarsfield Bridge, and was once patronised by the Barringtons, Charles and Croker, who rowed for Trinity and won the Visitors' Senior Cup at the Henley Regatta in 1873. They introduced eight's' rowing into Limerick, having seen it at Henley, in 1870. The Athlunkard Boat Club was founded in 1898 and has premises at Park Bridge on the Abbey River. St. Michael's Rowing Club was founded in 1900 and has its premises on O'Callaghan's Strand, north of the Shannon Bridge, and the Curraghour Boat Club, founded in 1877, has a boat house, with separate entrance, at the eastern end of the Potato Market, to the side of the court-house.

Shannon Island or Wellesley Pier, is a man-made structure, one that was designed to serve as a bulwark to the western wall of the lock that gave access to vessels travelling to and from the harbour. The foundation stone for the bridge project was laid by John Fitzgibbon, Earl of Clare, the son of Black Jack Fitzgibbon, on 24 October. 1824. The work was completed eleven years later, at a cost of £89,601, fifty percent more that the original estimate. The bridge had five arches of equal span, extending from the man made island to the Clare shore. A swivel bridge extended from the island to the Limerick shore and Brunswick Street (now Sarsfield Street); and there were two land arches, on the city side, for the convenience of quay traffic. The Wellesley Bridge was built as a toll bridge and levies were collected until 1883. Then a town council that "had many who are of the National League and Home Rule type, who desire a severance of the Union" succeeded in having the toll payments suspended. The same body was also responsible for having the name changed to Sarsfield Bridge in the same year. Jerome Counihan, mayor of the city in 1882 and 1883, is commemorated in a stone plaque on the bridge, near its centre, on the northern side. The swivel bridge has not been opened for river traffic since 1928 and it was officially closed in 1963.

St. Patricks Well and Shrine in 1904. Limerick City Museum.

The South Liberties

The South Liberties extended from four to five statute miles about the city and comprised 14,754 Irish acres in the 1830s. In 1831 Limerick City contained 4,862 houses. The principal residences six years later were Mount Shannon, Hermitage, Clarina, Doonass and the mansions of the Earl of Limerick and the Church of Ireland bishop within the city. In the vicinity of Limerick there were several good houses and neat villas, but by no means so numerous as its wealth would lead strangers to suspect. The rich merchants chiefly resided in Newtownpery, the spacious streets of which still intersect each other at right angles, and were occupied by elegant houses, splendid and well-stocked shops, and merchants' stores. Patrick Street, George's Street (now O'Connell Street), and The Crescent formed, and still do, a continuous line of elegant houses, extending about a mile from Mathew Bridge. The environs of the city were described as flat but beautiful in 1837. The soil was extremely rich and the sinuous course of the Shannon presented the appearance of a succession of lakes although the landscape was deficient in wood. The city was then the headquarters of the south-western region, which comprised the counties of Clare, Limerick, Tipperary (including Nenagh but excluding the barony of Lower Ormond) and that part of county Kerry north of the Flesk, and contained four military barracks.

Singland, or St. Patrick's Parish, is on the southern banks of the Shannon, close to the city, where the river sweeps round the eastern, northern and western sides of the parish. During the various sieges of the city the military camps of Cromwell, Ireton, William III and Ginkel were located here. Traces of their camps and entrenchment's have been discovered over the centuries, military weapons were frequently found, and the remains of the ancient military roads from Dublin and from Cork could still be traced by Samuel Lewis in 1837.

St. Patrick's Parish Church and Round Tower were destroyed during the war of 1641. Most of the remaining buildings were taken down by an English army to build batteries during one of the sieges, and the portions that were left standing were demolished in 1766. In 1837 the graveyard remained and Samuel Lewis claimed that only Catholics were interred here. St. Patrick is believed to have baptised Cairthenn, a Dalcassian king, here in ancient times. St. Patrick's Well was still the scene of an annual pilgrimage on 17 March, into the 1990s. In 1750 another St. Patrick's Catholic Church was built in Pennywell, mainly at the expense of a Mr. Harrold. This appears to have been replaced by a newer church built in 1816, in the form of a letter T, which was small but "neatly fitted up". This was improved in 1835.

St. Joseph's Psychiatric Hospital opened for the reception of patients in 1826. It was constructed for £30,000 over a period of two years. The design was by the firm of Johnson and Murray and the construction was carried out by a Dublin

ST. JOSEPH'S PSYCHIATRIC HOSPITAL WAS SIMPLY DESCRIBED AS THE LUNATIC ASYLUM IN THIS DRAWING OF 1827.
Fitzgerald and Mc Gregor.

builder, Williams. This limestone edifice was lined with brick and extended 429 feet in front and 314 feet in depth. The centre formed an octagon from which four wings diverged with cells for patients from Limerick, city and county, as well as the counties of Clare and Tipperary. Eugene O'Curry (1794-1862), the eminent Gaelic scholar, worked as a warder here before joining the Ordnance Survey Office in 1835.

Limerick Prison was designed by James Pain, an architect more renowned for his work on the big houses of Ireland. In 1816 three acres of ground on the New Cork Road were purchased for £958.33. In 1817 work commenced on the "New County Jail" which was completed in 1821 at a cost of £23,000. A further £2,000 was expended on the erection of a kitchen, laundry, tread-mill-house, and sheds for fuel, straw and other materials. The building was described in 1827 as castellated in appearance. The basic structure seems unchanged from the exterior but because of the prevailing need for security a more complete description of the building cannot be given here. The grand, or main, entrance is formed of very fine cut stone. "In the centre is a polygonal tower", wrote Samuel Lewis in 1837, "60 feet high, containing on successive stories the governor's residence, the committee room, a chapel, and an hospital, and having round the second story an arcade commanding the several yards. Five rays of building diverge from this tower, forming ten yards, each communicating by a cast-iron bridge with the chapel, and containing in the whole 22 apartments for debtors, and 103 cells for criminals. Between the wall immediately surrounding these and the outer wall is a space containing two tread-wheels, the female prison, various offices, and some ornamented plots. The whole is supplied with excellent water from the springs". John O'Donoghue, the Minister for Justice, opened an extension to the prison on Monday, 8 December, 1997. This consisted of forty-eight single cells and nine double ones which cost three million pounds to construct, and raised the total of prisoners who could be accommodated from 150 to 210.

Mount St. Lawrence Cemetery is the burial-place of Maurice Lenihan (1811-1895), the Bard of Thomond, Michael Hogan (1832-1899), Kevin Hannan (1917-1996) and Jim Kemmy (1936-1997).

The John O'Grady Monument at the top of Mulgrave Street was erected in the shape of a large weight. This commemorates John O'Grady (1892-1934), a world's champion weight-thrower who was born in Ballybricken.

THE O'GRADY MONUMENT.

The Pike is the name of an area at the junction of Blackboy Road, Ballysimon Road and the old Tipperary Road. It is now commemorated in the place-name of Pike Avenue and the name of the public-house in which Jim Kemmy, a local, held his clinic. Pike is actually an abbreviation of turnpike, a gate set across a road, watched by an officer appointed to collect a toll from animal drovers, horsemen, drivers of carriages, carts and wagons and, occasionally, travellers, such as peddlers. An Act of Parliament placed all turnpike roads under the management of trustees or commissioners, who were empowered with the authority to construct, manage and repair such roads. The Blackboy Pike was the name of the toll-gate leading towards the old highway to Tipperary and was in existence by 1741.

Blackboy Road is an anglicised corruption of the original *Bealach Buidhe*, the yellow way, path or road. It was altered to Blackboy over the years and gave its name to an ancient public-house or inn called the *Black Boy*, according to Maurice Lenihan in 1866.

The United London Gas Company contracted to light the city with gas in 1824. The original engagement was confined to Newtownpery but the corporation had the gas extended to the Irishtown, Dublin Road and parts of the Englishtown. Public lighting was not new to Limerick, however, as Alderman Thomas Rose erected the first street lamps in 1696.

The Groody River passes through St. Patrick's Parish and enters the Shannon east of the canal. Most of the land through which it flows was under tillage in the 1830s;

> and supplies the city with large quantities of vegetables; along the banks of the Groody is a tract of rich meadow, liable, however, to casualties from floods. On the river are a bleach-green, a paper-mill, and a flour-mill: at the salmon weir near the Shannon, is a very extensive flour-mill which commands the whole water of that river; in the city suburbs is a large brewery... The city water-works and the county infirmary are in the parish. There are several very elegant seats, with small but highly ornamented demesnes; the principal are Park House, the residence of the Rt. Rev. Dr. Ryan, R.C. Bishop of Limerick; Corbally House, of Poole Gabbett, Esq.; and Corbally Park, of Pierce Shannon, Esq.

Over 150 years later this is one of the two large tributaries, the other is the Ballinacurra Creek south-west of the city, into which surface water is discharged. A short canal from the Abbey River to the Shannon intersects the parish from east to west. The Lock Quay, at the city end, is one of the few cobbled quays left in the city. The canal walks, like the quay and adjoining works are now disused, derelict, and deteriorating, a far cry from the busy workplace envisaged in 1758. Over forty individual sewer outfalls discharge directly into the Shannon as it passes through the city. Seven pumping stations within the city and two in the environs regulate the flow of the treated effluent.

The Sewers of Newtownpery are in all probability the city's least mentioned Georgian architectural features. As the new town developed a vast network of sewers was built on the original ground level to cater for the population envisaged by the city planners. These sewers are quite literally streets beneath the streets of Limerick. A deep central channel, or gutter, carried raw sewage and water from the overhead drains to the Shannon. As internal plumbing was only in its infancy during the late eighteenth and early nineteenth century each house, on either side of a street had its own access to the sewer. This was located off the basement area where a door opened directly onto the sewer, allowing house staff to walk directly onto the service pavement which ran parallel to the channel on either side, Slops were then emptied into this rather unsavoury stream from the safety of the pavement. Several of these access doors can still be seen off the basement areas of Limerick's Georgian buildings, although the majority of them have long since been sealed off by the corporation. Like the streets, the sewers too were named. In fact some of Britain's monarchs are commemorated in the sewer's place-names. Several streets were once called after these imperial rulers as the sewers took their names from the streets above them.

The Parish of Kilmurry is located on the southern bank of the Shannon, east of Limerick City. It derives its name from *Cill Mhuire*, St. Mary's Church, the Mary in this instance being St. Mary Magdalene. The parish was once known as Kilmurry Magdalene and an earlier medieval church stood on the site now

Sarsfield Bridge and Curraghgower Falls in 1902. Limerick City Museum.

occupied by the present disused church. The original building was destroyed during the Williamite sieges of 1690 and 1691 and was replaced with another structure which was demolished in 1810. In 1812 a Church of Ireland church was built on the site of the original parish church, which had long since been converted to Protestant use, while the nearby glebe house had been erected in 1790. There was a well dedicated to St. Mary Magdalene on the bank of the Groody River, in the townland of Kilbane, a short distance from Singland mill. The site has been vandalised over the last few years but it was the scene of an annual pilgrimage, on the 22 July, into the 1920s. Local people made their traditional "rounds" here and left candles, coins, flowers and medals at the well, the waters of which were said to cure sore eyes and other complaints.

In 1837 the parish contained 1,803 inhabitants on its 3277 statute acres; the land was mostly meadow or pasture; and well planted near the Shannon. Limestone was quarried at Newcastle, and elsewhere in the parish. There was a paper and an oil mill at Ballyclough, a paper-mill at Annacotty, and flour-mills at Ballysimon. The big houses of the period were Newcastle, the residence of M. O'Brien: Milford, of T. Fitzgerald: Shannon View, of T. Kelly; Willow Bank, of Captain Hickey; Shannon Cottage, of G. McKern; Killonan Cottage, of H. Rose; Ballyclough of P. Cudmore; and Plassey of R. Harvey. In 1840 Killonan grave-yard was used for the burials of children and strangers and was then known as Killeen, the little church. The term *stranger* was in widespread use as a euphemism for suicide into modern times.

Kilmurry Church was recently restored as it had become rather dilapidated since its closure. The length of low wall running parallel with the southern wall and part of the eastern wall may well be remnants of the medieval church. The most intriguing memorial in the graveyard carries the following inscription;-

In Memory of
John
The infant son of Lieut. Colonel Sir
Guy Cambell Bart.
And Pamela his Wife
Died at Plassy
4th Feb. 1828

Sir Guy Campbell (1786-1849) was a major-general in the army, a colonel in the 3rd West Indian Regiment and was created a baronet on 22 May, 1815. He married Frances Elizabeth Burgoyne of Mark's Hill, Essex, on 13 January, 1817. She died on 1 May, 1818, leaving an infant daughter. He married Pamela Fitzgerald, the older daughter of Sir Edward Fitzgerald (1763-1798), on 20 November, 1820. She bore him four sons and seven daughters and survived him for over twenty years, dying on 25 November, 1869. Lord Edward Fitzgerald was mortally wounded by Major Henry Charles Sirr while resisting arrest during the 1798 rebellion. The older graveyard contains the memorials and tombs of Mary Colens (1696-1766), Richard Sargint Sadleir Ross Lewin (1848-1921) who was rector of this parish for thirty-five years, Robert de Ros Rose (1852-1900), Wyndham Magrath Fitzgerald (1865-1907), Nora Moloney who died on 5 April, 1948, John Moloney who died on 19 March, 1973 and the large Matterson-Langford memorial that commemorates Agnes Southerland Langford (1879-1968), Vera Langford (1891-1981), Colonel R.C. Langford (died 1922), Joseph Matterson (1840-1906), Agnes Matterson (1853-1932) and William Southerland Matterson (1876-1948).

New Castle is located north of the well, on a rocky promontory close to the Limerick-Dublin road. About 1800 its west side, and a square tower on its south-western corner, collapsed. It has changed but little since John O'Donovan and Eugene O'Curry described it in 1840. This castle was built by the Roche family. It was called Castlenoo or *Caisleán Nua*, the new castle, in 1583 and is the most prominent landmark on this side of the city, standing on the edge of the Dublin Road. Alderman Jordan Roche and Edmund Roche were listed amongst the twenty exempted from pardon by Henry Ireton and were hanged by the Cromwellians in 1651.

The Castletroy Golf Club is located to the south of the Dublin Road, on the boundary of the townlands of Newcastle and Kilbane. This is the second golf club founded in Limerick and it was established by Major H. K.

NEW CASTLE, AT THE TURN OF THE LAST CENTURY.
Limerick City Museum.

Murphy and a number of men who believed there was a need for a new club. In 1936 they enlisted the financial aid and expertise of Malcolm and Eric Shaw, of W.J. Shaw and Sons, Michael J. Clancy, a building contractor, Patrick Heffernan, a bank manager, and Dermot G. O'Donovan, solicitor, and decided to search for a suitable site for a golf course. Robert Nolan, a local farmer and golfer, leased fifty-three acres of land to the club, and members of the committee played over the new golf course for the first time in November 1936. The land was leased for £106 per annum, contained a nine-hole course, and was adjacent to the site that the Nolan family had let to the Limerick Golf Club in 1901 and 1902. Sixty to seventy members joined the club, paying an annual subscription of three pounds each, and the first club-house was a small tin shed which was added to from time to time. The Hurlers' public-house became the golfers *nineteenth hole* and the first Castletroy Golf Club dance was held there. In 1939 Judge McElligot granted a bar license to the club.

Dan Murray was the first professional golfer to work in Castletroy. He was enlisted during the spring of 1937 and supervised the construction of temporary tees and greens with Dr. Michael J. Roberts. He was succeeded by Denis Cassidy, another professional, who reported for duty on 9 September 1937 and guided the fledgling club through its gruelling formative years, with Dr. Michael J. Roberts and a staff of fourteen. In 1938 debentures were issued to raise money for additional land and an extra thirty-four acres were added to the grounds, sufficient land for the construction of an eighteen-hole course. James McNamara sold the land for £1000 and received an additional £1,200 for his cottage which stood near the present third tee. A special meeting was held in Cruises' Hotel on 23 March, 1938, at which new rules were considered and drafted by the committee, and the course became substantially as it is today. The first mens' trophy was the Shaw Cup which was presented in 1937. The first ladies' branch was formed in 1938, and the first ladies' competition was won by Judy Good.

NEWCASTLE RACE CARD, 3 OCTOBER, 1860. Limerick City Museum.

Golf was introduced into Limerick during the late nineteenth century but the game itself can be dated back to at least 1457, when James II of Scotland was at war with the English. An act of the Scottish Parliament ensured that "the golfe be utterly cryit down and not to be used" because it interfered with the practice of archery. The first golf club in Ireland was opened in Bray, in 1762; the first planned golf course was laid out in the Curragh in 1852; and the Golfing Union of Ireland was established in 1891 to regulate the game. Golf became a popular pastime in Limerick during the 1880s. It was played in an informal way by landowners who had twenty or thirty acres to spare, on which they could indulge their love of the game. They laid out six or nine hole courses and just started playing. Many of these landowners were businessmen who had seen the game played in Scotland or had some association with the Scottish regimental officers who were posted to Limerick, especially members of the Black Watch Regiment. The Golfing Union of Ireland was established after a meeting held in the Northern Counties Railway Hotel in Portrush, County Down, on 12 October, 1891. By then golf had become a popular pastime and eight or nine new clubs were opening every year. The new union was set up as an administrative body and its first resolution stressed the desirability of having its membership composed of representatives of every gold club in Ireland. The Limerick Golf Club became affiliated to the Golfing Union of Ireland in 1909.

The Limerick Golf Club owes its origins to Alexander W. Shaw (1847-1923), a prominent Limerick businessman, the owner of Shaw's bacon factory, W. J. Shaw & Sons, on Mulgrave Street, and a director of the Waterford Limerick and Western Railway Company. He was a keen sportsman and was instrumental in holding a meeting in the library of the Athenaeum on 11 December, 1891. Thirty-two men attended. Alexander Shaw was elected as chairman, B. Plummer as corresponding secretary, E. G. Fitt as financial secretary and J. E. Murphy as treasurer. Seven committee members were elected, and the new club adopted the Limerick Golf Club as its name. A subscription fee of ten shillings, fifty pence in today's money, was decided upon for the first season and any person who joined after 1 January, 1892, had to pay an entrance fee. Ladies were admitted to the membership at half of the entrance and subscription fees. The Limerick Golf Club had a nomadic existence in its earlier days. The first committee proposed that a course be laid out on ground at Greenpark Race Course, in Ballinacurra, with the permission of the Race Committee. This was done by Alexander Shaw, E. G. Fitt, Captain Willington and Captain Wylie of the Black Watch Regiment, who laid out a course of nine holes for the men and a short course for the women, within two weeks. The first game of golf under the auspices of the Limerick Golf Club took place on Christmas Day, 1891, with a large crowd in attendance. The first competition was held on 5 February, 1892, for a medal presented by Alexander Shaw, the first captain, a position he held from 1891 to 1894. The club moved to Hogan's Farm, in Dooradoyle, in the autumn of 1892. This farm was located in the area now occupied by Woodlawn Drive, Hilltop Drive and Lawndale Drive and the club used the course on it until 1897. The County Cricket and Tennis Club, off the Ennis Road, accommodated the golfers from 2 December, 1897. In those days the grounds of the County Cricket and Tennis Club were bounded by Shelbourne Road, to the east, The Ennis Road to the south, Lansdowne Road, to the West, and the Limerick Workhouse to the north. Golfers had the run of the grounds during the winter months as no cricket

ADVERTISEMENT FOR SHAWS MEAT PRODUCTS. 1907.

or tennis was played at that time of year. The Limerick Golf Club appears to have gone into abeyance from January 1898 to November 1901, possibly because the members had to negotiate for a suitable piece of land almost every autumn. Most of the members had played in Lahinch and Kilkee during the summer months and some of them were founders of other clubs in Ballybunion, Newport and Nenagh.

A new committee was elected on 2 November 1901 and Sir Charles Barrington (1848-1943) was in the chair when a resolution was passed to call the revitalised association by its old name, the Limerick Golf Club. Thomas Phelps, one of the committee, rented ground for a suitable course on the Nolan farm at Newcastle for a yearly rental of fifteen pounds. Coincidentally, this course was located between the Limerick Corporation reservoir and the eastern end of the present northern boundary of the Castletroy Golf Club and it was used by the club until October 1903. In that month the Limerick Golf Club relocated to Clancy's farm in Ballysheedy. Even though the golfers had the use of a small house and a coach-house behind Ballysheedy House the site was too small and did not lend itself to the playing of competitions. On 27 September, 1904, the Limerick Golf Club moved back to Hogan's farm and erected a pavilion they had bought from the Garrowen Rugby Club for twelve pounds. On 30 September, 1907, the committee decided to seek a permanent home for the club. In 1908 the Limerick Golf Club leased the Furnell farm in Ballyclough, on a twenty-one-year lease, at a yearly rent of seventy pounds. The members removed the pavilion from Hogan's farm and installed it on concrete foundations at Ballyclough; appointed a full-time professional, Thomas McNamara of Rushbrooke Golf Club, County Cork; hired a tea-lady and groundsman; and installed a public telephone. During the winter of 1912 and 1913 the members discovered that a Mrs. Laffan, whose family had been evicted from the farm, had a valid claim to most of their grounds. She recovered ownership in 1914 but leased the course back to the club. One field, retained by Mrs Furnell, was replaced by a field leased temporarily from a Mrs. Crawford. A man named Hartigan bought the Laffan land in 1915 and leased it to the club until 1919. In the meantime the Limerick Golf Club had made nine attempts to change locations because of title

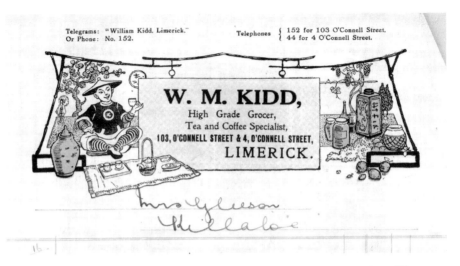

WILLIAM KIDD WAS A GROCER, PROVISIONS MERCHANT AND COLONIAL PRODUCE IMPORTER AT 4 AND 103 O'CONNELL STREET. ON 5 JANUARY, 1916, HE CHARGED MRS. GLEESON OF TINERANA, KILLALOE, FIFTY-NINE PENCE FOR NINE POUNDS OF IRISH BACON, SEVENTEEN-AND-A-HALF-PENCE FOR ONE HUNDRED ORANGES AND FORTY-TWO-AND-A-HALF PENCE FOR FOURTEEN POUNDS OF THE BEST CURRANTS. DESPITE LIMERICK BEING A MAJOR PRODUCER OF BACON, IN THAT YEAR, CANADIAN BACON WAS CHEAPER TO BUY, BEING A FRACTION LESS THAN FIVE PENCE A POUND, AGAINST THE LOCAL BACON WHICH WAS JUST OVER SIX PENCE A POUND.

difficulties. It stayed in the immediate area, however, and on 11 March, 1919, the committee decided to purchase the Crawford farm which had been up for sale. On 21 June 1919, the Limerick Golf Club bought the bulk of the land it now owns from Mrs Crawford for the sum of £2,000. Further purchases made in the 1950s and 1960s completed the present grounds. An army hut was bought and erected on the site in 1920. It served as the club-house until 1966. Roxboro Castle once stood on the site of the present club-house which was opened on Saturday, 16 April, 1966. The Limerick Golf Club had a low profile during the first seventy years of its existence but this changed when Thomas E. O'Donnell became president of the Golfing Union of Ireland for the 1967-1968 term. Patrick J. McPolin held the same office for the 1973-1974 term and both men helped to focus attention on Limerick's golfing fraternity. Up to 1945 the club had won only one Munster title but had annexed twenty-nine Munster titles between then and 1989 when it had a membership of 1,100. In 1967 the Barton Shield Team won the club's first Irish crown. The unique distinction of winning the big three, Irish Junior Cup, Senior Cup and Barton Shield, in the one year, fell to the club in 1976. Over the next twelve years it won fifteen Munster titles and six Irish ones. In 1980, as holders of the Irish Senior Cup, the Limerick Golf Club was invited to compete in the European Club Championship which was held at the Ponza Golf Club in Majorca. The team members were Vincent Nevin, Jackie Harrington, Ivan Morris and Pat Cotter (Captain). They created

Irish sporting history in winning the European Crown, the first club in Ireland to win a senior European title.

The Milford Hospice is located east of the entrance to Plassey. This was originally known as Milford house and was the home of a Limerick banker, George Maunsell of Milford. He was a collector of customs; was married twice; and was admitted as a freeman of Limerick in 1788. He married his first wife, Anne Smyth, the daughter of a former collector of customs, in 1786. They had a daughter who later married Thomas O'Grady. In 1796 he married Sir Richard Quin's niece, Frances Magrath of Redmondstown, by whom he had eleven children.

Plassey derives its place-name from the more distant place of the same name in India. The townlands of Annaghbeg, Dromore, Gurrane, Rivers and Shravokee are now merged into one collective identity, Plassey, by the many visitors who avail of this area's various amenities, especially the magnificent riverside walks.

Robert Clive (1725-1774), Clive of India, was born in Market Drayton, Shropshire. He was a wild youth, and his parents were quite glad to ship him off to India at the age of eighteen. While there he distinguished himself in war, fighting against the French and the Indians. His victory at the decisive battle of Plassey on 27 July, 1757, resulted in the British domination of India which lasted for almost two centuries. In this battle he defeated Surajah Dowlah and an Indian force of 60,000 men with a small force of 3,000 men, 2,000 of whom were Indians. This epic action enabled Clive to promote one of Surajah Dowlah's former officers as Nabob of Bengal in Dowlah's place. The new ruler, Mir Jaffir, enriched Clive, who was also rewarded with an Irish title by the grateful British. To qualify for this honour he had to buy an estate in Ireland, so he purchased a disjointed patchwork of several thousand acres stretching from Bunratty to the Fergus, including Rineanna (now Shannon Airport), Tullyglass and Drumgeely, on the Clare side of the Shannon, while nearer to the city of Limerick he acquired Cappantymore in the Clare Hills, other holdings in Gortatogher, Corbally, Rosmadda, three houses in St. Mary's parish, and Ballykilty Manor and lands in Kilmurry. From these assorted lands he took his title, Baron Clive of Plassey, County Clare, Ireland. On his return to India he practically became the governor of that sub-continent through his own connivance, and that of the English East India Company. He eventually retired to England but killed himself shortly afterwards, cutting his throat with a penknife in a lavatory.

Plassey House, in the townland of Sreelane, was re-named by Robert Clive soon after he purchased it from Thomas MacMahon. The present structure is a

PLASSEY HOUSE, IN THE 1920s, Limerick City Museum.

Victorian Italiante building which was built for the Russell family and completed in 1863. It is believed to incorporate part of the late-eighteenth-century house built by the Maunsell family and, quite possibly, may retain some features of the original house known as Ballykilty Manor. Richard Maunsell was mayor of Limerick in 1734, high sheriff in 1743 and was a member of parliament for the city from 1740 to 1761. His grandson, Thomas Maunsell (1732-1814) of Plassey, was a well-known banker who had served as a British official in the East Indies. The house and grounds have taken on a new role since the National Institute for Higher Education was established here in the 1970s and it is now an integral part of the college complex, linked by corridors at first-floor level. It is the administrative centre of a new university, the foundation of which was mooted by a Fianna Fáil cumann from Newmarket on Fergus in 1934. The resolution was drawn up by members of the cumann who pointed out the necessity.

> For the foundation of a constituent college of the National University of Ireland. Such a college would be of cultural and material advantage to the people of Limerick and of the neighbouring counties. The centre is an ideal one and can support easily a university college.

Copies of the resolution were forwarded to all public bodies in the city and county and in December of that year Limerick County Council adopted another resolution to take action with a view to having a college established in Limerick City. The government, however, had other priorities. Despite the efforts of the Limerick Chamber of Commerce, the Limerick City Vocational Educational

Committee, the Limerick branches of the Irish National Teachers' Association and Association of Secondary Teachers, the Limerick Employers' Federation, concerned individuals and local Dáil members the government of the day did not encourage the establishment of any such institution. The University Committee was founded on 24 October, 1945, and was eventually advised by the Taoiseach's (Eamonn de Valera's) private secretary to get in touch with the authorities of University College Cork to work out a satisfactory scheme that would not affect Cork interests. After Dr. O'Rahilly, president of University College Cork, stated his position, or rather opposition, to the idea he outlined his objections. He did not want to violate the existing charter of the National University, was wary of losing the religious atmosphere of the colleges to power-hungry governments and civil servants, and felt that Limerick would have an inadequate supply of students, qualified staff, administrative officers and finances.

THE CAMPUS IN THE 1980s, Shannon Development Photo Library.

Dr. O'Rahilly's objections to the foundation of the university had persuaded many of the University Committee to seek a substitute a college of technology. Little was heard about either type of college over the next decade. In 1957 Limerick City Council revived the idea and met with the representatives of the local schools. A new working committee was formed. University College Galway and University College Dublin supported its efforts and the committee submitted its report to the Limerick City Council on 12 November, 1959. The report was a timely one as *The University Commission Report 1959* the same year, reported on overcrowding in UCD and recommended a programme which resulted in the transfer of that university to Belfield. The universities of Cork

PLASSEY HOUSE IS INCORPORATED INTO THE FABRIC OF THE UNIVERSITY'S MODERN BUILDING COMPLEX.
PROFESSOR G.H DOWNER WAS INAUGURATED AS PRESIDENT OF THE UNIVERSITY OF LIMERICK BY THE
CHANCELLOR, DR. MIRIAM HEDERMAN-O'BRIEN, ON TUESDAY, 15 SEPTEMBER, 1998.
Shannon Development Photo Library.

and Galway benefited from the same programme as both were improved and extended. The Limerick City Council adopted the committee's report on 23 November, 1959, and passed a resolution asking the government to take the necessary steps to establish a constituent college of the National University of Ireland. The University Project Committee was established in 1959 at the instigation of the Limerick City Council and the past pupils' unions of the Limerick Schools. It came into existence on 23 October, 1959, campaigned for the establishment of a third-level college over an eleven-year period, and brought its work to successful fruition with the establishment of the National Institute for Higher Education in September 1972. Donough O'Malley (1921-1968), the Limerick-born Minister for Education, proposed another kind of institution, a "New College", in a report that was published the following August, on 22 March 1967. This would be a Limerick New College that would have lower entrance requirements but would be empowered to award pass degrees in the humanities, science and commerce. He was informed by the University Project Committee that they were not satisfied with such a solution but would accept it on three conditions, that honours degrees would also be awarded, that entry requirements would be of the same standard as the existing universities and that the name be changed to Limerick University College. Donough O'Malley was the minister who established free education in primary and secondary schools. He died suddenly in March, 1967, and was succeeded by Brian Lenihan as Minister for Education. In July of that year the government decided to establish a new body to deal with higher education and in August, 1968, the Higher Education Authority came into existence. The Government Information Bureau issued a statement on 12 December, 1968, stating that the government had decided to allocate the necessary funding for a third-level educational institution in Limerick and that negotiations for an eighty-acre site were in progress. In January, 1970, sites were examined at Clonmacken, Plassey, Raheen and Redgate and, although it was neither a university or university college, the new institution was officially opened in September, 1972.

The National Institute for Higher Education opened with a faculty staff of eleven, a general staff of eleven and 113 students, on a seventy-acre campus. Dr. Edward Walsh, the president of the University of Limerick, was the director of the new third-level institution which pioneered initiatives which are taken for granted by today's students. Credit transfer schemes allowed students to study abroad. Modular courses enabled other students, especially mature ones, to qualify outside of a set time frame, and the co-operative educational scheme valued work experience as a factor in all third-level courses. The National Institute for Higher Education became the University of Limerick on 12 January, 1989, had 9,400 students and a staff of 735 in September, 1997.

The Grounds of Plassey form an attractive campus today. The wooded demesne was established by Robert Clive but was retained and developed by the Campbell, Maunsell, Harvey, Baily and Keating families, owners of the estate over two centuries. The extensive damage wrought on the demesne in the early 1960s was stopped by Kevin Hannan and Donough O'Malley. The campus now covers an area of 250 acres and is still parkland to a certain extent, despite the large-scale building programme initiated over the last quarter of a century. From 1972 onwards the Plassey estate was cared for by the National Institute of Higher Education and its woodland and trees form an attractive backdrop for the various university buildings. The old stables have been expanded into a complex that includes a private bar and other services. At the launch of the thirty-fourth issue of *The Old Limerick Journal* on Monday, 20 July 1998, Dr. Edward M.

THE PLASSEY BANK, WITH PLASSEY HOUSE, THE UNIVERSITY CAMPUS AND CASTLETROY IN THE BACKGROUND.
Shannon Development Photo Library.

Walsh mentioned that Limerick University had acquired 100 acres of land on the Clare side of the River Shannon. Professor Roger G.H. Downer was inaugurated as the new president of the university on Tuesday, 15 September, 1998, at the University Concert Hall.

The Plassey Bank is one of Limerick's finest amenities. The footbridge leading towards it can be found behind the Physical Education building, close to a large block of stone with the inscription *Thomond College of Education* on one face and a longer inscription on the other side;

> *Oh Youth thou magician*
> *one hour on thy stage*
> *is worth all the gray-*
> *bearded wisdom of Age.*
> > *The Bard of Thomond*

This stone once identified the college of that name and originally stood outside what is now the Science and Technology building, the former Thomond College of Education. A tow-path constructed in the late 1820s to connect the canal harbour with Plassey and the Plassey Bank, became a particularly popular excursion area for people who walked here from the Irishtown, Englishtown and the developing Newtownpery. The remains of a ruined mill stand near the

ADVERTISEMENT DATED 1902

Plassey, or Black, Bridge, a footbridge across the River Shannon that leads off towards Corbally and Gilloge Bridge, parallel with the River Blackwater. There are six fishermen's' huts or cottages, some of them occupied, west of Ferry House and the mill. Near one of the cottages is a milestone indicating distance and inscribed *Limerick 2 Miles, Killaloe 10 Miles*. There was a ten-foot drop in the river level between Bohogue and Drominveg prior to 1929.

The Plassey Bridge was designed by 1837 at the behest of the Commissioners for the Improvement of the Navigation of the Shannon. The detailed map and plans used soundings taken at low water in July 1836. The bridge was constructed shortly afterwards and connected the Plassey Bank to the towpath and lock of the canal to Killaloe which, like the Blackwater River, emptied into the Shannon, opposite the Plassey Mill. The Annaghbeg Lock was the name of this first lock; the Gillogue Lock was east of Gillogue Bridge; and there was a limestone quarry in the vicinity of the second lock.

Shannys' Pub was established by the Shanny sisters, the two daughters of an Abbey fisherman. Their surname is a derivative of *Ó Seanaigh*, the descendant of Seanch, the old or the wise, an old Clare surname. The public-house was located on the Clare side of the river, a few hundred yards upriver from Plassey Bridge. It was sometimes known as *The Thatch* and up to the early 1900s it could only be approached by a track leading through three fields on the river side of the Gurrane Road. After High Court proceedings a right of way to Shannys' Pub was established along the canal bank. The pub sign was a wine-coloured board,

261

between the front door and the parlour window, that bore the legend *Catherine Shanny, licensed to sell beer, wine and spirits to be consumed on the premises.*

The Towing Path is the name of a path built in the 1820s to connect the two sections of the Limerick to Killaloe Canal that utilised that short stretch of the Shannon River between the Plassey Mill and Arthur's Ferry (and the Illaanaroon Islands). Strictly speaking, this place-name refers only to that part of the path leading from Plassey Bridge to the canal and Park Lock. The name, corrupted to the Tow Path, is often applied incorrectly to parts of the Plassey Bank.

The Plassey Mill was erected by Major Hodges Maunsell in 1824 but the remaining stairwell, rising to a height of seven stories, has features that look almost medieval. He built a dam known as the Plassey Falls almost as far as the Clare bank in order to harbour water for his mill-race. The hydroelectric scheme on the River Shannon resulted in a change in water levels from 1929 onwards and the dam was described by the late Kevin Hannan as being "swallowed up in alluvial deposits" becoming a "mass of vegetation". Reuben Harvey leased the mill, which was badly burned in 1841, with only the stone fabric remaining. He had to rebuild it at his own expense, as he had been in dispute with his insurance company at the time of the fire and his policy had been revoked. The mill closed shortly afterwards as the mill workers had gone on strike, demanding payment for the time they spent on travelling to and from work on Reuben Harvey's barges. Richard Russell installed a turbine, a type of hydraulic engine that was considered preferable to ordinary water wheels, to increase output during the 1860s. It was of little benefit and the mill closed a few years later. Its floors of pitch pine were ripped out, its machinery sold as scrap, and the main structure was demolished in 1957, leaving only the stairwell intact. The foundation stone of Mungret Gate had been placed in the riverside facade of the mill but was lost during the demolition by dynamite. It bore the Limerick City arms and was inscribed:

Carlo Rege
Regnante
Petro Creagh
Prietore
Anno Dmn
1643

Parts of the stonework in the stairwell, especially around the windows, doorways and steps, may have been quarried from older buildings within the city and shipped upriver to Plassey. William Wellington Baily purchased the Plassey

A Bronze Sun-dial, for the Parish of Kilmurry, including the Liberties of Limerick.
Limerick City Museum.

estate at the turn of the century. He died in 1911 and the estate became the property of his nephew, Eric Baily. Plassey was purchased by Patrick Keating in 1933, but after his death in 1961, the Rehabilitation Institute of Ireland bought the estate and cut down much of its extensive and well-maintained woodland.

The Ferry House stands next to the mill, on its eastern side, and was occupied by the Madden family at the time of the War of Independence. In March 1920, John Madden found the body of a young man on the small bridge over the mill-race overflow on the western side of the mill. There was a label tied around the boy's neck on which the warning *Spies and informers beware* was written. Some time later a mixed force of Royal Irish Constabulary and Black and Tans opened fire on a group of people making their way homewards on the Plassey Bank. Thomas Creamer was killed in the fusillade. A short distance beyond the Plassey Bridge, around the bend, are the remains of a barge which is said to have been sunk by Black and Tans firing on it. The house was built for the ferry-keeper, as the Shannon Navigation Company had operated a ferry here before the footbridge was built. Peg O'Brien, the last ferry-keeper on the Clare side, had a similar house on her side of the river. This has long since disappeared but she is commemorated on the site which is called Peg's Height.

A New Canal Bridge, to link Corbally with Rhebogue, now enables people to walk the river bank from Corbally almost as far as Castleconnell. The *Limerick Leader* of Saturday, 9 November, 1996, carried a report of this new project on the same page that bore Kevin Hannan's obituary. Mayor O'Hanlon was one of the dignitaries who visited Jim O'Donnell's engineering works, on the Dock Road, to examine the new crossing which was to be put in place a few weeks later. He said that the bridge had been sponsored by Guinness and would be the catalyst for major improvements in the canal and Plassey areas. He continued-

> I understand that the bridge is to be called the Guinness Bridge, but perhaps it could be called after Kevin Hannan, our great historian who died this week and who loved the area so well.

The Garrison Wall pre-dates the mill. This was erected to dissipate the force of the river current along the southern shore of the Shannon and protect the horse-ferry which operated here until the Shannon Navigation Company built the Black Bridge in the late 1830s. In 1949 this bridge was reconstructed. Mrs. Sheehy owned the ferry-keeper's house on this side of the river in 1979.

The American Ground was the name applied to the low-lying field to the west during the middle years of the nineteenth century when the ballast from the returning coffin ships was dumped here to fill the area.

Castletroy Tower House is located on the bank of the Shannon River and lies about midway between Plassey House and Annacotty. It is in extremely poor condition and has been fenced off in case of accident. This tower house may have been built by Dermot O'Brien during the reign of Henry III (1216-1272). O'Donovan and O'Curry were unable to ascertain when it was built, or by whom, but they doubted that it had been erected by a family of the O'Treos or Troys. Thirteen years earlier, in 1827, Fitzgerald mentioned the "ruins of Castle Troy ... and the rich plantations of Mr. Arthur of Glanomera [sic] on the opposite side of the river". In 1837 Lewis wrote of a modern gazebo near the castle "and not far distant are the ruins of the ancient church of Killonan or Killowen". By 1840 only the eastern and northern sides were in a state of "tolerable preservation" and the other two sides were "nearly destroyed". In 1997 the self same description still held true. Cement blocks have been used to repair parts of the remaining walls and to prevent people from trying to reach a staircase visible on the second level. The northern wall seems to have contained seven floors to judge from the windows and is slightly more complete than the eastern wall which contains the staircase and remains of five-and-a-half floors. Remnants of two barrell-vaulted ceilings are visible within the castle interior. Follow the Plassey Bank eastwards to find the castle. The Mulkear River flows into the Shannon east of Castle Troy and is spanned by what at first glance seemed to be two cast-iron footbridges and a large curved cast-iron pipe in the shape of an arch or bow. The apparent bridges are frames designed to bear the weight of heavy cast-iron pipes bearing water into the city from Clareville. The bowed cast-iron pipe over the river was a marvellous piece of engineering and a siphon-type system forced the water through the pipe from the far side.

The Earlier City Water-Works were commenced in 1834 by a London company which placed two tanks, about a mile from the city at Cromwell's Fort, near Gallows Green, one of the forts erected on the high ground of Singland Hill during the Cromwellian siege. The second fort, Ireton's Fort, was constructed to the east, above the Penny Well. The tank's elevation was fifty feet above the highest part of the city, and 72 feet above the river, from which the water was raised through a metal pipe, twelve inches in diameter, by two steam-

SHIELD OF BRONZE, IRISH, MADE FROM A SINGLE PIECE OF HAMMERED METAL, USED FOR DISPLAY ABOUT 3,000 YEARS AGO, AND NOW IN THE HUNT MUSEUM.

engines, each of twenty horse-power. During the process of excavating a foundation for the tanks, several skeletons, cannon, musket balls, armour and a selection of old military weapons were found. The water-works near Cromwell's Fort was later known as the Garryowen Reservoir.

Castletroy is actually a misnomer and the original place-name was *Caladh Uí Throighthigh*, the *caladh* of the Troys. The word *caladh* may refer to a port, harbour or ferry and the surname *Ó Troighthigh* means descendant of Troighthigh, the foot-soldier. The *Ó Troighthigh* originated in or near Corcomroe in north-west Clare but spread into Cork, Limerick, Tipperary and

Offaly in early medieval times. A similar surname *De Treo*, meaning of Troyes, a French city, was introduced into Kilkenny and Waterford by Anglo-Norman invaders. This latter name is also anglicised as Troy but the former surname is more likely to have been associated with the O'Briens as it was widespread throughout the old territory of Thomond. The *Ó Troighthigh* owner of the *caladh* may have been a tenant of Dermot O'Brien or the Clanwilliam Bourkes. The name has been linked with Limerick since 1200; Henry Troy was mayor of the city in 1237 and either he or his namesake held the mayoral office in 1260 and 1269. John Troy was sheriff in 1274 and 1281; Richard Troy was mayor in 1281; Henry Troy was mayor and John Troy a sheriff in 1282; the position of mayor was filled by various Troys in 1296, 1299, 1303, 1311, 1314, 1328, 1383, 1411, 1420, 1422, 1425 and 1430; and other members of the Troy family were sheriffs in 1296, 1303, 1315, 1317, 1334, 1338, 1354, 1356, 1361, 1370, 1373, 1383, 1400, 1405, 1420, 1422 and 1462.

The Plassey Bank can be followed almost as far as Annacotty. Shortly after passing over a stone and concrete footbridge a stile gives one access to the Bohemian Rugby Club Grounds from which one can stroll down the road to Annacotty.

Annacotty derives its name from *Áth na Coite*, the ford of the cot or river-boat. In ancient times this was an important crossing-point over the Mulkear River. Until quite recently this was a small village on the main road to Dublin from the city. It was so busy that one elderly lady used to leave her lights on at night to

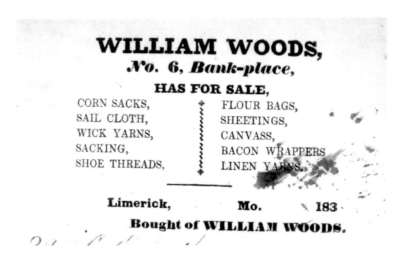

WILLIAM WOODS WAS A SUPPLIER OF CORN SACKS, SAIL CLOTH, CALICO, CANVAS, SACKING, SHEETINGS, SHOE THREADS, WICK YARNS, FLOUR BAGS, BACON WRAPPERS AND LINEN YARNS IN THE 1830S. HIS PREMISES WAS LOCATED AT 6 BANK PLACE.

prevent motorists from driving into her house. A monument to Jackie Power, a local hurler, now stands on the site of this lady's house. Walk onto the old stone bridge and look upriver to see the dam built by Joseph Sexton to harness the Mulkear and power his paper mills. The ruins of his mills can be seen next to a new housing development advertised as the Salmon Weir complex of townhouses and detached houses. Joseph Sexton's paper mill is about to undergo restoration, at the time of writing. The large modern bridge dwarfs the older structure and the extended highway now bypasses the village. Annacotty was the site of the now-closed Ferenka factory. The area achieved prominence in 1975 when Dr. Tiede Herrema was kidnapped here. As Limerick City extended south-eastwards from the 1950s onwards it covered a lot of the intervening region with residential estates. The population of the village of Annacotty was 523 in 1986 while that of Kilmurry was 760 persons.

The Annacotty Fountain Memorial commemorates Charles Richard George Fitzgibbon, the eldest son of Lady Louisa and her first husband Gerald N. Fitzgibbon, who died on 30 April, 1870, at the age of twenty-one. Louisa's uncle, John, had erected the pump here, near Finnegan's public house, at an earlier stage, and Louisa renovated it and erected the memorial in 1875.

The Earl of Clare's Desmene was located near the western boundaries of Killeenagarriff parish. In 1837 the principal seats were Thornfield, the residence of Major-General Sir R. Bourke; Woodsdown, of Major Gough; Mulcaher, of the Rev. J. Crampton; and Rich Hill, of W. Howley.

Woodsdown House is now a convent. William Gough Gubbins succeeded his relation, Major Gough, in 1853. He moved from Woodsdown House to Castletroy in the 1860s and eventually sold Woodsdown for £3,000 in 1875.

William Howley, the son of John Howley of Charlotte's Quay, Limerick, was one of Caleb Powell's grand jurors in 1858. He lived in Rich Hill and played a prominent part in the Limerick celebrations that preceded the proclamation of Queen Victoria in 1837.

Derrygalvan Parish was located within the Liberties of Limerick City in 1840 when the only trace of antiquity was a small burial-ground east of the Limerick-Tipperary road, in the townland of Ballysimon. Some small fragments of a ruined church were "visible among the luxuriant weeds" but little else remained to indicate how large it had been, or to reveal anything else about it. The land was considered remarkably good, with about half of it under tillage and the remainder attached to the large dairy farms which supplied the city with milk and butter. The principal houses were Coolanave, Ballyclough House and Killonan House.

St. Patrick's Church at Ahane was described in the 1830s as a large new chapel. It replaced a mud-and-wattle "Mass house" which had been erected near Biddiford in 1785. During penal times the people of the locality had resorted to a Mass rock near Ardvarna, and the hill on which they placed look-outs is still known as *Cnoc an Aifrinn*, Mass hill. St. Patrick's church was partially destroyed on the Night of the Big Wind, 6-7 January, 1839, but was repaired soon

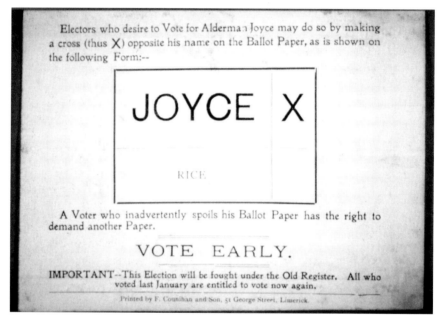

VOTING CARD OF 1910. Limerick City Museum.

afterwards. It was last renovated in 1977-1978 and is still in use. The arch around the door is believed to have been taken from Quin Abbey in County Clare.

Scart Townland is unique insofar as the dioceses of Limerick, Cashel and Killaloe meet here.

Derrygalvan derived its name form *Doire Uí Ghealbháain*, the derry or oak grove of O'Galvan, a family name still found within the city and Liberties. It was in Derrygalvan townland that the original parish church was built.

Galvan, Galvin, Galven, Gallivan, *O Gealwaine, O Gallivain* and *O'Galvane* are all derivatives of *O Gealbháin*, the descendants of Gealbhán, the Bright-white. This is a Dalcassian name once prevalent in Derrygalvan, found throughout Munster, and most numerous in Kerry. It is also found in County Roscommon.

Mountshannon House was a two-story eighteenth-century structure with a seven-bay entrance, erected by the White family in 1750. They later sold it to the Fitzgibbon family of Ballysheedy. Black Jack Fitzgibbon (1749-1802) may have renovated the house at a later stage. He was notorious as an opponent of Catholic Emancipation, an architect of the Act of Union and Lord Chancellor of Ireland. In 1795 he was created Lord Clare. He suppressed the Rebellion of 1798. At his funeral a dead cat was thrown at his coffin in memory of his boastful taunt that he "would make Ireland as tame as a mutilated cat". Lewis Wyatt remodelled Mountshannon for Black Jack's son, John, after 1813, while James Pain is also believed to have contributed to the overall design. John, Second Earl of Clare, was a close friend of Lord Byron. The pair of them invaded a Turkish harem on one memorable occasion. Byron escaped but John Fitzgibbon was captured and received the unkindest cut of all in punishment. After his death, in 1851 he was succeeded by his brother, Richard, the Third, and last, Earl of Clare. Richard lacked the government pension of his two predecessors. His personal fortune had been diminished during the *Great Hunger* by contributions to famine relief. His only son was listed as missing, presumed dead, after the Charge of the Light Brigade, and he left an impoverished estate to his daughter, Lady Louisa Fitzgibbon. She was the last of the Fitzgibbon family to reside in Mountshannon. Her first husband assumed her name on marrying her. After he died she married a Sicilian nobleman in the hope of repairing the family fortunes, only to discover he had married her for a similar reason. She left Ireland in 1887. In 1888 she sold the contents of the house, and in 1893 the house was purchased by Thomas Nevins, a wealthy Irish-American. Louisa was buried in a convent on the Isle of Wight. Mountshannon House was burned down in 1920 during the War of Independence and the Land Commission divided the 900 acre estate after Thomas Nevins died. Even today, the gaunt ruins of Mountshannon House form an impressive monument.

3,000 YEARS OLD CAULDRON, SHIELD AND SWORDS FROM IRELAND, IN THE HUNT MUSEUM.

Killeenagarriff derives its name from *Cillín na nGarbh*, the little church of the rough people. This may also be a corruption of *Cillín Aith Gairbh*, the church of the rough place. The ruin of this old parish church still stands in the graveyard to which it gives its name on the northern bank of the Annacotty River, which is here called the Killeenagarriff river. Tradition maintains that Mass was last celebrated here in 1648, but this is at variance with the Lewis account which refers to it as a Church of Ireland church which was destroyed in the war of 1641. It was rebuilt and re-used as a Protestant parish church but lapsed into ruin by 1837.

The Jewish Burial Ground is located opposite The Hurlers' public-house, at the end of a pot-holed boreen. The Jewish community decided to acquire land for use as a cemetery in the late 1890s and purchased this plot of ground in 1902. The graveyard had become overgrown with vegetation by the 1980s but was restored by the Limerick Civic Trust and rededicated by the Chief Rabbi of Ireland, Rev. Ephraim Mirvis, on 14 November 1990. The commemorative plaque on the side of the small prayer house refers to the restoration and bears an interesting motif, a Star of David with an Irish harp within its centre. The prayer house was known locally as the *Tahara*, or "the wash-house" and contained a ceremonial bath in which bodies were cleaned before burial. The bath was stolen about thirty years ago by two local men. A pathway through the graveyard now leads to a modern housing development in what was formerly Briar Field. There seems to have been a total of nine burials in the graveyard. Eight are marked by memorial stones and the ninth seems to have been unmarked, the grave of a Jewish lady who killed herself in Limerick. Her name was Elsa Reininger (1882-1938). She was born in Neulistritz, Bohemia, married Berish Hofler, a Polish Jew, and lived in Vienna until 1938. She fled to Ireland with her husband after the fall of Austria, and, for a time, lived with her daughter, Margaret Kaitcher, at 74 Wolfe Tone Street, and with the Tobin family at 18 Newenham Street. She had to abandon her money on fleeing Austria, suffered from depression and booked herself into the Hotel Crescent, at 87 O'Connell Street, on Thursday, 27 October, 1938. Some time between 6.45 p.m. and 11.45 p.m. that day, she committed suicide by shooting herself in the head. Most of the memorials bear Hebrew lettering and were carved in Dublin, with the exception of at least one that was made by T. O'Doherty & Sons of Mathew Bridge. The majority of the tombstones bear both the Christian and Jewish calendar year and commemorate Simon Gewurtz (1887-1944) from Bratislava, Limerick's last serving rabbi, Samuel Sochat (1847-1917) who died on 4 March, 5677, Asher Coen (1857-1914) who died on 22 May, 5674, Zlato Maissel (1841-1906) who died in 5666, Maurice L. Morrison who died in 1930 or 5690 and two others that were indecipherable because of my lack of Hebrew. The late Louis Fine (1921-

1996), a popular businessman in the city, was the last person interred here at the time of writing.

Ballinacurra derives its name from *Beal Átha an Curraigh*, the mouth of the ford of the marsh.

Greenpark Racecourse replaced Newcastle as a racing venue for the city with the establishment of the Limerick Race Company in 1890. Maurice Lenihan wrote in 1866:

> About two miles south from Limerick, at a place called Newcastle, is a very fine race ground with a permanent stand, where sporting events celebrated in a well-known ballad are generally held. These races have latterly attracted a great deal of attention even in England.

The Newcastle Races were regulated by stewards of the Turf Club which had its offices at 27 George's Street. In 1839 these stewards were drawn from some of the leading families of both city and county, William Cox, John Cripps, George E. Massey, Richard Quin Sleeman, John Westropp and two military men, Captain Croker (17th Lancers) and Captain Mac-Quirrie (Scots Greys). In 1860 the name of William H. Barrington (1815-1872) appeared on a programme listing the stewards for the Newcastle Races. William Hartigan Barrington succeeded to his father's title and became the third baronet on 1 April, 1861. He died on 14 July, 1872, so another member of the Barrington family became the first chairman of the Limerick Race Company, eighteen years later. The

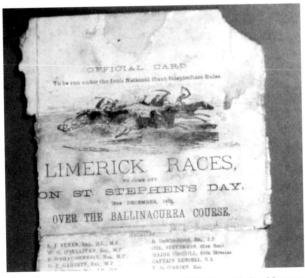

BALLINACURRA RACE CARD, 25 DECEMBER, 1879. Limerick City Museum.

Newcastle Races boasted a natural grandstand, Blackguard Hill, which not only provided race-goers with a spectacular view of each race from start to finish, but also epitomised the unruly nature of much of the audience. Faction-fighters, three-card-trick men, ballad singers, beggars, hawkers, hucksters and ordinary spectators frequented the course and patronised the bar tents, some of which sold alcohol of inferior quality. Disturbances, fights and violent scenes marred the races as the unruly elements in the crowd provoked incident after incident and drunken spectators died from alcohol poisoning or suffered fatal accidents. In 1865 six people died. One, the wife of James Nash, died of shock on hearing that her servant, Bridget Roche, had fallen into a quarry after drinking bad whiskey at the races. George Ballard (1847-1865) fell off a jaunting car into the path of another at Pennywell on his way home. Another unidentified man died in a similar accident on the same day, coming home from the races drunk. J. Hilliard (1785-1865) was on his way to the races to beg, when he was struck and killed by a jaunting car in Pennywell, and a fireman named Sullivan, with the Limerick Steamship Company, was found dead of alcohol poisoning the day after the races. In 1867 a special meeting of the total Abstinence Association moved the following resolution.

> In consequence of the dissipation, crime, loss of life and financial ruin arising annually to all classes from the holding of the Newcastle Races and the sale of intoxicating drinks thereon, that these field sports should in future be carried out in a manner befitting a civilised community, by prohibiting the licensing of tents thereon.

In 1868 the races were held in Ballinacurra for the first time, but even then the event was marred by an incident noted in the *Limerick Chronicle* of 15 October:

> Shortly after the start of the horse races at Ballinacurra, a faction fight took place near the entrance to the course in the vicinity of what is known as the "Water Leap"

Limerick has on old hunting tradition that dates back to mythological times. The Anglo-Normans introduced hunting from horseback and the origins of the Scarteen Black and Tans can be traced back to dogs brought ashore from

A DRINKING HORN WITH SILVER MOUNTS, FIFTEENTH-CENTURY, IN THE HUNT MUSEUM.

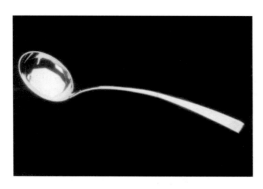

SILVER SOUP LADLE MADE IN LIMERICK IN THE EIGHTEENTH-CENTURY, AND NOW IN THE HUNT MUSEUM.

an Armada shipwrecked off the Kerry coast. These dogs came into the possession of the Ryan family who then lived in Ballyvistea, Emly, near Knocklong. The first authentic record of the Ryans dealing in hunting dogs dates back to 1642 and the family's association with the present mode of hunting dates back to its inception in England, towards the end of the seventeenth century. In 1735 Jack Ryan introduced another strain from the south-west of France to produce the distinctive black-and-tan coloured foxhound known as the Kerry Beagle. The County Limerick Foxhounds were established in 1828, the Limerick Harriers in 1872, and, as late as the 1960s, there were several packs in Limerick and the adjoining counties that used the Greenpark venue to show their horses paces. The Croom Harriers, the Clare Hunt, the Scarteen Black and Tans, the Golden Vale Foxhounds and the North Tipperary Foxhounds were the other hunts that collaborated with the County Limerick Foxhounds and the Limerick Harriers in regulating the Limerick Horse Show and boosting the attendance for two days each August. The Limerick Race Company built a large grandstand in 1893, but two of the largest audiences that ever attended the Greenpark Racecourse did not come to view the horses, visit the trade displays or examine the shows of cattle, dogs, flowers, fruit, or any agricultural exhibits.

John Fitzgerald Kennedy (1917-1963), President of the United States of America, visited Ireland for four days, from 26 June to 29 June, 1963. Mayor Frances Condell, the first woman to hold mayoral office in Limerick, received John F. Kennedy at Greenpark Racecourse as his schedule did not allow him sufficient time to visit the city. She conferred the freedom of the city on him, on Saturday 29 June, 1963, saying:.

> I would like you to know that we of Limerick, have a lovely city in there beyond those fields and trees - a city of which we are very proud steeped as it is in history and antiquity, with its charter and its first mayor reaching back to the year 1197.
>
> It was from our docks, Sir, that many emigrant ships set sail for your shores and from which point of departure our people became yours ...

President Kennedy thanked the mayor for conferring the freedom of the city on him and alluded to the Americans of Irish descent in his own speech:

> ...You can be proud of them and they are proud of you. Even though a good many years have passed since most of them left, they still retain the strongest sentiments of affection for this country and I hope that this visit that we have been able to make has reminded them not only of their past, but also that here in Ireland the word freedom, the word 'independence', the whole sentiment of a nation, are perhaps stronger than in almost any place in the world.
>
> I don't think that I have passed through a more impressive ceremony than the one I experienced yesterday in Dublin when I went with your Prime Minister to put a wreath on the graves of the men who died in 1916.

Pope John Paul II was conferred with the freedom of the city at Greenpark Racecourse during his visit to Limerick on 1 October, 1979. Mayor Bobby Byrne bestowed the honour on three other notable churchmen on the same date and occasion, Tomás Cardinal Ó Fiaich, Archbishop of Armagh, Archbishop Gaetano Alibrandi, Apostolic Nuncio of the Holy See to Ireland, and Dr. Jeremiah Newman, Bishop of Limerick.

The Quaker Cemetery is located a short distance south of Punch's Cross. The graveslabs are of equal size to signify the equality of man both in life and death. The Society of Friends, the Quakers, arrived in Limerick in 1655. They were persecuted by the authorities and were unable to set up a regular establishment until after the Restoration. In 1671 they erected a meeting-house in Creagh Lane. This was rebuilt in 1735 and remained in use until they moved to another

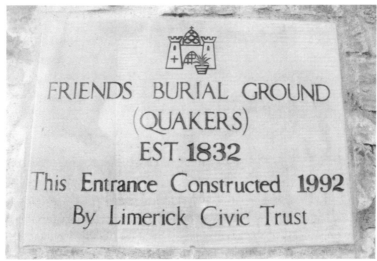

PLAQUE AT THE QUAKER BURIAL GROUND.

meeting house in Cecil Street, which they built for £1, 242.45 in 1807. This building is now owned by the Red Cross. One room was retained at the back, for the use of the Society of Friends until they built their new meeting house in Ballinacurra in 1997. During the Great Hunger the Quakers set up auxiliary relief committees throughout Ireland. Their reputation for involvement in charitable works is legendary. They are the most respected Protestant sect in both the Republic and Northern Ireland, the one sect accepted by Republicans and Loyalists alike as mediators, especially within the prison system.

The Quaker Meeting House, off Southville Gardens, is located behind the cemetery. Francis Howgill and Edward Burrows, both of Westmoreland, James Tickleman of Youghal and Edward Cook of Bandon were the first Quaker's to speak, or attempt to speak, in Limerick, in 1655. They converted John Love, Richard Pearce and Thomas Phelps and by the following year there were about seventy Quakers in the city. Meetings for worship took place in the house of Thomas Holmes and Richard Pearce's house in Bow Lane. Henry Ingoldsby, the governor of the city, banished Barbara Blagden and issued a proclamation;-

.... that no inhabitants of Limerick should receive or entertain a Quaker in his house upon penalty of being turned out of the City.

In 1656 the magistrates "forbid any person to purchase" from the Quakers and fined Edward Tavernor two pounds when he would not serve on a jury. In 1661 John Cobb, James Craven, Richard Pearce, Thomas Phelps and six of their co-religionists were fined forty pounds each after having been remanded in prison for four months on the orders of Thomas Miller, who served as mayor in 1660. In 1662 Edward Kemp was driven out of the city when he refused to contribute ten pounds for the repair of a church. His house was seized by the bishop and his wife and two children evicted. George Fox founded the Society of Friends in 1646. This new movement he set in train was averse to institutional religion, was devoted to peaceful Christian principles and eschewed formal doctrine, sacraments and ordained ministers. Its members became known as Quakers and were considered a serious menace by the Established Church. They were persecuted by the Star Chamber during the reign of Charles II (1660-1685), had their goods confiscated, and were imprisoned, tortured, oppressed and hounded in "every way short of actually putting them to death". From 1656 onwards several of the leading Quakers thought of relocating in the Americas, but when Ann Austin and Mary Fisher landed in Boston in July of that year they were whipped at a cart's tail before they and their baggage were forcibly returned to the ship on which they had arrived. The Puritans of New England resorted to whipping, branding and mutilating Quaker men and women who arrived into the colony. Many Quakers were put to death and others were sold to the plantations as slaves. The Cromwellians had a certain limited toleration of the new movement as Oliver Cromwell had guarded the "liberty of prophecying" but still subjected the Quakers to ill-usage. Matters became worse after the Restoration, as the Established Church brought the full rigour of the law to bear on all dissenters. In 1669 George Fox visited Ireland and was a guest in Richard Pearce's house in Bow Lane. King Charles II allowed dissenters limited religious liberties in 1671 and the Limerick Quakers availed of this opportunity to build a meeting-house in Creagh Lane and to acquire a burial ground, near Peter's Cell.

In 1687 James Craven, William Craven and Samuel Tavernor, three Quaker merchants, served on the corporation. Richard Pearce died in 1690; his mentor, George Fox died in 1691; James Craven died in 1695; and Thomas Phelps died in 1697. William Penn, Thomas Storey and fourteen other Quakers from the Americas visited Ireland in 1698. In his journal, Thomas Storey wrote:

> We had meetings in Charleville and Limerick where we viewed some of the effects of the last siege and observed the walls of some of the houses as well as of the City which had been much shattered with many large cannon shot and that great breaches had been made at the siege by King William's Army in which I had two brothers - one of whom had been killed at the siege of Charlmont and the other a chaplain to a regiment under command of Sir Thomas Gower. A relation of ours survived, wrote the history of the wars and afterwards was made Dean of Limerick in which he died.

Women seem to have been particularly active in the ministry of the Society of Friends. Elizabeth Jacob (1675-1740) of Ardee, County Louth, arrived into Limerick in 1699. She travelled throughout Ireland, particularly Ulster, Scotland, Wales, England and Holland and in 1712 was accompanied on a Scottish journey by Abigale Craven (1642-1752) of Limerick. The persecution of Quakers came to an end during the reign of William and Mary. Thomas Storey returned to Limerick in 1716 and was regarded as an object of curiosity because his brother, George Storey, was then dean of the city. The mayor, Tock Roche, expelled some Quakers from the city in 1723, because they were preaching

A ROMAN ROCK CRYSTAL GOBLET WITH SIXTEENTH-CENTURY FOOT AND LID, IN THE HUNT MUSEUM

in the streets. In 1735 the Quakers met in William Richardson's store while a larger meeting house was being built on the site of the older one, next door. On 9 April, 1805, the Society of Friends concluded an agreement with John Thomas Meade for a plot of land, fifty-four feet in breadth by ninety-two feet in length, on Cecil Street, at a yearly rent of £28.44. The most prominent Quaker surnames associated with the commercial life of the city during the nineteenth century were Alexander, Bennis, Fisher, Grubb, Harvey, Malchomson, Mark, Pike, and Unthank.

Mary Immaculate Teacher Training College, the oldest third-level college in the city, was founded by Bishop Edward T. Dwyer and the Sisters of Mercy in 1898 to train teachers for the primary school system. It was visited by Micheal Martin, Minister for Education, on Monday, 26 January, 1998. Sr. Angela, the college principal, spoke of the prevailing ethos that is considered more important than degrees, programmes of study, student numbers and facilities:

> True to its founding tradition, Mary Immaculate College maintains an active Christian life where Christian values and personal responsibilities are honoured and inculcated.

MARY IMACULATE TEACHER TRAINING COLLEGE CELEBRATED ITS CENTENERARY EARLIER THIS YEAR.

The minister thanked the nuns for their contribution and commitment to Irish education and spoke of his wish to see a partnership between the college and the Department of Education in the development of primary education. Dr.

MARY IMMACULATE TRAINING COLLEGE, THE SMALL LECTURE ROOM AS IT ONCE WAS.
Limerick City Museum.

Edward T. Dwyer laid the foundation stone of the college with a silver trowel and it was recognised as a college of the National University of Ireland in 1974. A new three-year degree course replaced the two-year diploma one in that year. In 1980 the college had 750 students but these numbers increased when it linked up with the University of Limerick to offer a liberal arts degree and post-graduate degrees in arts and education. The college campus has also been extended and in January of 1998 there were 1600 students here.

South Hill possesses the largest corporation estate in the city, a total of 1,201 houses containing 6,500 inhabitants, built between 1966 and 1972. In October, 1986, one shop, one public house, a church which doubled as a community centre, two small playgrounds, a swimming pool, a junior school, a park and two playing-pitches catered for the growing population, over half of whom are unemployed. South Hill House was built by the Evans family and gives its name to the area, part of the former demesne. This house was later occupied by Peter Tait and is now used as a community centre.

Rossbrien, or Rosbrien, is a derivative of *Ros Uí Bhriain*, the *ros* of O'Brien, *ros* meaning a level tract of arable land, in this instance, rather than a bluff, copse, isthmus, point, promontory, wood or the site of an old cemetery. The name came into use during the later years of the reign of Henry VIII (1509-1547), as the land had come into the possession of Murrough O'Brien, 1st Earl of Thomond and 1st Baron Inchiquin, at the time of the suppression. It was originally known as *Fearann na gCailleach*, the ploughland of the veiled women and had belonged to the Augustinian nuns of St. Peter's Cell. Rossbrien was still known under an anglicisation of *Fearann na gCailleach*, Farrine Gallach, as late as 1596 and both place-names were used in the Cromwellian accounts of the 1650s.

St. Dominic's Well is located on the lands of Rossbrien, east of Greenfields Road, a short distance beyond the level crossing. Its place-name may be a corruption of *Tobar Rí an Domhnaigh*, the well of the King of Sunday, that may have been anglicised as Domhnach's Well, rather than Sunday's Well, from *Domhnach*, meaning Sunday. There were at least five other Sunday's Wells in the county, at Ballingarry, Ballyshonby,

HOLY FAMILY JUBILEE MEDAL, 1918.
Limerick City Museum.

Cloncagh, Dromkeen and Gortadrumna, and there would have been pattern or patron days held at each up to 160 years ago. *Tobar Rí an Domhnaigh* could also be translated as the well of the king of the world and many wells bearing this name were the sites of *Lughnasa* gatherings, pre-Christian pilgrimages honouring the god Lugh and his feast or *nasad*. Domhnach could easily be corrupted to Dominic and there are also two St. Modhomhnocs, either of whom could have been commemorated here. The more famous one is St. Modhomhnoc of Tobroughney, possibly a variant of *Tiobroid Domhnach*, Domhnach's Well, in County Kilkenny. He was a sixth-century monk, who studied under St. David in Wales and his feastday falls on 13 February. Very little is known about the second St. Modhomhnoc other that the date of his feast, 18 May. The well is in a very poor state of preservation and the ancient right of way leading to it has been closed to the public since the early 1990s.

St. Dominic's Church probably derived its name from the well rather than an association with any saint. Only the faint outline of a church is now discernible in the tangled overgrowth that marks the site. The high cast-iron gate that marked the entry to the church and cemetery from the roadway has disappeared, concrete blocks were placed in the gateway to deny access to the public, and a barbed-wire fence has been strung around the graveyard, which was used as a *cilleen* or children's burial ground into the 1960s. The church is located about halfway between the site of the well and the level crossing on the old railway line to Foynes which was completed in 1858. St. Dominic's church is unlikely to have been a Dominican foundation, as these lands belonged to the Augustinian nuns who may have erected a church of their own here. Very little of whatever church stood here is now visible and Maurice Lenihan mentions how the graveyard was closed in the early 1850s. In 1849 Margaret Duhy erected a memorial to her husband, Timothy Duhy, in what may be part of the church's eastern gable. Anne Eustace commemorated her husband, James Eustace (1800-1839), with another monument inserted on the internal face of the western gable. Michael Hayes is commemorated on a gravestone to the north-west of the church; Patrick Civil erected a tombstone to the south-west of the church, in memory of his wife, in 1857; and Ellen O'Flaherty's grave is to the south of the Civil one. According to John O'Donovan (1809-1861) this was a burial place for children only until 1835, when the Dominicans consecrated it. By 1840 there was only the appearance of a church ruin in the centre of a circular graveyard. The stone stile, near the north-western corner of the graveyard wall, was virtually covered by brambles on 11 January, 1998.

Donaghmore is an anglicisation of *An Domhnach Mór*, the big *Domhnach*. In this instance, however, the word *Domhnach* is a term reserved for a church, especially one founded by St. Patrick. *Domhnach Mór Maighe Áine*, the great church of the plain of Ainy, Anye or Áine, was the original name of this early church, the ruins of which are quite extensive. Áine is remembered in folklore as the daughter of a Tuatha Dé Danann chieftain or as the banshee whose appearance and keening heralded the imminent death of a Fitzgerald of Desmond. Áine has also been described as a Celtic goddess and may be equated with Anu, who is described in *Cormac's Glossary* as the mother of the deities of Ireland. As the Irish language changed, glossaries of obsolete words were prepared to help students understand words found in ancient manuscripts. *Cormac's Glossary* was written by Cormac Mac Cuilleanáin, the scholar, bishop and king of Cashel who was killed at the battle of Ballaghmoon in 908. Áine is remembered in the folklore of Knockainy, Áine's hill, as the fairy queen who presided over a palace on that hill. St. Patrick stayed in Donaghmore as the guest of Lonan, a local chieftain. He is said to have met St. Nessan for the first time in this spot and founded the church which is commemorated in the place-name. Donaghmore is the burial place of the Connells of Garryowen and the Roche, Fitzgerald and Kelly families.

Mungret may derive its name from *Muine Gairid*, the short hill, but this is "a mere etymological guess" on the part of John O'Donovan in 1840. In earlier times it was known as *Imungram* and *Moungairid*. John O'Connor, the author of *Mungret History and Antiquities* (1971), accepts Mungairit as an acceptable form because it has the sanction of antiquity and believes it is derived form *Mong Ghairid*, the short swamp or morass, an apt description of the land between Mungret and Limerick, in earlier times.

Mungret Monastery was one of Ireland's earliest and greatest foundations. John O'Donovan claimed that an abbey was erected here in the fourth century long before the coming of St. Patrick and his supposed appointment of St. Nessan as prior here. The fifth century is generally accepted as the date of its foundation. St. Munchin is a likelier candidate to associate with St. Patrick, as he was also an abbot of Mungret and died in the later part of the fifth century. According to the long lost *Psalter of Cashel* this monastery had six churches within its walls and, exclusive of numerous scholars, 1500 monks, of whom 500 were learned preachers, 500 psalmists, and 500 wholly employed in spiritual exercises. The *Psalter of Cashel* disappeared from Cashel in 1647 after Murrough the Burner O'Brien attacked Cashel and killed 3,000 of its inhabitants. Mungret Monastery was raided and plundered by Viking marauders in 820, 834, 840 and 843, a long time before their conversion to Christianity. In 908 the king-bishop of Cashel, Cormac Mac Cuilleanáin, bestowed three ounces of gold and a satin chausible on this foundation. In 1080 the abbey was damaged by fire. Donal MacLoughlin and a raiding party of Ulstermen destroyed Mungret in 1088. The Augustinian rule may have prevailed here during the twelfth century although this has never been proved, nor is there any evidence to support a link with the Dominicans. The Knights Templars may have had a hospital here some time before 1312. In 1152 Mungret claimed diocesan status as it would have been the obvious centre of what had earlier become the diocese of Limerick. The Synod of Rathbreasail established the dioceses of Ireland in 1111. It failed to recognise the claim of Mungret since the city had been established as the O'Brien capital in 1106. No bishops were recorded here during the twelfth century and Brictius, the bishop of Limerick, received the monastic lands of Mungret from Domhnall Mór O'Brien between 1192 and 1194.

St. Nessan, St. Nessan the Deacon, or St. Neasan the Leper, was a disciple of St. Patrick, according to the folklore of the region, but as Nessan did not die until 551 or 561 this is extremely unlikely. He is also said to have been a disciple of St. Ailbe of Emly, a contemporary of St. Patrick whose feast falls on 12 September, but this is also an unlikely claim unless there was an earlier saint of the same name.

Baunacloka Townland may derived its name from *Bán a Chloiche*, the bawn or cattle enclosure of the stones or stone huts, as the earliest monastery probably consisted of a series of *clochans*, huts made of stone, wood or mud and wattle, in which the monks lived, clustered around a small church and other communal buildings located within an enclosure.

St. Nessan's Church, or the Monastery Church, is located on the edge of the road. It contains a monumental east window dating from the twelfth century but

St. Nessan's Church, Mungret Limerick City Museum.

the building is much older, possibly dating from the tenth century, and may have been erected before 1100. This tall building with its high walls also contains two blocked-up windows in its south wall and a lintelled doorway in the west wall.

The Oldest Church on this site is also the smallest. This is located a short distance south of St. Nessan's Church and is a narrow rectangular building containing two small windows in the south wall and a similar window in the eastern gable. The western gable and original doorway have disappeared, replaced by a modern wall. John O'Connor in *Mungret History and Antiquities* believes it was constructed between 800-1100.

Mungret Abbey was built between 1251 and 1272. This is the largest and most important of the three ruined churches, and is divided into three parts. The eastern section, or chancel, dates from the thirteenth century; the nave is of doubtful date as no details by which it could be dated are in *situ;* and the western portion probably dates from the fifteenth century as the workmanship is in the style of that period. A Gwynn and R.N. Hadcock described this medieval parish church as partly-fortified in *Medieval Religious Houses Ireland*

THE MUNGRET HOARD CONTAINS ANGLO SAXON COINS FROM THE REIGNS OF EDWARD THE ELDER (900-925) AND AETHELSTAN (924-939).
Limerick City Museum.

(1988). The residential quarters, and the unusual square tower at the western end of the church, date from the fifteenth century. The tower, on the northern side of the priests' residence contains a staircase and belfry, although its topmost storey is more modern than the rest of the building. This church, known as The Abbey, was later used for Protestant worship and remained in use as a parish church until 1822. In 1880 the three churches were vested in the Board of Works and repairs were carried out on them in 1932. The graveyard is

MUNGRET ABBEY. Limerick City Museum.

still in use. A few yards from the north-eastern end of the church is an old tombstone erected in memory of James Daly (1750-1810), the Loughmore poet, better known as Seamus O Dálaigh, a tailor of Croom. The inscription on this stone is in Irish. Another tombstone was originally placed about fifteen yards east of the eastern gable of the church and was possibly erected in 1811 in memory of Robert MacNamara. This carries an Irish inscription, as well as a *Crucifixion* scene showing the instruments of the *Passion*. The most interesting inscription in the graveyard, however, is that on the Holohan Stone. This unique memorial was originally located about twelve yards south-west of the south-western corner of The Abbey. It depicts a *Crucifixion* scene on the front, with the legend *I.N.R.I.* above it, and carries an inscription in both Roman and Ogham lettering beneath. The dedication on the back of the tombstone is in English and commemorates John Holohan (1752-1809), his mother and his brother. In more recent the ashes of Angela McCourt were deposited in Mungret Abbey. A modern *cillín* can be seen in the graveyard of the Abbey. This small burial ground originally stood outside the graveyard wall but was included within the cemetery in modern times. *Cillins* were originally reserved for the burial of unbaptised children and strangers.

Holohan, *O hUallacháin*, the descendant of *Uallachán*, the diminutive of *Uallach* or the Proud, was the name of several distinct families in Offaly and Thomond. Variants of this surname include *O Holohan, O Houlihan, O Huolighane, O Holeghane, Hoolihan, Houlihan, Holland* in west Cork, and Nolan in Mayo and Roscommon.

The Monks' Mill, or Shannillian Mill, was located about halfway between Mungret and Limerick. By 1971 only one wall remained.

Mungret Castle, or Castle Mungret, was mentioned as early as 1201 and seems to have been occupied by the Knights Templars at one stage. Part of its basement still survives beneath a farmhouse south of the modern corcass road to Limerick Docks. Bishop de Rupefort mentioned the castle in 1336 and it contained two towers in 1583, when it was mentioned in another account. Bishop Adams was in possession before 1621 and in 1655 David Roche and H. Bindon held Castle Mungret and Temple Mungret respectively. The castle remained in a good state of preservation until the early nineteenth century when part of it was demolished. By 1840 only an arch over the ground floor and one wall remained.

The Manor of Mungret comprised the lands granted to Brictius by Domhnall Mór O'Brien. In 1201 Donough O'Brien, as bishop of Limerick, set up a commission consisting of twelve Irishmen, twelve Vikings, and twelve Anglo-

Normans, to inquire into church possessions and before that, he gave the church and district of Mungret to Colm O'Regan. About 1216 Edmund, bishop of Limerick, received a royal grant of Omayl, possibly the lands of the O'Malleys, near Mungret. When Hubert de Burgo was bishop of Limerick (1223-1250) he got permission from King Henry III (1223-1272) to have a weekly market, on Tuesdays, here. By the time Hubert died in 1250 the main ecclesiastical positions in the diocese of Limerick were held by Anglo-Norman clergymen.

A THIRTEENTH-CENTURY FRENCH RELIQUARY CASKET DECORATED WITH ENAMEL, IN THE HUNT MUSEUM.

The Breteuil Laws were privileges bestowed on the town of Breteuil, in Normandy, by William the son of Osbuir, later the Earl of Hereford. These rights, the *Consaietudines de Breteuil*, were conferred on the burgesses of Mungret by Robert of Emly when he became bishop of Limerick (1251-1272). This gave them the right to choose their own rulers, hold their own courts, fix their annual rents at a set rate of five pence for each tenure of land in the town, and the right to levy fines or establish punishments for all but the more serious offences. The burgesses were also allowed a certain independence from the lord of the manor, as they could limit the period for which he could have credit, deny him any rights or wardship or marriage, and restrict him from imprisoning burgesses. These inducements attracted a lot of Anglo-Norman settlers into the area, particularly from the Welsh boroughs. The people of Mungret were divided into three classes by the fourteenth century: the native *Betagi, Betaghs or Biadhtaigh*, tenants who were classed as serfs until Bishop Rochefort recognised then as free tenants in 1336; the free Anglo-Norman tenants; and the burgesses of the *vill* of Mungret.

The Loftus Family were associated with the area from an early date. Folklore relates that, at one stage, 140 monks had assumed the pseudonym John Loftus on joining the monastery. The road from the monastery to Raheen Cross was known as Loftus Road and was marked as such in the 1844 Ordnance Survey Map. The surname Loftus, *de Lochtús*, de Lofthouse or Loftis is found mainly in Wexford and may have been of Danish or Viking origin as it was derived from *Loffi* or *Lloft*. The surname is also found in England and Normandy but there is a possibility that the family, in Limerick, may have been of Irish origin. In 1434 the *Papal Letters* mentioned the excommunication of John Loftus, who was later appointed bailiff of Limerick. Piers Loftus served as mayor in 'the same century. Another Piers Loftus of Mungret sought a pardon from Queen Elizabeth after the Desmond Rebellion. The Loftus family appear to have held the lands of Dooradoyle, Ballykeefe, Sluggary and Gouldavoher, for which they paid an annual rent of £80, in the early seventeenth century. The name does not appear in the *Civil Survey* list of proprietors in 1641.

A GILT ALTAR CRUET IN THE HUNT MUSEUM

Temple Mungret contained one plowland with a thatched house, fifteen cabins, four ruined churches and other stone walls in 1654 when its lands stretched from Mungret to Dooradoyle and from the Shannon to Ballycummin. Some time before 1865 a coin hoard was discovered in a quarry near the churches. It was hidden around the middle of the tenth century and is the earliest Viking hoard found in Thomond. It contained eight Anglo-Saxon pennies dating from about 905 to around 950; a rare Viking coin struck at York for one of the Hiberno-Norse kings about 942; and seven small ingots of silver. A bell of "very rude workmanship" was found at Loughmore about 1837 and, twelve years later, a bronze bell was discovered near Mungret Abbey.

Mungret Manor was profitable for the Protestant bishop of Limerick. On 1 January, 1871, an act of parliament disestablished and disendowed the Church of Ireland. At that time the bishop owned 3,700 acres of land here from which he derived an annual income of £2,100 in rents and fines. Colonel Gough of Fethard held the former Loftus estate, of 1,570 acres, from the bishop for an annual rent of £447. He held 100 acres for his own use and sublet the rest at £2 to £4 an acre. Sir David Roche leased 700 acres at Ballycummin from the bishop, as well as the lands of Ballyhourigan, which he held in perpetuity from the diocese. The Compton family leased 185 acres for £144 and sublet it for £2 to £3 an acre and in 1868 Edward L. Griffin leased the lands of Ballymacashel and Castle Mungret which had been leased to Robert Wogan Studdert in 1850. Tenants at will occupied farms in the townlands of Rathmale and Loughanleigh. These holdings varied from six to eighty-four acres and were let at an average rent of £1 an acre.

MUNGRET COLLEGE, A VIEW OF THE INTERIOR IN FORMER DAYS.
Limerick City Museum.

Mungret College evolved from a college and model farm established by the trustees of the Bindon estates after they had purchased 70 acres of land at Drumdarrig in 1852. This model farm closed in 1878 but the college re-opened as a non-denominational school on 23 September, 1880. Lord Emly, First Baron Maunsell, and Postmaster-General, became a Catholic through the efforts of a French Jesuit refugee, M. L'Abbe l'Heritier. He used his influence to acquire the model farm for the Jesuits. In 1882 Fr. W. Ronan became the first rector of Mungret College. Lord Emly later lost his fortune, his mortgaged property, and his home, Tervoe House. The college closed over a century later but its front entrance is still adorned by the pillared portico from Tervoe House, Clarina, which was demolished in 1953.

The Knights Templars were an international military order established to protect pilgrims after the recapture of Jerusalem in 1099. They operated under the Augustinian rule until 1128 when they adopted a rule similar to that of the Cistercians. The order was introduced into Ireland before 1180 and their chief house, or preceptory, was located in Clontarf. They were similar to the Knights

Hospitallers in many respects but the rivalry between both orders was the main reason for the fall of Jerusalem in 1187 and the capture of Acre in 1291. After 1312 all of the Irish possessions of the Knights Templars should have become the property of the Knights Hospitallers but this matter was still unresolved in 1329. The Knights Templars are believed to have had a preceptory in Temple Mungret ·which later became the mansion house of the prior. Samuel Lewis claims that their establishment here was granted to the Augustinians. A hospital for lepers was located on the ruins of a hermitage opposite Ballinacurra, near the eastern boundary of the parish, in ancient times but no record remains of the founder.

Mount Mungret was built as the Church of Ireland glebe house in 1832. This is a neat three-storey structure.

The Church of Ireland Church was a small handsome cruciform structure with an octagonal tower. This was built in 1822. It was closed down in 1877 and the roof was removed in 1900.

Conigar House was originally built in 1774, as a county residence for the Protestant Bishop of Limerick. In 1827 a new two-storey farmhouse was built near the old mansion which had fallen into ruin by then. By 1837 Conigar House had been sold to Charles Wilson. *The Griffith Valuation* states that a Mrs. Wilson leased 200 acres at Conigar Farm from the bishop in 1855. In 1837 Lewis reported that the constabulary police had converted the entrance lodge into a barracks. Conigar is an anglicised form of *Coinicear*, the place of rabbits.

Ballycummin derives its name from *Baile Uí Chománn*, the townland of Commons, Comane or Hurley.

Ballycummin House is a fairly modern castellated house. It is now the property of Joe O'Brien.

Dooradoyle derives its name probably from *Tuar an Daíl*, the tribe's bleach green. Other explanations given are *Túr an Daill*, the blind one's tower, or *Turradh an Daill*, the blind one's crypt or souterrain. The Limerick Regional Hospital is located in Dooradoyle.

The Mormon Church in Dooradoyle was erected in 1982-1983. The building may be new, but the Church of the Latter Day Saints in Limerick can trace its history back to the dissenting Protestant Palatines of Rathkeale. These Palatines contributed to the establishment of the Mormon faith after they left Ireland to start new lives in England and America during the 1830s and 1840s. A few Mormon missionaries arrived into Limerick in the late 1960s. They left but returned to open a meeting-place in Thomas Street in 1972-1973. The Church of the Latter Day Saints in Limerick had 130 members in March 1989. Genealogical records play a major role in the Mormon faith. Records are compiled and kept but not for the usual bureaucratic reasons. Special ceremonies are held in their temples in order to baptise the dead and to "seal families for time and eternity". Temples should not, however, be confused with churches. The nearest Mormon temple to Limerick is in London, and the nearest collection of records is in Cork. One of the earliest Mormon churches

LIMERICK TOKEN, ISSUED BY JOHN BENNETT IN 1668. Limerick City Museum.

LIMERICK TOKEN, ISSUED BY ANTHONY BARTLETT IN 1671. Limerick City Museum.

LIMERICK TOKEN, ISSUED BY WILLIAM RIMPLAND, A CHANDLER IN 1669, Limerick City Museum

established outside of America was founded in Rathkeale in the early nineteenth century by Palatine converts.

Sluggery Ring Fort is located almost directly behind the Limerick Regional Hospital. This fort, about an acre in size, was polygonal in plan and consisted of two concentric sets of banks and ditches with a third dry-stone built bank on the outside. Dr. Elizabeth Shee, University College Cork, and Liam Irwin, Thomond Archaeological Society, excavated here in 1973 and 1974. They found an ornamented bone comb, a bronze ring-headed pin, nails, pins, iron knives, a central cist-like hearth, and numerous post holes and pits. The fort has been preserved and landscaped. *Slogaire* has been translated as a swallower, a glutton, a gulf, a quagmire or as a common river-name.

Loughmore derives its name from *An Loch Mór,* the big lake. This is supposed to be an enchanted lake which disappears every few years. Grattan's Volunteers trained here and it was used for military tattoos or musterings into the early twentieth century. Loughmore Catholic church was a small thatched building in 1837 and the parish was known as Loughmore, rather than as Mungret, because both the church and the priests' residence were located here.

Raheen Catholic Church was partly built and roofed by Fr. Jeremiah Halpin, who was parish priest here for only one year before he died on 5 October 1845. The church was later completed by Fr. Michael Casey and his parishioners in 1862. Between Raheen Cross and Willow Park the remains of another earth fort can be seen in the centre of a built-up area.

THE NORTH LIBERTIES WERE DEVELOPED IN THE 1830S AS THE CITY SPREAD ONTO THE CLARE SIDE OF THE RIVER SHANNON . THE REGIONAL MATERNITY HOSPITAL, ON THE ENNIS ROAD, HAS REPLACED THE LYING-IN HOSPITAL IN BEDFORD ROW; BARRINGTON'S HOSPITAL, IN GEORGES QUAY AND CAHERCALLA IN ENNIS.
Shannon Development Photo Library.

Thomondgate and the North Liberties

Thomondgate takes its name from what was once the only entrance to the city from the Clare side. The name is now applied to a region which became a suburb of considerable extent as the Viking settlement gave way to the Norman development, especially after a bridge was constructed across the river. The rebuilt Thomond Bridge, dating from the late 1290s, contained fourteen arches of unequal size and had two gateways guarding the entrance to the city. One gateway stood at the Englishtown end of the bridge and another gateway, castellated with a drawbridge, was located on the seventh arch from the city end. By raising the drawbridge between the seventh and eighth arches the defenders of this fortified gateway created a gap to foil attacks from the Thomond or North Munster side of the river.

The Treaty Stone is the name given to a roughly hewn rock which was located near the northern side of Thomond Bridge until it was moved to the southern

The Treaty Stone, with Thomond Bridge , the Toll House and King John's Castle in background.
Shannon Development Photo Library.

side of the bridge in 1865. It was then placed on a pedestal. With the increase in traffic it became a hazard and was moved to its present location in 1990. The treaty of Limerick is supposed to have been signed on this stone in 1691 but it is most unlikely that either of the opposing forces was unable to provide a writing-table for such a momentous occasion. In all probability it marked the site on which the actual signing took place, some distance away. It is quite posible that the military articles, which were signed by the French as commanders of the Jacobite Army, were signed on the stone, which was then located half way between Thomond Bridge and the Williamite camp. The French did not attend the signing of the civil articles in Ginkel's tent as they were not involved. This stone has changed, drastically, since it was drawn by Edward Jones in 1836. It seems to have been used as a mounting block by horsemen, was located outside the *Black Bull* public house and had its shape altered over the years as souvenir hunters chipped pieces off it.

St. Munchin's Catholic Church, on the North Strand (now Clancy's Strand) was built in 1744. In 1827 it was described as "a commodious place of worship, but destitute of any particular object of interest". In 1837 the parishes of

St. Munchin and St. Nicholas with the North Liberties formed the composite parish of St. Lelia's, the original parish church of which was replaced with the present edifice in 1922. Samuel Lewis claimed that the "chapel, situated at Thomond-gate, is a large cruciform structure ... the first R.C. place of worship publicly erected in Limerick since the revolution".

Osmington Terrace may have derived its name from a former resident according to Rev. Michael Moloney (1894-1964) who was appointed as parish priest of St. Munchin's in 1946. He believed that the Osmington surname had nothing whatsoever to so with the Ostmen of Limerick.

Michael Hogan (1832-1899) is better known under his more popular name, the Bard of Thomond. He was born at New Road, Thomondgate, on 1 November, 1832. The critics and literati of his day, and later, considered his verse abominable but it found great appeal amongst the ordinary people. His mixture of patriotism, satire and humour was appreciated in the pages of *The Nation* and other periodicals to which he contributed articles. His *Lays and Legends of Thomond* could easily be listed as a tribute in verse dedicated to the more famous people and events in the history and folklore of North Munster. Within its pages can be found some extremely fascinating footnotes, some of which are more interesting than the lays and legends themselves. Over the years he produced small editions of many poetry pamphlets, most of which are now quite scarce. *Drunken Thady and the Bishop's Lady* is reputedly his masterpiece:

> 'Tis true she lived - 'tis true she died,
> Tis true she was a Bishop's bride:
> But for herself 'tis little matter
> To whom she had been wife or daughter.

Michael "The Bard" Hogan, a nominal employee of the Limerick Corporation, was buried in Mount St. Lawerence Cemetry.

The Thomondgate Distillery of Stein, Browne and Company produced 455,000 gallons of whiskey annually in 1837. In the same year the city possessed seven breweries, which brewed a total of 5,000 barrels of porter, ale and beer annually, mainly for local consumption. Several cooperage's, iron-foundries and comb-manufacturers also existed locally.

HOUSE OF INDUSTRY, IN 1786.

The House of Industry on Clancy's Strand had its foundations laid on 10 March, 1774, by Joseph Johns, mayor of Limerick, after legislation was introduced in 1772 to establish poorhouses and workhouses in every county. Bishop Gore granted the land at an annual rent of one peppercorn for ever and

*THE LIMERICK HOUSE OF INDUSTRY, BUILT ON THE NORTH STRAND (NOW CLANCY'S STRAND) IN 1774, RECENTLY RESTORED. **Shannon Development Photo Library.***

the Grand Juries of both city and county donated £500 towards the erection of the house of industry. Launcelott Hill supervised the building of this "respectable edifice, forming a large square, built in courses, with a handsome front of cut stone", designed by Rev. Deane Hoare. Doctor Edward Smyth of Dublin gave £200 towards the provision of a number of cells for lunatics in the infirmary which was behind the main building, in the garden. By 1827 the building was considered inadequate as 450 inmates were confined in space meant for 200. In 1838 the *Irish Poor Relief Act* led to the establishment of work-houses in the unions of Limerick, Croom, Kilmallock, Rathkeale and Newcastle West. It was used as the Strand Barracks into the early 1920s. The corporation used the building for storage and as offices before its conversion into apartments during the recent urban renewal of the 1990s.

Sarsfield Bridge was originally known as the Wellesley Bridge. The overall design was based on that of the Pont Neuilly in Paris by its architect, Alexander Nimmo. The foundation stone was laid on 2 October, 1824, and the work was completed, at a cost of £89,000, when it was officially opened by the lord lieutenant of Ireland on 5 August, 1835. The expansion of Limerick, stemming from the Newtownpery development of the 1760s, had extended mainly to the west and down river, so a bridge had to be constructed before further growth could take place. John Grantham surveyed the Shannon for the city fathers who eventually decided on a suitable site: "Said bridge shall be built over the said river, adjoining or near to the end of Brunswick Street in the parish of Saint Michael in the suburbs of the said city, to the north strand on the opposite side of the said river". The bridge consists of five large and elegant elliptic arches crossing the Shannon from Newtownpery to the northern, or County Clare, shore. The structure is basically unchanged since 1837 when the roadway was described as level with a parapet formed of a massive open balustrade. The swivel bridge on the city side is no longer functional but some of its heavy machinery is still intact underneath the roadway. This bridge could once swing aside to allow vessels through the lock on their way to or from the upper basin and quays. Sarsfield Bridge was the main bridge into Limerick from Clare for over a century and a half.

THE RIVER SHANNON WITH THOMOND GATE ON THE LEFT. CLANCY'S STRAND IS ABOVE, AND O'CALLAGHAN'S STRAND BELOW, SARSFIELD BRIDGE, ON THE SAME SIDE. THE CITY QUAYS AND HENRY STREET ARE ON THE OPPOSITE BANK WITH THE ENGLISHTOWN AND KING'S ISLAND IN THE BACKGROUND. **Shannon Development Photo Library.**

The War of Independence Memorial at the northern end of Sarsfield Bridge consists of four stone seats, a fountain and two inscribed commemorative plaques enclosed within a tiny park at the corner of the Ennis Road and O'Callaghan Strand. One plaque inscribed in English is located on a small monument above ground level while the Irish-inscribed plaque is mounted on the wall behind the park. This reads:

Tógadh an leacht seo mar chuimhneachán ar cheannairí mhuintir chathair agus chontae Luimní
A thug a n-anam ar son na saoirse sna blianta 1919 go dtí 1921
Micheál O Ceallacháin méara Luimní 1920
Seoirse Mac Fhlanncadha méara Luimní 1921

A dúnmahraíodh ina dtithe féin óiche an 7ú Márta 1921

Agus

Seán De Báll Cathaoirleach Chomhairle Chontae Luimní a thit sa ghleo in Áth na

Carte an 6ú Bealtaine 1921

Is cuimhneachán an leacht seo freisin ar an óglach Seosamh O Donnchú ar

dúnmharaíodh freisin leis óiche an 7ú Márta 1921

Agus ar na fir go léir ó chathair agus ó chontae Luimní a maraíodh de linn chogadh na

saoirse.

This monument was erected to commemorate the leaders
    of the people of the city and county of Limerick
who gave their lives on behalf of freedom in the years 1919 to 1921.
    Michael O'Callaghan mayor of Limerick 1920
    George Clancy mayor of Limerick 1921
Who were murdered in their own
    houses on the night of 7th March 1921
        And
Sean Wall Chairman of Limerick County Council who fell in the fight
    at Annacarty on 6th May 1921
This monument is a remembrance also for volunteer Joseph O'Donoghue
    who was murdered also on the night of 7th March 1921
And for all of the men of the city and county of Limerick who were
    killed during the war for freedom.

The Sarsfield Bridge Monument commemorates **1916.** The earlier monument on this site was flanked by two small Russian cannon captured during the Crimean War. The original monument was a statue of Viscount Fitzgibbon, grandson of Black Jack, Earl of Clare, who was posted as missing, presumed dead, after the Charge of the Light Brigade at Balaclava, on 25 October, 1854. During the second Afghan War (1878-1880) a "bowed and tattered figure" approached a British officers' mess. His English appeared to be rusty from disuse but he was entertained by the officers who discovered he was familiar with their customs and those of other regiments. In the course of conversation he mentioned that he had been living in Siberia and they, the officers, assumed that he had once served in the 8th Hussars. Some time afterwards when a roster of that regiment was checked it was discovered that the only officer, or ex-officer, of that mysterious stranger's approximate age had been Viscount or Lord Fitzgibbon. Kipling based a short story, *The Man who Was,* on this incident. The statue was blown up by the Irish Republican Army in 1930.

THE VISCOUNT FITZGIBBON MEMORIAL. Limerick City Museum.

The Ennis Road became the main road into Clare from the city with the erection of Sarsfield Bridge. When the new line of road was under construction in the 1830s heaps of skeletons were found laid out in rows about fifteen yards in length and six feet in depth. They were supposed to have been the remains of those who died in the great plague. In the latter half of the nineteenth century it became an exclusive residential area in much the same way as Newtownpery did in the previous century. The new Shannon Bridge with its auxiliary road and traffic roundabouts has already altered the traffic flow but it is still too early to gauge the long term effects this will have on the area. In 1859 the corporation built a reservoir here which gave the population of the time, 44,500 people, an average supply of 20 gallons each. In more recent times the reservoir was converted into a swimming pool. The Ennis Road was originally named Lansdowne Road to commemorate William Petty Fitzmaurice (1737-1805), Second Earl of Shelbourne and Marquis of Lansdowne, a prominent landowner whose former house, Shelbourne House, is now part of the Ard Scoil Rís complex. In 1760 he was an aide-de-camp to King George III (1760-1820); served as a major-general in 1765; was a principal secretary of state in 1766; was first lord of the treasury in 1782; and was created Marquis of Lansdowne,

Somerset, Earl of Wycombe, Buckinghampshire, and Viscount Calne and Calnestone, on 6 December, 1784.

Elm Park is north of the Ennis Road and east of the Limerick Tennis Club.

Michael Terence Wogan was born in 18 Elm Park on 3 August, 1938, the first child of Michael and Rose Wogan. Six years later, his brother, Brian, was born. Michael Wogan was the manager of the Leverett and Fry grocery store in the city centre. His older son, nowadays, more familiarly known as Terry, attended a small private school run by the Salesian Nuns until he was eight. He continued his education with the Jesuits in O'Connell Crescent and once partnered Dessie O'Malley in a debate against Mungret College. Terry Wogan's education was continued in Belvedere College, Dublin, which he entered at the age of fifteen. He excelled in English, Greek, Latin and the Classics, sat his Leaving Certificate examination at the age of seventeen, and spent an additional year in school, studying philosophy under Rev. Francis Schrenk, Society of Jesus. He joined the Royal Bank of Ireland after passing an examination, was first assigned to the Cornmarket branch in central Dublin, and was then transferred to the branch in Phibsboro. One day he spotted an advertisement for a trainee announcer in the newspaper, applied to Radio Éireann for the position and became a full-time radio broadcaster in November, 1961. Radio Telefís Éireann transmitted its first televised programmes in December, 1961, a month after Terry Wogan had joined the company. The Limerick broadcaster had found the medium that would propel him to fame at home and abroad as a chat show host extraordinary.

THE YARMOUTH FISH STORES WAS OWNED BY WILLIAM F.PIKE AND WAS LOCATED AT 2 WILLIAM STREET. IN MARCH, 1926, HE CHARGED SIXTY-SIX PENCE FOR TEN POUNDS OF COD AND £1.75 FOR EIGHT-AND-THREE-QUARTER-POUNDS OF SALMON.

The Limerick County Borough is a separate and quite distinct entity from County Limerick. The easiest way to describe it would be as a county within the county encompassing the city and its immediate environs.

The Population of the County Borough varied considerably over the years as the following chart illustrates:

YEAR	TOTAL	MALES	FEMALES
1831	44,100		
1841	48,391		
1851	55,448		
1861	44,476		
1891	37,153		
1911	38,518		
1936	41,061		
1951	50,820	24,103	26,717
1956	50,886	24,047	26,839
1961	50,786	24,134	26,652
1966	55,912	26,747	29,165
1971	57,161	27,626	29,535
1979	60,665	29,593	31,072
1981	60,736	29,723	31,013
1986	56,276	27,537	28,742
1991	52,083	25,318	26,765
1996	52,042	25,100	26,942

The Official Population stands at a figure of 52,042, making Limerick City the fourth largest city in the Republic of Ireland, after Dublin, Cork, and Galway. The city infrastructure, however, extends into the suburbs of Castletroy and Raheen, the populations of which are not returned with the Limerick County Borough. The Limerick County Council rejected the Limerick Corporation proposal to extend city boundaries to these suburbs on Monday 13 October, 1997. This proposal is still with the Minister and if it is accepted Limerick City would have a population of 82,000, restoring it to its old position as the third largest city in the Republic. Galway City has a population of 57,000 which is expected to reach a total of 63,000 by 2001; is officially the third largest city in the state; and plans to rezone 500 acres of land, east of the Corrib River to cater for the expected increase in population.

Ardhu House on the Ennis Road was built by Thomas Revington and became the residence of Robert de Ros Rose who married the daughter of Benjamin Frend of Boskell. It is now a hotel.

The Whining Bridge was the name bestowed on Limerick's newest bridge before it was officially opened, and unimaginatively named the Shannon Bridge. On Tuesday, 9 February, 1988 a storm passed through the country and the bridge emitted a whistling sound as gale force winds swept across it. Because of this piercing noise, it soon became known as the Whiner, the Singing Bridge, the Banshee Bridge or the Whistling Bridge. The Taoiseach, Charles. J. Haughey, opened it formally on 30 May, 1988. Two plaques located on each end commemorate the event and name some of the dignitaries involved. A railway bridge of the same name is located upriver, north of the Island.

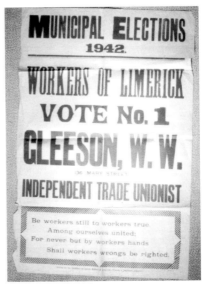

LOCAL ELECTION POSTER FOR 1942.
Limerick City Museum.

Thomas Henry Cleeve (1844-1908) was a son of Edward Elms Cleeve, Plumstead, Woolwich, England. He was reared and educated in Quebec, Canada, and first came to Limerick, on holiday, in 1864. The Irish agricultural scene offered him opportunities he was quick to avail of. His career commenced with the purchase of hay from Limerick farmers, which he baled and sold to the cavalry stationed within the city and county. He persuaded his brothers to join him. They established a chain of creameries, opened factories in Limerick and Tipperary to process the cream and skim milk, and then branched out into the manufacture of butter, sweets, and tinned condensed milk and cream. Golden Vale have now taken over the old Cleeves factory which contains the tallest remaining chimney stack in the city. This is built out of red brick and was originally 150 feet high - but it is believed that the height was lowered by 30 feet some years ago. Thomas Henry Cleeve and his brothers dominated the milk trade of the region into the opening decades of the twentieth century. Thomas became a justice of the peace, high sheriff (1899-1900), deputy lieutenant, and was created a knight in 1900. The business was at its most prosperous during World War I when they possessed a condensed milk factory on the north bank of the Shannon, a cooperage, a box factory, a toffee factory at Charlotte Quay and several creameries. Many of the latter were burned out by the British Forces in 1920. Cleeves were amongst the largest employers in the city and, in their heyday, had a staff of almost one thousand.

Barrington's Bank is the name of a large embankment that was constructed to contain the tidal waters of the Shannon by Sir Joseph Barrington (1764-1846) and one of his landlords, Henry Petty Fitzmaurice, 3rd Marquis of Lansdowne (1780-1863). This development took place before the Wellesley Bridge project was completed in 1835, as an account published in 1834 mentions:

> Some extensive embankments are now in course of being constructed below
> Limerick, with the view of reclaiming land ... by Lord Lansdowne and by Mr.
> Barrington.

Henry D. Inglis wrote the above description in his *Journey Through Ireland* (1834) and would have been extremely fastidious in how he addressed or referred to prominent people. As Joseph Barrington was referred to as "Mr. Barrington" this would indicate that the travel writer's description would relate to the days before Joseph Barrington was created a baronet, on 30 September, 1831. This, in turn, would confirm that the works had probably commenced prior to 1831. Barrington's Pier was reconstructed, rather than built, at a cost of £700, by

BARRINGTON'S BANK WITH CONDELL ROAD ON THE NORTHERN BANK OF THE SHANNON, STEAMBOAT QUAY ON THE SOUTHERN BANK, SHANNON BRIDGE AND THE RIVERFRONT OF THE ENGLISHTOWN AND GEORGIAN LIMERICK. Shannon Development Photo Library.

Joseph Barrington in 1830. The original builder seems to have been Benjamin Barrington, Joseph's grandfather, a prominent merchant who was a sheriff of Limerick in 1729. The lands between Coonagh and the city were subject to flooding until this great embankment was put in place. The opening of Wellesley Bridge in 1835 made the embankment more accessible and the city people turned the bank between the bridge and Barringtons' Pier into a popular promenade. It fell into disuse in the 1950s and 1960s but the opening of the new Approach Road has popularised this attractive walkway since 1989.

Spillane's Tower, a small Gothic-style round tower cum harbour light or marker-buoy, dates from the days when the shipowners of Limerick had to fund their own requirements. It is now visible from the Approach Road into the city from the Clare side and is known locally as the "Snuff Box". The Spillane family were the largest tobacco importers in Munster.

The Christian Brothers opened a school in Thomondgate in September 1844. By 1852 they had four schools in the city, in Sexton Street, Clare Street, St. Mary's Parish and St. Munchin's Parish. On 12 September 1888 they laid the foundation-stone of the Brother Welsh Memorial School, in John Street, on a site purchased from Crehan McMahon for £100. This last was built and furnished for £1,700. The Christian Brothers were asked to establish schools in Limerick by the Catholic bishop, Dr. Charles Touhy (1814-1828). Three brothers, Austin Dunphy, Francis Grace and Aloysius Kelly, arrived in Limerick on 26 June, 1816. They hired the assembly rooms in Charlotte's Quay, at an annual rent of £75, and on 11 September, 1816, they opened their first school in the city. Within six months the Christian Brothers had enrolled 648 pupils. They lived in Hill's Lane, north of Curry Lane at first, moved to Denmark Street in 1817, until 1824, and then settled into the diocesan college in Corbally where they opened a school in 1824.

The North Circular Road contains the residences of both bishops of Limerick. The Church of Ireland bishop, Dr. Edward Darling, resides in the Bishop's House which was constructed in the grounds of Portland House while Dr. Donal Murray, the Roman Catholic bishop, lives in Kilmoyle House. The latter building is an early-nineteenth century one built in classical style.

Belle Vue Gardens, on the North Circular Road, owes its name to the three Alexander brothers who were amongst the first developers to construct houses here, three of which are still standing, Beechlawn, Bellevue and Evergreen. Kilcornan is now the new name for Evergreen.

TREATY STONE SOUVENIRS, CUFF LINKS MADE FROM PARTS OF THIS HISTORIC MONUMENT, CHRISTMAS 1898. Limerick City Museum.

Belle Vue Mews, off Iona Drive and to the rear of Belle Vue Gardens, also owes its name to one of Limerick's leading Quaker families, the Alexanders.

Kilrush, *Cill Rois,* may mean the church of the wood or peninsula although it is also supposed to derive its name, Rose's church, from a sister of St. Munchin's. The location of the old church suggests that in former times it was located on an island or a promontory of some kind and up to a few years ago some traces of a causeway were evident. The area was zoned for development in 1837 and it was "in contemplation ... in consequence of the facilities of communication recently afforded by the erection of Wellesley Bridge". Despite much development in the area since 1837 it was not until 1979 that the old church from which the area took its name stood in some danger of demolition, even though it was listed as a national monument.

Kilrush Church, Old Church, St. Munchin's or St. Mainchin's Church is possibly the oldest building with its walls still standing in the city. Bulldozers damaged all but a small portion of the surrounding site before it could be excavated in 1979. Even so, the area almost directly beneath the Quinlivan window contained forty one human burial deposits. These burials were post-medieval and dated from the sixteenth or seventeenth centuries. Some had been buried in coffins, others in shrouds, as both coffin nails and shroud pins were discovered during excavations. These burials lay quite close to the surface, no more than 16 inches (40 cm) below the modern surface, with only a shallow covering of soil over bedrock. The burials were mainly of infants, and there was evidence of late weaning, which would suggest that the site had been used as a *cillín* or children's burial ground. Twenty-three of the bodies were of infants under five years of age and one of them had been buried, face-downwards, in a prone position. The adults were all buried in "the modest man" position, and one of them had worn a copper bracelet on the left wrist. Kilrush Church was first mentioned in 1201 but it is generally believed to be much older, possibly dating from the tenth century. It is now located in an attractive cul-de-sac off the North Circular Road, off Barrington's Pier and the new roadway, and is the chief focal point in the centre of a new housing complex. A modern brick-buttress and frame supports the west wall with its flat-headed doorway. The church is a small rectangular structure and contains a round-headed east window. The window in the south wall dates from the fifteenth century but, despite its age, it was only inserted here in 1900 by Robert Vere O'Brien. This window is believed to have belonged to the old Franciscan church in St. Mary's Lane and the eastern portion of it is inscribed with the name of the Quinlivan family.

The Quinlivan name is derived form *O Caoindealbháin*, the descendant of *Caoindealbhán*, the Gracefully-shaped, who died in 925. Variants of the name include Guindelane, O Kennellan, O Kenolan, O Quinelane, Kindellan, Kennellan, Connellan, Kinlan, Kinlen, Kenlan, Conlon, Quinlan, *O Caoinliobháin*, *O Caoinleáin* and *Quinlivan*. Originating in *Cinel Laoghaire* in Meath, the name can be found in Leinster and all the counties of Munster.

St. Camillus's Hospital was originally built by Sir Thomas Deane and Company as the Limerick Workhouse to replace the House of Industry on Clancy's Strand. Opened in May, 1841, it has undergone many changes over the years but is still in operation as a hospital. The oldest part is a large Tudor-Gothic-style edifice with pointed arches over the upper windows, and pointed gables.

Páirc na nGael, the park of the Gaels, on the Ennis Road, is the principal playing-pitch of Limerick's Gaelic Athletic Association. Hurling and football were played at Ballinacurra Racecourse, Rosbrien, Derryknockane, Corkanree, the Island Bank and the Grocer's Field (on the Ennis Road) until 1888. In that year the Gaelic Athletic Association moved to the Market's Field, in Garryowen; held its first inter-county game there in 1899; staged the 1901, 1915, 1919 and 1992 hurling finals there; hosted the football finals there in 1899, 1900, 1903, 1906 and 1924; and continued to share the grounds with their rugby rivals until 1928. William P. Clifford, president of the G.A.A., proposed the idea of acquiring their own grounds to the county committees in 1926, with the proviso that these grounds be retained exclusively for Gaelic games. The Limerick G.A.A. purchased a twelve-and-a-quarter-acre site on the Ennis Road at

Monument in O'Connell Street, showing rugby player and hurler, representatives of Limerick's rich sporitng heritage.

Coolraine for £1,209.45, and established a limited liability company to run the new grounds, The Limerick Gaelic Grounds Ltd. Its first directors were W.P. Clifford (chairman), Tim Humphries (secretary), Con Browner, Charlie Holland, Denny Lanigan, Pat McGrath and Albie Quillinan. In the early 1930s a development committee was formed to level the playing pitch, provide sideline seating and banking and erect a surrounding wall. The continual development, into the 1940s, meant that the grounds could accommodate a record crowd of 43,236 supporters at the Munster final in 1951, paying £6,207.47 at the toll-gates. These figures were later beaten by an attendance of 50,071 in July, 1954, and an attendance of 61,174 in 1961. On the latter occasion the figure may even have been upwards of 70,000, as the gates had to be thrown open halfway through the minor game to forestall a possible riot or panic. This last event convinced the directors of the necessity of acquiring and enclosing some of the lands surrounding the grounds in order to accommodate future expansion. The new acquisitions allowed for later development and provided crucial parking facilities.

The Gaelic Athletic Association, *Cumann Luthcleas Gael* or, more familiarly today, the G.A.A. came into existence with a circular issued by Michael Cusack (1847-1907) and Maurice Davin (1864-1927) on 27 October, 1884. The circular persuaded various individuals to attend a special meeting in the billiard-room of Hayes's Hotel, in Thurles, on 1 November, 1884, and resulted in the formation of a Gaelic association charged with the preservation of national pastimes and amusements. *Peil* (football), *iománaídheacht* (hurling) and *liathróid láimhe*, (handball), were the three principal sports that were sponsored, and thrived, under the patronage of the new association. Hurling was a popular sport in Georgian Limerick, as can be attested to by an account of 1776, and remained so into the 1840s. Early meetings of the newly-formed G.A.A. were often disrupted by members of the Irish Republican Brotherhood being at odds with its president, Maurice Davin, in 1886 and 1887. Frank Dinneen, Patrick Hassett and Anthony Mackey of Limerick were amongst the I.R. B. men who managed to make major revisions of the G.A.A. rules. Gaelic football and hurling gained a new popularity in 1887 when the newly-formed association introduced a novel idea, inter-county championship competitions in both sports. The first finals were played in April, 1888, and the city's Commercials club, representing the county, became the first All-Ireland football champions.

Hurling has been associated with Ireland for almost four thousand years, according to the old legends that speak of the Fomorians and the Tuatha Dé Danann playing a game before the first Battle of Moytura, near modern Sligo.

G.A.A. MEDALS, WON BY P. SCANLON BETWEEN 1927 AND 1940. Limerick City Museum.

Gaelic Football, soccer and rugby have evolved from ball games played in the distant past by such diverse peoples as the Aztecs, Celts, Chinese, Egyptians, Greeks, Israelis, Japanese, North American Indians, Persians, Romans and Vikings.

Soccer is an English modification of football that can be dated to 1846. H. de Winton and J. C. Thring met with representatives of major public schools at Cambridge University in order to regulate the game. The Cambridge Rules were published as a result of this meeting and were later adopted by the Football Association. The Football Association of Ireland was founded in 1921; regulates play in the Republic of Ireland, and has played in internationals since 1924. One of the oldest rules of soccer states:

Hands may be used only to stop a ball and place it on the ground before the feet.

Rugby evolved from a specific incident, some call cheating, that occurred at Rugby School. In 1823 William Webb Ellis "took the ball into his arms and ran with it". The game derived its name from the school and town in Warwickshire, Rugby, the place-name of which means the fort of Rook, in Old English, or the farm of Rook, in Old Norse.

Charles Burton Barrington (1848-1943) was the founding father of Limerick Rugby. The game had been introduced into Ireland by the 1840s; was played in Trinity College, Dublin, from 1848 onwards; and a club had been established in the university in 1854, the second oldest club in the world. The young Charles B. Barrington was introduced to the game in 1859 when he was a pupil in St. Columba's College, Dublin;-

> O.R. Strickland, a member of the T.C.D. football club, came to St. Columba's to instruct the boys in the game as played at Trinity College. Strickland was collared and lay on the ball and could not be removed by the united efforts of the St. Columba's team and remained on the ball until the headmaster intervened.

This exhibition impressed the young Charles B. Barrington and gave him an interest in the game that remained with him lifelong. On leaving St. Columba's College, he continued his education at Rugby School and then attended Trinity College in Dublin. He captained the Trinity team from 1867 to 1870 and also became involved in the regulation of the game. From 1867 onwards he worked with Richard M. Wall, secretary of the Trinity club since 1865, and they drew up a set of rules, similar to those passed by the Blackheath Club in 1862. The Barrington-Wall rugby rules, containing twenty-three clauses, were accepted and passed by the Trinity Club in 1868 and were adopted by the Irish Rugby Football Union when it was formed in 1874. In 1898 the IRFU arranged for the Irish team to play Wales at Lansdowne Limerick, possibly on the site occupied by the County Cricket and Tennis Club, the city's only rugby international until 1977. Rugby almost ground to a halt when World War I erupted. Hurling became more entrenched in the war years and the

BOATING IN THE SHANNON, OFF HOWLEY'S QUAY AND LOWER CECIL STREET.
Shannoon Development Photo Library.

Munster Cup games were not resumed until 1920. Cruise's Hotel was the unofficial headquarters of Limerick rugby into the 1930s, just as the Markets' Field was the principal rugby grounds. By the mid-1930s it became necessary for the rugby players to acquire a playing pitch of their own. A site to the east of Hassett's Cross was purchased and the first match was played there on 17 November, 1934. This "unsheltered plateau" witnessed its first Munster Cup game, a tie, on 29 February, 1936, a game that was replayed on the Markets' Field. A stand was completed in the new grounds, Thomond Park, in 1938 and it became the official venue for all cup matches in Limerick. There were five senior teams in the city by 1954 as the Shannon Rugby Football Club and Old Crescent Rugby Club had become senior clubs since 1952.

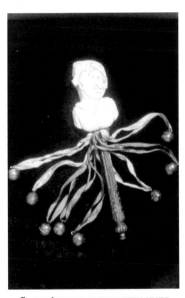

JESTERS' BAUBLE OF IVORY WITH SILVER BELLS, GERMAN OR FRENCH - IN THE HUNT MUSEUM

The Limerick County Football Club was founded by William L. Stokes and Charles B. Barrington in 1876 and was the only club in the city for a number of years. William L. Stokes captained the team from 1876 to 1886 and was vice-president of the Irish Rugby Football Union in 1885. In 1884 C.B. Barrington and A.W. Shaw were, respectively, elected president and vice-president, D. Hall became vice-captain, B. Lucas was treasurer and A.R. Redding was elected secretary. The Munster Cup was inaugurated on 12 January, 1886. It was first won playing against Limerick County F.C. by the Bandon Rugby Club, composed mainly of Royal Irish Constabulary men, and Limerick County lost again to Garryowen in the Markets' Field, in 1889. At the turn of the century the club ceased to exist.

Shannon Rugby Football Club is located in Thomond Park and its foundation can be dated back to 19 February, 1884. Dan Duggan, Richie Gleeson, Pierce Hartney, Joe Hegarty and Paddy Lynch, the first captain, were the founding members. It became a senior club during the season of 1953 and 1954 and won its first Munster Cup in 1960. *There is an Isle* was not written as a rugby song but is now indelibly planted in Limerick memory as the anthem of Shannon R.F.C., known locally as the "Parish". Shannon became tenants of Thomond Park soon after achieving senior status. Eugene Davy, president of the Irish Rugby Football Union, opened the clubs pavilion, inside the main gate, on 27 December, 1967.

Sr. M. Barbara Down, an English nun, died in St. Mary's Convent, in 1966. The words of *There is an Isle* appeared in the *Limerick Chronicle* during the 1860s referring to a Scottish island, and were adapted by Sr. M. Barbara to suit St. Mary's Parish - The Parish - in the 1940s. She was a skilled musician, instrumentalist and soprano, and composed the music to accompany the song.

ST. MARY'S CONVENT. Limerick City Museum.

Garryowen Football Club is now located in Dooradoyle. This club was originally founded as Park Rangers but adopted its present name after a meeting in the Athenaeum, on 19 September 1884. The first president of the renamed club was William L. Stokes, the first secretary was J. Gogarty, the treasurer was M.L. Joyce and the first captain was J. O'Sullivan, all four and the committee having been elected at the Athenaeum meeting. In the absence of W.L. Stokes, the meeting was chaired by Michael Joyce who had represented Limerick as a member of parliament as Westminster for several years. Five years later, as the "bell of the asylum clock struck three", the men of Garryowen faced the Bandon team that had defeated them in their first bid for the Munster Cup, in 1886. This time, in 1889, Garryowen won its first Munster Cup, in the Markets' Field, in front of an audience of more that 3,000. By the turn of the century Garryowen dominated the Limerick rugby scene. In 1932 Stephen J. Coffey, a former Young Munster player, was captain of the Garryowen team. In 1958 Garryowen Football Club opened a new pavilion and grounds at Dooradoyle. Garryowen players had used the Markets' Field into the mid-1950s, but as they had to share the pitch with hurlers, footballers and soccer players the pitch was not always available. Since John Glynn, the president of the Irish Rugby Football Union, opened Dooradoyle in September, 1958, Garryowen has extended its grounds.

Lansdowne Rugby Football Club was founded in 1901. It achieved senior status immediately but did not survive the war years, 1914-1918.

The Young Munster Rugby Football Club is now located at Greenfields but, its formation dates back to 1895 when the Tyler Shoe Company presented a cup to be competed for by junior players of eighteen or under. This created great excitement amongst the boys living in the Boherbuoy, Carey's Road, Dixon's

ATHLUNKARD BOAT CLUB, A SCENE FROM THE PAST. **Limerick City Museum.**

Lane (now part of Hyde Road), Lord Edward Street and Parnell Street areas and those employed by the bacon factories, flour mills, railway station, sawmills and other firms. They banded into various groups and ten junior teams were entered for the competition, Clare Street Academy, Crescent College, Intermediate, Kiely's Academy, Lansdowne, St. Munchin's, Shannon, Sexton Street Rovers, Villiers and Young Munsters. Young Munsters won the cup, captained by M. Gilligan. Patrick Flavin and Michael O'Brien guided the young team and merged it with the older Treaty Club in 1896, retaining the name of the longer-established club. The combined clubs had five very successful seasons but re-emerged under the Young Munster name in 1901, under the guidance of Michael

Keyes, Con Carey, Thomas Hannon, Richard Matthews and Michael Quigley, following a meeting in the club rooms, then located in Bedford Row. Many of these early players were also members of the Gaelic Athletic Association. They were forced to adopt pseudonyms such as "Mack" to hide their true identities while playing rugby, as the All-Ireland Gaelic Convention adopted a resolution in 1902 to disqualify Gaelic footballers who took an active part in rugby matches. The Young Munster Rugby Football Club achieved senior status in 1922 and Nick Butler was the first senior captain. In 1923 Young Munsters competed, unsuccessfully, for their first Munster Cup under the captaincy of Nick Butler. Phonny Neilan was captain in 1929. Gerry Kileen was the captain in 1930 when the panel of players included P. Brazier, J. Brennan, J.J. Connery, M. Cosgrave, P.Deegan, F. Garvey, G. Griffin, T. Hickey, T. Kirkland, J. McCormack, J. McNeice, A. Neilan, J. O'Dea, M. O'Flaherty, M. D. Sheaman and C. St. George. Young Munster played in the "Bombing Field" from 1901 until the Prospect Hill housing estates were built in 1939. The club moved to the Catholic Institute grounds in Rossbrien, which it had to share with other clubs and associations. The Young Munster R.F.C. acquired its own grounds in 1958, purchasing a stretch of land on the opposite side of Greenfields Road. Jack Siggins, president of the Irish Rugby Football Union, opened their new grounds and pavilion in September, 1962.

The Old Queens Rugby Club was founded about 1918 to cater for the surplus players in Young Munster's.

Pirates Rugby Club was founded as an offshoot of Young Munsters as the latter's membership swelled, about 1918.

Bohemians Rugby Football Club is located in Thomond Park. This club was

AN IRON-AXE-HAMMER FOUND AT LONG PAVEMENT MAY DATE FROM PRE-CHRISTIAN TIMES.
Limerick City Museum.

founded in 1926 by Dr. Matt Graham, Larry Harkness, Jack McNiece, Tom Maher, Ned Stokes and Jack O'Sullivan, its first president. By 1927 the new club had upstaged Garryowen by winning the Munster Cup, under the captaincy of H. P. McMahon.

The Old Crescent Rugby Club became a senior club in 1953, beating Bohemians in a Munster Cup match on 7 March, 1953. Old Crescent was originally based at Priory Park, south of the railway station, where it shared the pitch with the Limerick Junior Soccer Council for a number of years; purchased their own grounds in the mid-1960s, and Chris Crowley, president of the Connacht Irish Rugby Football Union, opened the new pitch at Rathbane on 8 December, 1968. The club purchased other grounds at Rossbrien from the Jesuit Order, about 900 metres down the road from the ruins of St. Dominic's Church.

Thomond Rugby Football Club is located at Woodview, near Woodview Close and Rosturra Crescent.

THE CASTLE AND CITY OF LIMERICK IN 1827 - Fitzgerald and McGregor.

The North Liberties varied from one to four statute miles, comprising 1714 Irish acres in 1837. St. Munchin's Parish was situated partly in the barony of Bunratty, County Clare, but chiefly in the North Liberties of the city of Limerick, on the River Shannon, and immediately adjoining the city. The main residences in the late 1830s were Castle Park; Ballygrennan, the home of Richard Smyth; and Clonmacken.

Castle Park may have been designed by Francis Bindon (c. 1698-1765) about 1750 for Edward Ormsby. It was then leased to a Limerick solicitor, Nicholas Smith and, apparently, sold to Christopher Delmege (1785-1863) who occupied it in 1837. The building contains the stump of an old tower house which was used as a pavilion and joined to the main structure by a screen wall. In 1839 John O'Donovan wrote that the first building on this site dated back to 1620 and had been built and occupied by the O'Briens of Thomond. In 1789 it became the property of the Ormsbys who changed the name to Blackland Castle. Christopher Delmege bought it in 1833 and he improved and restored the building, rebuilding the greater part of it. The screen wall, the castle remains and the single-storey wing at one end of the house were crenellated with Irish battlements of a type in vogue during the early years of the nineteenth century. The house was sold in 1969.

BRONZE SOCKETTED-AXEHEADS FOUND AT MOYROSS DATE BACK TO THE BRONZE AGE, MOST LIKELY TO A TIME LONG BEFORE 500BC WHEN IRON STARTED TO REPLACE BRONZE.
Limerick City Library.

Caherdavin was recorded as Caherdavy in an inquisition of 1615 and appears as Caherdavyne and Caherdavine in a civil survey prepared by the Cromwellians between 1654 and 1656. It seems to be a derivative of an older Irish name such as *Cathair Daimhin*. The term *cathair* may refer to a city, court or mansion but was usually applied to circular stone forts, many of which were associated with the Celts. *Cathairs* were erected, of earth or stone, from about 300 BC onwards and remained in use into the early 1600s. *Daimhín* is an old Gaelic personal name that has long been associated with the Oirghialla, a great Ulster clan descended from the legendary three Collas. It is a diminutive of the term *Damh*, a poet or bard, and is the basis of *Ó Daimhín*, a surname that has been anglicised as O'Devine, Davine, Devine, Davin, Deven, Devin, Devon, Devins and, occasionally, Davy and Davis.

Clonmacken House is mentioned in Hugh Weir's *Houses of Clare* as a two-and-a-half storey gable-ended house with chimney stacks on each gable. Thomas Dineley wrote of it in 1680 as "a small house belonging to Mr. John Clenett, a Fleming (Dutchman), a gentleman of extraordinary civility towards strangers". He continued to relate that the house "is situated very pleasantly and commodiously upon the river Shannon, where the shipping passes by daily". In 1827 it was occupied by a Mr. D'Esterre. It was unoccupied in 1837 but listed as the property of the Marquess of Lansdowne. John O'Donovan, however, wrote that this house was built by Rev. Edmund Walker in 1700, was occupied by Captain Vereker in 1834, and was the seat of Jonathan Finch in 1839. Some time later John Browne Finch of Clonmacken married Maria Singleton of Quinville. The house later came into the possession of the Dixon and O'Brien-Kelly families. Hugh described the building as standing but uninhabited in 1985.

The Church of Our Lady of the Rosary was designed as a temporary wooden church by W.H.D. McCormick and F.M. Corr. Erected in 1949-1950, it serves a dual purpose as both a church and a show-place for modern Irish ecclesiastical

A Special Edition, to honour the heroes of Easter 1916. Limerick City Museum.

art. Oisin Kelly designed the teak statue, *Our Lady of Fatima*, on the tower; the *Annunciation* is by Imogen Stuart; the *Deposition from the Cross* by Andrew O'Connor is a plaster model for the bronze now in London's Tate Gallery; the sanctuary figures of the *Sacred Heart* and *Our Lady* are by Yvonne Jammett; the *St. Anne* is by Eamonn Costello; the font is by T. Quinn; and the single-light window, the *Baptism of Christ*, in the baptistry, is by Evie Hone.

Coonagh Airfield is situated north-west of the city. Dr. Robert Wyse Jackson described Coonagh as "that ancient fishing village of Viking origin". The flying club started the aerodrome here in 1945 under the tutelage of Arthur Topin who, before his death, was the oldest practising pilot in Ireland. This is still the only airfield within the county boundaries. The next nearest one is Shannon Airport, twelve miles west of here, in County Clare.

Killeely or Meelick Parish was known under both names in 1837. It was located "partly within the North Liberties of the city of Limerick, but chiefly in the Barony of Bunratty". There were then 5,141 inhabitants living on 5,135 statute acres which were nearly equally divided between tillage and pasture. The old entry into Limerick is still guarded by the castles of Cratloemoyle and Cratloekeel nearby, in County Clare, on the road to Bunratty, Shannon, Ennis and Galway. In 1837 Samuel Lewis wrote:-

> It extends nearly to the old Thomond bridge, at Limerick, and includes the extensive distillery of Messrs. Brown, Stein, and Co. ... There are stations of the constabulary police at Cratloe, Meelick, and Thomond Gate. Cratloe House is the residence of Stafford O'Brien, Esq.,; the demesne and wood of Cratloe, which are chiefly in this parish , extend into the adjoining parish of Kilfentinan ... The [Church of Ireland] church, a small plain structure is picturesquely situated at Meelick; it was built by the grandmother of the present Marquess of Conyngham, and subsequently made parochial ... In the R.C. divisions this parish is partly in the district of Meelick, and partly in that of Thomond Gate, or St. Lelia.

Killeely is believed to derive its name from one of two sources, both associated with early saints. *Cill Faoile*, the church of Faoile, a virgin saint commemorated in the name of a holy well in the Clare parish of Killmurry and in the name of a religious establishment in County Galway, is one explanation of the place-name. Killeely is generally believed to be a corruption of *Cill Liadhaine*, the church of Liadhain, a saint reputedly of Dalcassian origin. Liadhain is said to have been a daughter of Diarmuid, the grandson of Cairtheann, who was converted to Christianity by St. Patrick. This would make her a contemporary of other saints of the late fifth, or early sixth, century. She is usually referred to as St. Lelia. Her feast is, or rather was, celebrated on 11 August; and she has long been associated

EIGHTEENTH-CENTURY BOHEMIAN
DRINKING GLASS WITH
'zwischengoldglas' DECORATION - IN
THE HUNT MUSEUM

with the dioceses of Kerry and Limerick. Folklore refers to her as a sister of St. Munchin. The original parish church was located in what is now the graveyard of Killeely and was listed amongst the churches of Limerick shortly after 1200. The church had fallen into ruin before the Cromwellian siege and occupation of the city and by 1840 was described as "level with the ground", with only the burial ground remaining.

Killeely Graveyard is located to the east of Killeely Road and is virtually surrounded by Smith O'Brien Avenue, O'Callaghan Avenue, Hogan Avenue and a stretch of wall backing onto a road junction. The entrance is just off Killeely Road, south of where it meets Smith O'Brien Avenue, and is marked by a small metal arch bearing the legend *Cill Lela*. This arch, and the regular footpath around the graveyard, can be attributed to Sonny Guerin, "Shocker" Shaughnessy and Marie Looney who looked after this ancient burial ground in the 1960s, 1970s and 1980s. The high ground in the centre of the cemetery may mark the site of the old church, as there is quite a lot of loose stone in the vicinity that may have come form the fabric of the old building. The O'Halloran vault was found in the early 1970s and was restored by St. Senan's Historical Society as a tribute to Sylvester O'Halloran (1728-1807). Mount St. Lawerence cemetery opened in 1849, but the people of Thomondgate continued to bury their dead in Killeely into the early 1900s. A caretaker was appointed in 1879, at seven pounds a year, but the graveyard was closed by order of the Local Government Board in the early 1900s. Some burials continued, however, as a few of the local families had a long-established right to burial here. In 1939 the city council announced its plans for the construction of 360 houses in Killeely and the graveyard had become neglected by the 1940s and 1950s. In the 1960s this ancient burial ground was used as a *cillín* for the burial of young children and one local man told me of how he had buried his infant son here. This was almost at the end of an era when the religious authorities condemned the burial of unbaptised children in consecrated ground. The local man ignored the clerical strictures and helped others to inter the remains of their dead children in their own family plots. Sonny Guerin and "Shocker" Shaughnessy, two of the self-appointed custodians of Killeely, are now laid to rest in the old graveyard in which they had laboured so diligently. Elsewhere in the cemetery is the grave of a legendary man who is said to have been the father of at least eighty-nine children. John Meany (1902-1982) of Crossroads is buried in a family plot that dates back to 1720. John Barry (1781-1839) of Sexton Street (North) is also interred here. There are numerous brick-lined stone vaults and several Celtic-style crosses that date from the early 1800s. The most imposing monument is that of John Vaughan (1818-1887) which mentions his daughters, Bridget (1846-1940), Katie (1856-1948), son John (1863-1928), his first wife, Lizzie (nee Dillon 1859 - 1887), his second wife, Bridget (*nee* Tierney 1858-1933), their daughter, Mary Kiely (*nee* Vaughan 1898-1983), and her husband, James Kiely (1890-1966). The Barry, Grimes, Massey, Meany and O'Brien surnames can be found throughout the graveyard.

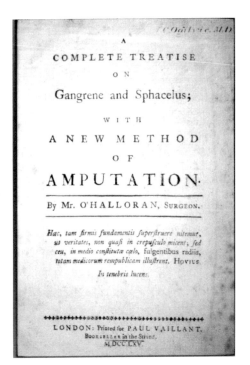

A MEDICAL TREATISE BY SYLVESTER O'HALLORAN,
TITLE PAGE.
Limerick City Museum.

Watch House Cross derives its name from a small house that stood close to what is now the intersection of New Road, Killeely Road and Long Pavement Road. Body-stealing or body-snatching was prevalent in Georgian times, and earlier, and the graves of the recent-dead had to be guarded. This was done, in some instances, by having caretakers live in, or close to , the cemeteries they were protecting. The houses in which these guardians lived were known as watch houses and the Killeely watch house was last occupied by Mick Cantillon, who died about thirty years ago. His former home was demolished by road-widening long before his death. In 1791 the government of the day passed a bill that allowed for the post-execution dissection of all criminals. John Scanlan, the murderer of the Colleen Bawn, was hanged in Limerick in 1820. His body should have been delivered to the Mulgrave Street hospital for dissection but his family used their influence to have it exempted from such treatment and he was buried at Crecora. This law remained in force until the Anatomy Act of 1832 was passed to endure an adequate supply of bodies. Even so, fear of body snatching was prevalent throughout Victorian times and the bodies of paupers remained at risk even into the 1920s or 1930s. In 1907 one of the guardians of the North

LIMERICK, FROM THE TOWER OF ST. MARY'S CATHEDRAL. Limerick City Museum.

Dublin Workhouse Union noted that an excessive amount of unclaimed bodies had been sent to the medical schools from that establishment.

St. Bridget's Graveyard is known locally as the paupers' graveyard. It is marked by a tall wooden cross on the hill behind Walters Fuels on the western side of Killeely Road; and may be reached by a pathway close to the northern wall of the fuel yard. The new Union Workhouse, now St. Camillus' Hospital, opened in 1841 and for several years most of its dead inmates were buried in Killeely graveyard. The Great Famine and its aftermath forced the hospital authorities to move burials elsewhere, as the cemetery at Killeely became overcrowded and the numerous burials created a health risk for the population of Thomondgate. In 1849 the Board of Guardians leased this plot of land from Daniel Cullen, a tenant of the Marquis of Lansdowne. It became notorious as the Yellow Hole, the burial place of so many paupers, in famine times. A fairy fort, the remains of a ring fort, was located within 150 yards of the cross up to about thirty years ago.

The Yellow Hole was the name bestowed on St. Bridget's graveyard by the inhabitants of Ballynanty, Killeely, Thomondgate and the city. During the worst days of the Great Hunger multiple burials were an everyday event and large pits were dug to accommodate the dead. Ballynanty was a boggy area and some distance below the surface of the soft boggy earth was a deep band of yellow

319

WEDDING THE SHANNON IN 1872. THIS ILLUSTRATION SHOWS THE MAYOR OF THE CITY WEDDING THE SHANNON, A CUSTOM THAT MAY HAVE ORIGINATED WITH THE VIKINGS. CASTING THE DART WAS ANOTHER CUSTOM BY WHICH THE MAYORS OF LIMERICK DISPLAYED THEIR JURISDICTION OVER THE RIVER AND SCATTERY ISLAND. UNDER A CHARTER GRANTED TO LIMERICK ON 3 MARCH, 1609, THE SUZERAINTY OF BOTH WAS CONFERRED ON THE MAYOR AS ADMIRAL OF THE SHANNON. TED RUSSELL EXERCISED THESE ANCIENT RIGHTS BY THROWING A TWO-FOOT-LONG SILVER DART INTO THE RIVER, ONE MILE OFF SCATTERY ISLAND, ON 16 MARCH, 1956. **The Graphic.**

mud. Mud of a yellow or off-white texture can be found six to thirteen feet below bogland. The presence of yellow mud at the bottom of the famine pit may have seemed remarkable to city dwellers but would not have merited any comment elsewhere. Yellow clay is the normal third soil layer throughout much of the country. Quicklime was in all probability used as a disinfectant and as a means of speeding up the decomposition of bodies which had been placed in peaty soil. Each layer of bodies was concealed beneath a shallow layer of earth, more bodies were laid on top of the earlier burials, and, even if no yellow mud had existed, the resultant effects of quicklime on human bodies would have produced a yellow soap-like substance at the bottom of such pits.

Wattle and Daub Construction has been in use since prehistoric times when men plastered light-timbered huts with a mud or marl known as *Dóib*. *Dóib buí* is the old Irish term for the yellow mud, clay or marl found in boggy areas. It was extensively used into the nineteenth century, may still be found in old chimney breasts and internal divisions within nineteenth-century houses, and was widely used by Limerick's first builders, the Vikings. One is inclined to wonder if burials commenced here simply because the Yellow Hole was already in existence, the worked-out marl or clay beds providing a ready made burial pit.

Kilquane Church derives its name from *Cill Chuain*, the church of Cuan, one of eight early saints who bore that name. Could this be Cuan the abbot, hermit and patron of Timahoe, County Laois, who died about 657? His feastdays are celebrated on both 24 December and 1 January and he appears to have been a man who travelled extensively. This ruined church, surrounded by its graveyard, is located on the bank of the River Shannon within view of, and only the width of the river from, Corbally. The townland derives its name from *Fearann Cille Chuain*, the land of the church of Kilquane, but was called Church Land in 1839. The swimming baths of Corbally are visible from the featureless remains of the old church, which are mainly of chest height. Kilquane is noted as the burial place of a local fisherman, Philip MacAdam, who, according to local tradition, pointed out the place where the Williamites could ford the river in order to attack Limerick City from the north. His descendant vigorously protested that this was not the case to Maurice Lenihan. His letter to Lenihan is in the Limerick Museum. The original *Áth an Longphuirt*, from which Athlunkard Bridge derives its name, may have been located at Kilquane which was also known in 1300 as Cluainanarny, from *Cluain na n-Áirne*, the river meadow of the sloes. The *longphort* was said to be an O'Brien stronghold of which no trace is evident. A nearby earthworks enclosure, close to the Lax Weir, is believed to have been a Viking base or *longphort*. Philip MacAdam, as a native of the region, knew the location of the ford which had passed out of use soon after Turlough O'Brien built a bridge, upriver, in 1071, near the site of another ford, *Vadum*

Silvae or *Áth Coille*, the ford of the wood. Philip MacAdam died on 26 November, 1700, and was buried outside the eastern gable of the church. His son and namesake died at the age of thirty-three on 24 June, 1729, and was interred in the same tomb, the damaged remains of which can be seen today.

The earliest documentation on this church is an agreement of 1240 between Gerard de Prendergast and Hubert, bishop of Limerick, which can be found in the *Black Book of Limerick*. It is also mentioned in the papal taxation lists of 1302 and 1306. It was desecrated in 1641 after the Confederate wars erupted, but seems to have remained in use as a Catholic church throughout penal times and later, until a new Catholic church was erected in Parteen in 1834. This is also the burial place of the Holmes family who have farmed the Church Land for over three centuries, own the land in the vicinity of the church, and have their home on the hill overlooking the ruins. Edward Appleyard (1710-1790) of Blackwater House, Charles Holmes (1758-1862) and the Piper of Limerick, Pádraig O'Briain (1773-1855), are all buried here. The Aherne, Beville, Beveridge, Cahill, Costelloe, Drew, Dundon, Egan, Galaher, Gough, Henly, Hogan, Keaten, Kennedy, McGrath, McKie, Minihan, Nihill, O'Brien, O'Connor, O'Mara, Ryan, Sliney and Sweeney surnames feature on the memorial slabs. The Parteen Historical Society erected a monument to Herr Feverstein, who was killed while working on the Shannon Scheme in 1926. He was one of three German nationals who died on this project, the other two being Josef Hainer and Rudolph Weigal. The wooden crosses that marked all three graves have long since deteriorated and only one grave is now distinguishable, the one identified by the historical society.

LIMERICK TOKEN, ISSUED BY THOMAS MARTEN IN 1669. Limerick City Museum.

Kilquane Parish is the alternative name of St. Patrick's North in the Lewis *Topographical Dictionary of Ireland* (1837). In 1839 John O'Donovan noted that it was called St. Patrick's Parish soon after the new Protestant church was erected in Parteen, about 1819. The parish was known to the Roman Catholic population of the day as Parteen Parish and comprised an area of 3,719 acres, most of it under tillage in the early 1830s. In 1837 Samuel Lewis wrote;-

> ... the state of agriculture has of late years considerably improved, from its proximity to the city of Limerick, of which it includes a small portion of the north liberties: midway between Corbally mills and St. Thomas's Island is the boundary mark called the "Liberty Stone". There is a considerable portion of bog; and limestone, containing fossil shells, is used for building and burnt for manure. On the river Blackwater, which runs into the Shannon, are two large flour-mills, the property of S. Caswell, Esq. Manorial courts for the recovery of small debts are occasionally held at Athlunkard and Parteen; and at Ardnacrusha is a station of the constabulary police. The seats are Spring Hill, the residence of P. McAdam, Esq.; Quinsborough, of Martin Honan, Esq. (formerly the residence of Lord George Quin); Whithall, of Capt. R. Kane; Fairy Hill, of E. Burnard, Esq.; Thomas Island, of J. Tuthill, Esq.; and Cottage, of R. Rogers. Esq. ... and at Parteen is a large national school, chiefly supported by a grant of £30 per ann. from the Board. The schoolhouse, erected by Mr. Honan in 1833, consists of a centre and two projecting wings, and contains apartments for the master and mistress.

FRANCIS HYNES AND COMPANY WERE HATTERS AT THE GEORGE STREET CORNER OF WILLIAM STREET IN 1846. IN AUGUST OF THAT YEAR MRS. BUTLER PAID £2.65 FOR TWO LADIES' HATS, A CASE AND A SERVANT'S HAT.

Parteen is a diminutive of *páirt*, a corruption of the old Irish word *port*, meaning a bank, landing-place, shore, earthwork or platform. *Páirín*, meaning the little landing-place, was a common place-name applied to several places on the Shannon between Limerick and Killaloe. In 1703 the village of Parteen comprised three ale-houses, a tan-yard, a malt-house a farmhouse, a mill and nine cabins. *The Moland Survey* of that year noted that large areas of land were still forested, stated that landowners were beginning to enclose land (the beginning of the "big house" era), and commented on how urban development was still affected by the recent Williamite wars. Castlebank contained two farmhouses, the ruins of an old castle and five or six cabins. Ballykealane consisted of a good slate house, three farmhouses, five cabins and the old church of Kilquane. Thomas Moland, a surveyor employed by the Earl of Thomond, wrote, in 1703:

> St. Thomases Island, situate as the former [Kilquane] and is part of it, has a good house, tan yard, mill and a store house for the fish caught in the Corporation of Limerick's weir which joynes it.

Parteen is now located on the Tail-race, a one and a half mile length of canal which carries the water from Ardnacrusha back to the Shannon River, above the city. The Head-race is the seven and a half miles section of canal leading from O'Briens Bridge to Ardnacrusha. The old bridge at Parteen bore a Latin inscription which referred to the *Via Strata*, the long pavement, a name still commemorated in Long Pavement Road, the road from Thomondgate to Parteen. This village is actually in County Clare but is rapidly becoming a suburb of Limerick City.

St. Thomas's Island commemorates St. Thomas Acquinas (c. 1225-1274), a notable Dominican teacher and theologian. He was canonised in 1323 and declared a doctor of the Church in 1567. In 1880 he was declared the patron saint of Catholic universities and study centres. The island belonged to the Dominicans of Limerick who are said to have built either a small monastery or a chapel of ease here. This building may have been erected some time after 1323 but no trace of it now remains. In 1691 the Williamites used pontoon bridges to ford the river at St. Thomas's Island and the rock to which their engineers hitched a chain became known as Carrig-a-Cluragh, the rock of the chain. This rock was shattered by a local landowner and vanished under alluvial deposits when the River Shannon was lowered in 1929. The Jacobite garrison, on the island, surrendered after the Williamites had crossed, but their barracks or headquarters had probably been a fortified house. In 1659 the tituladoes of St. Thomas's Island had been named as Edward Gould, William Stritch and Thomas Poore. One of these may have built a house or converted a building erected by the friars or the corporation to watch over the salmon weir. The ruins of the Tuthill house are still visible but local folklore also tells of two other men associated with the island. One was a *poitín*-maker and the other was a Sunday-man. The last term was reserved for one who lived "on the water" to avoid being sued for debt. An anomaly of the law did not allow process-servers to sue such

*THE SHANNON SCHEME, A LITHOGRAPH. **Limerick City Museum.***

individuals if they lived on a barge, boat or island and as Sunday was a Sabbath day nobody could serve them with a warrant on that day.

Ardnacrusha is believed to derive its name from a large wooden cross that was erected on the high ground, near the present Catholic Church, at Dundon's Corner, in 1111. It was one of three such markers, the other two being at Glenagross and Blackwater, that marked the diocesan borders of Limerick. *Ard na Croise*, the height of the cross, need not have been a wooden cross but may have been a termon or boundary cross, possibly of stone.

The Ardnacrusha Power Station evolved from the Shannon Scheme, the brainchild of Thomas A. McLaughlin, an Irish engineer who had left Ireland in December, 1922, to work with the firm of Siemens Schuckert in Germany. The German company specialised in supplying electrical power to parts of their country and this inspired Thomas A. McLaughlin to work out a plan for utilising the waters of Ireland's largest river to generate electricity for the entire country. He then approached Siemens Schuckert and the Irish government and outlined his idea which became known as the Shannon Scheme. Patrick McGilligan, (1889-1979), minister for Industry and Commerce in the new Free State, supported the scheme and on 13 August, 1925, the government and the German firm signed a five-point two million pound contract to implement the scheme, within a three-and-a-half-year deadline. Dr. Michael Fogarty (1859-1955), the bishop of Killaloe, turned the first sod in Ardnacrusha in August, 1925. The Electricity Supply Board was established on 11 August, 1927, to operate, manage, maintain and sell the power station's output. It was officially opened on

THE DAM AT ARDNACRUSHA. Limerick City Museum.

22 July, 1929. Three construction camps were established for the project, the largest one being at Ardnacrusha. It had living quarters for 750 construction workers, a dining-room which could accommodate 600 men, a kitchen, canteen and general store. The majority of the skilled workers and engineers were Germans. After the opening, the canal was slowly filled, the embankment thoroughly checked and great turbines set the generators in motion, two months later. The Shannon Scheme put an end to traffic on the Limerick to Killaloe canal which had come into operation by 1799 but it led to the electrification of rural Ireland. From 1936 onwards the Electricity Supply Board began to restore the salmon pools and, under its management, the Shannon Fisheries restored the fish hatcheries at Parteen Weir. In 1987 this was a major centre for the rearing of trout or salmon which were kept in 125 small, and eighteen large pools, at egg and fry stages, up to April of each year.

TOURIST INFORMATION OFFICE ON ARTHUR'S QUAY. Shannon Development Photo Library.

Bibliography

Books

Allen, R.E., Editor, *The Concise Oxford Dictionary of Current English*, Eighth Edition, Oxford 1990.

A Memory of John Fitzgerald Kennedy, Dublin

Baigent, Michael, and Richard Leigh, *The Temple and the Lodge*, London, 1993.

Barry, Michael, *Across Deep Waters, Bridges of Ireland.*

Begley, Rev. John, *The Diocese of Limerick, Ancient and Medieval*, Dublin, 1906.

Begley, Rev. John, *The Diocese of Limerick in the 16th and 17th Centuries*, Dublin, 1927.

Begley, Rev. John, *The Diocese Of Limerick From 1691 to the Present Time*, Dublin, 1938.

Bence - Jones, Mark, *Burke's Guide to Country Houses, Ireland*, London, 1978.

Bennis, Ernest H., *Reminiscences of Old Limerick*, Tralee, 1951.

Bolster, Evelyn (Sister M. Angela), *The Knights of Saint Columbanus*, Dublin, 1979

Bord Fáilte, *Limerick and Tipperary North 1980/1981*, Shannonside Tourism Organisation.

Bourke, Rev. Joseph, *A Letter Addressed to the Lord Bishop and the Clergy of the Diocese of Limerick by Rev. Joseph Bourke, a priest of the Diocese*, Mungret, 1881 - printed privately and intended for the clergy alone.

Brady, Anne M., and Brian Cleeve, *A Biographical Dictionary of Irish Writers*, Mullingar, 1985.

Byrnes, Ollie, *Against the Wind, Memories of Clare Hurling*, Cork, Dublin, 1996

Carew, Sir George, *Pacata Hibernia or A History of the Wars in Ireland during the Reign of Queen Elizabeth especially within the Province of Munster under the government of Sir George Carew and compiled by his direction and appointment*, edited and annotated by Standish O'Grady, London, 1896.

Castleconnell Guild, Irish Countrywomen's Association, *Castleconnell, Co. Limerick. A Walking Tour and Historical Notes*, 1987.

Census of Population of Ireland 1996. Preliminary Report, Dublin, July 1996.

Census 91. Local Population Report - 1st Series. No. 11 Limerick County Borough, Population by Age, Sex, Marital Status and Household Composition, Dublin, 1991.

Central Statistics Office, *Census 86, Local Population Report No. 19 County Limerick (excluding Limerick County Borough), Population by Age, Sex, Marital Status and Household. Composition in towns, D.E.D.'s, urban and rural districts*, Government Publications sales office, November, 1987.

Central Statistics Office, *Census 86. Local Population Report, No. 24. Limerick City Borough - Population by Age, Sex, Marital Status and Household Composition*, Government Publications, December, 1987.

Conil, Jean, and Richard Marchbank, *Banquet Cuisine, Modern Banqueting Gastronomy*, London, 1933.

Corporation of the City of Limerick, Limerick. *Treorán Oifigiúil do Luimneach, Official Guide to the City of Limerick*, 1988.

Corporation of the City of Limerick, *Official Guide to the City of Limerick*, Dublin, 1965-1966.

Cottle, Basil, *The Penguin Dictionary of Surnames*, Middlesex, 1967, 1978.

Cronin, Jim, Seamus Ó Ceallaigh and Patrick C.Walsh, *Munster G.A.A. Story*.

Cronin, Sean, *Irish Nationalism. A History of its Roots and Ideology*, 1980.

Crossle, Philip, *Irish Masonic Records*, published by the Grand Lodge of Ireland, 1973

De Breffny, Brian, and George Mott, *Castles of Ireland*, London, 1977.

De Breffny, Brian, Rosemary ffolliott and George Mott, *The Houses of Ireland, Domestic Architecture from the Medieval Castle to the Edwardian Villa*, London, 1984.

De Búrca, Marcus, *The G.A.A.: A History*, Dublin, 1980.

Delany, V.T.H., and D.R. Delany, *The Canals of the South of Ireland*, Newton Abbot, 1966.

De Paor, Liam, Editor, *Milestones in Irish History*, Dublin, Cork, 1986.

De Vere, Aubrey, *Recollections of Aubrey de Vere*, New York, London, 1897.

Dinneen, Rev. Patrick S., *Foclóir Gaedhilge agus Béarla - An Irish-English Dictionary*, Dublin, 1927.

Donnelly, Kevin, Michael Hoctor and Dermot Walsh, *A Rising Tide. The Story of Limerick Harbour*, Limerick Harbour Commissioners, 1994.

Doran, Patrick F., *50 Treasures from the Hunt Collection*.

Dowd, Rev. J., *St. Mary's Cathedral, Limerick*, Limerick, 1899.

Dowling, John A., John Weaving, Dom Roche and Eric Erskine, Editors, *The Shannon Guide - A navigational pilot, fishing and touring guide*, Irish Shell and B.P., November 1962 to April 1963.

Dowling, P.J., *A History of Irish Education. A Study in conflicting Loyalties*, Cork, 1971.

Dowling, P.J., *The Hedge Schools of Ireland*, Cork, Dublin, 1968.

Edwardes, Michael, *The Dark Side of History, Subversive Magic and the Occult Underground*, London, 1980.

Egan, Fr. Bartholomew, *Franciscan Limerick, The Order of St. Francis in the City of Limerick*, Limerick, 1971.

Fallon, Niall, *The Armada in Ireland*, 1978.

Fennelly, Mary, Editor, *Limerick Lives*, Limerick, 1996

Ferrar, John, *History of the City of Limerick*, Limerick, 1767.

Ferrar, John, *Ferrar's Limerick Directory*, 1769.

Ferrar, J, *The History of Limerick, Ecclesiastical, Civil and Military, From the Earliest Records to the year 1787, Illustrated by Fifteen Engravings, To which are added The Charter of Limerick and an Essay on Castle Connell Spa, On Water in General and Cold Bathing*, Limerick, 1786.

Finerty, John F., *Ireland in Pictures*, Chicago, 1897.

Fitzgerald, Rev. P., and J. J. M'Gregor, *The History, Topography and Antiquities of the County and City of Limerick with a preliminary view of the History and Antiquities of Ireland*, Vol. II, Limerick, London, 1827.

Fitzgibbon, Constantine, *The Irish in Ireland*, London, 1983.

Fleming, John, *St. John's Cathedral, Limerick*, Blackrock, 1987.

Fleming, John, and Sean O'Grady, *St. Munchin's College Limerick 1796-1996*, Limerick, 1996.

Foster, R.E., *Modern Ireland 1600-1972*, London, 1988

Fógra Fáilte, Official Guide, *Limerick City and County*, The National Tourist Publicity Organisation for Ireland, Dublin.

Frost, James, *The History and Topography of the County of Clare*, London, 1893, Cork, 1978.

Fourth Report of the Commissioners for the Improvement of the Navigation of the River Shannon, with maps, plans and estimates, and an appendix, Dublin, 1839.

Gibson, William H., *Early Irish Golf. The First Courses, Clubs and Pioneers*, Naas, 1988

Gilhooly, John T., *Stair Chaisleán Uí gConaing Athaín The Annals of Castleconnell and Ahane since Prehistoric Times.* Castleconnell, 1988

Gleeson, Dermot F., *A History of the Diocese of Killaloe*, Dublin, 1962.

Graves, Robert, *Goodbye to All That*, London, 1929.

Graves, Robert, *Claudius the God*, London, 1934, recent edition.

Green, Alice Stopford, *Irish Nationality*, London, 1911.

Green, Jonathon, *Famous Last Words*, London, 1979.

Gwynn, Aubrey, and R. Neville Hadcock, *Medieval Religious Houses Ireland*, London 1970, 1988.

Hall, S.C., and A.M. Hall, *Halls' Ireland, Mr. And Mrs. Hall's Tour of 1840*, originally published in three volumes between 1841 and 1843, edited by Michael Scott, 1984

Hamilton, Frank, *Limerick in Days gone by ... A guide to the olde citie. A Walk through Thomondgate, the Parish and Johnsgate*, Limerick, 1978.

Hannan, Kevin, Limerick. *Historical Reflections*, Castletroy, 1996.

Hannan, Kevin, *Patrick's People. Historical Perspectives of an Ancient and Developing Community*, Limerick

Harbison, Peter, *Guide to the National Monuments in the Republic of Ireland including a selection of other monuments not in State care*, Dublin, 1970, 1975, 1992.

Haydn, J. A., *Misericords in St. Mary's Cathedral, Limerick*, Revised by Rev. M. J. Talbot, Limerick, 1969.

Healy, James N., *Irish Ballads and Songs of the Sea*, Cork, 1967.

Herbert, Robert, *Worthies of Thomond; being a compendium of short lives of the most famous men and women of Limerick and Clare to the present day*, Limerick, 1944.

Hickey, D. J., and J. E. Doherty, A *Dictionary of Irish History*, Dublin, 1980.

Hill, Judith, *The Building of Limerick*, Cork, Dublin, 1991, 1997.

Hogan, Robert, *Dictionary of Irish Literature*, Dublin, 1980.

Hyman, Louis, *The Jews of Ireland from Earliest times to the year 1910*, Reprint, Shannon, 1972.

Inglis, Henry D. *Journey Through Ireland*, 1834

Irish Freemasons' Calendar and Directory for the Year A.D. 1996, published under the sanction of the Most Worshipful, The Grand Lodge of Ireland.

Jackson, Robert Wyse, *The Story of Limerick*, Cork, 1973.

Jehovah's Witnesses, *1988 Yearbook of Jehovah's Witnesses*, Pennsylvania, 1987.

Joyce, Gerry, *Limerick City Street Names*, Limerick, 1995.

Joyce, P.W., *A Short History of Ireland, from the earliest times to 1608*, Dublin, 1893

Joyce, P. W., *A Smaller Social History of Ancient Ireland*, Second Edition, 1908.

Joyce, P. W., *The Origin and History of Irish Names of Places*, London, 1912, Wakefield, 1973.

Kemmy, Jim, and Larry Walsh, *Limerick in old picture postcards*, Zaltbommel, The Netherlands, 1997.

Kemmy, Jim, Editor, *The Limerick Compendium*, Dublin, 1997.

Keogh, Dermot, *Jews in Twentieth-Century Ireland, Refugees, Anti-Semitism and the Holocaust*, Cork 1998

Killanin, Lord, and Michael V. Duignan, *Shell Guide to Ireland*, London, Revised Edition, 1967.

Kilroy, Roger, and McLachlan, *Illuminated Limericks*, London, 1982.

Kohl, J.G., *Ireland, Scotland and England*, London, 1844.

Lee, David, Editor, *Remembering Limerick. Historical essays celebrating the 800th anniversary of Limerick's first charter granted in 1197*, Limerick Civic Trust, 1997.

Lee, David, and Bob Kelly, Editors, *Georgian Limerick*, Limerick Civic Trust, 1996

Lenihan, Maurice, *Limerick; Its History And Antiquities, ecclesiastical, civil and military, from the earliest ages, with copious historical, archaeological, topographical and genealogical notes and illustrations; maps, plates, and appendices, and an alphabetical index, etc. Compiled from the ancient annals, the most authentic ms and printed records, recent researches, etc., etc.*, Dublin, 1866.

Lewis, Samuel, *A Topographical Dictionary of Ireland*, London, 1837.

Limerick City Trust, *Limerick, An Appreciation*, Limerick, 1987.

Limerick City Trust, *Limerick, Street Antiquities*, Limerick, 1986.

Lilburn, Hugh, *Presbyterians in Limerick*, Limerick, 1946.

Lodge, Edmund, *Lodge's Peerage, Baronetage, Knightage & Companionage of the British Empire for 1912*, London, 1912.

Logan, John, Editor, *With Warmest Love, Lectures for Kate O'Brien, 1984-93*, Limerick, 1994.

Logan, Patrick, *The Holy Wells of Ireland*, Gerrard Cross, Buckinghamshire, 1980.

Longfield, Ada Kathleen, *Anglo-Irish Trade in the Sixteenth Century*, London, 1929.

Loveday J.F.T., Editor, *Diary of a Tour in 1732 through parts of England, Wales, Ireland and Scotland made by John Loveday of Caversham*, Edinburgh, 1890.

Lucas, Richard, *A General Directory of the Kingdom of Ireland*, 1788.

Lyons, F.S.L., *Charles Stewart Parnell*, London, 1977.

Macardle, Dorothy, *The Irish Republic - A documented chronicle of the Anglo-Irish conflict and the partitioning of Ireland, with a detailed account of the period 1916-1923 with a preface by Eamon de Valera*, Dublin. 1951.

McCaffrey, Rev. James, *The Black Book of Limerick*, Dublin, 1907.

MacCarthy, Colonel J. M., Editor, *Limerick's Fighting Story - From 1916 to the Truce with Britain*, Tralee.

McCourt, Frank, *Angela's Ashes. A Memoir of a Childhood*, New York, 1996, London, 1997.

MacDonald, A.M., Editor, *Chamber's Shorter English Dictionary*, Edinburgh, London, 1949, 1955.

MacLysaght, Edward, *Irish Families. Their Names, Arms and Origins*, Blackrock, 1985.

MacLysaght, Edward, *Irish Life in the Seventeenth Century*, Cork, 1939, 1950, 1969.

Marquis Who's Who, *Who's Who in America*. 45th Edition 1988-1989. Volume I, Wilmette, Illinois.

Maxwell, Constantia, *Irish History from Contemporary Sources (1509 - 1610)*, London, 1923.

Menton, William A., *The Golfing Union of Ireland*, Dublin, 1991.

Millard, Dom Bede, Editor, *The Book Of Saints - A Dictionary of Servants of God Canonized by the Catholic Church*, sixth edition, entirely revised and re-set, London, 1989.

Molony, W. Brother Alfred, *Notes on the Minutes, 1785-1863, of the Dunboyne Masonic Lodge, No. 60, Ennis, County Clare*, Masonic Lodge Headquarters, Molesworth Street, Dublin.

Moody, T. W., and F. X. Martin, *The Course of Irish History*, Cork, Dublin, Revised and Enlarged, 1994.

Mulligan, Fergus, *One Hundred and Fifty Years of Irish Railways*, Dublin, 1983.

Mulqueen, Charles, *Limerick's Rugby History*, Limerick, 1978.

Mulqueen, Charles, Club History, *Garryowen F.C. 1884-1984*, Limerick, 1984.

Munter, Robert, *A Dictionary of the Print Trade in Ireland 1550-1775*, New York, 1988.

Murphy, Charlotte M., *Limerick City - An Architectural Guide*, Shannon, 1986.

Nash, Ogden, Edward Lear, Charles Barsotti, Dean Walley and Others, *New Comic Limericks, Laughable Poems*, Edited by Ivanette Dennis, Illustrated by Louis Marak, 1969.

National Monuments and Historic Properties Service 1997, *Record of Monuments and Places as Established under Section 12 of the National Monuments (Amendment) Act 1994 - County Limerick*, 1997.

National Parks and Monuments Service, *Visitor's Guide, King John's Castle*, Limerick.

Neeson, Eoin, *The Book of Irish Saints*, Cork, 1967.

Nolan, Myles, *Dominicans in Limerick 1227 - 1997*, Limerick, 1997.

O'Brien, Conor, *From Three Yachts*, Revised, 1949.

O'Brien, Ivar, *O'Brien of Thomond - The O'Briens in Irish History 1500 - 1865*, Chichester, 1986.

Ó Ceallaigh, Seámus P., *History of the Limerick G.A.A., from earliest times to the present day*, Tralee, 1937

Ó Ceallaigh, Tadhg, *Limerick: A Handbook of Local History*, Coiste Oideachais Múinteoirí Luimnigh, as dáta.

Ó Céirín, Kit and Cyril, *Women of Ireland. A Biographic Dictionary*, Newtownlynch, Kinvara, 1996.

Ó Cléirigh, Nellie, and Veronica Rowe, *Limerick Lace. A Social History and a Maker's Manual*, Gerrards Cross, 1995.

O'Connor, G. B., *Elizabethan Ireland. Native and English*, Dublin.

O'Connor, John, *Mungret, History and Antiquities*, 1971.

O'Connor, Patrick J., *Exploring Limerick's Past. An historical geography of urban development in city and county*, Newcastle West, 1987.

Ó Corráin, Donncha, *Ireland before the Normans*, Dublin, 1972.

Ó Corrbuí, Máirtín, *Kenry, The Story of a Barony in County Limerick*.

O'Donovan, John, and Eugene Curry, *The Antiquities of County Clare - Letters containing information relative to the Antiquities of the County of Clare collected during the progress of the Ordnance Survey in 1839; and letters and extracts relative to Ancient Territories in Thomond*, 1841, based on the typescript produced under the direction of Rev. M. O'Flanagan, Bray, 1928, edited and indexed by Maureen Comber, Ennis and Barr Trá, by permission of the director of the Ordnance Survey, Ennis, 1997.

O'Farrell, Padraic, *Who's Who in the Irish War of Independence 1916 - 1921*, Cork, 1980.

O'Flaherty, Michael, *The Story of Young Munster Rugby Football Club, 1895/1896- 1995/1996. A Celebration of 100 years of Football,* Edited by Sean Curtin.

Ogilvie, John, *The Imperial Dictionary, English, Technological and Scientific, adapted to the present state of literature, science and art; on the Basis of Webster's English Dictionary,* Glasgow, Edinburgh, London, 1850.

O'Kelly, Eoin, *The Old Private Banks and Bankers of Munster,* Cork, 1959.

O'Mahony, Seán, *Frongoch, University of Revolution,* Killiney, 1987.

O'Malley, Ernie, *The Singing Flame,* Dublin, 1978

O'Meara, John F., *Gerard of Wales - The History and Topography of Ireland,* London, 1951, Revised 1982.

Oram, Hugh, *The Newspaper Book. A History of Newspapers in Ireland,* 1649-1983, Dublin, 1983.

Ó Riain, Dónal, agus Séamas Ó Cinnéide, *Stair agus Béaloideas - Páirtín agus Míliuc, The History and Folklore of Parteen and Meelick,* edited by Eilís Uí Shuilleabháin.

Ó Tuama, Seán, *An Duanaire, 1600 - 1900: Poems of the Dispossessed,* Translated into English verse by Thomas Kinsella, 1981

Otway - Ruthven, A.J., *A History of Medieval Ireland,* London, 1968.

Patterson, Richard Ferrar, and John Dougal, Editors, *Virtue's English Dictionary, Encyclopaedic Edition,* London, Dublin.

Patterson, R.E., *History of the Grand Lodge or Free and Accepted Masons of Ireland,* Vol. II, Dublin, 1957.

Price, Charles, *The World of Golf, a panorama of six centuries of the game's history,* London, 1963.

Quinlan, Arthur J., *History of Castletroy Golf Club*

Radnedge, Keir, General Editor, *The Ultimate Encyclopedia of Soccer,* England, 1994.

Read, Charles A., *The Cabinet of Irish Literature, Selections from the works of the chief poets, orators, and prose writers of Ireland*, London, 1902.

Reid, Austin, *Limerick Golf Club 1891-1991*, Limerick, 1991.

Roche, Richard, *The Norman Invasion of Ireland*, Dublin, 1979.

Rolleston, T.W., *Celtic Myths and Legends*.

Ronan, Myles V., *The Reformation in Ireland under Elizabeth 1558 - 1580*, London, New York, Toronto, 1930.

Rules and Regulations for the controul and government of the North Munster Provincial Grand Lodge of the Most Ancient and Honorable Society of Free and Accepted Masons Enacted in Full Lodge, on the 12th Day of July, 5842, Limerick, 1847.

Rynne, Etienne, *North Munster Studies, Essays in Commemoration of Monsignor Michael Moloney*, Limerick, 1967.

Scott, George Ryley, *History of Torture*, London, 1971.

Sanderson, Edgar, *A History of the British Empire*, London, 1909.

Seaby, Peter, *Coins and Tokens of Ireland*, Part 3, London, 1970.

Second Report of the Commissioners for the Improvement of the Navigation of the River Shannon, with maps, plans and estimates, and an appendix, Dublin, 1837.

Seoighe, Mainchín, *A Walking Tour of Historic Limerick*, Shannonside Tourism, 1982.

Seoighe, Mainchín, *Portrait of Limerick*, London, 1982.

Seoighe, Mainchín, *The Limerick Guide - Official Irish Tourist Board Guide to County Limerick*, Bórd Fáilte.

Sheehy, Maurice, *When the Vikings came to Ireland*, Cork, 1975.

Shepherd, Sandy, Project Editor, **Reader's Digest Illustrated Guide to Ireland.** London, New York, Sydney, Montreal, Cape Town, 1992.

Shiel, Michael, *The Quiet Revolution. The Electrification of Rural Ireland, 1946-1976*, Dublin, 1984.

Smith, Gus, Wogan. *Chat Show Host Extraordinary*, Dublin, 1986

Smith, Peter, and Keith Mackie, *The Guinness Book of Golf*, Enfield, 1992.

Smyth, Alfred P., *Scandinavian York and Dublin, The History and Archaeology of two related Viking Kingdoms*, Volume II, Dublin, 1987.

Spellissy, Seán, *Clare County of Contrast*, with photographs by John O'Brien, Ennis, 1987.

Spellissy, Seán, Limerick *The Rich Land*, with photographs by John O'Brien, Ennis, 1989

Spellissy, Seán, *A Portrait of Ennis*, with photographs by John O'Brien, Ennis, 1990.

Spellissy, Seán, Editor, *The Royal O'Briens - A Tribute*, with photographs by John O'Brien, Dromoland, 1992.

Spellissy, Seán, *The Merchants of Ennis*, with photographs by Richard Wilson, Cloghroe, Blarney, County Cork, 1996.

Spellissy, Seán, Suicide: *The Irish Experience*, Cloghroe, Blarney, County Cork, 1996.

Stalley, Roger, *The Cistercian Monasteries of Ireland*, London, 1987.

Stalley, R.A., *Architecture and Sculpture in Ireland 1150 - 1350*, Dublin, 1971.

Stewart, R.J., *Celtic Gods. Celtic Goddesses*, London, 1990.

Sykes, J. B. Editor, *The Concise Oxford Dictionary of Current English - based on the Oxford English Dictionary and its supplements*, Oxford, 1976.

Talbot, Rev. M. J., *A Pictorial Tour of Limerick Cathedral.*

Talbot, Rev. M. J., *The Monuments of St. Mary's Cathedral, Limerick*, Limerick, 1976.

Thom, Alex., *Thom's Official Directory of the United Kingdom of Great Britain and Ireland: for the year 1897*, Dublin, 1897.

Telecom Éireann, *Eolaí Telefóin na hÉireann, 06 Area 1997/1998.*

Trevelyan, G. M., *English Social History. A Survey of Six Centuries. Chaucer to Queen Victoria*, London, 1944.

Walford, Edward, *The County Families of the United Kingdom or Royal Manual of the Titled and Untitled Aristocracy of England, Wales, Scotland, and Ireland*, London, 1892.

Wallace, Martin, *100 Irish Lives*, London, 1983.

Walsh, Larry, *Historic Limerick - The City and its Treasures*, The Irish Heritage Series, Dublin, 1984.

Warwick, *The Warwick English History, a sketch of the development of England and the Empire from 55 BC to the present time*, London

Weir, Hugh W. L., *Historical Genealogical Architectural Notes on some Houses of Clare*, Whitegate, 1986.

Weir, Hugh, W. L., *O'Brien People and Places*, Whitegate, 1983.

Weir, Hugh, W. L., *Ireland - A Thousand Kings, Words, Academic and Otherwise, on Irish Kings and Queens*, Whitegate, 1988.

Westropp. T. J., *The Antiquities of Limerick and its Neighbourhood*, Dublin, 1916.

White, Rev. P., *History of Clare and the Dalcassian Clans of Tipperary, Limerick, and Galway*, Dublin, 1983.

Woodham-Smith, Cecil, *The Great Hunger 1845-1849*, London, 1962.

Woulfe, Rev. Patrick, *Sloinnte Gaedheal is Gall, Irish Names and Surnames*, Dublin, 1923.

Younger, Calton, *Ireland's Civil War*, London, 1968.

Bibliography

Journals, Magazines, Maps, Newspapers,
Unpublished Material, Etcetera.
Asterisk denotes unpublished material.

Ahern, Richard, "A History of the Christian Brothers in Limerick", *The Old Limerick Journal*, Autumn, 1987.

Ahern, Richard, "Limerick in 1689", *The Old Limerick Journal*, Number 26, Winter, 1989.

* Ashton, Geoffrey G., "Correspondence and Notes on the Provincial Grand Lodge of North Munster"

"Athlunkard Boat Club's unique and historic gates", *Limerick Leader* (Date unknown, supplied by Desmond M. Long)

"Athlunkard Viking 'longphort' identified", *Archaeology Ireland*, Volume 12, No.2, Issue No. 44

Barry, James Grene, "Old Limerick Bridges", *Journal of North Munster Archaeological Society*, 1909.

Boland, S. J., "Fr. John Creagh in the Kimberleys", *The Old Limerick Journal - Australian Edition*, No. 23, Spring, 1988.

Bowles, Sister Joan, *Limerick Youth Service, 1996/1997*, Annual Report

Bracken, Dymphna, "City toasts Gaisce gold recipients", *Limerick Leader*, Saturday, January 31, 1998

Bracken, Dymphna, "Minister praises role of religious in education as Mary I celebrates", *Limerick Leader*, Saturday, January 31, 1998

Bracken, Dymphna, "County Says 'No' to City Extension, *Limerick Chronicle*, Tuesday, October 14, 1997.

Brennock, Mark, "Passionate worker for disadvantaged", *The Irish Times*, Saturday, September 27, 1997.

* Browne, Tony, "Houses and Families of Limerick City and County".

"City mourns local noted historian, Kevin Hannan", *Limerick Leader*, Saturday November 9, 1996.

Clark, William Smith, "The Limerick Stage 1736 - 1800", Part One, *The Old Limerick Journal*, Winter, 1981.

Clark, William Smith, "The Limerick Stage 1736 - 1800", Part Two, *The Old Limerick Journal*, Summer, 1982.

Connolly, John, "University Challenge. How Limerick fought and won its place under the third-level sun", *Education and Living. The Irish Times*, Tuesday, September 30, 1997.

Corporation of Limerick, *A List of the Mayors and Sheriffs of Limerick, from 1197 to 1990 - 1991*, Limerick.

Culhane, Rev. James, "Monsignor Michael Moloney: His life and work", *North Munster Studies*, Limerick, 1967.

Cussen, Robert, "Caleb Powell, High Sheriff of County Limerick, 1858, sums up his Grand Jury", *North Munster Studies, Essays in Commemoration of Monsignor Michael Moloney*, Edited by Etienne Rynne, 1967

Danaher, Patricia, "An Uphill Battle for People of Southill", *The Irish Press*, 6 October, 1987.

Devereux, Dr. Eoin, "The Life and Writings of Seamus Ó Cinnéide", *Limerick Christmas Gazette*, 1996.

"District Link - State of health of 17th century citizenery was generally good", *Limerick Leader*, Saturday, December 20, 1997.

"District Link - Sir Harry's Mall will be closed .... 200 years after its construction," *Limerick Leader*, Saturday, January 31, 1998.

Dolley, Michael, "The Mediaeval Coin-Hoards of Thomond", *North Munster*

Antiquarian Journal, Volume XII, 1969.

Dolley, Michael, and William O'Sullivan, "The Chronology of the first Anglo-Irish Coinage", *North Munster Studies, Essays in Commemoration of Monsignor Michael Moloney*, Edited by Etienne Rynne, 1967.

Doran, Patrick F., "The Hunt Museum", *North Munster Antiquarian Journal*, Volume XX, 1978.

Duffy, Paul, "A Limerick Pawnshop Farthing", *North Munster Antiquarian Journal*, Volume XXV, 1983.

Feeley, Pat, "Aspects of the 1904 Pogrom", *The Old Limerick Journal*, Summer, 1982.

Fitzgibbon, Constantine, "A Visit to Limerick - 1952", *The Old Limerick Journal*, Summer, 1982.

Galvin, Anthony. *"Inside the Freemasons"*, Limerick Leader, 23 November, 1996.

Galvin, Anthony, "Loosening the strings on the Masons' apron" *Limerick Leader*, 30 November, 1996.

Gleeson, Willie W., "R.I.C. and the Black and Tans", *Limerick Leader*, Saturday, 27 March, 1982.

Gleeson, Willie W., "City of Commerce", *The Old Limerick Journal*, Summer, 1982.

Gleeson, Willie W., "The Brazen Head", *The Old Limerick Journal*, Autumn, 1981.

Glin, The Knight of, "A Baroque Palladian in Ireland. The architecture of Davis Duckart - I", *Country Life*, September 28th, 1967

Glin, The Knight of, "The last Palladian in Ireland. The architecture of Davis Duckart II", *Country Life*, October 5th, 1967.

Glin, The Knight of, "The Limerick Custom House", *50 Treasures from the Hunt Collection.*

Graphic, The, October 5, 1872

Graphic, The, November 13, 1880

Hanly, David, "I long for the Vikings' long ship", *The Sunday Tribune*, 14 June, 1998.

Hannan, Kevin, "A Forgotten Limerick Genius", *The Old Limerick Journal*, Autumn, 1987.

Hannan, Kevin, "Garryowen", *The Old Limerick Journal*, December, 1979.

Hannan, Kevin, "How Plassey Got Its Name", *The Old Limerick Journal*, December, 1979.

Hannan, Kevin, "The Irishtown", *The Old Limerick Journal*, Spring, 1982.

Hannan, Kevin, "The Sandmen", *The Old Limerick Journal*, Autumn, 1981.

Hannan, Kevin, "St. Michael's", *The Old Limerick Journal*, Winter, 1981.

Harrold, Patsy, "The Park Danes", *The Old Limerick Journal*, Autumn, 1982.

Harvey, Rev. Patrick, *St. Mary's Cathedral*, (1168 AD), A Guide, Limerick, 1997.

Haydn, J.A., "Essay on the Bicentenary, 1732-1932 of Ancient Union Lodge No. 13, Limerick"

Herbert, R., "The Lax Weir and Fishers Stent of Limerick", *North Munster Antiquarian Journal*, Volume V, 1946-1949, Limerick.

Herbert, R, *Limerick Printers & Printing*, Limerick City Library 1942.

Herbert, Robert, 'The Antiquities of the Corporation of Limerick", *North Munster Antiquarian Journal*, Vol. IV. No. 3, Limerick, Spring 1945.

Hewson, Michael, "Emigration to the North American Colonies from the port of Limerick in 1841", *North Munster Antiquarian Journal*, Volume XXIII, 1981.

Hickson, Miss, "Names of Places and Surnames in Kerry", *Journal of Royal Society of Antiquaries*, 1892.

Hodkinson, Brian, "127. St. Mary's Cathedral; Limerick. Medieval Cathedral" *Excavations 1992. Summary of archaeological excavations in Ireland*, edited by Isabel Bennett on behalf of the Organisation of Irish Archaeologists.

* Honan, Joseph S., "The Real Irish", and "Men of Stature - Collins, Griffith and O'Higgins".

Howard, Leonard, "The Penal Laws in Limerick 1670 - 1684", *North Munster Antiquarian Journal*, Volume XII, 1969.

Hutton, Seán, "Fionn Mac Cool. An Irishman's Diary ... Stalwart to the last", *The Irish Post*, October 4, 1997.

Illustrated London News The, October 8, 1853.

Illustrated London News The, October 29, 1881.

Janssens de Varebeke, Dom Hubert, "The Barringtons of Limerick", *The Old Limerick Journal.* Barringtons' Edition, Number 24, Winter, 1988

Johnston, Karl, "The Sporting Barringtons", *The Old Limerick Journal, Barringtons' Edition*, Winter, 1988.

Keane, John, "Limerick Breweries", *The Old Limerick Journal*, Autumn, 1981.

Kearney, Pat, "Towards A University For Limerick 1934 - 1972", *The Old Limerick Journal*, Autumn Edition, 1990.

Kemmy, Jim, *The Granary*, Limerick City Library, Limerick, 1987.

Kemmy, Jim, "How Garryowen got its name Owen's Garden, Famous Limerick Gardens - III", *The Old Limerick Journal*, Autumn, 1981.

Kemmy, Jim, "How Plassey Got Its Name", *The Limerick Compendium*, Dublin, 1997.

Kemmy, Jim, "The Death of a Cabin-Boy", *The Old Limerick Journal*, Winter, 1981.

Kemmy, Jim, "The Siege of Clampett's Bow", *The Old Limerick Journal*, December, 1979.

Kemmy, Jim, "The Park Danes - The Daily Labourers", *The Old Limerick Journal*, Winter, 1985.

Kilfeather, Frank, "Spring Leads Tributes To A Giant Of A Limerick Man", *The Irish Times*, Saturday, September 27, 1997.

* Leonard , Denis, "Notes on the Inner City Development".

* Leonard , Denis, "Notes on the Limerick Civic Trust".

* Leonard , Denis, "Notes on Limerick Jewish History - Limerick Civic Trust, Labour History Workshop".

Limerick Christmas Gazette, 1987, "Recalling the day that Limerick's city centre came to a standstill - Todd's Great Fire, August 25, 1959.

"Limerick Freedom Box", *North Munster Antiquarian Journal, Vol. V, Nos 2 & 3*, Limerick, Autumn 1946-Spring, 1947.

"Limerick Quakers", *The Clare Champion*, Friday, 16 September, 1988.

Llywelyn, Morgan, "The O'Brien Dynasty", *Ireland - A Thousand Kings*, Whitegate, 1988.

Logan, John, "Family and Fortune in Kate O'Brien's Limerick", *With Warmest Love, Lectures for Kate O'Brien*, 1984-93, Limerick, 1994.

Lovett, Phil, "The Development of the Port of Limerick in the 19th Century", *The Old Limerick Journal*, Spring, 1982.

Lovett, Phil, "The Wellesley Bridge", *The Old Limerick Journal*, Winter, 1981.

Lydon, J.F., "Reviews and Short Notices", *Annual Report of the I.C.H.S., 1962-3*, a report approved on 30 May, 1963, at the Conference of Irish Historians held at Magee University College, Derry.

* Lynch, Dr. Patricia A. "The European Connections of two Irish Writers: Maria Edgeworth and Kate O'Brien": A paper presented to the Triennial Conference of the International Association for the Study of Anglo-Irish Literature, the New University of Ulster at Coleraine, July 1988.

Lynch, P.J., "Obituary, Patrick Weston Joyce, LL.D., M.R.I.A.", *Journal of the North Munster Archaeological Society*. Vol. III, No. 2, January, 1914.

Mac Bradaí, Yann Philippe, *Limerick Leader*, 15 January, 1983

McElduff, Marese, "Traditional Chinese Medicine-Acupuncture" *Clare County Express*, January, 1997, Ennis.

MacLeod, Catriona, "The Statue of Our Lady of Limerick: a gift in reparation", *North Munster Studies, Essays in Commemoration of Monsignor Michael Moloney*, 1967.

MacMahon, Tony, "Studiisque Asperrima Belli", *The Old Limerick Journal*, Autumn, 1981.

MacMahon, Tony, "The Evolution of Local Government", *The Old Limerick Journal*, Spring, 1982.

MacSpealáin, Gearóid, "Notes on place-names in the City and Liberties of Limerick", *North Munster Antiquarian* Journal, Vol. III, No. 2, Autumn, 1942.

Maloney, Patrick, "With the Mid-Limerick Brigade Second Battalion" *Limerick's Fighting Story 1916 - 21, Told By The Men Who Made It*, Tralee.

Marrinan, Seán, "Dickens in Limerick, 1858", *North Munster Antiquarian Journal*, Vol. XXIV, 1982.

Marrinan, Seán, "Limerick Tokens of the 17th Century" *North Munster Antiquarian Journal*, Volume XXIX, 1987,

Meghen, P.J., "Turnpike Roads in Co. Limerick", *The Old Limerick Journal*, Winter, 1986.

Mitchell, James, "The Ordination in Ireland of Jansenist Clergy from Utrecht, 1715-16: The Role of Fr. Paul Denny ODC of County Galway (Concluded)", *Journal of the Galway Archaeological and Historical Society*, Volume 43, 1991

Murphy, Charlotte, "The Limerick to Killaloe Canal", *The Other Clare*, Vol. 8, Shannon, 1984

Ní Chinnéide, Síle, "A Journey from Cork to Limerick in December 1790", *North Munster Antiquarian Journal*, Vol. XIV, 1971.

Nevin, Jackie, *The C.A.R.I. Foundation*, Brochure.

Newman, Jeremiah, "Scattery: An Unknown part of the Diocese of Limerick:, *North Munster Antiquarian Journal, Volume XXXIV,* 1992, Limerick.

Newman, Rev. Jeremiah, "John McEnery - Limerick Priest Palaeontologist 1796 - 1841", *North Munster Studies*, 1967.

Ó Ceallaigh, Tadhy et al, *Limerick: A handbook of local history*, Coiste Oideachas Múinteoirí Luimnigh, no date.

Ó Corráin, Donnchadh, "Brian Boru and the Battle of Clontarf", *Milestones in Irish History*, Dublin, Cork, 1986.

Ó Dálaigh, Brian, "An early nineteenth - century painting of Ennis", *The Other Clare*, Vol. 10, Shannon, 1986.

Ó Dálaigh, Brian, "A history of an O'Brien stronghold c. 1210 - 1626", *North Munster Antiquarian Journal*, Vol. XXIX,1987.

Ó Dálaigh, Brian, "The O'Brien Strongholds of Clarecastle and Clonroad 1200 - 1600", *The Royal O'Briens - A Tribute*, Dromoland, 1982.

Ó Dálaigh, Brian, "Thomas Moland's Survey of Ennis", *The Other Clare*, Volume IX, Shannon, 1987.

O'Dea, Trish, "Sr. Joan Bowles", *Limerick Lives*, 1996.

* O'Donovan, John, "Ordnance Survey Name Books and Letters for Limerick, 1839- 840", typescript by Rev. M. O'Flanagan, Bray, 1928, unpublished.

* O'Donovan, Reenie, "Notes on Kilrush Church", Prepared for a lecture on that site to members of the Shannon Archaeological and Historical Society, 31 August, 1988.

O'Grady, Desmond, "Shawn-a-Scoob", *The Old Limerick Journal*, December, 1979.

Ó Lochlainn, Colm, "The Irish Book Lover", *Ceist agus Freagra*, Dublin, 1933.

* O'Mahony, Chris, and Mary Pyne, "Family History in Limerick".

* O'Mahony, David, "Potted History of O'Mahony's", notes on origin of the business.

Ó Maidín, Pádraig, "The Building of the Sarsfield Bridge", *Old Limerick Journal*, 1981

Ó Murchadha, Ciarán, "The Dal gCais (Dalcassians) and the territory of Tuamhumhain (Thomond)", *The Royal O'Briens - A Tribute*, Dromoland, 1992.

Ó Murchadha, Ciarán, "Brian Boru", *The Royal O'Briens - A Tribute*, Dromoland, 1992.

O'Rahilly, Celie, "Recent Research in Limerick City", *Archaeology Ireland*, Vol. 2, No. 2, Winter, 1988.

Ordnance Survey Office, *Street Map of Limerick, Tercentenary of Sieges of*

Limerick 1691 - 1991, Phoenix Park, Dublin, 1989.

O'Riordan, Manus, "Anti-Semitism in Irish Politics", *Dublin Jewish News*, March - April, 1979.

O'Riordan, Manus, "The Sinn Fein tradition of anti-Semitism :- from Arthur Griffith to Sean South", Published as "Anti-Semitism in Irish Politics" in *The Irish-Jewish Year Book 1984 - 1985*.

O'Sullivan, Thomas F., "The City of Limerick in the 17th Century - A Topographical study", *Tercentenary Commemoration of the Cromwellian Siege of Limerick 1651 - 1951*, Limerick, 1951.

Phelan, Eugene, "Canal bridge provides new links", *Limerick Leader*, Saturday, November 9, 1996

Place, J.A., and Joe MacMahon, "The Lax Weir", *Limerick Christmas Gazette*, 1988.

"Portrait Gallery. Mr. Robert Herbert", *The Irish Times*, Saturday, September 12, 1953.

Prendergast, Frank, "Limerick's Viking Era", *Remembering Limerick*, Limerick, 1997.

Quinlan, Arthur, "Hunt Museum appoints author". *The Irish Times*, Tuesday, December 9, 1997.

Quinlan, Arthur J., *Irish Professional Golf Championship 1955 Official Programme*

Quinlan, Arthur, "Limerick City Marks 800 Years", *The Irish Times*, Saturday, October 4, 1997.

Quinlan, Arthur, "Limerick prison extension opened", *The Irish Times*, Tuesday, December 9, 1997.

* Reddan, Hilary, and Noreen Elleker, "St. Mary's Cathedral - notes on its restoration", unpublished.

Rowe, Veronica, and Nellie Ó Cléirigh, *A Stitch in Time Limerick Lace, Art & Economy, the Hunt Museum, 1 July to 30 Sept, 1998*, Brochure.

Ryan, P. J., "The Royal Irish Constabulary", *The Old Limerick Journal*, Summer, 1982.

Ryan, P. J., "Some Local Industries", *The Old Limerick Journal*, Autumn, 1981.

Ryan, Des, "The Jews of Limerick, Part 2", *The Old Limerick Journal*, Winter, 1985.

Ryan, Des, "Remembering Elsa Reininger", *The Limerick Compendium*, Dublin, 1997.

Rynne, Etienne, "John Daly and the Bard of Thomond", *North Munster Antiquarian Journal*, Vol. XIX, 1977.

Rynne, Etienne, "A Late Medieval Casket from Knockmore, Co. Clare", *North Munster Antiquarian Journal*, Vol. XIV, 1971.

* Sheaff, Nichols, "Historical Survey of the Chamber of Commerce premises, 96 O'Connell Street, Limerick".

* Shee-Twohig, Elizabeth, and Liam Irwin, "Notes on Sluggery Ring Fort"

Siggins, Lorna, "'Uniqueness' pledge in Galway city plan" The Irish Times, Thursday, February 26, 1998.

"Silver chalice is found in church" *The Irish Times*, Saturday, May 16, 1998

Simms, J. G., "The Siege of Limerick, 1690", *North Munster Studies*, Limerick, 1967.

Spellisy, Seán, "Peter the Packer - A Man for the Times" *Dal gCais*, No. 7, Miltown Malbay, 1984.

Spellisy, Seán, "Ballinalacken Castle - A Stronghold in Corcomroe", *The Royal O'Briens - A Tribute*, Dromoland, 1992.

Spellissy, Seán, "Scattery Island", *Clare Association Yearbook 1987.*

Snoddy, Oliver, "The Limerick City Militia and the Battle of Collooney, 1798," *North Munster Antiquarian Journal*, Vol. IX, No. 3, Limerick, 1964.

Stewart, Dolly, "The Goose's Corner", *The Old Limerick Journal*, December, 1979.

Talbot, Rev. M. J., "The Memorial to Prior Johannes ffox in St. Mary's Cathedral, Limerick", *North Munster Studies*, 1967.

Wallace, Patrick F., "The Organisation of pre-railway public transport in counties Limerick and Clare", *North Munster Antiquarian Journal*, Vol. XV, 1972.

Wallace, J.N.A., "Limerick Silver Freedom Boxes", *North Munster Antiqurian Journal*, Vol. IV, No. 3. Limerick, Spring 1945.

Walsh, Larry, "The Mayoral Myth", *Remembering Limerick*, Limerick, 1997

Westropp, M.S.D., "The Goldsmiths of Limerick," *North Munster Antiqurian Journal*, Vol. I. No. 4, Limerick, 1939.

Westropp, T. J., "Ancient Places of Assembly in the Counties of Limerick and Clare", *Journal of the Royal Society of Antiquaries of Ireland*, Vol. XLIV, 1919.

Westropp, T. J., "Carrigogunnell Castle and the O'Briens of Pubblebrian, in the County of Limerick", Part I and Part II, *Journal of the Royal Society of Antiquaries of Ireland*, 1906.

Westropp, T. J., "Cromwellian Account Books, Limerick", Journal of the Royal Society of Antiquaries of Ireland, Part II, Vol. XXXVI, 30th June, 1906.

Westropp, T. J., "St. Mary's Cathedral, Limerick: Its Plan and Growth", *Journal of the Royal Society of Antiquaries of Ireland*, Part II, Vol. VIII, June, 1898.

* Westropp, T. J., "Miscellanea", Unpublished notes, available in The Manse, Harmony Row, Ennis (The Clare Local History Workshop)

Wiggins, Kenneth, "Strange Changes at King John's Castle", *Archaeology Ireland*, Vol. 5, No. 3, Autumn, 1991.

* Wood, Hiram, "History of the Quakers in Limerick".

Woulfe, Jimmy, "Nuns prayer: Stop singing The Isle as a rugby anthem", *Limerick Leader*, 20 December, 1997.

Woulfe, Rev. Patrick, "Names and Surnames in County Limerick", *Journal of the North Munster Archaeological Society*, 1919.

.

Index

The Celtic Bookshop

2 Rutland Street,
Limerick City,
Republic of Ireland.
Tel: 061-401155 Fax: 061-340600.
e-mail: celticbk@iol.ie

The Celtic Bookshop specialises in books relating to Ireland and offers customers, both individuals and institutions a comprehensive service in the acquisition of Irish interest books. We stock a comprehensive selection of new and out of print books relating to all aspects of Irish Studies including historical, literary, genealogical, language and cultural titles. We also offer an out of print book service. We search for particular out of print books for customers. The Celtic Bookshop also issues catalogues of out of print titles to a world-wide mailing list. If you wish to receive our catalogues please advise. We also display a selection of our stock on our world wide web page.